Emerging E-Collaboration Concepts and Applications

Ned Kock
Texas A&M International University, USA

Cybertech Publishing
Hershey • London • Melbourne • Singapore

Acquisition Editor: Kristin Klinger
Senior Managing Editor: Jennifer Neidig
Managing Editor: Sara Reed
Assistant Managing Editor: Sharon Berger
Development Editor: Kristin Roth
Copy Editor: Julie LeBlanc
Typesetter: Michael Brehm
Cover Design: Lisa Tosheff
Printed at: Integrated Book Technology

Published in the United States of America by
CyberTech Publishing (an imprint of Idea Group Inc.)
701 E. Chocolate Avenue
Hershey PA 17033
Tel: 717-533-8845
Fax: 717-533-8661
E-mail: cust@idea-group.com
Web site: http://www.cybertech-pub.com

and in the United Kingdom by
CyberTech Publishing (an imprint of Idea Group Inc.)
3 Henrietta Street
Covent Garden
London WC2E 8LU
Tel: 44 20 7240 0856
Fax: 44 20 7379 0609
Web site: http://www.eurospanonline.com

Library of Congress Cataloging-in-Publication Data

Emerging E-Collaboration Concepts and Applications / Ned Kock, editor.
p. cm.
Summary: "This book presents a state-of-the-art discussion of conceptual and applied e-collaboration issues. Business organizations increasingly rely on collaborative processes to maintain their competitiveness. E-collaboration technologies are at the source of something that underlies most business, political, and even societal developments - intense human collaboration"--Provided by publisher.
Includes bibliographical references and index.
ISBN 1-59904-393-9 (hardcover) -- ISBN 1-59904-394-7 (softcover) -- ISBN 1-59904-395-5 (ebook)
1. Business enterprises--Computer networks 2. Business networks. 3. Computer networks. 4. Communication--Technological innovations. I. Kock, Ned F., 1964-
HD30.37.A28 2007
658'.044 dc22
2006031351

British Cataloguing in Publication Data
A Cataloguing in Publication record for this book is available from the British Library.

Emerging E-Collaboration Concepts and Applications

Table of Contents

Preface

E-collaboration technologies have been around for a long time. If we look only at computer-based e-collaboration technologies, arguably the first instances date back to the emergence of the ARPANET (the precursor of the Internet) in the late 1960s. We can safely say that e-collaboration technologies have been developed and used for more than 35 years. Many new technological developments have taken place during this period. Those developments have both shaped e-collaboration technologies and pushed them in particular directions. For example, the emergence of local area networks in the 1980s has led to the development of e-collaboration technologies aimed at supporting the work of small groups. The ascendance of the Internet in the 1990s as a global infrastructure for business transactions and personal interactions, on the other hand, has led to the development of e-collaboration technologies to support the creation of large virtual communities.

One cannot help but be somewhat surprised at the amount of interest, in both academic and industry circles, that e-collaboration has commanded during those 35 years. That interest does not seem to be showing any signs of dissipating; something that has happened with many technological advances that at some point in time seemed to be the center of all of the world's attention. Perhaps the reason is that e-collaboration technologies are at the source of something that increasingly underlies most business, political, and even societal developments–intense human collaboration. Business organizations in the last 10 years, in particular, seem to have to increasingly rely on distributed collaborative processes to maintain their competitiveness. E-collaboration technologies are a sine qua non condition for the successful implementation of those types of processes.

This book is a collection of chapters on emerging e-collaboration concepts and applications. The volume is organized in three main sections – Section I: Conceptual and Methodological Issues; Section II: Applied Research and Challenges; and Section III: Research Syntheses and Debate. The chapters are by and large based on articles published recently in the *International Journal of e-Collaboration*, for which

I have had the pleasure of serving as editor-in-chief since its inception. Some of the chapters are reprinted here with permission. Other chapters are revised versions of previously published articles, with the revisions made by the authors specifically for inclusion in this volume.

Section I of the book includes chapters I to V, and is dedicated to the discussion of conceptual and methodological issues in connection with e-collaboration. Chapter I, by Kock, presents six key conceptual elements that arguably make up most e-collaboration interactions; going from technology-related elements to the social environment surrounding the e-collaborators. Chapter II, by Markus, develops a "tool view" of e-collaboration, and contrasts it with the previously developed and widely cited "ensemble view". Markus does that through a chapter that is essentially a revised version of an award winning article, selected as the best article published in the *International Journal of e-Collaboration* in 2005. Chapter III, by Munkvold and Zigurs, focuses on the discussion of organizational and behavioral challenges associated with the integration of different e-collaboration technologies. Chapter IV, by Nosek, cogently argues that individual and group "sensemaking" is a better starting point for the development of effective e-collaboration environments and features. Chapter V, by Kock, concludes Section I of the book by discussing the action research approach and pros and cons of its use in e-collaboration research.

Section II of the book is made up of chapters VI to X, and is dedicated to the discussion of applied e-collaboration research findings and related challenges. Chapter VI, by Fjermestad, discusses a longitudinal experiment that investigated the efficiency, effectiveness, and group member perceptions of two approaches to strategic decision making in distributed e-collaboration environments. Chapter VII, by Evaristo and colleagues, discusses a field experiment involving two graduate information technology student classes that collaborated electronically; one located in Porto Alegre, Brazil, and the other in Chicago. Chapter VIII, by Miranda and Carter, reports on a field study conducted during the migration of a business unit to a new communications system, which suggested the existence of a counterintuitive positive effect of "telework" on the use of face-to-face communication. Chapter IX, by Schultze and Bhappu, develops a contingency theory of customer co-production designs, and then uses cases of Internet-based services to highlight the benefits and challenges of relying on Internet technology to implement customer co-production. Chapter X, by Dennis and colleagues, concludes Section II of the book by discussing a study that examined two key factors through which group size may affect brainstorming performance, namely synergy and social loafing.

Part III of the book is made up of chapters XI to XV, and focuses on the discussion of syntheses of prior research and issues that are likely to lead to future debate. It starts with Chapter XI, by Kock and Hantula, where the authors claim that human beings are not genetically designed to efficiently use e-collaboration technologies and provide a discussion of counterintuitive implications in the context of e-collaboration. Chapter XII, by Smith and Hayne, follows with an integration of recent theories of cognition (distributed cognition, transactive memory, and template theory) from the perspective of e-collaboration. Chapter XIII, by Dennis and Williams, reports on a meta-analysis of the effects of group size on electronic brainstorming, verbal brainstorming, and nominal group brainstorming; concluding that as group size increases, the relative benefit of electronic brainstorming also increases. Chapter XIV, by Pinsonneault and Caya, reviews the extant empirical literature on virtual teams and presents, in the words of the authors, "what we know and what we don't know about them", following that with the proposal of a framework that integrates the most important variables affecting virtual teams. Chapter XV, by George and Marett, concludes Section III of the book by discussing how the art of deception in e-collaboration can potentially affect both the current and future efforts of those involved, and offers the authors' thoughts on some of the factors e-collaboration practitioners should consider when trying to combat electronic deception.

The range of topics covered in this book is certainly broad and representative of the state-of-the-art discussion of conceptual and applied e-collaboration issues. If one looks at the broad literature on e-collaboration, as well as its impact in academic and industry circles, it becomes clear that this book brings together the best in terms of thinking in the field. The authors of the chapters in this book are among the most accomplished and influential e-collaboration researchers in the world. I thank them for being contributors to this book, and am honored to have been able to serve as its editor.

Ned Kock

Editor-in-Chief

Emerging E-Collaboration Concepts and Applications

Acknowledgments

I would like to thank the team at Idea Group Publishing for their excellent support of this book project. I am particularly grateful to Lynley Lapp and Michelle Potter for allowing me to streamline the process of exchanging materials with them, even though that streamlining led to time savings on my end and not necessarily on theirs. Special recognition here goes to Mehdi Khosrow-Pour and Jan Travers, who have provided the initial impetus for this book. Many thanks are also due to Jennifer Neidig and her team for their editorial support of the *International Journal of e-Collaboration*; without which many of the chapters published here would not exist.

I have been blessed to have joined Texas A&M International University several years ago, and have thoroughly enjoyed the working environment there—as well as the beautiful Laredo weather. I would like to thank Ray Keck, president of Texas A&M International University, and Dan Jones, provost, for their unwavering support of quality scholarship at that wonderful institution. Special thanks also go to Jacky So, dean of the College of Business and Economics, for giving me the flexibility to plan my time so that I can still conduct scholarly activities while doing my best at being an effective chair of the Department of MIS and Decision Science. Last, but certainly not least, I would like to thank my family for their love and support—this book is dedicated to them.

Section I

Conceptual and Methodological Issues

Chapter I

A Discussion of Key Conceptual Elements of E-Collaboration

Ned Kock, Texas A&M International University, USA

Abstract

This chapter defines e-collaboration, and provides a historical glimpse at how and when e-collaboration emerged. The discussion suggests that the emergence of e-collaboration had more to do with military considerations than with the solution of either organizational or broad societal problems. It is also argued that e-collaboration, as an area of research and industrial development, is broader than what is often referred to as computer-mediated communication. The chapter concludes with a discussion of six key conceptual elements of e-collaboration: (1) the collaborative task, (2) the e-collaboration technology, (3) the individuals involved in the collaborative task, (4) the mental schemas possessed by the individuals, (5) the physical environment surrounding the individuals, and (6) the social environment surrounding the individuals.

E-Collaboration Defined

Electronic collaboration (e-collaboration) is operationally defined here as collaboration using electronic technologies among different individuals to accomplish a common task (Kock & D'Arcy, 2002; Kock, Davison, Ocker, & Wazlawick, 2001). This is a broad definition that encompasses not only computer-mediated collaborative work, but also collaborative work that is supported by other types of technologies that do not fit most people's definition of a computer. One example of such technologies is the telephone, which is not, strictly speaking, a computer—even though some of today's telephone devices probably have more processing power than some of the first computers back in the 1940s. Another example of technology that may enable e-collaboration is the teleconferencing suite, whose main components are cameras, televisions, and telecommunications devices.

The above operational definition, which I will use as a basis to discuss other related issues in this chapter, is arguably very broad. Yet, it is probably clearer than the general view of e-collaboration in industry, which some may also see as a bit unfocused. For example, some developers of e-collaboration tools, such as Microsoft Corporation and Groove Networks, emphasize their technologies' support for the conduct of electronic meetings over the Internet. There seems to be a concern by those developers with offering features that make electronic meetings as similar to face-to-face meetings as possible.

Industry information technology publications such as *CIO Magazine* and *Computerworld*, on the other hand, often tend to favor a view of e-collaboration technologies as tools to support business-to-business electronic commerce and virtual supply chain management over the Web. These are business activities that are arguably substantially different from electronic meetings, both in terms of scope and main goals. The primary audiences of industry information technology publications are information technology managers and professionals, who are the consumers of e-collaboration technologies. Given that, one can imagine the possible misunderstandings that may take place when those managers and professionals get together with developers' sales representatives to discuss possible e-collaboration technology purchases.

The First E-Collaboration Technology

As far as buzzwords are concerned, *e-collaboration* is still in its infancy, even though the technologies necessary to make e-collaboration happen have been around for quite some time. Strictly speaking, e-collaboration could have happened as early as the mid-1800s, with the invention of the telegraph by Samuel F. B. Morse. The telegraph allowed individuals to accomplish collaborative tasks interacting primarily electronically. If one assumes that the telegraph was too cumbersome to support e-collaboration, it may be more reasonable to argue that the birth of e-collaboration could have been soon after that, in the 1870s, with the invention of the telephone by Alexander Graham Bell.

Yet, for a variety of reasons, true e-collaboration had to wait many years to emerge. Did the commercialization of the first mainframe computers in the 1950s, following the ENIAC project, help much in that respect? Not really, and that was not necessarily due to technological obstacles to developing e-collaboration systems for mainframes. The real reason seems to have been the cost of mainframes (Kock, 1999; 2005), which was then seen as too high for them to be used: (a) by anyone other than very specialized workers, who often dressed like medical doctors; or (b) for anything other than heavy data processing-intensive and/or calculation-intensive applications. Of course, e-collaboration was not seen as one of those applications. Moreover, worker collaboration was not even a very fashionable management idea by the time the mainframes hit the market big time in the 1960s (Kock, 2002).

Then the ARPANET, the precursor of today's Internet, happened in the late 1960s. The ARPANET Project's main goal was to build a geographically distributed network of mainframes within the U.S. that could withstand a massive, and possibly nuclear, military attack by what was then known as the Soviet Union. By that time, mainframes were used in ballistics calculations without which intercontinental missiles would not be as effective in reaching their targets as they were expected to be. The Project was motivated by the Cold War between the U.S. and the Soviet Union, which reached a tense stage in the early 1960s. The main sponsor of the ARPANET Project was the U.S. Department of Defense.

One of the tools developed to allow ARPANET users to exchange data was called "electronic mail" (e-mail). E-mail was initially perceived as a "toy" system, which researchers involved in the ARPANET Project used to casually interact with each other. This perception gave way to one that characterizes e-mail as the father (or mother) of all e-collaboration technologies (Sproull & Kiesler, 1991). To the surprise of many, serious use of e-mail grew quickly, primarily as a technology to support collaboration among researchers, university professors, and students—the primary users of the ARPANET while it was in its infancy.

So, in spite of the fact that other technologies already existed that could have been used for e-collaboration, e-mail was arguably the first technology to be used to support e-collaborative work. Interestingly, e-mail's success as an e-collaboration technology has yet been unmatched—at least in organizational environments (college dorms do not qualify). This is somewhat surprising, given e-mail's granddaddy status as far as e-collaboration is concerned. Helping it hold that enviable position is e-mail's combination of simplicity, similarity to a widely used "low-tech" system (the paper-based mail system), and support for anytime-anyplace interaction.

E-Collaboration vs. Computer-Mediated Communication

What I refer to in this chapter as e-collaboration research is in fact made up of several research streams, with different names and traditions. One such research stream is that of computer-mediated communication, also known as CMC, which has been traditionally concerned with the effects that computer mediation has on individuals who are part of work groups and social communities. One common theme of empirical CMC research is the investigation of the effects of computer mediation on group-related constructs by using as a control condition the lack of computer mediation—what some prefer to simply call "face-to-face interaction."

E-collaboration is not the same as computer-mediated communication. Earlier in this chapter, I defined e-collaboration as collaboration using electronic technologies among different individuals whose goal is to accomplish a common task. I would argue that, following from that definition, e-collaboration research should be seen as encompassing traditional CMC research, as well as other lines of research that do not necessarily rely on computer-mediated communication to support collaborative tasks. One example would be the study of telephone-mediated communication. This argument also applies to another area of research normally referred to as computer-supported cooperative work (CSCW), for similar reasons. That is, e-collaboration research should also be seen as encompassing traditional CSCW research.

Another distinction that I would like to point out, and that may be seen as controversial by some, is that e-collaboration may take place in situations where there is no communication per se, much less computer-mediated communication. Let us consider for example a Web-based e-collaboration technology that allows different employees of an insurance company to accomplish the same collaborative task, namely the task of preparing a standard insurance policy for a customer. Since we are assuming that the collaborative work is on a standard insurance policy, it is not unreasonable to picture a case in which different employees would electronically input pieces of information through the e-collaboration technology that will become part of the final product (i.e., the policy), without those employees actually communicating any information to one another. In this case, the e-collaboration system would pull together different pieces of information from different individuals into what would in the end become an insurance policy, and in such a way that the individuals may not even have been aware of one another. Some, of course, will argue that this is not *really* e-collaboration. But it fits our definition of e-collaboration, presented earlier in this chapter: "... collaboration among different individuals to accomplish a common task using electronic technologies."

Today, many technologies exists that do not involve computer-mediated communication, and that nonetheless are becoming increasingly important as tools for e-collaborative work. Mobile e-collaboration devices, from cell phones to wireless personal digital assistants (PDAs), are a good example. Some may see those devices as computers, while others may not. Regardless of that, those devices are likely to be a key target of e-collaboration research in the near future.

Six Key Conceptual Elements of E-Collaboration

What are the main *conceptual elements* that define an e-collaboration episode? This is a general question whose answer, I believe, can further shed light on what e-collaboration is (and what it is NOT). Moreover, identifying the key conceptual elements that make up e-collaboration will inevitable lead us to the identification of constructs that can be targeted in e-collaboration research, which is a desirable outcome for an inaugural issue of a journal that wants to establish a clear identity.

Based on past research on e-collaboration, one could contend that the following conceptual elements define e-collaboration, in the sense that changes in those elements can significantly change the nature of an e-collaboration episode: (1) the collaborative task, (2) the e-collaboration technology, (3) the individuals involved in the collaborative task, (4) the mental schemas possessed by the individuals, (5) the physical environment surrounding the individuals, and (6) the social environment surrounding the individuals. Each of these elements is discussed next.

The Collaborative Task

An example of generic collaborative task that is often conducted with support of e-collaboration technologies today is that of writing a contract, particularly when the parties involved are geographically distributed. The nature of the collaborative task (e.g., whether it is simple or complex) can have a strong effect on its outcomes when certain e-collaboration technologies are used (Zigurs & Buckland, 1998; Zigurs, Buckland, Connolly, & Wilson, 1999).

The E-Collaboration Technology

This comprises not only the communication medium created by the technology, but also the technology's features that have been designed to support e-collaboration. The implementation of a particular feature (e.g., video streaming) in a particularly type of e-collaboration technology (e.g., instant messaging) can have a strong effect on how the technology is actually used by a group of individuals to accomplish a given collaborative task (DeSanctis & Poole, 1994; Poole & DeSanctis, 1990).

The Individuals Involved in the Collaborative Task

This conceptual element refers primarily to certain characteristics of the individuals involved in the collaborative task, such as their gender and typing ability (which would be relevant in text-based e-collaboration contexts). This conceptual element also refers to the "number" of individuals involved in the e-collaboration episode, or the size of the e-collaborative group. An individual's gender, for example, may have a significant effect on how that individual perceives a particular e-collaboration technology (Gefen & Straub, 1997), which may affect that individual's behavior as part of a group of e-collaborators (Kock, 2001).

The Mental Schemas Possessed by the Individuals

This conceptual element refers to mental schemas (also referred to as "knowledge" or "background"; see, e.g., Kock, 2004; Kock & Davison, 2003) possessed by the individuals involved in the collaboration task, including socially constructed schemas that may induce the individuals to interpret information in a particular way (Lee, 1994). This conceptual element also refers to the degree of similarity of the mental schemas possessed by the individuals. The degree of similarity among the task-related mental schemas possessed by different individuals engaged in a collaborative task (e.g., whether task experts are interacting with other experts, or novices) may significantly affect the amount of cognitive effort required to successfully accomplish the task using certain types of e-collaboration technologies (Kock, 2004).

The Physical Environment Surrounding the Individuals

This comprises the actual tangible items that are part of the environment surrounding the individuals involved in the collaborative task, as well as the geographical distribution of the individuals. Geographically dispersed individuals are more likely than co-located ones to use e-collaboration technologies that are perceived as "less rich" than face-to-face interaction, and spend time and effort adapting the features of the technologies to their task-related needs (Kock, 2001; Trevino, Daft, & Lengel 1990).

The Social Environment Surrounding the Individuals

This conceptual element refers primarily to aspects of the social environment surrounding the individuals involved in the collaborative task that can be characterized as being social influences on those individuals. Those aspects may involve expressed perceptions and/or behavior by peers, managers and other individuals (e.g., customers) toward e-collaboration technologies. For instance, an individual's behavior toward a particular e-collaboration tool, or certain features of that tool, may be significantly influenced by peer pressure (Markus, 1994), which may take the form of other individuals heavily using the e-collaboration tool and expressing positive opinions about the tool. That behavior may also be significantly influence by the position that the individual occupies in an organization's hierarchical management structure (Carlson & Davis, 1998).

The above discussion on key conceptual elements should be followed by a couple of caveats. First, the list of key conceptual elements presented is not comprehensive. There are certain elements that are relevant for e-collaboration research that are not covered by the above list. Second, the conceptual elements above may be (or have been) given different names by different researchers, or the same name but different meanings.

Nevertheless, I hope to have been able to accomplish one main goal by discussing the conceptual elements—to provide a glimpse at the complexity of e-collaboration and its many behavioral facets. Each of the conceptual elements above, if significantly manipulated in, say, a laboratory experiment or action research project (Kock, 2003), would potentially lead to variations in key variables. Among those key variables are two favorites of e-collaboration researchers: task outcome quality and task efficiency. Task outcome quality is frequently assessed based on how *good* the task *product* is, often in terms of customer perceptions. Task efficiency is usually assessed based on how much time and/or cost is involved in accomplishing the task.

Conclusion

The field of e-collaboration has a promising future, in terms of both academic research and commercial software development. As an area of academic research, e-collaboration has flourished since the 1980s and particularly the 1990s, which led to the need for new publications outlets—a need that, one recently launched journal, the *International Journal of e-Collaboration*, tries to address by its very existence. As an area of commercial software development, e-collaboration is likely to benefit from a critical assessment of how it can be applied to the benefit of individuals, organizations and society.

In this chapter, I provided an operational definition of e-collaboration, and a historical glimpse at how and when e-collaboration emerged. I also argued that e-collaboration, as an area of research and industrial development, is broader than what is often referred to as computer-mediated communication—an argument that also applies to another field called computer-supported cooperative work (CSCW). Finally, I discussed key conceptual elements in connection with e-collaboration, which I hope will provide a relatively easy to understand conceptual basis for future research design and implementation. While the conceptual elements discussed have consistently been targeted individually in past research, rarely interaction effects among those conceptual elements have been investigated. There are tremendous research opportunities, and challenges (mostly methodological), for researchers that decide to conduct research projects addressing those interaction effects.

The view that I propose here of e-collaboration is hopefully focused enough to allow for a clear understanding of what types of research would constitute e-collaboration research, and hopefully help shape this new and promising field of inquiry. At the same time, I hope such view of e-collaboration is comprehensive enough to leave room for likely technological developments that are not seen today as enabling e-collaboration, but that may be seen as doing so in a not so distant future. One such likely development is that of virtual reality applications (Briggs, 2002), and their increasing use to support e-collaborative work. Other related technological developments are likely to arrive in other areas such as wearable computing and speech recognition, with significant impacts on how e-collaboration takes place in the context of certain collaborative tasks (Parente, Kock, & Sonsini, 2004).

References

Briggs, J. C. (2002). Virtual reality is getting real: Prepare to meet your clone. *The Futurist*, *36*(3), 34-42.

Carlson, P. J. & Davis, G. B. (1998). An investigation of media selection among directors and managers: From "self" to "other" orientation. *MIS Quarterly*, *22*(3), 335-362.

DeSanctis, G. & Poole, M. S. (1994). Capturing the complexity in advanced technology use: Adaptive structuration theory. *Organization Science*, *5*(2), 121-147.

Gefen, D. & Straub, D. W. (1997). Gender differences in the perception and use of e-mail: An extension to the technology acceptance model. *MIS Quarterly*, *21*(4), 389-400.

Kock, N. (1999). *Process improvement and organizational learning: The role of collaboration technologies*. Hershey, PA: Idea Group Publishing.

Kock, N. (2001). Compensatory adaptation to a lean medium: An action research investigation of electronic communication in process improvement groups. *IEEE Transactions on Professional Communication*, *44*(4), 267-285.

Kock, N. (2002). Managing with Web-based IT in mind. *Communications of the ACM, 45*(5), 102-106.

Kock, N. (2003). Action research: Lessons learned from a multi-iteration study of computer-mediated communication in groups. *IEEE Transactions on Professional Communication, 46*(2), 105-128.

Kock, N. (2004). The psychobiological model: Toward a new theory of computer-mediated communication based on Darwinian evolution. *Organization Science, 15*(3), 327-348.

Kock, N. (2005). *Business process improvement through e-collaboration: Knowledge sharing through the use of virtual groups*. Hershey, PA: Idea Group Publishing.

Kock, N., & D'Arcy, J. (2002). Resolving the e-collaboration paradox: The competing influences of media naturalness and compensatory adaptation. *Information Management and Consulting* (Special Issue on Electronic Collaboration), *17*(4), 72-78.

Kock, N., & Davison, R. (2003). Can lean media support knowledge sharing? Investigating a hidden advantage of process improvement. *IEEE Transactions on Engineering Management, 50*(2), 151-163.

Kock, N., Davison, R., Ocker, R. & Wazlawick, R. (2001). E-collaboration: A look at past research and future challenges. *Journal of Systems and Information Technology* (Special Issue on E-Collaboration), *5*(1), 1-9.

Lee, A. S. (1994). Electronic mail as a medium for rich communication: An empirical investigation using hermeneutic interpretation. *MIS Quarterly, 18*(2), 143-157.

Markus, M. L. (1994). Electronic mail as the medium of managerial choice. *Organization Science, 5*(4), 502-527.

Parente, R., Kock, N., & Sonsini, J. (2004). An analysis of the implementation and impact of speech recognition technology in the heath care sector. *Perspectives in Health Information Management, 1*(5), 1-23.

Poole, M. S., & DeSanctis, G. (1990). Understanding the use of group decision support systems: The theory of adaptive structuration. In J. Fulk & C. Steinfield (Eds.), *Organizations and communication technology* (pp. 173-193). Newbury Park, CA: Sage.

Sproull, L., & Kiesler, S. (1991). Computers, networks and work. *Scientific American*, 265(3), 84-91.

Trevino, L. K., Daft, R. L. & Lengel, R. H. (1990). Understanding manager's media choices: A symbolic interactionist perspective. In J. Fulk & C. Steinfield (Eds.), *Organizations and communication technology* (pp. 71-94). Newbury Park, CA: Sage.

Zigurs, I., & Buckland, B. K. (1998). A theory of task-technology fit and group support systems effectiveness. *MIS Quarterly*, *22*(3), 313-334.

Zigurs, I., Buckland, B. K., Connolly, J. R., & Wilson, E. V. (1999). A test of task-technology fit theory for group support systems. *Database for Advances in Information Systems*, *30*(3), 34-50.

Chapter II

Featuring Technology in Studies of E-Collaboration Technology Effects

M. Lynne Markus, Bentley College, USA

Abstract

For the 2005 launch of the International Journal of e-Collaboration *I wrote an essay in response to Orlikowski and Iacono's (2001) call for enhanced theorization of the IT artifact. Specifically, I set out to develop a "tool view" of IT, arguing that this perspective was deeply engrained in the IS worldview, but poorly conceptualized. In what I called "the technology-shaping[1] perspective", I hypothesized that, although IT does not determine outcomes, the use of IT might be associated probabilistically with patterns of consequences that can be attributed to the material features of IT. Technologies pose problems for users who want to use them for particular goals; the solutions users arrive at for those problems during recurrent IT use may exhibit certain regularities across different contexts. Consequently, small differences in the features of apparently similar tools could be associated with variations in usage patterns and social outcomes. I gave examples to illustrate the argument and explained that, despite hundreds of studies of group support systems, the technology-shaping hypothesis has not yet been tested.Since the article was written, I have received comments from a number of colleagues. I have continued to explore the ideas proposed in the article, concluding that the development task is bigger than I thought at that time—but still worth pursuing. Because I have not yet resolved the issues to my satisfaction, this chapter does not represent a comprehensive revision. Instead, the chapter contains a few updates, many annotations, and a postscript in response to some of the readers' comments.*

Introduction

The point of departure for this chapter is Orlikowski and Iacono (2001)'s observation that the IS field has not sufficiently engaged the problematic nature of its subject matter. Orlikowski and Iacono (2001) analyzed conceptualizations of IT in articles published in a leading IS journal. They found that descriptions of the IT artifact were absent in 25% of the articles and that the remaining articles exhibited many specific conceptualizations, which they grouped into four categories[2]. Two categories are particularly relevant here: the tool view and the ensemble view. The "tool" view, described as "the common, received wisdom about what technology is and means" (p. 123), was present in 20% of the articles in the journal they examined. The "ensemble" view, to which Orlikowski and Iacono have both made highly important contributions, views technology as only one element in a package of resources; this view was found in 13% of the articles in their analysis.

Orlikowski and Iacono (2001) concluded that more work needs to be done to theorize the subject matter of the field, so that it does not "disappear from view, [become] taken for granted, or [be] presumed to be unproblematic" (p. 121). Although they acknowledged that "no single, one-size-fits-all conceptualization of technology ... will work for all studies" (p. 131), they offered five premises as a starting point for further theorizing. These premises included the non-neutrality of IT artifacts, their embeddedness in space, time, and context, their multiplicity of components, their dynamism, and so forth.

What Orlikowski and Iacono (2001) neglected to point out is that those five premises are accepted cornerstones *of the ensemble view*, a class of IT artifact conceptualizations that is well articulated in the IS literature. Those premises might *not*, however, be appropriate for other views, such as the tool view.

The premises of the ensemble view are well understood, but those of the tool view are less so[3]. Perhaps because the tool view has always been so deeply engrained in the IS worldview, its proponents have rarely found it necessary to clearly articulate their assumptions. By contrast, researchers who advocated alternative (i.e., ensemble) views (e.g., Lamb et al., 2003, Kling & Scacchi, 1992, Kling & Iacono, 1988, Orlikowski, 1992; Orlikowski, 2000; DeSanctis & Poole, 1994; Poole &

DeSanctis, 1990) found it necessary to craft finely articulated and highly persuasive conceptual platforms to challenge an implicit worldview that had never been sharply delineated.

If one agrees with Orlikowski and Iacono (2001) that additional effort is needed to conceptualize the IT artifact and that no single conceptualization will work for all research purposes, then the task for the field would now seem to be to carefully articulate *alternatives to the ensemble view*[4], such as the tool view. I say this not because I intend to criticize the ensemble view. Indeed, I believe it characterizes some of my own research[5]. Instead, I base my assertion on the prominence of the tool view in prior e-collaboration research. Orlikowski and Iacono (2001), for example, cite George et al.'s (1990) study of the impacts of GDSS on group decision making as their one illustration of the tool view.

My point is that, if the tool view is important for e-collaboration research, it should be as articulated as carefully as the ensemble view. Such an articulation should spell out basic premises, in a manner similar to that done by Orlikowski and Iacono (2001) for the ensemble view, so that the differences (if any) between them are clear. In this essay, I explore some aspects of a tool view of e-collaboration technology, and I invite others to continue developing it—or to build a case for abandoning the attempt.

The Ensemble View of Technology as Artifact

Orlikowski and Iacono describe the tool view as focusing on equipment, software applications, and techniques with particular capabilities; it presents technology as bundles of "specifiable *features* hypothesized to produce more effective ... outcomes than would result ... without those tools" (2001 p. 123, emphasis added). Although they do not further discuss it, the taken-for-granted IS concept of *features* provides a useful starting point for conceptualizing the tool view. Below, I briefly review how the concept of features has figured explicitly in prior conceptualizations of IT and e-collaboration technologies.

Loosely (for now), features can be thought of as specific technological capabilities for, and potential constraints (e.g., restrictiveness, Silver, 1991) on, users; examples include asynchronous message handling or electronic brainstorming and text-only communication or anonymous contributions. Analysts disagree whether the features that matter are the result of designers' deliberation intentions, accidental by-products of technology development, users' perceptions, or some combination. They also disagree about the level of granularity or detail at which features should be described. Setting these important issues aside momentarily, let's consider how recent literature has dealt explicitly with the concept of technology features.

Features in Structuration Theory

Building on the work of sociologist Anthony Giddens, Orlikowski (1992) sought to reconceptualize technology and its relationship with organizations in a way that would resolve the "false dichotomy" (p. 406) in prior literature between "overly deterministic or unduly voluntaristic [e.g., strategic choice] perspectives" (p. 403), or between views of technology as "objective force or as social constructed product" (p.406). She restricted the scope of the concept "technology" to *material artifacts* (defined as "various configurations of hardware and software"); she made a theoretical distinction between "the material nature of technology and the human activities that design or use those artifacts" (p. 403); and she focused mainly on the latter.[6]

In doing so, Orlikowski (1992) took pains to elaborate her views of the relationship between the concepts of technology and technology use. During technology design (or use), human actors were said to build into technology artifacts (or to appropriate for their own purposes) *social structures*, that is, rules and resources (interpretive schemes, facilities, and norms)[7] (p. 410). Thus, social structures were viewed as *embedded in* the material properties of technology, such that technology could be said to both *facilitate* the performance of work and to *constrain* it (p. 411). Some technologies were posited as more or less "interpretively flexible" (flexible or rigid in terms of how people design, interpret, and use them, cf. p. 409, 421), and that interpretative flexibility was said to be a function of *both* the material characteristics of the technology and the institutional context and the power of human actors (p. 409, 421). She illustrated these ideas clearly in an interpretive study of CASE tool usage.

In more recent work, Orlikowski (2000) continued to develop her structuration theory for the IS context, and she applied it to an analysis of e-collaboration technology. However, her newer work makes a significant departure from the earlier work in its treatment of structures and their relationship with technology features. Therefore, I will discuss her newer work after reviewing other research in the "embedded structures" tradition.

By the time Orlikowski had published her 1992 analysis of the duality of technology, a considerable body of empirical research (much of it experimental) had been conducted on the effects of group decision support systems (GSS) on such outcomes as decision quality and member satisfaction. (Much more research has been published in the intervening years, cf. Briggs, Nunamaker & Sprague, 1998-99; Fjermestad & Hiltz, 1998-99.) The results of these studies were seen as disappointingly inconsistent (Chin, Gopal & Salisbury, 1997; Contractor & Seibold, 1993; DeSanctis & Poole, 1994). To account for them, the field was said to need a theory "capable of explaining how groups with similar composition, working on identical tasks, perceive and use the same technologies differently" (Contractor & Seibold, 1993 p. 529). Adaptive structuration theory (DeSanctis & Poole, 1994;

Poole & DeSanctis, 1990), a further extension of Giddens' and Orlikoswki's work, was viewed as a theory that would accomplish that goal.

Adaptive structuration theory was based on the premise that technology "structures (e.g., data and decisions models)" (DeSanctis & Poole, 1994 p. 122) and "specific features or properties" (p. 123) are important: "*There is no doubt* that technology properties and contextual contingencies *can play critical roles in the outcomes* of [GSS] use. [However], there are not clearcut patterns indicating that some technology properties ... consistently lead to either *positive or negative outcomes*." (p. 124, added emphasis). Furthermore, more reductive experiments with ever-finer feature comparisons were not likely to provide more consistent results. Therefore, a change in conceptual orientation was called for.

> *Although some of these variations [in GSS research findings] may be attributable to systematic sample and measurement differences, it was equally apparent that the hypotheses in the studies were rooted in the (flawed) premise that the impact of the technology* ***ought to be consistent across groups using it***. (Contractor & Seibold, 1993 p. 531, original emphasis)

DeSanctis, Poole, and colleagues conducted painstaking observational studies of groups using GSS, coding transcripts in minute detail (Poole & DeSanctis, 1992). Generalizing from this work, DeSanctis & Poole (1994), proposed a "more complete view [that] would account for the power of social practices without ignoring the potency of advanced technologies for shaping interaction" (p. 124). Two sets of concepts were relevant in this theoretical perspective: technology properties (*structural features*) and technology uses (*appropriations*). Technology properties could be understood in terms of *structural features* (the capabilities built into a system) and *spirit* (a system's "general intent with regard to values and goals underlying a given set of structural features", p. 126). As defined by DeSanctis and Poole (1994), spirit was neither entirely the designers' intentions (since it is impossible for a designer to fully realize his/her intentions) nor users' perceptions and interpretations (which may not comprise the whole or the essence of the technology). Instead, spirit refers to the researcher's interpretive reading of the technology as text. Appropriations—which I understand to be uses that do not necessarily conform to designers' intentions, spirit, or the system's material properties—are not determined by technology designs; instead they are choices made by users. Various kinds of appropriations are possible; among other kinds of appropriations, groups may use a technology in ways that are faithful or unfaithful to its spirit[8].

DeSanctis and Poole's theoretical essay (1994) could be read today as providing solid prescriptive guidance on how IS researchers should approach the study of IT features. Yet, possibly because their comments on prior features-oriented work were so dismissive ("So how far must the analysis [of GSS features] go to bring consistent, meaningful results?" p. 124), most subsequent research in the adaptive structuration tradition has focused almost entirely on technology appropriation, not on structural features or spirit. For example, Gopal, Bostrom, and Chin (1992-3) considered technology to be an input to a process in which faithfulness of users' appropriations and users' consensus on faithfulness of appropriation lead to the observed outcomes of GSS use (e.g., decision quality and member satisfaction). Chin et al. (1997) and Chudoba (1999) pursued survey and observational approaches respectively to assessing faithfulness of appropriation, and Salisbury, Chin, Gopal, and Newsted (2002) developed an approach to measuring group consensus on appropriation. As far as I can tell, no comparable effort has gone into the measurement of GSS structural features or GSS spirit.

Features in Social Construction Theory

The concept of technology features has also figured prominently in e-collaboration research grounded in the social construction of technology perspective. Griffith and Northcraft (1994) defined communication media as "socially constructed convenient fictions for describing and discussing particular constellations of features" (p. 273). Features were categorized as the objective (e.g., transmission speed) and the psychosocial (e.g., anonymous communication) characteristics of communication media that result from designers' or users' choices. The features of communication media include some that are known and recognized by designers and/or users (e.g., anonymity of messages); they may also include characteristics unrecognized by either party. Communication media were assumed to affect the outcomes of communication media use, but not to cause them, because the effects were believed to result from *users' intentional choices*[9] of which features to use:

> ***These distinctions [between recognized and unrecognized features] are important because*** *communication media themselves do not have organizational effects; those effects result from the use of features (acknowledged or unacknowledged) which comprise the medium.* (p. 273, original emphasis)

Griffith and Northcraft (1994) observed that the majority of prior empirical research on computer-mediated communication had employed two research designs, both of which potentially confounded media (packages or constellations of features) and features. One design, which compared, for example, electronic mail to face-to-face communication, ran the risk of attributing "*to media characteristics which are, in fact, the effects of features*" (p. 274, original emphasis). The other design, which compares different features of a single medium, runs the risk of attributing "*main effects to features which, in fact, may be interactions between features and media*" (p. 275, original emphasis). In other words, although Griffith and Northcraft (1994) believed that most important "media" effects resulted from use of particular recognized features, they also acknowledged that some unrecognized or "residual" features might not be empirically separable from the medium (package of features) as a whole; thus residual features might also have some effects.

To tease out such possible interactions, they designed an experiment in which media and features were fully crossed. They found significant main effects for both features and for media, as well as significant interaction effects. These results suggested that "the effects of the same features ... differ when operationalized in different media" (Griffith & Northcraft, 1994, p. 282). And, although not specifically addressed by their study (which compared computer-mediated to paper-and-pencil negotiations), the findings also suggest that the effects of the "same" feature (e.g., documentation) might differ when operationalized *in different implementations of the same medium*—for example, in different group support systems).

Griffith and Northcraft's findings, they argued, imply opportunities for further features-based research; for example, "...what unspecified features ... account for the medium's effects?" (1994 p. 283). They acknowledged some conceptual difficulties with features-based research, such as "the infinite decomposition problem: How should researchers decide which features to explore and which to control?" (p. 283). But the challenges of features-based research need to be compared to "the costs of designing [or selecting and implementing] communication media without a basic understanding of their features' effects" (p. 283).

Although Griffith and Northcraft (1994) largely attributed e-collaboration technology effects to people's (groups') intentional choice of features for use, their assumption that technology use causes effects still connotes a determinism that many analysts would reject. Perhaps to address such criticism, Griffith's later work on features (1999) focused on how people socially construct, or make sense of, features prior to appropriating them. The starting point of her analysis was that "features *that are noticed by users then can be socially constructed* into an organizational system—for example, as described by adaptive structuration theory" (p. 476, added emphasis). This observation led her to inquire about the conditions under which features would be noticed[10]. Drawing on prior literature in cognitive psychology, she identified three such conditions: novelty, discrepancy (relative to expectations, schemas, or frames), and deliberate initiative (when the user is provoked by external events to think). She differentiated features on two dimensions with hypothesized links to novelty, discrepancy, and initiative—whether the features were concrete or abstract and whether the features were core versus tangential to the technology. She generated a set of propositions to the effect that "concrete, core technology features are most likely to trigger sensemaking" (p. 483).

Recently, Jasperson et al. (2005) drew on Griffith's work on technology sensemaking to develop a "feature-centric view of technology". However, system features are understated in the Jasperson et al. model, except insofar as "post-adoptive behaviors" are understood in terms of the subset of a system's features actually employed by a user.

As a model intended to augment the theory of adaptive structuration, Griffith's (1999) work raises some intriguing questions. First, is it possible for users only to notice and make sense of features that were put there by designers (either intentionally or unintentionally)? As earlier noted by Orlikowski (1992), Griffith argued that users can create new features during the social construction and use of a technology, but she was silent on whether they could only notice features "as designed" into a technology (diagram, p. 474) or whether they might also perceive and make sense of features that are not "really" there. Second, if only *noticed* features are available for sensemaking, does it follow that only noticed features are available for appropriation and/or creations into new features? Put differently, can users become directly, or "prereflectively" aware of some features and use them without explicit intentionality and reflective cognitions (Mohr, 1996; Heft, 2003)[11]?

Features in Practice Theory

As mentioned earlier, Orlikowski (1992) originally argued that the process of technology design embeds social structures (rules and resources) in technology. In more recent work, Orlikowski (2000) rejected the notion of embedded structures, because:

> ***While these notions have been extremely valuable in explaining the various outcomes associated with*** *the use of given technologies in different contexts,* ***they are*** *less able to account effectively for ongoing changes in both technologies* ***and their use. This insufficiency is particularly acute in the context of internetworked and reconfigurable technology (such as groupware and the Web)...*** (p. 405, added emphasis)

Orlikowski (2000) again differentiated technology use (called "technology-in-practice") from the technology artifact. She acknowledged that: "From the users' point of view, technologies come with a set of properties crafted by designers and developers" (p. 409). Researchers can examine these properties to identify expected technology uses, but technology does not determine these uses; rather they emerge as people interact with tools in particular situations. "Use of a technology is not a choice among a closed set of predefined possibilities" (p. 409); nevertheless, "it is important to keep in mind that the recurrent use of a technology is not infinitely malleable" (p. 409).

Increasing use of e-collaboration technologies creates new challenges for research on technology use and effects: e-collaboration technology is often "radically tailorable" and integrated into complex configurations with other tools (Orlikowski, 2000, p. 424). The material properties of such technologies are not solely those initially created by designers; they are also the product of users' actions. Users can change their technologies by downloading plug-ins, developing (or commissioning development of) specialized applications, or modifying how features work through customization. Because the nature of technology changes during technology use, social structures are not embedded in technology, but only emerge when "people interact recurrently with whatever properties [features] of the technology are at hand, whether these were built in, added on, modified, or invented on the fly" (p. 407).

This "practice" perspective on information technology, so elegantly detailed by Orlikowski, is extraordinarily powerful and useful for students of e-collaboration technology. Its key strength is its ability to explain how, where, and why "slippage" occurs between the intentions of designers and the practices of users. Her application of this perspective to the e-collaboration technology of Lotus Notes shows, as Contractor and Seibold (1993) required, how and why people can "enact different technologies-in-practice with the same type of technology across various contexts and practices" (Orlikowski, 2000, p. 420). Although this premise undoubtedly applies to most types of IT, it is particularly important for the specific case of e-collaboration technologies, in contrast with the less interpretively flexible (Orlikowski, 2000) (or more restrictive, Silver, 1991) ITs, such as individual decision support systems or enterprise resource planning systems.

The power of Orlikowski's analytical distinction between technologies as artifacts (bundles of features) and technologies-in-practice is not limited to those who take an ensemble view of technology. Her research provides an invaluable reminder to tool view researchers that technology does not determine use or outcomes. Therefore, one should not expect the "same" technology to be used in precisely the same way in different contexts. Consequently, researchers who adopt a tool view of technology should reject the flawed premise that, "...the impact of [a] technology *ought to be consistent across groups using it.*" (Contractor & Seibold, 1993, p. 531, original emphasis)

Moreover, Orlikowski's work cautions tool view researchers that *no two implementations or installations of today's complex e-collaboration technologies may be identical in material properties or features*. Two different installations of a single packaged system, e.g., Lotus Notes, can be quite different, not just in use, but also *as artifacts,* because of choices make by the organizations and individuals that adopt the Notes package. The features available to users may differ because of "properties ... built in, added on, modified, or invented on the fly" after initial development (Orlikowski, 2000 p. 407). If material properties can differ across installations of the same packaged e-collaboration technology, it is even more likely to be the case that one vendor's implementation of e-collaboration functionality will have significantly different features than another vendor's offering (e.g., Notes versus Groove), even when those two systems purport to do the same thing. Therefore, researchers who adopt a tool view of technology must give as careful attention to differences in technology's material features as ensemble view researchers give to differences in "technologies-in-practice".

In the next section of this essay, I discuss how tool view theorists might approach technology features differently in light of these understandings.

A Tool View of the IT Artifact

Tool view researchers have fundamentally different objectives than ensemble researchers do. Tool view researchers try to understand and explain technologies' "effects" (or "impacts"). By contrast, many ensemble view theorists aim to demonstrate that technology *does not have impacts* (or that technology effects differ substantially from those predicted by technology determinsts). Howcraft, Miteve and Wilson (2004) described proponents of the "social shaping of technology approach" (which includes the social construction of technology perspective and actor-network theory), in terms that may also characterize structuration theorists:

> [S]*ocial shaping researchers are united in their aim to critique the predominance of technological determinism* [which] *comprises two key ideas: firstly, technology development is seen as autonomous; and societal development is determined by technology....* [In technological determinism] *society is merely responsive, as technology moulds society according to its needs.* (pp. 332-3)

Although some ensemble theorists, such as the late Rob Kling, adhere to the "weak constructivist" position that "the specific nature of the technology itself (computing and information systems specifically) has some bearing on its effects" (Howcraft et al., 2004) [12], others strenuously reject that idea. "Strong constructivists" strive to show how society shapes technology (rather than the other way around); naturally, they tend to study technology development and technology-in-use and to eschew studies of technology features and purported "impacts".

Because of their theoretical and ideological commitments, social constructivists have generally pursued studies likely to reveal how *the same technology* is used in *different ways* owing to *different contexts*, institutional arrangements, local motivations, etc. Conversely, they have *not* pursued studies that are likely to reveal technology-shaping effects, if any, such as studies that examine the uses of *different technologies in generally similar*[13] (that is, not systematically different) *contexts*. Ironically, the same is also true of the vast majority of *tool view* studies of e-collaboration technologies—which could go a long way to explaining their disappointing results. Before justifying that last assertion, however, it is important to be explicit about why, although it is *not* realistic to expect *consistency* in use practices and outcomes *within a technology*, it *is* reasonable to look for *systematic differences* in uses and outcomes *across technologies*.

Systematic Differences Across Technologies

The ensemble perspective explains how the same IT artifact (e.g., Lotus Notes) can be used differently across various social contexts. It does not help us see how different IT artifacts purporting to do the same or similar things (e.g., Lotus Notes versus Groove; Eudora versus Outlook) might be associated with *systematically* different *patterns* of technology use practices.

Why is it reasonable to expect, and meaningful to look for, systematic differences across such different technologies? After all, knowing that the *same* technology can be used differently in different contexts also strongly implies that *different* technologies would be used differently. Think about the answer in statistical terms. The different use practices of a single technology could represent statistical variations around a central tendency described by what Orlikowski (2000) calls the "expected uses" (p. 409) of a technology's material properties as crafted by designers. Although these expected uses do not represent "a closed set of predefined possibilities" (p. 409); they are "not infinitely malleable" (p. 409). Thus, one would expect to find that usage patterns cluster around the central tendency of "expected uses". Another superficially similar technology might likewise exhibit variable usage patterns around a central tendency, but, if it differed in features from the first technology, *its central tendency might be different* in a way consistent with its different features (Griffith & Northcraft, 1994).

An analogy from a different field of inquiry might clarify this reasoning. When one compares societies in which the subsistence technology is hunting and gathering, one can observe enormous differences in social organization and cultural beliefs. However, when one compares hunter-gatherer societies with agricultural societies, striking *patterns of differences* in social organization and belief systems become visible (Lenski & Lenski, 1970). Similarly, in agricultural France, noticeably different plow designs were used in different social arrangements in two locales with different ecological conditions (Stinchcombe, 1983); despite these large pattern differences, there were undoubtedly also numerous variations in tool design and social arrangements within each region.

The type of argument I'm using here is similar to one used in several branches of sociology and anthropology in the 1980s, known under names such as "cultural materialism" (Harris, 1980), "economic sociology" (Stinchcombe, 1983) or "political economy." Today, that style of argument is unfashionable in some circles[14], probably because of its origins in Marxist historical materialism. Stripped of some of its more unpalatable elements, however, the idea of "probabilistic" technology effects (Harris, 1980) could provide a foundation for a "technology-shaping" view.

When people want to use a technology to achieve certain goals, the technology not only has certain material properties that may suggest "expected usages" (which Norman, 1990 called "affordances"[15]), it also evokes what Stinchcombe (1983) called "derived motivations"[16]—that is, motivations to do those things that have to be done in order to use the technology to achieve people's goals. For example, because I want to use my computer system to write this chapter, I am also motivated to do many things that are only indirectly related to writing but are directly related to the characteristics of the computer system I use. Examples include coping with a screen size that doesn't let me read multiple pages at once, leading me to rely on my printer, which I have to support by buying toner, clearing jams, and so forth. Using my computer system to accomplish my writing goals has shaped my writing-with-computer behavior in ways that I believe differ systematically from that of colleagues who have access to multiple, large and linked display screens. Consider two additional examples of technology-shaping effects from published research on e-collaboration technologies.

E-Mail Features and Use Patterns

Using data from my case study of e-mail use in the late 1980s (Markus, 1994a; Markus 1994b), I recently (Markus, 2004) listed a large number of problems that managers at HCP Inc. had to overcome because they wanted to gain efficiency benefits by using a primitive e-mail system. These problems included:

- The Mail system permitted 12-character user IDs that did not adequately identify the senders and intended receivers of e-mail messages.
- The Mail system lacked a "cc" feature, requiring all recipients to be listed on the "to" line, making it difficult to know who was expected to respond or take action.
- Someone using the Mail system's REPLY feature would only reach the sender of the original message, no matter how many other recipients had been listed on the original message's "to" line; when this happened, it broke the chain of group communication.
- Non-response to messages challenged continued use of e-mail, because the likely reaction in the case of non-response is a follow-up telephone call, which

is costly for the sender and fails to discipline the recipient for not responding to the message. (See Markus 2004, Table 2.1 pp. 41-3.)

Mangers at HCP Inc. evolved several recurrent solutions to these problems, including the following:

- Users originally chose mnemonic e-mail IDs that signified their organizational position; however, they were reluctant to change e-mail IDs when they changed organizational roles, which led to great confusion over the identity of e-mail senders; users adapted by nearly always using redundant salutations and signatures in the body of their messages.
- Using redundant salutations to name particular recipients when there were multiple individuals on the "to" line made it clearer who was expected to take action and for whom the message was an "FYI" (i.e., people on the "to" line but not in the salutation).
- Users routinely used the FORWARD feature in lieu of the REPLY feature, even though this involved more work (reentering the ID of the sender), because, in this particular e-mail system, the FORWARD feature would automatically "cc" the message with history to all e-mail IDs listed on the original message's "to" line.
- Users sent important information only through e-mail, thereby penalizing those who had not logged on; they subordinated the telephone to e-mail by delaying responses to telephone messages, by requiring e-mail scheduling of telephone calls and so forth, thus ensuring that recipients continued to use Mail; senders sometimes used "shotgun [broadcast] messages" to get a response quickly without going through channels; this created enough havoc that people were motivated to check e-mail regularly, so they would have a chance to contain the damage. (See Markus, 2004, Table 2.1 pp. 41-43.)

It would be wrong to conclude that the Mail system *determined* the technology use patterns of HCP Inc. managers. Had they not wanted to achieve a certain goal (i.e., to improve efficiency per their President's mandate), they might not have experienced feature-related problems when they tried to use Mail, and they might not have invented solutions for those problems through their recurrent use of the technology. They might have invented different solutions to the problems posed to them by the Mail system.

However, although the Mail system did not *determine* their technology use patterns, it did *shape* them. If the Mail system had had different features—if, for example, it had had a "cc" line, as most e-mail systems do today, HCP Inc. managers would likely not have evolved their practices regarding salutations[17]. If they had had a feature to archive communications by topic, as in PROFS or Lotus Notes, they might not have evolved their use of FORWARD in lieu of REPLY.

At the same time, some of their behavior patterns seemed to have been shaped, not by particular features of the Mail system, but by the whole package of features we call the e-mail medium (Griffith and Northcraft 1994). For example, HCP Inc. managers complained of "shotgun messages" in which a query was sent to everyone in hopes that anyone (or the right someone) would reply. That problem has now come to be viewed as intimately linked with the medium, regardless of context: "For instance, if we are seeking assistance on a matter, sometimes it is easiest to broadcast a message to multiple recipients in the hope that someone will respond" (Weber, 2004 p. vi). By contrast, broadcasting to everyone is not seen as a negative social "impact" of listservs, but rather as one of their beneficial features. In that sense, one would expect to see different "impacts" (patterns of use and different outcomes) for the two superficially similar technologies of e-mail and listservs[18].

As Orlikowski (2000) also argued, the Mail illustration shows that the features of technology (especially e-collaboration technologies) are rarely binding constraints. Binding implies that no other course of action is possible to users. The materialist position is, not that technology causes[19] people to behave the way they do, but only that it makes it expensive for them to do otherwise, and hence they often don't. Stinchcombe (1983) noted that most technological "constraints" can be removed, but only at a cost (often denominated in users' effort, rather than in money). Thus, a technology is said to be constraining if alternative technologies "cost" more, such that the usual course of action is to use the first technology, with all the "derived motivations" and recurring patterns of behavior that using the technology entails (Stinchcombe, 1983).

In this example, my evidence for the thesis that technology shapes behavior is the tight correspondence between the features available to users and the behavior patterns of people who were motivated to work with the technology to achieve particular goals. More likely to be persuasive, however, is evidence of behavior patterns that vary systematically with the features of apparently similar technologies. A study of electronic calendar systems provides suggestive evidence along those lines.

Electronic Calendars, Use Patterns, and Social "Impacts"

Palen and Grudin (2002) studied the use of different electronic calendar systems at Microsoft Corporation and Sun Microsystems. The two systems varied significantly in their privacy default settings. The default setting on Microsoft's SCHEDULE+ system highly restricted the amount of calendar information that others could access; the default setting on Sun's Calendar Manager permitted everyone on the network to read the full contents of others' calendars.

Consistent with other studies showing that users rarely modify the default settings of their IT systems, Palen and Grudin (2002) found that over 80% of users surveyed in each company maintained the default privacy settings. They also found "remarkable" differences in patterns of technology-in-use, which they attributed in part to those privacy defaults. Sun employees used their scheduling system, not just to schedule meetings, but also to learn what was going on in their organization. They could assess whether someone was in her office and whether she would need time to get back from a meeting across town. To schedule a group meeting, Sun employees would identify a possible time by inspecting attendees' calendars and suggesting a specific time to the others in a regular e-mail message (although they could have used the calendar system itself to set up the meeting). By contrast, Microsoft employees checked others' availability then sent an automatic SCHEDULE+ message announcing a proposed time. Recipients would then accept or decline the meeting with a keystroke, without an explanation. According to Palen and Grudin (2002), this hit-or-miss (and apparently blunt) approach evolved in response to the relative lack of information available in people's calendars.

Let's for the moment suppose that the patterns of behavior observed by Palen and Grudin (2002) in these two companies were generally replicated in other settings where the two different calendar packages were used. (This *is* a hypothetical. Sun and Microsoft are very different companies, and it is possible that institutional factors alone explain the findings there; the different privacy defaults could represent a spurious correlation.) If so, the findings would constitute reasonable support for the hypothesis that technology shapes behavior (and related social outcomes). A small difference in features could mean a noticeable difference in social outcomes for companies choosing between these packages. Knowledge that such a link existed, even a weak one, could lead to efficacious changes in companies' technology selection decisions or in their implementation practices (e.g., changing defaults before a package is released to users, educating users, and so forth).

This hypothesis of a link between features and uses or outcomes is not deterministic. It allows for the possibility of choice, not just by implementers, but also by users: when using an electronic calendar system, individuals can disregard both privacy defaults and implementers' guidance. The hypothesis also allows for the possibility of emergence—an organization might enact use practices similar to Sun's while using Microsoft's package, or it might enact altogether different practices. It is agnostic about a priori fit between features and context—some organizations might select well, some might not. It is also agnostic about the type of technology-in-practice that might be enacted: inertia, application, change (Orlikowski, 2000)—or outright rejection. It merely asserts that differences in technology features might explain variations in usage patterns at an aggregate level.

Features and Impacts in The "Tool View"

Ironically, not only have ensemble view researchers not sought systematic evidence of technology-shaping effects, neither have e-collaboration researchers who adopt the tool view of technology. To find technology-shaping effects requires careful attention to both technology features and to technology use patterns, and much prior e-collaboration research has been limited on both dimensions. The single largest body of research on e-collaboration technologies has focused on group support system "impacts". Fjermestad and Hiltz (1998-99) reviewed 184 unique experiments, the vast majority of which compared face-to-face group work to the use of GSS. Of these studies, I counted only 3 (Davey & Olson, 1998; Gopal et al., 1992-3; Sia, Tan, & Wei, 1997) that compared the use of different GSS packages (e.g., GroupSystems to OptionFinder) and only four more studies that compared the Level 1 (communication only) to Level 2 (decision support) capabilities of the same package (e.g., SAMM). An additional 54 case and field studies of GSS use involved *no* detailed comparisons of different GSS technologies (Fjermestad & Hiltz, 2000-2001). Study designs such as these are simply not able to reveal convincing evidence of technology-shaping effects.

What underlying assumptions in GSS research might have prevented a focus on technology-shaping effects? Fjermestad and Hiltz (1998-99) opined that: "[M]ost experiments seem (mistakenly) to assume that all GSS are a standard 'package' that will have the same effect" (p. 15). But additional factors might also be involved. GSS are a class of IS tools that were developed by IS researchers with the explicit goal of improving group work following social science theory and practice (DeSanctis & Gallupe, 1987). From the very beginning, GSS research has largely adopted an evaluation stance in which *the objective is to learn whether the tools fulfilled the designers' intentions*. Over time, the assertion that "a [GSS] *aims to* improve the process of group decision making" (DeSanctis & Gallupe, 1987, p. 589, added emphasis) has become the largely accepted belief that improving group outcomes *is* what GSS do: "GSS is an enabling technology that can promote constructive social interactions, which in turn will increase meeting performance" (Reinig & Shin, 2002 p. 305). The continued focus on what GSS *are supposed to do* is not conducive to seeing what *other* (or different) effects they might have when people recurrently use them. Perhaps it should not be surprising that GSS research has had disappointing results, when it has not yet fully pursued the research agenda laid out as its foundation:

> ***We propose that research into the design and use [I'd add "and effects"] should proceed in an iterative manner, beginning with Level 1 and Level 2 systems and advancing to the study of Level 3 systems after some understanding of the needed [I'd substitute the word "actual"]***

> ***features and impacts of the lower level systems has been achieved. With this approach in mind, how do researchers begin? A critical first step is to construct a software environment [I would add "or find suitable software environments in the field"] in which*** *alternative [GSS] designs can be compared...* (DeSanctis & Gallupe, 1987 p. 595, added emphasis)

In other fields of inquiry that focus on technology, scholars have found it useful to put aside the notion that cultural evolution and technological advance mean *progress* "in the sense of improvement" (Lenski & Lenski, 1970). Thinking of technology development and social change in terms of temporal *progression*, as in "the progress of a disease" (Lenski & Lenski, 1970) is a much healthier way to keep the focus on technology-shaping effects.

A Research Agenda on Technology-Shaping Effects

The aim of a technology-shaping research agenda (a type of "tool view", Orlikowski & Iacono, 2001) is to learn whether, when, how, and why the features of e-collaboration tools shape technology use practices and social outcomes. The hypothesis guiding this agenda is that focusing directly on two concepts (features and patterns of use) that have largely been controlled in prior e-collaboration research might lead to a better understanding of technology effects. Such an agenda offers both opportunities and challenges for future e-collaboration research.

Opportunities

When DeSanctis and Gallupe (1987) first published their foundation for GSS research, GSS were not generally commercially available, and there were relatively few other good examples of e-collaboration tools besides GSS. Accordingly, DeSanctis and Gallupe (1987) based their research agenda on tool building and laboratory experimentation. Today, the options are far greater. Not only are there quite a number of commercial and open source packages, some tool categories have several offerings: e-mail packages, document database systems, e-learning systems, technology for the support of virtual communities (e.g., listserves), electronic calendars, and knowledge management systems (like AskMe and Tacit's ActiveNet), and group authoring tools (Wikis versus hypertext and XML). This proliferation can enable the design of interesting comparative field studies.

For example, virtual community environments[20] offer a range of technical variations that are plausibly associated with different patterns of use and social outcomes. For example, whether or not messages are threaded and whether or not multiple identities are allowed and users' identities are validated by community monitors are plausibly associated with behaviors such as searching previously posted information (versus asking without searching), making supportive remarks (versus flaming), and making financial transactions with other members. In some interest areas (e.g., rock star fan clubs), it is possible to find several virtual community environments with different features, allowing for comparison of outcomes.

Furthermore, the technology-shaping perspective affords new opportunities for experimental studies. Here, the focus would not be on comparing the presence of media or features to their absence but rather on comparing *different implementations of the same feature*. For example, software defaults, as in Palen and Grudin's (2002) study of electronic calendar systems, lend themselves nicely to experimental controls. Similarly, one could experimentally compare different ways of implementing a feature such as anonymity. In GroupSystems, each comment is randomly numbered. Consider an alternative implementation in which each comment was coded with a participant number so that users could see all comments made by each unnamed individual. Would users be more likely to try to guess others' identities in the second condition? Would they be more accurate in their identifications than they are with GroupSystems (cf. Hayne, Pollard, & Rice, 2003)?

Another opportunity lies in trying to find linkages between organizations or individuals and the technology selections they make. A great deal of effort goes into technology selection, yet very little academic research assesses how these choices are made and what their implications are. (See Ginsburg & Duliba, 1997 for an exception.) Is there any regularity in the kinds of organizations that select AskMe versus ActiveNet? If so, what does it tell us about the nature of the fit between technology features and "ecological" conditions?

Yet another opportunity lies in analyzing the development trajectories of particular e-collaboration technologies in terms of features and the problems users experience when trying to use them. How do the changing features of a technology shape (or co-evolve with) social understandings of how the technology should be used?

These examples hardly exhaust the possibilities of a technology-shaping research agenda. At the same time, several challenges need to be addressed to make this research agenda vibrant and productive.

Challenges

Researchers who pursue a technology-shaping agenda face a number of challenges as well as opportunities. High among them is the dearth of carefully articulated theoretical statements to guide the work. Whether features should be conceptualized and operationalized as designers' intentions, users' perceptions, material properties (structural features), researchers' assessment of spirit (DeSanctis & Poole 1994), or the interplay among them is undoubtedly a key concern.

This conceptual challenge can be turned into a research opportunity. Some of the most fascinating work in the materialist tradition has explored the tensions between what people say and what they actually do (and why) (Harris, 1980). It might similarly be possible to exploit these tensions in e-collaboration research. For example, de Vreede and de Bruijn (1999) carefully delineated the GSS spirit and then showed how it did not fit numerous interorganizational policy making contexts. One could also: compare and explain the divergence between designers' intentions and package spirit or between package spirit and users' perceptions of package capabilities; compare a package's structural features, spirit, and users' perceptions to observed patterns of use; or compare the spirits of different e-collaboration packages from the same tool category. The slippages between designers' intentions, the material properties of the technologies they produce, users' perceptions and uses, and researchers' points of view offer endless research opportunities for scholars who work on the technology-shaping agenda.

A related theoretical problem is whether technology effects are believed to require users to notice or be aware of relevant features. In this area, too, I would argue against premature theoretical closure: There is reason to believe that some technology use is skilled behavior that takes place outside of people's awareness (Markus, 2004; Heft, 2003). Thus, technology-shaping effects could occur even when people don't notice features.

Several authors have pointed out the (related) methodological challenges of deciding (and controlling) the level of feature granularity (DeSanctis & Poole, 1994; Griffith & Northcraft, 1994). If one is concerned about demonstrating causality and ensuring consistency of research results from one study to the next, one always faces problems of how finely one needs to categorize features. From an experimental control perspective, comparing whole packages (e.g., Notes versus Groove) used in different settings is hopelessly problematic; if one did find systematic differences in use patterns, to what could they be attributed? On the other hand, if the goal is to find broad patterns of regularities or to provide guidance to practitioners, excessive concern with control could be misplaced. Every day business executives compare packages that differ on innumerable features, but they generally have to choose on the basis of package entirety. Knowledge about systematic technology effects at the gross package level could be useful to them, even if the precise source of these effects remains somewhat unclear. In general, the technology-shaping perspective outlined in this chapter is not concerned with tight correlations between specific features and specific uses, but rather with plausible linkages and broad patterns that could stimulate new design research or better implementation.

This still begs the question of where to start looking for features likely to have effects. Although no one approach is likely to fit all research purposes, I can offer a few suggestions. One could start with a priori theoretical interests, such as decision making (where features that might restrict or give guidance would be a place to start, cf. Silver, 1991) or privacy (where anonymity and opt-out features might be of prime concern). Alternatively, one could start by looking at the technologies of a type and seeing where they differ most, such as in the privacy defaults of electronic calendars, the threading and member registration of virtual community environments, or whether the expert profiles of knowledge management systems are generated by the expert or by the system. Still another place to start is in the level and type integration of various packages—does a user have to go to another piece of software if s/he wants to communicate with someone who does not use a particular e-collaboration tool? There are many possible starting places, each likely to lead in interesting research directions.

The technology-shaping agenda also raises challenges in terms of describing and measuring technology and use patterns. Orlikowski's (2000) work tells us that, where e-collaboration tools are concerned, one cannot reasonably assume that either categories of tools (e-mail systems), or individual tools in a category (Lotus Notes), have fixed material properties. It's not good enough to refer to labels like "mobile devices" when searching for effects. Whether it's a Palm or a Blackberry probably makes a difference. Furthermore, a Palm onto which a user has downloaded numerous add-on applications is not the same thing as one that has not been so customized. It is also the case that the Palm III and the Treo 600 are very different tools. Therefore, researchers will need to develop ways to characterize features, to cluster variations into manageable categories, and to be explicit about the dynamic nature and temporal boundedness of their subject matter (Orlikowski & Iacono, 2001). Similarly, researchers will need new approaches for analyzing technology use patterns and social outcomes. Fortunately, e-collaboration tool designers have already started thinking about this problem, and their solutions may provide guidance to technology-shaping researchers (Martin & Sommerville, 2004).

Conclusion

This chapter has proposed the basics of a technology-shaping perspective on e-collaboration technologies as an alternative both to the ensemble view (Orlikowski & Iacono, 2001) and to the nominal (absent) view that seems to characterize such a large amount of the GSS literature (Fjermestad & Hiltz, 1998-99). The technology-shaping perspective can be summarized as follows: Technologies pose problems for users who want to use them to accomplish particular goals; the solutions users create for those problems during recurrent use may exhibit certain regularities across different contexts[21]. Consequently, small differences in the features of apparently similar tools could be associated with noticeable variations in usage patterns and social outcomes.

Like the ensemble view, the technology-shaping perspective eschews technological determinism. When one compares the technology-shaping perspective with the five premises Orlikowski & Iacono (2001) offer as a starting point for theorizing about IT artifacts, one sees that they are not very different: Both the ensemble view and technology-shaping view can accommodate the beliefs that IT artifacts are shaped by people, embedded in historical and social contexts, made up of a multiplicity of components, emergent from social and economic practices, and dynamic. But what these two different perspectives do with these premises is different. Ensemble view researchers look for differences across contexts attributable to human action; technology-shaping researchers would look for regularities across contexts attributable to the material properties of technology.

Like GSS research, the technology-shaping perspective looks for effects that can be attributed to technology's material features, but the technology-shaping perspective looks for those effects in a different place—in broad probabilistic patterns observable across different contexts in which different tools are used, not in tightly controlled comparisons with conditions in which tools are not used. The hypothesis is that conducting future research on a technology-shaping agenda could yield cumulative results that are less "disappointing" than many scholars find GSS research, the largest single body of work on e-collaboration technologies.

Postscript

Jennifer Xu (Bentley College) appropriately challenged me to articulate the premises of the tool view (personal e-mail, 12/29/05), a task that I side-stepped in the original article. I attempt that task provisionally here, for the technology-shaping view, if not for the tool view writ large:

1. IT artifacts are not necessarily better than the artifacts and manual activities they replace. When used, they do not always have beneficial consequences. Unintended consequences are the rule, rather than the exception. Consequently, there is no role in the technology-shaping research agenda for naïve notions of technological progress or the assumption that "problematic" technology uses and outcomes can be attributed to problematic users.

2. Like all other students of technology, technology-shaping researchers need to locate themselves theoretically in terms of the two orthogonal dichotomies of materialism/realism (concerned with the causal role of the environment and technology) versus idealism (concerned with the causal role of cognitions and ideologies) and determinism (belief in the external control of human behavior) versus volunteerism (belief in the possibility of individual and social choice) (Barley 1998). Barley argued that "empirical evidence undermines any warrant for taking a strong stance on either dimension" (p. 251), and I generally agree. However, the technology-shaping perspective is more compatible with the *materialist/realist* side of the first dichotomy. This side has been woefully neglected in IS research, which generally views technology in terms of users' cognitions (cf. Jasperson et al., 2005). Therefore, technology-shaping research could be productive of important new insights. On the other hand, the technology-shaping perspective as outlined above is *not deterministic* on the second dichotomy, but retains a role for individual and organizational choice. (At the same time, it does not necessarily assume that all human behavior is intentional.) In other words, the technology-shaping perspective holds that, although IT artifacts with particular features might have certain effects if used in particular ways, there is no guarantee that people will actually use those artifacts in those ways. This, in turn, makes describing and explaining how technologies are used an important part of the technology-shaping agenda. However, unlike the typical IS research approach of looking for *user* characteristics or cognitions to explain the uses of IT, the technology-shaping perspective looks for explanations in the characteristics of the *technology* available to particular users.
3. The *effective* features of an IT artifact—that is, the features to which a technology's effects can be persuasively attributed—may not be invariant across users and situations. That is, an artifact's effective features may vary depending on who uses it, when, and for what purposes. Put differently, a single IT artifact can provide different affordances to different groups of organizations or individual users, according to the nature of their business, their expertise in IT or in the subject matter of a particular IT (cf. Markus et al., 2002), or some other factor. Yet another way of saying this is that technology affordances (or material agency, cf. Pickering, 1995) can be viewed as an emergent property of human interaction with technology. This means that technology-shaping researchers must take great care in adopting a point of view from which to describe and analyze features. At least three different perspectives on features can be differentiated: the designers' point of view, the individual and organizational users' point(s) of view, and the researcher's point of view. The designer's point of view should serve only as a point of departure for analysis, because an IT artifact may imperfectly reflect the designer's intentions, and because individual and organizational

users might have modified the tool. Therefore, depending on the purposes of a study, multiple points of view might be required. And researchers or other analysts might have a perspective on a tool (e.g., its spirit) (DeSanctis, Snyder & Poole, 1994; Heft, 2003) that is not shared by either the tool's designers or its users. These observations suggest, 1) the value of research exploring the features of IT artifacts from multiple points of view and, 2) the importance of justifying the point(s) of view used in particular technology studies.

4. The features of an IT artifact (and hence, its expected uses and consequences) may be different at different points in time. A software package has different features in each new release. Organizations can alter the package by modification, customization, integration, support, etc. And end-users can made additional changes. These observations highlight the challenges involved in ensuring "comparability" of IT artifacts in cross-sectional technology-shaping studies. At the same time, careful attention to the temporal dimension is critical for maintaining a role for human agency in material/realist analyses (Archer, 1995).
5. A corollary of the above points is that, depending on the temporal orientation and purposes of a study, the effective features of an IT artifact may include elements that extend well beyond the boundaries of the "material" (i.e., hardware and software). An expanded view of the IT artifact might include "social" features such as business process changes, support services, and charges for use—elements that economists refer to as "complements" in their studies of when and why IT delivers business value. Ensemble theorists caution against viewing technology as "stripped of use" (Kling et al., 2003; Star et al., 1996); their solution is to restrict the scope of the term "technology" to the narrowly "material" (Orlikowski, 2000) and to consider social complements as parts of the "technology-in-use". However, technology-shaping researchers have a different research agenda than many ensemble theorists do. Because technology-shaping researchers set out to study technology effects, they need to push back the boundaries of the technology-in-use concept somewhat and to take a somewhat larger view of the technology concept. Taking this larger view of technology is an explicit acknowledgement that technology is "social" in the sense that people and institutions create, recreate, and reinvent technology. However, acknowledging the social nature of technology does not diminish the value of looking for effects that might occur when people use technology. Only by tracing the effects of technology-in-use back to the real social and technical features of IT artifacts can we make concrete recommendations for changes in the design of IT artifacts that might be successful in altering those effects. Consequently, a core challenge for technology-shaping researchers is to develop ways to characterize (describe, measure, compare) IT artifacts "made up of a multiplicity of … [social and technical] components" (Orlikowski et al., 2001 p. 131).

To my eyes, these five points are similar to the five premises listed by Orlikowski et al. (2001), but they are framed differently—in terms of what they mean for researchers who are interested in exploring the possibility, the nature, and the causes of technology effects. Does this mean, as Steve Sawyer pointed out that "we can take BOTH a social shaping and technology shaping view… that [we] must take BOTH and privilege NEITHER" (personal e-mail 1/27/2006)? Maybe so. At the same time, I'd like to read the results of research conducted using the technology-shaping view.

Acknowledgments

This chapter is dedicated to the memories of Rob Kling and Gerry DeSanctis. The ideas in the chapter originated in conversations with Sabine G. Hirt. I am grateful for the comments and encouragement of Andrew Dutta, Matthew Jones, Ana Ortiz de Guinea Lopez de Arana, Mark Silver, Steve Sawyer, Mike Tyworth, Jennifer Xu and the members of the Bentley Invision project team: Jane Fedorowicz, Joe Gelinas, Janis Gogan, Amy Ray, Cathy Usoff, and Chris Williams.

References

Archer, M. S. (1995). *Realist social theory: The morphogenic approach*. Cambridge, UK: Cambridge University Press.

Barley, S. R. (1998). What can we learn from the history of technology? *Journal of Engineering Technology Management, 15*, 237-255.

Briggs, R. O., Nunamaker, Jr., Jay F., & Sprague, Jr., Ralph H. (1998-99). GSS insights: A look back at the lab, a look forward from the field. *Journal of Management Information Systems, 15*(3), 3-6.

Chin, W. W., Gopal, A., & Salisbury, W. D. (1997). Advancing the theory of adaptive structuration: The development of a scale to measure faithfulness of appropriation. *Information Systems Research, 8*(4), 342-367.

Chudoba, K. M. (1999). Appropriations and patterns in the use of group support systems. *The Data Base for Advances in Information Systems, 30*(3,4), 131-148.

Contractor, N. S., & Seibold, D. R. (1993). Theoretical frameworks for the study of structuring processes in group decision support systems: Adaptive structuration theory and self-organizing systems theory. *Human Communication Research, 19*(4), 528-563.

Davey, A., & Olson, D. (1998). Multiple criteria decision making models in group decision support. *Group Decision and Negotiation, 7*(1), 55-75.

de Vreede, G.-J., & de Bruijn, H. (1999). Exploring the boundaries of successful GSS application: Supporting inter-organizational policy networks. *The Data Base for Advances in Information Systems, 30*(4), 111-130.

DeSanctis, G., & Gallupe, R. B. (1987). A foundation for the study of group decision support systems. *Management Science, 33*(5), 589-609.

DeSanctis, G., & Poole, M. S. (1994). Capturing the complexity in advanced technology use: Adaptive structuration theory. *Organization Science, 5*(2), 121-147.

DeSanctis, G., Snyder, J. R., & Poole, M. S. (1994). The meaning of the interface: A functional and holistic evaluation of a meeting software system. *Decision Support Systems, 11*(319-335).

Fjermestad, J., & Hiltz, S. R. (1998-99). An assessment of group support systems experimental research: Methodology and results. *Journal of Management Information Systems, 15*(3), 7-149.

Fjermestad, J., & Hiltz, S. R. (2000-2001). Group support systems: A descriptive evaluation of case and field studies. *Journal of Management Information Systems, 17*(3), 115-159.

Ginsburg, M., & Duliba, K. (1997). Enterprise-level groupware choices: Evaluating Lotus Notes and intranet-based solutions. *Computer Supported Cooperative Work: The Journal of Collaborative Computing, 6*, 201-225.

Gopal, A., Bostrom, R. P., & Chin, W. W. (1992-3). Applying adaptive structuration theory to investigate the process of group support systems use. *Journal of Management Information Systems, 9*(3), 45-69.

Griffith, T. L. (1999). Technology features as triggers for sensemaking. *Academy of Management Review, 24*(3), 472-498.

Griffith, T. L., & Northcraft, G. B. (1994). Distinguishing between the forest and the trees: Media, features, and methodology in electronic communication research. *Organization Science, 5*(2 (May)), 272-285.

Harris, M. (1980). *Cultural materialism: The struggle for a science of culture*. New York. Vintage Books.

Hayne, S. C., Pollard, C. E., & Rice, R. E. (2003). Identification of comment authorship in anonymous group support systems. *Journal of Management Information Systems, 20*(1), 301-330.

Heft, H. (2003). Affordances, dynamic experience, and the challenge of reification. *Ecological Psychology, 15*(2), 149-180.

Howcraft, D., Miteve, N., & Wilson, M. (2004). What we may learn from the social shaping of technology approach (pp. 329-371). In J. Mingers & L. Willcocks (Eds.), *Social theory and philosophy for information systems*. London: John Wiley & Sons Ltd.

Ingold, T. (1996). Situating action VI: A comment on the distinction between the material and the social. *Ecological Psychology, 8*(2), 183-187.

Jasperson, J., Carter, P. E., & Zmud, R. W. (2005). A comprehensive conceptualization of post-adoptive behaviors associated with information technology enabled work systems. *MIS Quarterly, 29*(3), 525-557.

Jones, K. S. (2003). What is an affordance? *Ecological Psychology, 15*(2), 107-114.

Kling, R., & Iacono, S. (1988). The mobilization of support for computerization: The role of computerization movements. *Social Problems, 35*(3), 226-242.

Kling, R., McKim, G., & King, A. (2003). A bit more to it: Scholarly communication forums as socio-technical interaction networks. *Journal of the American Society for Information Science and Technology, 54*(1), 47-67.

Kling, R., & Scacchi, W. (1992). The web of computing: Computer technology as social organization. *Advances in Computing, 21*, 1-90.

Lamb, R., & Kling, R. (2003). Reconceptualizing users as social actors in information systems research. *MIS Quarterly, 27* (2), 197-235.

Lenski, G., & Lenski, J. (1970). *Human societies: An introduction to macrosociology* (2nd ed.). New York, NY: McGraw-Hill.

Markus, M. L. (1994a). Electronic mail as the medium of managerial choice. *Organization Science, 5*(4 (November)), 502-527.

Markus, M. L. (1994b). Finding a happy medium: Explaining the negative effects of electronic mail on social life at work. *ACM Transactions on Information Systems, 12*(2), 119-149.

Markus, M. L. (2004). Fit for function: Functionalism, neofunctionalism, and information systems. In J. Mingers & L. Willcocks (Eds.), *Social theory and philosophy for information systems.* (pp. 27-55). London: John Wiley & Sons.

Markus, M. L., Majchrzak, A., & Gasser, L. (2002). A design theory for systems that support emergent knowledge processes. *MIS Quarterly, 26*(3), 179-213.

Martin, D., & Sommerville, I. (2004). Patterns of cooperative interaction: Linking ethnomethodology and design. *ACM Transactions on Computer-Huamn Interaction, 11*(1), 59-89.

Mohr, L. B. (1996). *The causes of human behavior: Implications for theory and method in the social sciences*. Ann Arbor: The University of Michigan Press.

Norman, D. A. (1990). *The design of everyday things*. New York: Doubleday.

Orlikowski, W. J. (1992). The duality of technology: Rethinking the concept of technology in organizations. *Organization Science, 3*(3), 398-427.

Orlikowski, W. J. (2000). Using technology and constituting structures: A practice lens for studying technology in organizations. *Organization Science, 11*(4), 404-428.

Orlikowski, W. J., & Iacono, C. S. (2001). Research commentary: Desperately seeking "IT" in IT research—a call to theorizing the IT artifact. *Information Systems Research, 12*(2), 121-134.

Palen, L., & Grudin, J. (2002). Discretionary adoption of group support software: Lessons from calendar applications. In B. E. Munkvold (Ed.), *Implementing collaboration technologies in industry*. London: Springer Verlag.

Pickering, A. (1995). *The mangle of practice: Time, agency, and science*. Chicago, IL: University of Chicago Press.

Poole, M. S., & DeSanctis, G. (1990). Understanding the use of group decision support systems. In J. Fulk & C. Steinfield (Eds.), *Organizations and communication technology*. Thousand Oaks, CA: Sage Publications.

Poole, M. S., & DeSanctis, G. (1992). Microlevel structuration in computer-supported group decision making. *Human Communication Research, 19*(1), 5-49.

Reinig, B. A., & Shin, B. (2002). The dynamic effects of group support systems on group meetings. *Journal of Management Information Systems, 19*(2), 303-325.

Salisbury, W. D., Chin, W. W., Gopal, A., & Newsted, P. R. (2002). Research report: Better theory through measurement—developing a scale to capture consensus on appropriation. *Information Systems Research, 13*(1), 91-103.

Sia, C. L., Tan, B. C. Y., & Wei, K. K. (1997). Effects of a GSS interface and task type on group interaction: An empirical study. *Decision Support Systems, 19*, 289-299.

Silver, M. S. (1991). *Systems that support decision makers: Description and analysis*. Chichester, UK: John Wiley & Sons.

Star, S. L., & Ruhleder, K. (1996). Steps toward an ecology of infrastructure: Design and access for large information spaces. *Information Systems Research, 7*(1), 111-134.

Stinchcombe, A. L. (1983). *Economic sociology*. New York, NY: Academic Press.

Weber, R. (2004). Editor's comments--the grim reaper: The curse of e-mail. *MIS Quarterly, 28*(3), iii-xiii.

Endnotes

1 Mark Silver (Fordham University) did not like the name I gave this perspective and used in the title of the original article, arguing that "technology shaped" would be more appropriate (telephone call 2/8/06). I explained that I chose the term to mirror the term "social-shaping of technology". However, I acknowledged that the term is not entirely appropriate, since "social-shaping" refers primarily to technology development, that is, social effects on the characteristics of technology, where as the term "technology-shaping" was meant to refer to the consequences of technology use. Steve Sawyer "loved the 'Bugs and Features' subtitle and wished [I'd] used this phraseology more through the paper" (personal e-mail, 1/27/06). The subtitle was a nod to the title of my long out-of-print book (*Systems in Organizations: Bugs and Features*, Marshfield, MA: Pitman, 1984). It related to a story first told to me by Stu Madnick of the Sloan School at MIT and apparently told in software development circles around the globe. It has the punch-line: "That's not a bug, it's a feature".

2 Sawyer and Chen ("Conceptualizing Information Technology and Studying Information Systems: Trends and Issues," in: *Global and Organizational Discourse About Information Technology,* Myers, Whitley, Wynn and DeGross (eds.), Kluwer, London, 2002, pp. 109-131) conducted a similar analysis around a broader range of concepts. They also concluded that the majority of the literature reviewed provided "little insight into the specifics of the [information technology] being discussed."

3 Steve Sawyer (Penn State University) commented that I overstated the development of the ensemble view and understated the development of the tool view. He claimed that although there are many articles discussing ensemble view premises, "empirical details and particulars are more sketchy". By contrast, tool view "particulars are detailed, but the principles are a bit murky. ... Through the rest of the paper, you move across these distinctions to make points (the points are valid, but often hard to link up)" (personal e-mail, 1/27/06).

4 Or, as Mark Silver suggested, variants of the ensemble view (telephone call 2/8/06).

5 Mark Silver wanted to know where I stand now. Was I distancing myself from the ensemble view in this sentence and elsewhere in the article? By contrast, the technology-shaping perspective seemed to Mark to be a version of the ensemble view, an "enlightened tool view" as it were, rather than a tool view per se (telephone call, 2/8/06). I explained to him that I still consider myself an ensemble theorist. My reason for waffling in this and a few later sentences was my awareness that "strong constructionists" strongly dispute my arguments about the importance of IT's material features and therefore probably

do not regard me as an ensemble theorist. My wording aimed at not claiming to be a member of a group that would reject me.

6 I have since learned through my reading that the definitions/meanings of the concepts of *material* and *social* are highly problematic, and the distinctions made between them (or denied) are controversial. Some believe the two concepts are inseparable; others claim that only by differentiating them can you equate them (cf. Ingold "Situating Action VI: A Comment on the Distinction between the Material and the Social," *Ecological Psychology* (8:2), 1996, pp. 183-187). I am still sorting out where I stand on this issue. It seems likely that the debate disguises a deeper issue that could be more fruitful to explore.

7 Also called "institutions" by some.

8 DeSanctis, Snyder, and Poole (1994) examined GSS features in detail for a preliminary evaluation of the SAMM system's interface.

9 I have since become aware of a branch of psychology that focuses the behavior of animals and humans in their environments. Most ecological psychologists appear to believe that routine use of tools rarely involves cognitive reflection and explicit intentionality; rather, they believe that much tool use involves action based on direct (prereflective) perceptions of the affordances in the environment or animal-environment system (cf. Heft 2003). This body of literature offers a very significant alternative to, or augmentation of, the intentional and cognitive models that are widely accepted in the IS literature (cf., the entire research stream on the Technology Acceptance Model, including Jasperson, Carter and Zmud "A Comprehensive Conceptualization of Post-Adoptive Behaviors Associated with Information Technology Enabled Work Systems," *MIS Quarterly* (29:3), 2005, pp. 525-557.). See also Mohr *The Causes of Human Behavior: Implications for Theory and Method in the Social Sciences*, The University of Michigan Press, Ann Arbor, MI, 1996 for a theory of the causes of human behavior in which intentionality plays a much more limited role than it does in most IS theorizing.

10 I read Griffith's work as consistent with the stream of IS research that assumes reflective cognition and explicit intentionality rather than the prereflective direct perception and action model favored by ecological psychologists (cf. note 8). Jasperson et al. (2005) appear to interpret Griffith's work the same way I do.

11 I subscribe to the view that some, perhaps much, technology use is automatic or prereflective.

12 I do, too.

13 Steve Sawyer noted that "making the case for not-alike is much easier than arguing differences ... about mostly-similar things" (personal e-mail 1/27/06). I agree, alas. I expect that strong constructivists will not be persuaded by studies

that look for the effects of differing features in mostly similar contexts, such as the study that Andrew Dutta (ICFAI, India) is currently conducting.

14 Matthew Jones called my attention to Pickering (1995), which develops and justifies the concept of *material agency*, and I have since read other works advancing similar views. I am currently working through the implications of these ideas for my work.

15 The term appears to have originated in the work of psychologist J.J. Gibson, a founder (if not the founder) of the field of ecological psychology. The definition of affordance is debated in that field (cf. Jones "What Is an Affordance?" *Ecological Psychology* (15:2), 2003, pp. 107-114)—some see affordances as properties of the environment in relation to a particular type of animal or human; others view affordances as emergent. In the field of computer-human interaction, affordances appear to be viewed as stable properties of systems or technologies.

16 See Mohr (1996) for the possibly related concept of "effective reasons".

17 Note that other scholars often explain the use of "redundant" signatures and salutations as a holdover from personal letters or as acts of politeness. My explanation of that behavior at HCP Inc. is quite different, centering on the features of the particular system in use there.

18 This argument highlights a major challenge facing a "technology-shaping" perspective—that of systematic identification and description of system and their features. I am in ongoing discussions with Mark Silver about this challenge.

19 Mohr (1996) makes the distinction between "make happen" and "let happen". Technology per se "lets" things happen rather than "makes" them happen. However, Mohr argues that when material objects are combined with particular human motivations, they can "make" things happen.

20 I am grateful to Mary J. Culnan (Bentley College) for this suggestion.

21 Kock (2001) makes a similar argument.

Chapter III

Research Challenges for Integration of E-Collaboration Technologies

Bjørn Erik Munkvold, Agder University College, Norway
Ilze Zigurs, University of Nebraska at Omaha,USA

Abstract

Integrated technology support for collaborative work is a topic of great interest to academics and practitioners alike. E-collaboration has become a vibrant and fruitful area of research and application from many perspectives. Integration remains a major challenge, however, and a significant opportunity exists to advance the state of practice as well as research. We provide an overview of different forms of integrated e-collaboration technologies, along with examples of key application areas. Based on these examples, we analyze the research opportunities and challenges and provide a set of recommendations for advancing our understanding of integrated e-collaboration technologies. The focus throughout is on behavioral and organizational issues related to these technologies and their underlying theoretical perspectives. The overarching goal of the chapter is to identify important needs for research, based on a clear understanding of the key concepts, issues, and existing knowledge.

Introduction

Developing integrated technology support for collaboration has been a major target for both research and industry since the early groupware era of the 1980s. Numerous prototypes have been developed in the area of computer supported cooperative work (CSCW), which integrate combinations of collaborative support tools for different working modes and contexts (e.g., Francik et al., 1991; Sohlenkamp & Chwelos, 1994; Geyer et al., 2001). While providing important illustrations of the potential and limitations of different design concepts and architectures, the evaluation of these prototypes in real use tends to be limited. As with most technologies, the road from prototype to commercial systems is long and complex.

With the widespread diffusion of the Internet and the Web, new possibilites have emerged for providing integrated support for flexible, anytime/anyplace collaboration. The current market for integrated e-collaboration products and solution providers is growing rapidly. This trend coincides with the current industry focus on enterprise integration, i.e., the integration of vital information from both internal systems and those of trading partners (Rabin, 2001).

Integrated e-collaboration technologies available in the marketplace today range from small-scale, Web-based team and project rooms, to enterprise-scale collaborative product suites. They include both new products developed exclusively for this market and established products that extend their functionality to collaboration. Examples of the latter include integration of document management and workflow functionality in enterprise resource planning systems. During the last few years, major vendors of e-collaboration suites have sought to broaden the scope of their platforms by acquiring vendors of conferencing and team support applications, e.g., the acquisition of PlaceWare and Groove Networks by Microsoft, and eRoom by IBM. Even standard office applications such as MS Word and MS Powerpoint today offer collaborative features for co-authoring and net meetings, which when used to their full extent comprise relatively advanced collaborative support.

While integrated e-collaboration technologies have finally become easily available in the commercial marketplace, we still know little about how the integration aspect of these technologies affects their appropriation and use, nor is it clear what their effects are on productivity and quality of task execution and work processes. Research on CSCW and groupware has provided a rich body of studies on the adoption and use of single technologies or services, such as electronic calendaring and scheduling (Grudin & Palen, 1995), workflow management support (Grinter, 2000), electronic meeting support (Fjermestad & Hiltz, 1998-1999, 2000-2001), or desktop conferencing (Mark et al., 1999). While these different technologies can also integrate several features, they mainly support one of the three major forms of collaboration–either communication, coordination, or information sharing (Grudin & Poltrock, 1997). Furthermore, the research rarely focuses on integration aspects *per se*. The more comprehensive set of tools integrated in collaborative product suites such as Lotus Notes do provide potential exceptions. However, the body of empirical research on Lotus Notes shows that organizations tend to make rather limited use of the varied functionality available in Notes (Karsten, 1999). Consequently, even this research rarely addresses aspects related to integration of tools, other than reporting how the flexible nature of this product suite may result in user perceptions of increasing complexity (Orlikowski & Gash, 1994).

Given the state of research and the importance of this area, our goals in this chapter are to provide the following: (1) an overview of different types of integrated e-collaboration technologies and solutions currently available in the marketplace; (2) examples from selected application areas that reveal key issues and practices; (3) highlights of existing research that reveal gaps and possibilities for next steps; and (4) questions for future research that would take us into the next phase of understanding and application of integrated e-collaboration technologies. Our primary focus is on behavioral and organizational issues relative to integrated technologies. We do not underestimate the important challenges of such technical integration issues as architecture, compatibility, or interoperability, but our viewpoint is that the current need in research is greatest in the behavioral domain. As integrated e-collaboration technologies are deployed on an increasingly greater scale, we need to understand how to assimilate and use these systems effectively in different collaborative contexts. Further, we need to develop appropriate theoretical foundations for this research.

The next section discusses the concept of integration in the context of e-collaboration technologies, and provides an overview of technologies. The third section summarizes findings from previous research in selected application areas that can provide a foundation for research on integrated e-collaboration technologies. The fourth section discusses opportunities and challenges for further research in this area. The final section concludes with a brief summary of the key contributions of the chapter.

Definition and Examples of Integrated E-Collaboration Technologies

Definition

Integration is a ubiquitous term that has no single meaning. We build our conceptualization on a framework developed by Mandviwalla and Khan (1999) that defines three collaborative integration factors: *mode, medium,* and *structure*. Mode refers to the time and space of interaction, i.e., face-to face vs. distributed, and synchronous (same time) vs. asynchronus (different time). Medium is the conduit provided for interaction, e.g., text, graphic, audio, video, or shared whiteboard. Structure is the support provided by the application for group development and productive outcomes, such as cognitive mapping, anonymity, or consensus building. A working definition of integration is thus provided as follows: "*A technology is integrated in the technological domain of interest if it combines support for more than one of the identified key factors. For example, a collaborative technology is integrated if it combines support for more than one mode, medium, and structure* " (Mandviwalla & Khan, 1999, p. 245). According to this definition, integration can take either a vertical direction or a combined vertical-horizontal direction. Vertical integration is accomplished by providing integrated support for more than one mode, medium, or structure. Vertical-horizontal integration is defined as combining vertical integration *across* more than one mode, medium, or structure (op.cit.). For example, a system that provides an integrated interface for brainstorming and ranking ideas, both synchronously and asynchronously, would be considered a vertically-horizontally integrated system.

Basically, there are two main approaches that an organization can use for providing integrated e-collaboration support: either through aquiring an integrated product that offers the necessary collaborative tools, or by building an *ad hoc* collaborative infrastructure based on integrating different e-collaboration products. The following discussion encompasses both these approaches.

Examples of Technologies

In this section we present examples of integrated e-collaboration technologies, including both research prototypes and commercial applications. We discuss the examples briefly in light of the definition of integration presented.

Research Prototypes

Table 1 shows examples of research prototypes that together illustrate various approaches to integration and the scope of the integration challenge. The table is not intended to provide a historical account of prototypes, thus it does not include early versions of commercial systems such as Meetingworks and GroupSystems (see Table 2). Instead, the purpose here is to show a range of approaches to integration in the prototype phase.

As the table shows, these prototypes provide different combinations of integration support and collaborative tools. Of the three integration factors discussed in the previous section, integrated support for several *modes* (synchronous and asynchronous) is clearly most predominant. An exception here is the VIVA project, which explicitly

Table 1. Examples of integrated e-collaboration research prototypes

Prototype (source)	Collaborative tools included	Integration support
DIVA Virtual Office (Sohlenkamp & Chwelos, 1994)	Audio/video conferencing, awareness support, shared graphics editor, document management, annotations, activity replay	Mode Media
TCBWorks (Dennis et al., 1998)	Project folders, structured discussion, voting	Mode Structure
COWS (Mandviwalla & Khan, 1999)	Awareness support, text chat, object templates and folders, shared whiteboard, group memory (log player and finder)	Mode Media Structure
TeamSpace (Geyer et al., 2001)	Audio/video conferencing, text chat, awareness support, document management, sharing and annotation of presentations, administration of agenda and action items, time-based capture and access of meeting records	Mode Media
VIVA (Pekkola, 2003)	E-mail, text chat, audio, file transfer, memo, co-authoring, shared whiteboard, awareness support	Media

focused on integration of multiple media for supporting real-time and distributed group work. Only two of the prototypes provide integration of several structures, in the definition of Mandviwalla and Khan (1999). In the COWS prototype, this integration was provided through integrating process structures such as access control and concurrency control with content structures such as categorization. TCBWorks provides combined structural support through its voting tool, discussion structure, and restrictiveness in user actions (guided by a project organizer). It is also interesting to note that three of the prototypes include tools for recording and accessing information from meetings/interaction sessions, a functionality that is now included in several desktop conferencing systems.

Commercial Systems

Table 2 shows examples of different categories of integrated e-collaboration systems in commercial use, along with typical tools or services provided within each type, specific product examples, and the integration factors that are typically supported within that category. The collaborative tools that are shown for each category are intended as representative examples, and the actual combination of tools that are implemented in each product will vary. The table reflects the growth that has occurred in recent years in the number of integrated applications available in the commercial marketplace.

Since this area is evolving rapidly, it is difficult to provide clear categorizations based on product functionality. The categories listed are thus not intended to be

Table 2. Examples of integrated e-collaboration products

Category	Examples of collaborative tools included	Product examples	Integration support*
Collaborative product suites	E-mail, group calendar, threaded discussions, document management, workflow	Lotus Notes/Domino, Microsoft Exchange, GroupWise (Novell)	Medium
Collaborative portals	Instant messaging, presence awareness, team workplaces, people finder, e-meetings, document management	IBM Websphere portal, MS Sharepoint	Mode Medium
Desktop conferencing systems	Instant messaging/chat, audio conferencing, presence awareness, videoconferencing, application sharing, shared whiteboard, polling, voting, recording of meeting information	MSN Messenger, Interwise, Centra 7, WebEx Meeting, Microsoft Live Meeting, Marratech	Mode Medium
Web-based team/project rooms	Group calendar, contacts, notes, tasks, file sharing, e-mail, chat, pinboard, project management, document management, threaded discussions, brainstorming, voting, time sheets, telegram, evaluation, scheduler	TeamSpace, Documentum eRoom, Lotus Workplace Team Collaboration, Microsoft Office Groove 2007	Mode Medium (Structure)
Electronic meeting systems (EMS)	Agenda, brainstorming, categorization & organizing, voting & prioritizing, action planning, surveys, shared whiteboard, meeting log, chat	GroupSystems, Facilitate.com, Meetingworks	Mode Medium Structure
E-Learning systems	E-mail, instant messaging, presence awareness, calendar, threaded discussion, learning objects repository, course administration	Blackboard, Centra 7, Aspen, Lotus Workplace Collaborative Learning, WebEx Training Center	Mode Medium (Structure)

**Since the integrated functionality offered by the products within a category varies, we can give only a broad indication of the type of integration support offered within each category. The parentheses indicate that support for this integration factor is only provided in some products within a category.*

mutually exclusive, but rather to reflect major concepts used in the marketplace today. Furthermore, the distinctions between these categories are becoming more and more blurred, both through extended functionality within products and by different products being merged through company acquisitions. Several major vendors offer products in more than one category, and some vendors integrate their different e-collaboration products into a total portfolio, such as the Lotus Workplace products.

The table also reflects the similarity in the range of tools integrated in each category, including support for both asynchronous and synchronous collaboration. Basic tools for asynchronous collaboration include e-mail, group calendar, threaded discussions, document management, and file sharing, while instant messaging is the most widespread tool for synchronous interaction. In addition, the categories can be distinguished somewhat on the degree of sophistication they offer in their solutions for asynchronous and synchronous work and the targeted organizational scope of the collaboration. Collaborative product suites and collaborative portals are the most comprehensive solutions, intended to provide for an organization's total need for collaborative support. While collaborative product suites such as Lotus Notes have so far provided stronger support for asynchronous work than for synchronous collaboration, e.g., document repositories and workflow, collaborative portals tend to provide support for both modes.

Desktop conferencing and Web-based team/project rooms offer many of the same tools, but are usually intended to support smaller workgroups. The first of these two categories offers strongest support for synchronous communication, e.g., audio/video conferencing or application sharing, while the second is more oriented towards providing shared document repositories. However, the capability for recording meetings also extends the application of desktop conferencing systems to the asynchronous mode. Both categories increasingly use the Web as their platform.

Electronic meeting systems (EMS) can be distinguished somewhat from the other categories by their integration of tools for structuring group interaction in a meeting process. Of the technologies listed, only EMS include explicit support for same-time, same-place collaboration. Although EMS can now also be used in distributed meetings, desktop conferencing systems are more commonly used in this meeting mode. However, desktop conference systems do not yet provide the same information processing and agenda structuring capabilities as electronic meeting systems.

Finally, e-learning systems are included as a more domain-specific example of products that integrate the same range of tools as the other categories but are tailored to an educational context. This area again comprises different types of systems. While synchronous collaborative learning is supported by so-called virtual classrooms, asynchronous collaborative learning is supported by learning management systems and learning content management systems (Bostrom et al., 2003). The two latter types of systems also include support for user/course administration and learning objects repositories, respectively. The trend here is towards integrating support for these different e-learning services into so-called enterprise learning systems. Integration of learning support tools with existing course management systems has been shown to be an essential aspect of these environments (Ellis & Hafner, 2006).

Overall, Table 2 shows that integration is strongest in terms of mode (asynchronous and synchronous) and media (e.g., text, audio, video). Integrated support for more than one structure is a standard feature only in EMS. In addition, some Web-based team products offer a subset of EMS functionality (brainstorming, evaluation/voting, etc.), and other products integrate tools for structuring team member interaction (e.g., Microsoft Office Groove 2007). Support for one type of structure, such as idea generation, group outlining, and evaluation, is included in some products that also provide integration on mode and/or media. For example, some e-learning systems provide mechanisms for sequencing learning objects into larger products such as topic or course. Integrated work process structure in the form of workflow management support is still limited to larger, enterprise-wide solutions such as collaborative product suites and collaborative portals.

Examples of Research in Key Application Areas

In this section, we provide examples of key issues and practices from selected application areas and discuss the current state of research in each area. The application areas covered are: virtual teamwork, distributed project management, integrated meeting support, and e-learning. These are areas in which integrated collaboration support may have a vital impact, and each area currently attracts a great deal of focus from both researchers and practitioners.

Virtual Teamwork

In a review of the empirical literature on virtual teamwork, two mechanisms were identified as essential for alleviating potential process losess of virtual teams: process structure mechanisms, and multiple communication media (Pinsonneault & Caya, 2005). Process structure mechanisms appear to foster group cohesiveness, support establishment of trust, and improve communication and information exchange effectiveness. Combinations of multiple communication media seem to result in greater satisfaction with the process, equalization of participation, and higher quality of outcomes, when compared to use of single communication tool only (ibid.). However, the studies that reported combined use of different media have so far mainly been experimental studies, while most field studies on virtual teams have included a relatively limited set of technologies, typically restricted to asynchronous tools such as e-mail and document repositories (Powell et al., 2004). Also, access to multiple media and e-collaboration tools does not automatically imply effective use, and there may be any number of challenges in the team members' appropriation of the media and tools.

An example of the challenge of multiple tools comes from a study of virtual teams of information systems graduate students in Norway and the United States (Munkvold & Zigurs, 2004). The virtual teams were supported by a Web-based intranet product that offered integrated document management, discussions, tasks, polling, group calendaring, e-mail, and instant messaging/chat. Designed as a typical *ad hoc* virtual team project, the study did not include technology training as an explicit activity, but instead had the students begin directly with project tasks. While each tool offered in the intranet was relatively easy and intuitive by itself, the combination of tools was confusing for the students in several ways. The students perceived the intranet to be "too cluttered" and difficult to navigate. The teams experienced particular difficulties in structuring their discussions in the electronic discussion forum and finding a way to maintain an overview of several parallel discussion streams. Other tools, like voting and polling, were not found to be of any use for this project. The only tool offered for synchronous communication was instant messaging. However, since this tool supported only one-to-one communication, it proved useless for synchronous team meetings. Thus, as a whole, user experiences with this integrated technology were not entirely positive in terms of user attitude and satisfaction, yet the students were able to complete the project and produce appropriate deliverables.

Other studies have found similar results in that users sometimes adopt and utilize only a subset of the available tools of an integrated technology. For example, the use of desktop conferencing among virtual teams in Boeing was reported mainly to include giving presentations in distributed meetings, with less use of the features for joint work on information objects (through shared whiteboard or application sharing), file sharing, and chat (Poltrock & Mark, 2003). Distributed facilitation in such cases has emerged as an important support mechanism for conducting effective, technology-supported virtual meetings.

A set of field studies of a variety of technologies and companies shows some common themes in terms of virtual teams and collaborative tools (Qureshi & Zigurs, 2001). The case studies reinforced the importance of several factors for success, including management motivation for virtual work; definition of explicit roles in collaboration; using virtual teams for appropriate tasks (in these cases, structured tasks and tasks that required detailed teamwork); providing training; and reinforcing the use of technology as a device and not a driver for collaborative activity. This latter point corroborates findings from early studies of Lotus Notes (e.g., Orlikowski, 1992). Not all of the field studies were conducted with integrated technologies, but they do reinforce the importance of simplicity in the technology, attention to the nature of the task, and explicit design and training for collaboration.

Distributed Project Management

The domain of project management is another area in which integrated e-collaboration technologies could make a major difference. A fundamental challenge in successful projects is communication and coordination among and across diverse people, locations, and tasks, thus integration on several dimensions is essential. Virtual, or distributed, projects are increasingly more common, yet we do not yet have a good understanding of the differentiating characteristics of such projects or how different kinds of technologies might best support them. A needed foundation is the characterization of project types in a way that helps to understand the differences among them (Khazanchi & Zigurs, 2005). While traditional project management has developed a substantive body of knowledge and a professional code (Project Management Institute, 2004), it is not clear how virtual projects fit into that structure. Typologies of projects typically focus on such characteristics as complexity, scope, risk, member characteristics, resource requirements, and knowledge domain (e.g., Shenhar, 1998; Project Management Institute, 2004). Virtual projects can be further defined in terms of the extent to which there is dispersion of team members, whether geographically, culturally, or by organizational or other affiliation (Katzy et al., 2000; Evaristo & Munkvold, 2002). The extent of dispersion is what creates the need for reliance on information and communication technologies.

If we look at existing project management tools in terms of the terminology of integration of mode, medium, and structure (Mandviwalla & Khan, 1999), there is ample opportunity for improvement. Most existing tools focus on traditional work breakdown structures and project tracking mechanisms, and they do not address the higher-level strategic implications of coordination. For example, Chen et al., (2003) examined existing tools and found them deficient in providing for project analysis, communication, process support, and an integrated project repository. In addition, with integrated systems, there is an even greater need for attention to providing protocols or guidelines for use (Evaristo & Munkvold, 2002).

Many of the empirical studies of virtual projects are in the context of systems development projects, given the increasing ubiquity of global software development (Carmel & Agarwal, 2001). A recent review of virtual team research summarized several studies of virtual projects conducted in universities, typically as part of systems development courses (Powell et al., 2004). Most of this literature is included generically in studies of virtual teams and rarely is there an emphasis on the project management issues or a longer-term analysis of virtual projects. Hence, the opportunity here is to focus specifically on the coordination, knowledge, and process challenges of virtual projects and the benefits that integration can bring.

Integrated Support for Meeting Processes

Electronic meeting systems (EMS), often referred to by the broader term group support systems (GSS) (Fjermestad & Hiltz, 1998-1999), fall under the category of technologies that provide integrated structural support in the framework of Mandviwalla and Khan (1999). These systems usually offer a range of tools for structuring information generation and analysis in meetings. The challenge of selecting tools that match the meeting agenda typically implies a need for trained meeting facilitators who guide participants through the agenda. However, we are seeing the emergence of systems that embed this form of structural support within the technology itself, with the intent of reducing some of the need for expert facilitators (Briggs et al., 2003). Thus, one of the research issues in this area is how to achieve the best mix of human, process, and technological support.

The use of electronic meeting systems has long mirrored the traditional practice of co-located meetings, but that use is now increasingly extended to supporting meetings that are distributed in time and/or space. While EMS can be used in asynchronous mode simply by extending the time period defined for a meeting and then having meeting participants access the system at different times over the company network, synchronous meetings in distributed settings still require integration with other communication technologies such as audio and/or videoconferencing with chat.

A study of meeting practices in a large oil company exemplifies the use of this type of integrated meeting infrastructure, enabling anytime/anyplace meetings (Anson & Munkvold, 2004). For example, in a synchronous meeting, participants would typically attend the meeting from several electronic meeting rooms that were equipped with integrated EMS, audio, and videoconferencing, as well as from their home offices through desktop conferencing. Further, asynchronous meetings were also conducted, e.g., for project reviews, where participants contributed at their leisure during a predefined period of time. The study also identified examples of multimode meetings, in which the meeting process incorporated multiple modes that were sequentially or synchronously linked. These meeting processes took advantage of the portfolio of collaboration technologies available in this company. In addition to the integration of synchronous technologies, other examples of integration included using survey tools for generating input to the EMS, or processing EMS output in Lotus Notes. In this context, mode thus became a meeting design instrument. Mode selection criteria might include task urgency, required access to distant or mobile participants, degree of engagement and focus needed among participants, or need for accessing external sources of information.

The study of the implementation of integrated meeting support technologies in this company also provided interesting findings on adoption processes for the different technologies (Munkvold & Anson, 2001). These processes were partly interrelated through competition for resources and key personnel, with different "technology camps" advocating "their" technology as the most important one. To better coordinate these resources, the company merged the different technology support groups into a central e-collaboration team, responsible for delivering support to consulting, deployment, adoption and facilitation of e-collaboration in the company. This example illustrates many of the issues involved in providing support for integrated meeting features, an area that has tremendous potential for enhancing the effectiveness of meetings, regardless of their mode.

E-Learning Environments

E-learning by definition covers technology-supported learning activities in any combination of time-place environments (Bostrom et al., 2003). Thus, this application area exemplifies well the potential for using integrated e-collaboration technologies to enable new and flexible forms of work. From being confined originally to a traditional classroom setting, the combined use of asynchronous and synchronous e-collaboration tools now supports anytime/anyplace learning environments. The core software in most e-learning environments is a Learning Management System, which provides a database repository for learning resources and a common interface to various collaboration tools such as e-mail, discussion databases, streaming audio/video (asynchronous), instant messaging, chat, and audio/videoconferencing (synchronous tools) (op.cit.).

Bostrom and his colleagues at the University of Georgia (UGA) provide an in-depth account of their experiences in establishing such an e-learning infrastructure for a joint university-corporate MBA program (Bostrom et al., 2003). In addition to the technological challenges involved in identifying and deploying a suitable mix of technologies and in training faculty and staff, there was also a gradual learning process for finding the best way to integrate the technology in the educational program. Blended learning emerged as a key concept, referring both to the blend between distance and face-to-face education, and the blending of different technologies. While use of e-learning technologies tends to be associated with distance learning, the program at UGA also integrated use of the e-learning tools as learning resources in the classroom setting itself. The process of finding the best blend between face-to-face and distant learning in various modes (synchronous and asynchronous) needed to take place at the individual course level and be adapted to the course content. Experimentation and sharing of best practices among faculty were essential, as was the concept of a learning community, i.e., virtual learning teams of four to five students who worked together both on and off campus.

Summarizing Key Themes in Current Research

The previous sections have provided a brief overview of key findings and issues related to the deployment and use of e-collaboration technologies in selected application areas. Here, we summarize common observations and themes:

- Despite the increasing use of integrated e-collaboration technologies in different application areas, there is still relatively little field-based research on such technologies.

- Greater theoretical foundation and development would help make sense of the diversity in research and conflicting findings.
- In terms of the three modes of integration, most of the vertical integration occurs on mode and/or medium, and not on structure. EMS are one exception, since they typically provide integration of two or more structures to support group process.
- The complexity of integrated systems is a real challenge for users, who tend to fall back on familiar patterns and simple solutions.
- Technological integration may enable new behavioral patterns of collaboration, but there is a lack of guidelines or best practices for developing such patterns. As a result, collaborative tools available in integrated technologies are often not used to their full potential.
- The metaphor for integrated systems, e.g., the virtual office or e-room, tends to reflect the well-known physical world. If we are to go beyond familiar patterns of technology use and communication, we might need new metaphors.

The next section discusses the implications of these observations in terms of opportunities and challenges for further research. Both theoretical and methodological issues are addressed.

Research Opportunities and Challenges

Scope and Definition of Integration

Technological integration in the e-collaboration domain is still at an early stage. The framework of mode, medium, and structure provides a useful starting point for thinking about how the scope of integration might be extended. In terms of *mode*, we see very few examples where asynchronous and synchronous integration are done successfully, as noted in the previous section. In addition, there is a need for integrating support for content management with support for asynchronous and synchronous collaborative work processes (Päivärinta & Munkvold, 2005). From a knowledge management perspective, this challenge corresponds to integrating the knowledge repository and knowledge networking models defined by Alavi (2000). Bieber et al. (2002) present an interesting vision of this type of integration, in the context of providing support for virtual communities. A possible architecture for this "community knowledge evolution system" is defined as comprising a multimedia document repository (digital library), augmented with tools that support computer-mediated communication, conceptual knowledge structures, community process support (process models and workflow support), decision analysis support, and advanced hypermedia features.

Integrating the *media* of collaborative technologies is an especially lively area, what with the rapid pace of technological development in media. Yet we need theory-based guidelines for understanding what is important. The studies of the differences between communication media are important, e.g., between audio and video (Olson et al., 1995), but it is also interesting to speculate how we might begin to make recommendations about multiple media. Integrated interfaces are relevant to this issue, for example, the use of virtual reality for creating 3D environments for synchronous interaction among distant individuals, often referred to as collaborative virtual environments (CVE) (Pekkola, 2003; Ragusa & Bochenek, 2001).

In terms of *structure*, integration could be especially useful for helping to create a unified and accessible record of the collaborative work of a group as it goes through different processes. Some EMS and desktop conferencing systems are beginning to provide recording capabilities in their meeting support tools. But with multiple media being used in integrated systems, there are different types of things that need to be recorded. Such multi-media data sets have to be easy to use and navigate. Research on these issues is being conducted in the area of enterprise content management, focusing on how to provide integrated search capabilities covering all types of digital content in an organization, regardless of media and formats, and based on corporate taxonomies of the organization's information resources (Päivarinta & Munkvold, 2005).

The above examples discuss how integration might be extended on each of the factors of mode, medium, and structure. However, there are other perspectives on integration that may complement the factor view. As Mandviwalla and Khan (1999) have noted, integration is not about "throwing everything into the pot." Yet, when we look at the products in the marketplace today, it is not always obvious what work process model or criteria underlie the combination of tools or media that are integrated in a specific product. Historically, the functional perspective of most technology designs made it fairly simple to identify what work process the tool was intended to support, e.g., workflow, learning/training, communication, or file sharing. Now, with the advent of different forms of integration, the functional perspective is not as helpful in differentiating tools or systems. For example, the integration of business intelligence with knowledge management technologies has the aim of providing real-time, personalized information to decision makers in a way that adapts to the context of a particular business process or workflow (Cody et al., 2002). These "infrastructural" types of systems represent both an opportunity and a challenge for defining what is meant by integration.

In sum, key research questions on the scope and definition of integration include:

- What kinds of comprehensive records of communication are required to enable stakeholders both inside and outside the collaborative team to understand what they need to know about the team's process or decisions?
- What kinds of contextual information are required to make a repository more useful, and how should personalized access to this information be provided for the users?
- How can we define the best blending of mode support (e.g., asynchronous and synchronous) for different collaborative processes and tasks?
- How can similar guidelines be developed for an appropriate mix of media for different circumstances, e.g., text, audio, video, sensory, or other kinds of interface?
- How does the definition of integration need to evolve in order to account for infrastructural systems?

Individual User Acceptance and Choice of Technologies

Despite the extensive body of research on individual user acceptance of information technologies (Venkatesh et al., 2003), there is little research that sheds light on how access to an integrated set of technologies influences users' perceptions of each tool or the integrated technology as a whole. The integration framework presented earlier included a set of behavioral propositions about technology use, specifically that users would prefer integrated features to non-integrated ones; that integrated systems would be harder to use for simple tasks and easier for complex tasks, and they would be initially more difficult to understand (Mandviwalla & Khan, 1999). These propositions remain to be tested.

A second important area for investigation in the context of integrated systems is the choice of technology and the impacts of that choice on use and effectiveness. Media richness theory (MRT) is one of the earliest theories to be applied to computer-mediated communication. MRT holds that a communication medium that matches the characteristics of the task is important for effective performance (Daft & Lengel, 1986). In MRT, media are defined in terms of fixed characteristics that relate to the medium's capacity to convey rich information. There is limited support for the theory with modern technologies (Dennis & Valacich, 1999), though it remains a popular area of study. Channel expansion theory represents an evolution beyond MRT (Carlson & Zmud, 1999), in that it recognizes that a fixed view of media characteristics is inconsistent with how people use modern technologies. Instead, the same medium can become "richer" as communication partners gain experience with each other, the task, or the context.

Another perspective on matching technology to task is task-technology fit theory (Zigurs & Buckland, 1998) and the follow-up Fit Appropriation Model (Dennis et al., 2001). Task-technology fit theory characterizes tasks on the basis of their complexity, and technologies on the extent to which they provide communication support, process structure, and information processing. The fit appropriation model goes one step further by incorporating the role of support provided to the group by such features as training, facilitation, or software restrictiveness. The model therefore integrates task-technology fit with adaptive structuration theory (AST). AST is one of the most influential theories in the research on group decision support (DeSanctis & Poole, 1994), and it addresses directly the challenge of explaining the balance between fixed and emergent processes in groups.

Both media richness theory and task-technology fit theory rely on characterizations of technology, tasks, and of the relevant aspect of the group or process. These issues suggest the following key research questions on individual user acceptance and choice of technologies:

- How well do existing characterizations of technology translate to the multi-mode and/or multi-media nature of integrated systems?
- How can we extend existing concepts of task-technology fit to a larger framework of task-technology-team fit?
- What new measures or methods are needed to study user acceptance of integrated technologies?

Procedural Guidance and Appropriation Support

Another key area of research concerns the need for building procedural guidance into integrated technologies. Integrated systems imply the challenge of not only providing guidance for specific aspects of the system but also for the overall approach to moving around the application among its different modes, media, and structures. The concept of procedural guidance from the world of decision support is relevant here (Silver, 1991). Procedural guidance refers to features of a system that direct a user during the process of interacting with that system. The features may be informational or more directive (Silver, 1991). In single-user systems, the examples are straightforward, e.g., a recommendation of the best format for displaying a specific data set, or a prompt for a next step in writing a letter. In collaborative systems, procedural guidance might provide a group agenda that prescribes each step, a voting procedure, or a recommended group decision rule.

A second theoretical perspective takes procedural guidance in a group context one step further, making it particularly relevant for integrated systems. The concept of collaboration engineering includes the idea of building structured support for group process into collaborative tools via the technique of thinkLets (Briggs et al., 2003; Vreede & Briggs, 2005; Santanenet al., 2006). ThinkLets are a bundle of steps in a collaborative process that group members can adopt and put together in a component-building way. ThinkLets address the context of a collaborative problem, the steps recommended for carrying out a process, and techniques for each step. They are particularly relevant for integrated e-collaboration because of their object-oriented nature, that is, the ability to build components (thinkLets) separately and then combine them dynamically in a specific process. The objective of collaboration engineering, and thinkLets in particular, is to be able to transfer process knowledge from expert facilitators to team members. An interesting question is the appropriate balance of engineering and flexibility in terms of prescribing what needs to be done in specific contexts.

Yet a third perspective–one which takes a broader view and is entirely consistent with the previous discussion–introduces the concepts of swift process and swift technology (Munkvold & Zigurs, 2004). Swift process is the idea of implementing a structure that quickly lays the foundation for continuing and effective development of the group. Swift process can be implemented at the beginning of a collaboration via introductory exercises, information sharing, and consensus building. Swift technology is a related concept that emphasizes the importance of groups being able to start using the essential features of an e-collaboration system immediately, without getting bogged down in the complexity of the system. The thinkLets discussed earlier have great potential for integrating swift process with swift technology. Combining thinkLets with the concept of swift technology could result in a set of procedural guidelines that take into account not just a process for the task and tool selection, but selection of the media as well. The system could prompt users for task characteristics and team configuration (e.g., number of members, geographical distribution, technical platforms), and then suggest a suitable combination of tools and/or media for that specific task. Providing this task-oriented interface to the tools, rather than the traditional functional interface, could also ease navigation. For new users who are inexperienced with an integrated technology, this form of guidance could provide both swift process and swift technology.

These different perspectives on procedural guidance relate directly to the earlier discussion of Adaptive Structuration Theory, in that various forms of procedural guidance provide support for users in the appropriation process. Key questions in this area include:

- What is the best way to train users in integrated technologies?
- What level and form of structure should be embedded in the system for effective appropriation to occur?
- How can we obtain an optimal balance of user experimentation and flexibility with detailed procedural guidance?

- What are the tradeoffs for using engineered process objects such as thinkLets for user-driven facilitation of collaboration?

Integrated Behavioral Patterns

One of the behavioral propositions suggested by Mandviwalla and Khan (1999) was that integrated collaborative applications would result in new and integrated behavioral patterns. An example of an integrated pattern that they observed in a study of their COWS prototype was the spontaneous combination of asynchronous with synchronous interaction among distributed students. Even though this specific example might be attributed to simple exploration by the students, the emergence of integrated behavioral patterns is nonetheless an interesting area for further research. The theoretical perspectives that could be useful for examining this phenomenon include Adaptive Structuration Theory, thinkLets, and theories related to time.

Adaptive Structuration Theory was introduced in an earlier section. Its characterization of rules and resources, and the process by which groups adapt and change them, could be very useful in searching for new patterns of behavior. ThinkLets (Briggs, et al., 2003) could also be a fruitful technique for creating new patterns of behavior and testing them in collaborative environments. While AST provides a framework for understanding what happens in groups, thinkLets can be used to impose novel structures on groups to examine how groups deal with them.

Theories related to time represent an opportunity that has yet to be examined fully. A theory that is relevant in this area is time-interaction-performance (TIP) theory (McGrath, 1991), which provides a set of propositions about how group functions are carried out during modes of interaction. According to TIP, groups go through four modes of interaction (inception, problem solving, conflict resolution, and execution) and also carry out three functions (production, well-being, and member support). Each group will take a different path through a combination of modes and functions, depending on the characteristics of the context of the problem and team members. TIP theory can be used to describe a particular group's process, but we suggest that it might also be used to discover new behavioral patterns. Unusual combination of mode and function within TIP theory might be tested to trigger new, integrated behavioral patterns.

We have seen increased attention to other perspectives on the role of time in collaborative activity. For example, Saunders et al. (2004) discuss different conceptions of time and how that might affect communication in global virtual teams. Another treatment of time deals with its role in coordination of virtual teams, and the ways in which members carry out temporal coordination (Massey et al., 2003). These studies suggest that we need to start to take time into account in our theorizing about collaboration technology and the behavioral patterns of collaborative process.

Key research questions on integrated behavioral patterns include:

- How do integrated behavioral patterns develop and how are they sustained over time?
- How can we identify integrated behavioral patterns that lead to successful and unsuccessful collaboration?
- How can such behavioral patterns be disseminated most effectively as guidelines for best practice?
- How can integrated behavioral patterns be linked with technologies through such techniques as thinkLets?

Organizational Implementation

The general complexity associated with implementing e-collaboration technologies has been well documented through a rich body of field studies, and several important implementation factors related to the different types of technologies have been identified (Munkvold, 2003). However, little of this research has studied organizational implementation of integrated technologies. The many field studies on Lotus Notes have documented how the flexible range of tools available in this product may impose greater challenges for users in understanding how to integrate these tools in their work, which might then require more comprehensive training and follow up (e.g., Orlikowski & Gash, 1994; Karsten, 1999). A study of the implementation of integrated meeting support (see earlier section on Integrated Support for Meeting Processes) showed how implementation of different collaboration technologies may follow different patterns of adoption and diffusion, even within the same organization (Munkvold & Anson, 2001). Further, these adoption processes may also intersect with political processes where different "technology camps" in an organization compete for the same resources in the form of personnel and budgets (Munkvold & Tvedte, 2003). In the implementation of data conferencing in Boeing, the implementation team also experienced how it can be difficult to place ownership of collaboration technologies with respect to financial and technical support. Typically, the IS organizations tend to give priority to more established enterprise systems.

Given that organizations need to manage and evolve their infrastructures and environments carefully, one of the key challenges in organizational implementation is the incorporation of emerging technologies. Web-based tools such as wikis and Web blogs (popularly known as "blogs") have begun to support collaborative communities, but their incorporation into organizational environments has yet to develop in a systematic way (Grudin, 2006). A challenge will be to incorporate these flexible tools and their "bottom-up" adoption into organizational environments.

Theoretical perspectives proven to be relevant for research on organizational implementation of e-collaboration technologies include adoption and diffusion of innovations (Applegate, 1991; Rogers, 1995), adaptive structuration theory (DeSanctis & Poole, 1994), change management (Orlikowski & Hofman, 1997), and IS implementation (Marble, 2000).

Key research questions on organizational implementation thus include:

- What is the best way of introducing an integrated e-collaboration technology into an organization, with respect to establishing ownership and developing an effective support infrastructure?
- For organizations developing *ad hoc* integrated solutions, what is the relationship between adoption and diffusion of the different technologies?
- What conditions should determine the preferred sequence of the implementation of these technologies in an organization?
- How can organizations incorporate emerging technologies and tools into their existing infrastructures and practices?

Methodological Challenges

While the literature on computer-mediated communication (CMC) is rich in experimental studies that compare the effects of communication mode and form of technology support on team process and outcome (Fjermestad, 2004), there exist few studies that evaluate the combined use of a set of integrated technologies with respect to user satisfaction and task efficiency. A study by Ocker et al. (1998) indicated that teams that were able to combine several modes of collaboration, in this case face-to-face and asynchronous computer conferencing, produced solutions of higher creativity and quality than groups working in a single mode only (face-to-face, synchronous computer conferencing, or asynchronous computer conferencing). The benefit of multiple modes of collaboration was reinforced in a review of virtual team research (Pinsonneault & Caya, 2005). One opportunity for further research could thus be to extend these experimental designs to encompass the combined use of multiple, integrated collaboration tools. However, as argued by Mandviwalla and Khan (1999), laboratory experiments necessarily will have to involve relatively simple tasks, and there would be little opportunity for studying the emergence of new behavioral patterns of the kind discussed earlier. The increasing proliferation of integrated e-collaboration technologies in industry also makes gaining field access less of a problem than it has been so far.

A potential challenge related to studying organizational appropriation and use of integrated e-collaboration technologies is defining an appropriate level of analysis.

As illustrated throughout this chapter, the concept of integrated e-collaboration technologies may encompass a wide variety of tools and technologies that are intended to support collaboration at different organizational levels. In analyzing 36 studies of e-collaboration published in several IS journals in the last five years, Gallivan and Benbunan-Fich (2005) found that over two-thirds of the studies contained one or more problems of levels incongruence related to the level of the theory, the level of the data analysis, and the unit of analysis. They argue that methodological problems in part may be responsible for the inconsistency of the results reported in the e-collaboration literature. There is thus a need for frameworks that may aid in identifying levels. The work by Gupta and Bostrom (2003) provides a starting point. They view collaboration as occuring at five different levels: individual, project/team, community of interest/practice, organizational, and across enterprises.

Measurement is always an issue in research, and the study of integrated systems creates a need for new measures. The prior sections imply what constructs might need to be operationalized for integrated systems, e.g., user satisfaction and other perceptual measures. This is also an area that is ripe for new techniques and multi-methodological approaches. Turoff (1997), for example, calls for conscious design and experimentation on social systems using computer simulation. Simulation as an analysis method is rarely used in collaboration research, but such a technique could be very useful for generating new ideas.

Research and Theory Integration

The challenge of integrating technology is mirrored in the equal if not greater challenge of integrating research. The call for interdisciplinary research in this area came early, as did the recognition of the difficulty of coordinating across diverse streams of knowledge and experience (Ellis et al., 1991; Grudin, 1994). We have taken a broad perspective in this chapter, but we are inevitably working from the frame of our own background as information systems researchers. The greater the integration of knowledge from such communities as CSCW and human-computer interaction, the greater the potential to build significant knowledge in the important area of integrated e-collaboration technologies and their application.

Interdisciplinary research implies integration of theory. The Fit Appropriation Model is one example of such integration, namely the integration of Task-Technology Fit theory with Adaptive Structuration Theory. Collaborative e-learning represents one application area in which those two theories have been integrated. The integrated learning model proposed by Gupta and Bostrom (2004) is a good example of how structure and process are combined to explain outcomes. Clearly, such models are complex, but the integration of theory is essential to extending our knowledge in such situations.

Table 3. Key Research Issues

Research issue	Relevant theoretical perspectives / research areas
Scope and definition of integration	
• Requirements for communication records that enable collaborative team stakeholders (both internal and external) to understand the team's process and decisions • Types of contextual information needed to make a repository more useful • Providing personalized access to contextual information for diverse users • Defining optimal blending of mode and media support for different collaborative processes and tasks • Evolving the definition of integration to account for infrastructural systems	Enterprise content management, Corporate taxonomies, Collaborative virtual environments, Media characteristics
Individual User Acceptance and Choice of Technologies	
• Translating existing characterizations of technology to multi-mode and/or multi-media integrated systems • Extending existing concepts of task-technology fit to a larger framework of task-technology-team fit • Developing new measures or methods to study user acceptance of integrated technologies	Individual user acceptance, Media richness theory, Channel expansion theory, Task-Technology fit theory
Procedural Guidance and Appropriation Support	
• Developing user training for integrated technologies • Embedding structure in systems for effective appropriation • Balancing user experimentation and flexibility with detailed procedural guidance • Determining trade-offs for optimal use of process guidance	Decision support, thinkLets, Adaptive structuration theory
Integrated Behavioral Patterns	
• Identifying how integrated behavioral patterns develop and are sustained over time • Identifying integrated behavioral patterns that lead to successful and unsuccessful collaboration • Developing guidelines for best practice for effective dissemination of behavioral patterns • Linking integrated behavioral patterns with technologies through such techniques as thinkLets	Adaptive structuration theory, thinkLets, Time-Interaction-Performance, Temporal coordination
Organizational Implementation	
• Best practices for introducing integrated e-collaboration technology into an organization • Defining the relationship between adoption and diffusion of different technologies in *ad hoc* integrated solutions • Identifying conditions for preferred sequence of implementation • Incorporating emerging technologies into existing infrastructures	Adaptive structuration theory, Diffusion of innovations, Change management, IS implementation

A recent review of interdisciplinary perspectives in small groups defines nine theoretical perspectives from which groups have been studied: psychodynamic, functional, temporal, conflict-power-status, symbolic-interpretive, social identity, social-evolutionary, social network, and feminist (Poole et al., 2004). We noted the growing interest in the temporal perspective earlier. We also indicated that the functional perspective is a very prevalent one in most existing research, and certainly in commercial products. Clearly, there is ample room for broadening the perspectives from which we examine the phenomenon of e-collaboration, as a step toward integrating theory and research in this area.

Summary

The previous sections presented numerous opportunities for further research on integration of e-collaboration technologies. Table 3 provides a summary of these research issues and related theoretical perspectives.

The issues that are summarized in Table 3 show the broad range of challenges that we face in the study of integrated e-collaboration technologies. The good news is that many theoretical perspectives exist to help in further development of these issues. Early efforts in a particular area of research are often criticized as being atheoretical, yet it is obvious from Table 3 that theory in e-collaboration has developed well. The continuing challenge is to stay ahead of technical developments with appropriate research and best practices for managerial action.

Conclusion

We have addressed the important topic of integration of e-collaboration technologies. We chose a broad approach that outlined possible avenues for further research related to design, implementation, and use of integrated e-collaboration technologies at various levels. As is typical in the information systems domain, technological opportunities can develop ahead of the related academic research that strives to accumulate and explain experiences. Blogs provide an example of a "grass roots" collaborative environment that is available in a flexible, easy-to-access, and ubiquitous way. The challenge is to study such rapidly-occurring phenomena in a theory-based way that provides lasting contribution even as technologies change.

As a variety of technologies become widespread in use, getting access to field sites constitutes less of a barrier. Field sites present both opportunity and risk, given the differences in contexts and complexity of such environments. Action research studies have the potential to provide a bridging mechanism between the desire to control collaborative phenomena and the value of studying them in natural contexts (Kock, 2005). Our point is that diverse methods will need to be used and accepted for this research. We anticipate a growing variety of research projects and perspectives for studying the phenomenon of integrated e-collaboration technologies in the hope of providing answers to the questions posed in this chapter.

Acknowledgments

The authors gratefully acknowledge Robert P. Bostrom for his invaluable comments on earlier versions of the manuscript.

References

Alavi, M. (2000). Managing organizational knowledge. In R.W. Zmud (Ed.), *Framing the domains of IT management: Projecting the future...through the past.* (pp. 15-28). Cincinnati, OH: Pinnaflex Educational Resources.

Anson, R., & Munkvold, B.E. (2004). Beyond face-to-face: A field study of electronic meetings in different time and place modes. *Journal of Organizational Computing and Electronic Commerce, 14*(2), 127-152.

Applegate, L.M. (1991). Technology support for cooperative work: A framework for studying introduction and assimilation in organizations. *Journal of Organizational Computing, 1*, 11-39.

Bieber, M., Engelbart, D., Furuta, R., Hiltz, S.R., Noll, J., Preece, J., Stohr, E.A., Turoff, M., & van de Walle, B. (2002). Toward virtual community knowledge evolution. *Journal of Management Information Systems, 18*(4), 11-35.

Bostrom, R.P, Kadlec, C., & Thomas, D. (2003). Implementation and use of collaboration technology in e-Learning: The case of a joint university-corporate MBA. In B.E. Munkvold (Ed.), *Implementing collaboration technologies in industry. Case examples and lessons learned* (pp. 211-245). London: Springer-Verlag.

Briggs, R.O., de Vreede, G-J., & Nunamaker, Jr., J.F. (2003). Collaboration engineering with ThinkLets to pursue sustained success with group support systems. *Journal of Management Information Systems, 19*(4), 31-64.

Carlson, J.R., & Zmud, R.W. (1999). Channel expansion theory and the experiential nature of media richness perceptions. *Academy of Management Journal, 42*(2), 153-170.

Carmel, E., & Agarwal, R. (2001). Tactical approaches for alleviating distance in global software development. *IEEE Software*, March/April, 22-29.

Chen, F., Nunamaker, Jr., J.F., Romano, N.C., & Briggs, R.O. (2003). A collaborative project management architecture. *Proceedings of the 36th Annual Hawaii International Conference on System Sciences* (pp. 15-26). Washington, DC: IEEE Computer Society.

Cody, W.F., Kreulen, J.T., Krishna, V. & Spangler, W.S. (2002). The integration of business intelligence and knowledge management. *IBM Systems Journal, 41*(4), 697-713.

Daft, R.L., & Lengel, R.H. (1986). Organizational information requirements, media richness and structural design. *Management Science, 32*(5), 554-571.

Dennis, A.R., Pootheri, S.K., & Natarajan, V.L. (1998). Lessons from the early adopters of web groupware. *Journal of Management Information Systems, 14*(4), 65-86.

Dennis, A.R., & Valacich, J.S. (1999). Rethinking media richness: Towards a theory of media synchronicity. *Proceedings of the 32nd Annual Hawaii International Conference on System Sciences* (p. 10). Washington, DC: IEEE Computer Society.

Dennis, A.R., Wixom, B.H., & Vandenberg, R.J. (2001). Understanding fit and appropriation effects in group support systems via meta-analysis. *MIS Quarterly, 25*(2), 167-193.

DeSanctis, G., & Poole, M.S. (1994). Capturing the complexity in advanced technology use: Adaptive structuration theory. *Organization Science, 5*(2), 121-147.

Ellis, C.A., Gibbs, S.J., & Rein, G.L. (1991). Groupware: Some issues and experiences. *Communications of the ACM, 34*(1), 39-58.

Ellis, T.J., & Hafner, W. (2006). ACLE: A communication environment for asynchronous collaborative learning, *Proceedings of the 39th Hawaii International Conference on System Sciences* (p. 9). Washington, DC: IEEE Computer Society.

Evaristo, R., & Munkvold, B.E. (2002). Collaborative infrastructure formation in virtual projects. *Journal of Global Information Technology Management, 5*(2), 29-47.

Fjermestad, J. (2004). An analysis of communication mode in group support systems research. *Decision Support Systems, 37*, 239-263.

Fjermestad, J., & Hiltz, S.R. (1998-99). An assessment of group support systems experimental research: Methodology and results. *Journal of Management Information Systems, 15*(3), 7-149.

Fjermestad, J., & Hiltz, S.R. (2000-2001). Group support systems: A descriptive evaluation of case and field studies. *Journal of Management Information Systems*, *17*(3), 115-159.

Francik, E., Rudman, S.E., Cooper, D., & Levine, S. (1991). Putting innovation to work: adoption strategies for multimedia communication systems. *Communications of the ACM*, *34*(12), 52-63.

Gallivan, M.J., & Benbunan-Fich, R. (2005). A framework for analyzing levels of analysis issues in studies of e-collaboration. *IEEE Transactions on Professional Communication*, *48*(1), 87-104.

Geyer, W., Richter, H., Fuchs, L., Frauenhofer, T., Daijavad, S., & Poltrock, S. (2001). A team collaboration space supporting capture and access of virtual meetings. In *Proceedings of the ACM 2001 International Conference on Supporting Group Work* (Group 2001) (pp. 188-196). New York: ACM Press.

Grinter, B. (2000). Workflow systems. Occasions for success and failure. *Computer Supported Cooperative Work (CSCW)*, *9*(2), 189-214.

Grudin, J. (1994). Computer-supported cooperative work: History and focus. *IEEE Computer*, *27*(5), 19-25.

Grudin, J. (2006). Enterprise knowledge management and emerging technologies. *Proceedings of the 39th Hawaii International Conference on System Sciences* (p. 10). Washington, DC: IEEE Computer Society.

Grudin, J., & Palen, L. (1995). Why groupware succeeds: Discretion or mandate? In *Proceedings of ECSCW '95* (pp. 163-278). Dordrecht: Kluwer.

Grudin, J., & Poltrock, S.E. (1997). Computer-supported cooperative work and groupware. *Advances in Computers*, *45*, 269-320.

Gupta, S., & Bostrom, R.P. (2003). Knowledge management and peer-to-peer collaboration technology: Key issues and research challenges. In *Proceedings of the 6th Annual Conference of the Southern Association for Information Systems (SAIS)* (pp. 175-185).

Gupta, S., & Bostrom, R.P. (2004). Collaborative e-learning: Information systems research directions. *Proceedings of the Tenth Americas Conference on Information Systems* (pp. 3031-3039).

Karsten, H. (1999). Collaboration and collaborative information technologies: A review of the evidence. *The DATA BASE for Advances in Information Systems*, *30*(2), 44-65.

Katzy, B., Evaristo, R. & Zigurs, I. (2000). Knowledge management in virtual projects: A research agenda. In *Proceedings of the 33rd Annual Hawaii International Conference on System Sciences*. (p. 5) Washington, DC: IEEE Computer Society.

Khazanchi, D., & Zigurs, I. (2005). *Patterns of effective management of virtual projects: An exploratory study*. Newtown Square, PA: Project Management Institute.

Kock, N. (2005). Using action research to study e-collaboration. Editorial Essay. *International Journal of e-Collaboration*, *1*(4), i-vii.

Mandviwalla, M., & Khan, S. (1999). Collaborative object workspaces (COWS): Exploring the integration of collaboration technology. *Decision Support Systems*, 27(3), 241-254.

Marble, R.P. (2000). Operationalising the implementation puzzle: an argument for eclecticism in research and in practice. *European Journal of Information Systems*, *9*, 132-147.

Mark, G., Grudin, J., & Poltrock, S.E. (1999). Meeting at the desktop: An empirical study of virtually collocated teams. In *Proceedings of ECSCW'99* (pp. 159-178).

Massey, A.P., Montoya-Weiss, M., & Hung, Y-T. (2003). Because time matters: Temporal coordination in global virtual project teams. *Journal of Management Information Systems*, *19*(4), 129-156.

McGrath, J.E. (1991). Time, interaction, and performance (TIP): A theory of groups. *Small Group Research*, *22*(2), 147-174.

Munkvold, B.E. *Implementing collaboration technologies in industry: Case examples and lessons learned.* London: Springer-Verlag.

Munkvold, B.E., & Anson, R. (2001). Organizational adoption and diffusion of electronic meeting systems: a case study. *Proceedings of the ACM 2001 International Conference on Supporting Group Work (Group 2001)* (pp. 279-287). New York. ACM Press.

Munkvold, B.E., & Tvedte. (2003). Implementing a portfolio of collaboration technologies in Statoil. In B.E. Munkvold (Ed.), *Implementing collaboration technologies in industry: Case in examples and lessons learned* (pp. 81-107). London: Springer-Verlag.

Munkvold, B.E., & Zigurs, I. (2004). *Global virtual teams in systems development: Starting swiftly in process and technology*. Working paper, Agder University College.

Ocker, R., Fjermestad, J., Hiltz, S.R., & Johnson, K. (1998). Effects of four modes of group communication on the outcomes of software requirements determination. *Journal of Management Information Systems*, *15*(1), 99-118.

Olson, J.S., Olson, G.M., & Meader, D.K. (1995). What mix of video and audio is useful for small groups doing remote real-time design work? *CHI '95 Proceedings*. New York: ACM Press.

Orlikowski, W.J. (1992). Learning from Notes: Organizational issues in groupware implementation. In *Proceedings of CSCW '92* (pp. 362-369).

Orlikowski, W.J., & Gash, D.G. (1994). Technological frames: Making sense of information technology in organizations. *ACM Transactions of Information Systems*, *12*(2), 174-207.

Orlikowski, W.J., & Hofman, J.D. (1997). An improvisational model for change management: the case of groupware technologies. *Sloan Management Review*, Winter, 11-21.

Päivärinta, T., & Munkvold, B.E. (2005). Enterprise content management: An integrated perspective on information management. In *Proceedings of the 38th Annual Hawaii International Conference on System Sciences*. Washington, DC: IEEE Computer Society.

Pekkola. S. (2003). *Multiple Media in Group Work. Emphasising Individual Users in Distributed and Real-time CSCW Systems*. Doctoral dissertation. Jyväskylä Studies in Computing 29, University of Jyväskylä.

Pinsonneault, A. & Caya, O. (2005). Virtual teams: What we know, what we don't know. *International Journal of e-Collaboration*, *1*(3), 1-16.

Poltrock, S. & Mark, G. (2003). Implementation of data conferencing in the Boeing Company. In M. Munkvold (Ed.), *Implementing collaboration technologies in industry: Case examples and lessons learned* (pp. 129-158). London: Springer-Verlag.

Poole, M.S., Hollingshead, A.B., McGrath, J.E., Moreland, R.L., & Rohrbaugh, J. (2004). Interdisciplinary perspectives on small groups. *Small Group Research*, *35*(1), 3-16.

Powell, A., Piccoli. G. & Ives, B. (2004). Virtual teams: A review of current literature and directions for future research. *The DATA BASE for Advances in Information Systems*, *35*(1), 6-36.

Project Management Institute (2004). *A guide to the project management body of knowledge (PMBOK)*. Retrieved August 13, 2004, from http://www.pmi.org

Qureshi, S., & Zigurs, I. (2001). Paradoxes and prerogatives in global virtual collaboration. *Communications of the ACM*, *44*(12), 85-88.

Rabin, S. (2001). *Collaborative Commerce and Enterprise Integration*. Auerbach Publications & CRC Press.

Ragusa, J.M., & Bochenek, G.M. (2001). Collaborative virtual design environments. *Communications of the ACM*, *44*(12), 41-43.

Rogers, E.M. (1995). *Diffusion of innovations* (4th ed.). New York: The Free Press.

Santanen, E., Kolfschoten, G., & Golla, K. (2006). The collaboration engineering maturity model. In *Proceedings of the 39th Hawaii International Conference on System Sciences*. Washington, DC: IEEE Computer Society.

Saunders, C.S., Van Slyke, C., & Vogel, D. (2004). My time or yours? Managing time visions in global virtual teams. *Academy of Management Executive, 18*(1), 19-31.

Shenhar, A.J. (1998). From theory to practice: Toward a typology of project management styles. *IEEE Transactions on Engineering Management, 45*(1), 33-48.

Silver, M.S. (1991). Decisional guidance for computer-based decision support. *MIS Quarterly, 15*(1), 105-122.

Sohlenkamp, M. & Chwelos, G. (1994). Integrating communication, cooperation, and awareness: the DIVA virtual office environment. In *Proceedings of CSCW'94* (pp. 331-343). New York: ACM Press.

Turoff, M. (1997). Virtuality. *Communications of the ACM, 40*(9), 38-43.

Venkatesh, V., Morris, M.G., Davis, G.B., & Davis, F.D. (2003). User acceptance of information technology: Toward a unified view. *MIS Quarterly, 27*(3), 425-478.

Vreede, G.J., de, & Briggs, R.O. (2005). Collaboration engineering: Designing repeatable processes for high-value collaborative tasks. In *Proceedings of the 38th Annual Hawaii International Conference on System Sciences.* Los Alamitos: IEEE Computer Society Press.

Zigurs, I., & Buckland, B. (1998). A theory of task/technology fit and group support systems effectiveness. *MIS Quarterly, 22*(3), 313-334.

Chapter IV

Collaborative Sensemaking Support: Progressing from Portals and Tools to Collaboration Envelopes™

John T. Nosek, Temple University, USA

Abstract

Sensemaking involves incomplete discovery, inaccurate interpretation, and imperfect action that will fail in someway and likely alter the situation in some unknowable way. Sensemaking demands intense, deep collaboration with participating agents, who many times are physically distributed and come from different groups and organizations. Incorporating collaboration functionality in a piece-meal approach in different ways as add-ons within a portal-based architecture can place heavy demands on users to learn, organizations to train, and ultimately limit the potential of collaboration technology to achieve organizational goals. It is proposed that individual and group sensemaking is a better starting point from which to build architectures to mitigate socio-cognitive limitations of participating agents collaborating to make sense of things. Three levels of Collaboration Envelopes™ are presented and architectural considerations presented to guide development of technology to better support collaborative sensemaking.

Introduction

... we expect KM (Knowledge Management) to become more people-centric as the recognition spreads that it is networking of competent and collaborating people that forms the basis for the behavior and success of any organization. ... People are the real intelligent agents, those that see and act on new opportunities that really are creations of the mind. (Wiig, 2000)

By their nature, innovative, forward-thinking organizations must empower their people and key stakeholders to engage in collaborative sensemaking. In collaborative sensemaking, participants accept that data discovery will be incomplete, their efforts to comprehend, interpret, and integrate data will be difficult and inaccurate to some degree, and their actions that emerge from sensemaking will fail in some ways and alter the situation in some unknowable way (Weick, 1979). In the future, organizational success will depend on how well organizations exploit synergies while minimizing risk in collaborative sensemaking.

The way to build better sensemaking technologies is to understand the strengths and limitations of human sensemaking, in other words, the strengths and limitations of how participants discover the right signals at the right time, make sense of them, and transmit signals to other participants at the right time as they collaboratively construct sufficient meaning to act.

Incorporating collaboration functionality in a piece-meal approach in different ways as add-ons within a portal-based architecture can place heavy demands on users to learn, organizations to train, and ultimately limit the potential of collaboration technology to achieve organizational goals. It is proposed that individual and group sensemaking is a better starting point from which to build architectures to overcome socio-cognitive limitations of participating agents, both human and non-human, collaborating to make sense of things. The notion of Collaboration Envelopes™ that wrap around sensemaking processes is introduced as a way to build more cohesive architectures to fully support sensemaking processes. First, sensemaking is explained through a framework of sensemaking cycles and linkages. Second, using this framework, three levels of Collaboration Envelopes™ are introduced. Third, some architectural considerations are introduced to better support collaborative sensemaking anytime, anyplace.

Single Sensemaking Cycle by Individual Agent

While aggregates can project a signal (which will be described subsequently), it is critical to remember that processing to make sense of a signal needs to occur at the individual-agent level. While many individual agents within an aggregate can be processing the same signal at the same time, although not necessarily in the say way, the aggregate, like a team or organization, can not process a signal. Before describing multi-level sensemaking and linkages, we briefly identify issues relevant to a single sensemaking cycle, which are basic to all levels of sensemaking. See Figure 1 below for an abstraction of a single sensemaking cycle.

Signal Out: The action or the constructed boundary object (something an agent consciously or subconsciously externalizes, like a message, picture, gesture…). A signal out:

1. May or may not be attended to by other agents.
2. Must be generated at the right time.
3. Must be directed to the right agents while denying it to the wrong agents.
4. That is transmitted by the sending agent is affected by such factors, as: degree that a sending agent evaluates that receiving agents do not share the same meaning of a situation, the effort to transmit, the available means to transmit, the perceived effectiveness of means, trust of receiving agents, dependence on receiving agents to accomplish sending agent's goals, task importance, time to achieve shared meaning, task equivocality, and so forth.

Signal In: A boundary object, otherwise known as something external to the cognitive domain and observable by an agent, that affords action opportunity to a class of agents of similar capabilities, for example, affordance (Nosek, 2004). A signal in:

1. Must be received at the right time.
2. Must be received from the right agent(s).
3. May be actively pulled in by the receiving agent, including action by the receiving agent to uncover/clarify signals.

Figure 1. Single sensemaking cycle

4. Must have sufficient signal strength, in other words, the inherent properties of the signal to project clearly over the noise in the environment.
5. Is affected by receiving agent factors, such as: sensing capabilities, cognitive workload, working memory capacity, goals, and hypotheses.

Constructing Meaning (Make Sense): Some factors that affect the process of construing meaning of a received signal include:

1. Available knowledge to process signal (attunement [Heft, 2001]), such as the episodic nature of elicited/accessible knowledge (Nosek, 2004; Yufik, 2003; Yufik & Georgopoulos, 2002) determines what knowledge is available within working memory for sensemaking at a given point in time (see Figure 2).
2. Task importance to which the signal is related.
3. Some cognitive limitations mentioned above related to signal in effect making sense of the signals: cognitive workload, working memory capacity, goals, and hypotheses.
4. Additional factors that affect meaning construction include: beliefs, trust in origin, dependence on others relative to the sign, in other words, how does the signal in affect a dependence that the receiving agent may have with other agents, etc.

Not surprisingly, there are a number of cognitive processing factors that overlap in attending to Signals In, making sense of these signals, and constructing and conveying Signals Out. However, it is important to understand how some of these overlapping aspects of cognitive processing affect the constituent processes within the overall sensemaking cycle.

Levels and Linkages

A primary reason for failure to act effectively in ill-structured domain situations is failure in sensemaking at the individual, team, organizational, and interorganizational levels. Sensemaking cycles must be linked among individuals within a team, the team must link the results of their sensemaking cycles to other teams in the organization by linking with one or more agents of those teams, and the organization must link their sensemaking cycles to agents within other organizations. Figure 3 below provides an abstraction of these sensemaking levels and linkages. In one way, the framework can be viewed as layering socio-cognitive cycles over the general systems theory model with at least two important and useful distinctions:

Figure 2. Dynamic, episodic nature of elicited/accessible knowledge

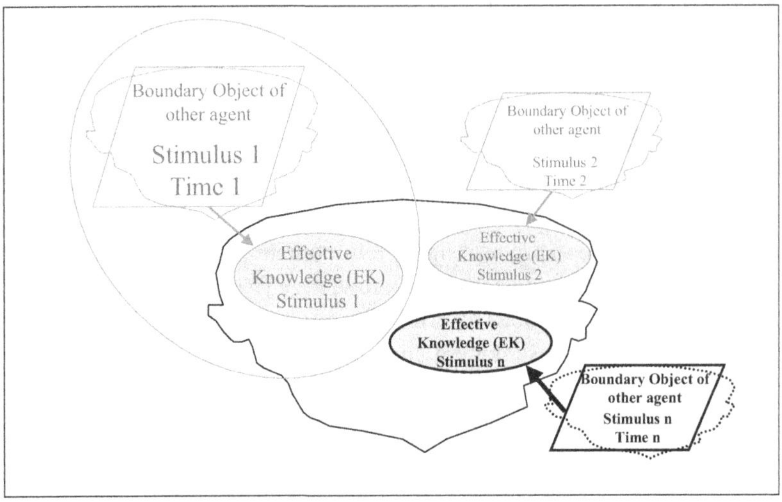

1. As opposed to systems theory where the output of one system is the input to another system, the signal in to systems is not necessarily perceived as being the same as the intended signal out of another system. In addition, if the right agent does not receive the signal out at the right time, it is functionally a lost signal.
2. While a higher level aggregate, such as a team, can create a single output signal, like a document, warning, or joint action, this can only be perceived by individual human and non-human agents within other higher level aggregates, such as teams or organizations.

Collaboration Envelopes™

There must be an intellectual break away from the notion of individual tools that incorporate collaboration functionality in their own unique ways in a non-integrative fashion. The notion of a Collaboration Envelope™ is introduced as a way to envision technology that seamlessly wraps around socio-cognitive work to augment individual-agent and aggregate sensemaking cycles. Essentially, participating agents should be able to perform their work within the technology that provides the greatest ease and power, while Collaboration Envelopes™ provide the collaboration functionality to achieve collaborative sensemaking. Table 1 provides a summary

Figure 3. Sensemaking cycles and linkages

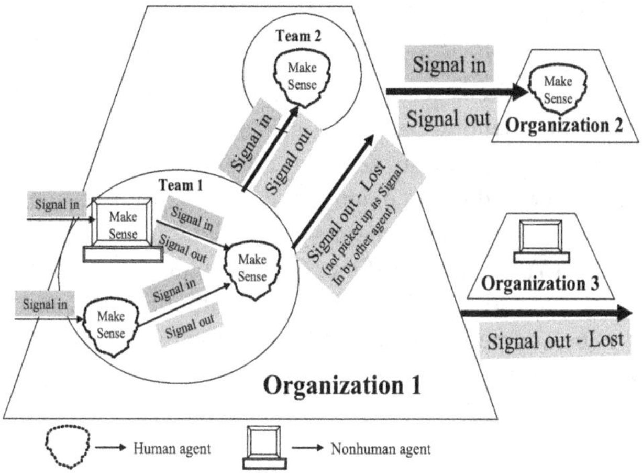

comparison between tool-centric and Collaboration Envelope™ Technology.

It is useful to view augmentation with Collaboration Envelopes™ at three levels:

Level 1: This level of augmentation is very limited. The focus is on sharing data to overcome the fact that *everyone can not be in the same room at the same time.* A Level 1 Collaboration Envelope™ supports data sharing, but in a way that is non-tool-centric and more of a natural wrapper around sharing, in other words, there is a consistent way to store, retrieve, and share data of all types, which makes it easier to learn and reduces training requirements.

Level 2: This technology addresses the issues of cognitive workload associated with attending to signals in and constructing and directing signals out. It can include the

Table 1. Tool-centric vs. Collaboration Envelopes™

Dimension	Tool-centric	Collaboration Envelopes™
Degree of Integration	Very limited, mostly stand-alone	High, integration of functions
Effort to Learn	High, separate unfamiliar environments to learn	Low, integrated environment with similar, familiar interfaces
Flexible Perspective Taking	Low, limited to perspective of the individual tool	High, permits flexible, multiple perspectives of work activity

use of computerized agents. They can range from non-human agents that perform simple actions and do not learn, for example, agents that search the Web for certain key words, to more complex agents that can learn to push and pull relevant signals.

Level 3: This technology focuses on helping to make sense of signals, otherwise known as help in comprehending, interpreting, and integrating signals to collaboratively construct meaning and subsequent actions. This can include artificial intelligence technology that directly extends the workload capacity of humans and mitigates weaknesses due to working memory limitations and the episodic nature of accessible knowledge (Yufik, 2003; Yufik & Georgopoulos, 2002; Yufik & Seridan, 2002). Since sensemaking deals with incomplete, conflicting data, existing AI techniques will need to be augmented with approaches such as situational logic-based technology and artificial intelligence incorporating non-axiomatic reasoning (Wang, 1995; Wang 1996; Wang 2004).

Architectural Considerations

For the most part, existing technologies focus on sharing data and not on supporting the sensemaking activities of participants engaged in a collaboration. Technology must fully support the sensemaking activities of participants who engage in various collaborations. The core idea of working within and among collaborations will be used as a basis to discuss some of the kinds of functionality that would be found in different levels of Collaboration Envelopes™.

Human and non-human agents may participate in multiple collaborations with different participating agents in parallel, switching among various collaborations. In some sense, an agent may even engage in a collaboration with himself. For example, during reflection on an issue, one's perspective and understanding may have changed since the last time the issue was visited. Figure 4 shows a schematic of how an agent is part of a collaboration at one time, Time 1, and then through some change in attention, becomes part of another collaboration at Time 2. Collaboration Envelopes must support the process of working within a collaboration and then shifting attention and working effectively within another collaboration. Collaboration Envelopes™ help build and maintain an understanding by each member of the group. As noted earlier, participating agents possess inherent working memory limitations that severely hinder sensemaking. Working memory has (1) limited capacity and (2) knowledge available within it is episodic, in other words, knowledge available shifts with signals received and the reflective processing of signals, so that what knowledge is available for processing signals within working memory at a given time changes.

Figure 4. Collaboration Envelope™ support within and among collaborations

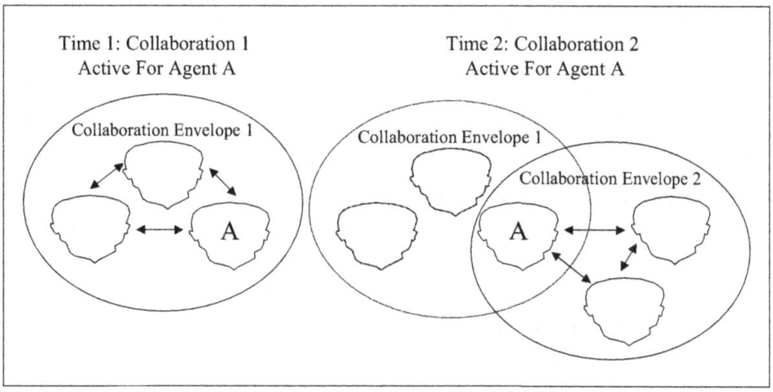

There must be ways to support sensemaking (signals in, signals out, and making sense) within a collaboration and among collaborations.

For example, within a collaboration, agents must be aware of important signals out at the right time, and at the same time, be open to important signals coming from another collaboration to shift attention at the right time. Several examples of the kinds of collaborative functionality that need to be incorporated within Collaboration Envelopes™ to comprehensively support collaboration excellence follow.

Co-Development of Work Products within a Collaboration

Joint work products that evolve as part of the sensemaking process include such things as plans, reports, budgets, specifications, architectures, contracts, designs, and software code. Collaboration Envelopes™ must support all phases (Mitchell, Posner, & Baecker, 1995; Salcedo & Decouchant, 1997):

- **Planning:** Collaborators establish the objectives, structure, and divide up parts of the shared work product to be created.
- **Creation:** Collaborators compose their portion of the joint work product. Although they may work alone, it is important that they are aware of what the other collaborators are doing.
- **Evaluation:** Collaborators review, propose changes, and add comments to each other's work.

- **Negotiation:** Collaborators discuss proposed changes with one another and decide on what changes should be made.
- **Consolidation:** The collaborators resolve conflicts and merge changes into the shared work product.

It should be stressed that these phases are normally not sequential. There is continuing cycling through these phases for different sections of the shared work product. For example, while negotiation is occurring for one part, creation could be occurring for another part. Dealing with these social, intellectual, and procedural complexities, collaborators work asynchronously and synchronously as they navigate through these phases (Tammaro, Mosier, Goodwin, & Spitz, 1997). They must establish and maintain a common understanding of the situation and solve problems such as work product structure, while adopting procedures that will enable them to get their work launched, circulate drafts, circulate comments, and incorporate changes in order to finalize the joint work product (Tammaro et al., 1997). Collaborators usual work synchronously when planning, negotiating, and consolidating and asynchronously when creating and evaluating, but this could be because of inadequate asynchronous technologies to support all phases. Maintaining situational awareness of what others are doing is especially difficult yet critical to effective joint development of shared work products (Ede & Lunsford, 1990).

Advanced Attention Management within and among Collaborations

Attention management includes basic ideas of push and pull technology. However, to be even more effective, attention management schemes must be integrated within collaborative activities such as joint work-product development to insure that the right signal is sent and received at the right time. For example, a change to a word within a document or a position on a map might automatically trigger notifications to certain agents so that this small change to the joint work product is identified. When receiving agents somehow recognize this change, notification of recognition to other cognizant agents could automatically be initiated. Integrating with other functionality listed in the previous section, this change may also initiate a structured dialog or review of assumptions. Advancing this idea further, instead of an actual change causing the above set of actions, the change may just be proposed. Just a proposed change may invoke similar activity and may require negotiation and the use of voting on the proposed change before being accepted.

Another example of integrated collaborative functionality is the integration of attention management and socially constructed knowledge (Fitzgerald, 1992; Nosek, 2004). Using knowledge interest profiles, Signals are dispersed within an organization as experts evaluate them. For example, some report is reviewed by a specialist at the African Desk of the State Department. The specialist stores the report for himself and adds the keyword, Africa, importance: Low. At the time this evaluation is added, the report is sent to the Embassy in Somalia, because the Embassy has a profile that indicates it should be notified about any report on Africa of any level of importance. Upon reviewing the report, the Embassy evaluates that it is important to Somalia and adds a keyword, Somalia, importance: High. At this time, the Joint Chiefs of Staff is notified of the report, because their profile indicates that they are interested in reports about Somalia of high importance. The watch-desk officer for the Joint Chiefs evaluates that for Somalia, the importance of this report is Urgent. This modification of importance causes the report to be sent to the National Security Advisor Team, because their knowledge profile indicates they are interested in only Urgent matters related to Somalia. Compare this process to where reports are just replicated and distributed without evaluation.

Reentering a Collaboration: Quickly Update Sensemaking State

To quickly make sense of these signals at the right time, there must be mechanisms that allow participating agents to understand what may have changed in the collaboration since the last time the agent was engaged within the collaboration, in other words, changes will occur within a collaboration that will affect the sensemaking state of a participating agent, and mechanisms must allow individual participating agents to understand changes in their state of understanding relative to their last sensemaking efforts within a collaboration. For example, a participating agent must be able to evaluate changes since the last time the agent was engaged within the collaboration, evaluated a collaboration state property, and perhaps modified it. This means that the participant who re-engages within a collaboration is not necessarily interested in all the incremental changes since the last time of engagement. The agent made judgments in reviewing a collaboration state property at a given point in time, the collaboration state property may have changed within a collaboration, now the agent must be supported to quickly evaluate what changes may have been made to the collaboration state property since the last evaluative act. Referring now to Figure 5, Agent 1 initiates some collaboration state property. When Agent 2 re-engages within the collaboration, Agent 2 must compare Version 4 against the last version that Agent 2 evaluated: Version 1 plus the suggested changes of Agent 2. When Agent 3 re-engages within the collaboration, Agent 3 must compare Version 4 against the last version that Agent 3 evaluated: Version 1 plus the suggested changes of Agent 3. Finally when Agent 4 re-engages within the collaboration, Agent 4 must compare Version 4 against the last version that Agent 4 evaluated: Version 2 plus the suggested changes of Agent 4.

Figure 5. Evaluation in collaboration state properties by participating agents since last evaluation

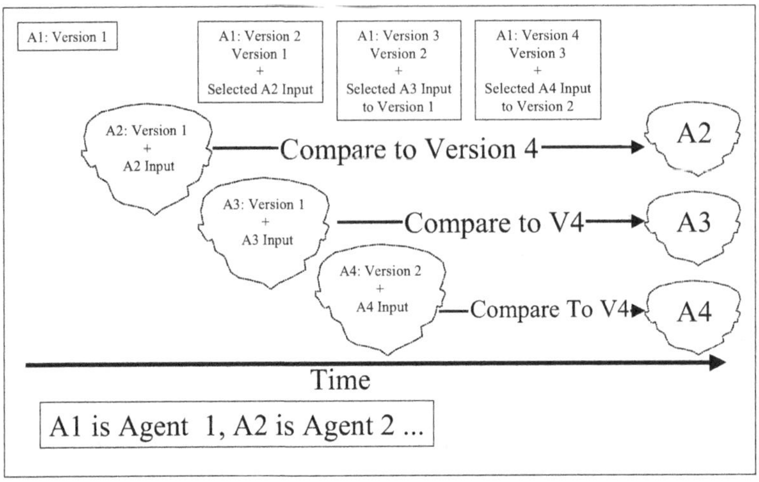

Possible Artificial Intelligence Component Enhancements

Figure 6 illustrates the integration of a specialized artificial intelligence collaboration component within a collaboration. As noted earlier, for the most part, collaboration technology has focused on overcoming limitations of people who can not be in the same place at the same time, and has not integrated advanced artificial intelligence techniques. At the same time, artificial intelligence (AI) has not integrated collaboration technology to enhance input to AI systems and to help make sense of output from AI systems. Signals (0) can be initially filtered using human and non-human agents (1). This means that the artificial intelligence collaboration component can be used with any filtering process and technology. Human agents access available signals (nodes of data) (2) and use judgment in making sense of these signals. Some of these signals that are enhanced through collaborative sensemaking (3) can then be used as input to the specialized AI collaboration component, composed of a translation component (4) and AI processing component (5) via a data exchange channel (6). A translation process must occur within the translation component (4) to make these signals meaningful to the AI processing component (5). Likewise, signals that result from AI processing component (7) can be made available for human agents to make sense of them by engaging in collaborative sensemaking around AI output. Also, the AI processing component (5) can accept signals that have not been collaboratively enhanced (8) and can return signals that are then available for processing (7) by collaborating human or non-human agents.

Figure 6. Integrating collaboration and artificial intelligence technology

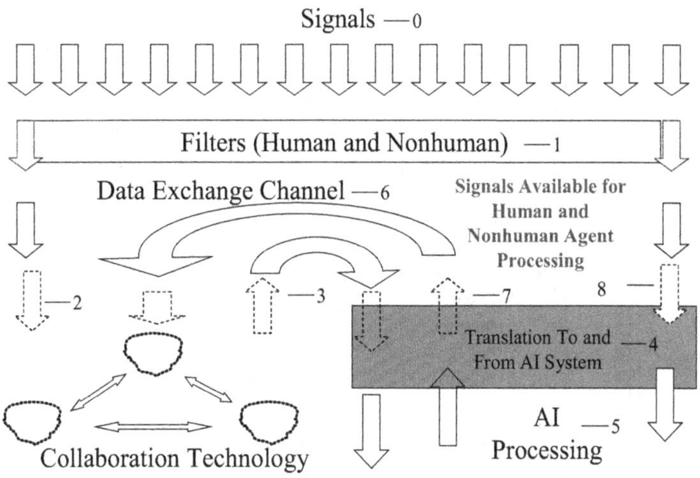

Referring now to Figure 7, there is an illustrated diagram of an aspect of AI enhancement that directly addresses the limitation of individuals and groups to simultaneously follow multiple inference chains. At any time individual or collaborating human agents (0) will be able to initiate an AI processing component (1, 2) to follow a different perspective. The initialized processing component (1, 2) will then take input from multiple collaborating agents or directly from filtered signals through a translation mechanism as described in Figure 6. AI processing agents can also be spawned (3). This is similar to initiating, but the spawned AI processing component (3) takes on all characteristics of the parent AI processing component (1). The spawned AI processing component (3) will be duplicates of the parent AI processing component (1), but will then follow different paths with different input and provide different output available for human collaborating agents via the data exchange channel as described in Figure 6. It is possible that an AI processing component (1) can spawn itself based on its own internal reasoning structure.

Architectural Considerations: Summary

As noted earlier, for the most part, existing non-Collaboration Envelope™ technologies focus on sharing data and not on supporting the sensemaking activities of participants engaged in a collaboration. Collaboration Envelopes™ must fully

Figure 7. Initiating and spawning to augment multiple inferencing

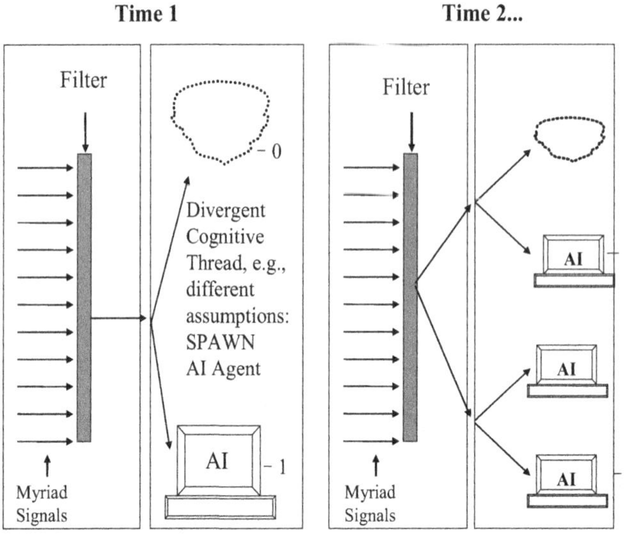

support the sensemaking activities of participants who engage in various collaborations. Some aspects of this support include:

1. Customized help for human and nonhuman agents to maintain the state of the agent's sensemaking within a collaboration.
2. Attention mechanisms to guide attention within a collaboration and support the shifting of attention among collaborations.
3. Help participating agents achieve changes in state between engagements within a collaboration by assisting agents in ascertaining the changes in collaboration state properties for a participating agent from one engagement within a collaboration to another engagement within a collaboration.
4. Support the construction of appropriate signals out (including joint work products) to the right agent at the right time, the reception of appropriate Signals In by the right agent at the right time, and assist participating agents in making sense of signals in by supporting the comprehension, interpretation, and integration of data signals in the most effective manner. This includes the following advanced artificial intelligence mechanisms to:
    a. Collaboratively enhance input to and clarify output from artificial intelligence components.
    b. Directly extended agent processing within collaborations through the initialization and spawning of AI agent components.

5. Multiple Collaboration Envelopes™ can be active simultaneously.
6. Collaboration Envelopes™ must be accessible from any computer that has access to other computers that are connected in some manner, either wired or wireless, over local area networks, intranets, or the Internet.
7. Collaboration Envelopes™ that are not on a local computer that is connected to other computers in some way may be accessed without loading specialized software on the client machine.

Summary

Portals are entry points to the web and the notion of portals affects architectural designs. In ill-structured situation domains, such as command and control, strategic planning, new product development, and information systems development, participating human and non-human agents engage in sensemaking. Sensemaking involves incomplete discovery, inaccurate interpretation, and imperfect action that will fail in someway and likely alter the situation in some unknowable way. Sensemaking demands intense, deep collaboration with participating agents, who many times are distributed and from different groups and organizations. Incorporating collaboration functionality in a piece-meal approach in different ways as add-ons within a portal-based architecture can place heavy demands on users to learn, organizations to train, and ultimately limit the potential of collaboration technology to achieve organizational goals. It is proposed that individual and group sensemaking is a better starting point from which to build architectures to overcome socio-cognitive limitations of participating agents collaborating to make sense of things. Three levels of Collaboration Envelopes™ were presented and sample integrated functionality explored. Architectural considerations for Collaboration Envelope™ Technology were identified that provide collaboration functionality to support sensemaking capabilities of participating agents. A major innovation of the Collaboration Envelope™ Method is the way it enhances the ability of participating agents to maximize their sensemaking effectiveness as they work within a collaboration and then support the shifting among collaborations. Each participating agent may initiate Collaboration Envelopes™ within many collaborations. It is possible to have multiple Collaboration Envelopes™ initiated simultaneously to support shifting among collaborations. Collaboration Envelopes™ can maintain Collaboration State Properties with customized views for each participating agent so that participating agents may ascertain what has changed in collaboration state properties since the last time that the participating agent evaluated them. Examples of integrating collaboration and artificial intelligence components as part of advanced Collaboration Envelopes™ were also presented. As noted earlier, "... it is networking of competent and collaborating people that forms the basis for the behavior and success of any organization" (Wiig, 2000). Establishing a comprehensive basis to direct the path to excellence in collaborative sensemaking is superior to piece-meal approaches that have no sense of direction.

References

Ede, L., & Lunsford, A. (1990). *Singular texts/plural authors: Perspectives on collaborative writing.* Carbondale: Southern Illinois University Press.

Fitzgerald, J. (1992). *Towards knowledge in writing: Illustrations from revision studies.* New York: Springer-Verlag.

Heft, H. (2001). *Ecological psychology in context.* Mahwah, NJ: Laurence Erlbaum.

Mithcell, A., Posner, I., & Baecker, R. (1995). Learning to write together using groupware. In *Proceedings of the ACM Conference on Human Factors in Computing Systems (CHI'95)* (pp. 288-295). Denver, CO: ACM.

Nosek, J. T. (2001). Social organization of knowledge in teams: Issues for computer support. In M. McNeese, M. Endsley, & E. Salas (Eds.), *New trends in cooperative activities: System dynamics in complex settings* (pp. 218-229). Human Factors and Engineering Society (HFES).

Nosek, J. T. (2004). Group cognition as the basis for supporting group knowledge creation and sharing. *Journal of Knowledge Management, 8*(4), 54-64.

Salcedo, M. R., & Decouchant, D. (1997). Structured cooperative authoring for the World Wide Web. *Computer Supported Cooperative Work: The Journal of Collaborative Computing, 6*, 157-174.

Tammaro, S. G., Mosier, J. N., Goodwin, N. C., & Spitz, G. (1997). Collaborative writing is hard to support: A field study of collaborative writing. *Computer Supported Cooperative Work: The Journal of Collaborative Computing, 6*, 19-51.

Wang, P. (2004). The Limitation of Bayesianism. *Artificial Intelligence, 158*(1), 97-106.

Wang, P. (1996). Heuristics and normative models of judgment under uncertainty. *International Journal of Approximate Reasoning, 14*(4), 221-235.

Wang, P. (1995). *Non-axiomatic reasoning system: Exploring the essence of intelligence.* PhD dissertation, Indiana University.

Weick, K. E. (1979). *The social psychology of organizing.* Reading, MA: Addison Wesley.

Wiig, K. M. (1999). What future knowledge management users may expect. *Journal of Knowledge Management, 3*(2), 155-165.

Yufik, Y. M. (2003). Transforming data into actionable knowledge in network centric warfare. *Journal of Battlefield Technology, 6*(1), 1-10.

Yufik, Y. M., & Georgopoulos, A. P. (2002). Understanding understanding: Modeling cognitive mechanisms of comprehension in complex dynamic tasks. In *Proceedings of Technology for Command and Control (TC3) Workshop: Cognitive Elements of Effective Collaboration* (pp. 91-96).

Yufik, Y. M., & Sheridan, T. B. (2002). Swiss army knife and Ockham's razor: Modeling and facilitating operator's comprehension in complex dynamic tasks. *IEEE Transactions on Systems, Man, and Cybernetics—Part A: Systems and Humans, 32*(2), 185-199.

The chapter was previously published in the International Journal of e-Collaboration, 1(2), 25-39, April-June 2005.

Chapter V

Action Research and its Use in E-Collaboration Inquiry

Ned Kock, Texas A&M International University, USA

Abstract

This chapter begins with a discussion of action research from a historical perspective. It then puts forth some ideas on how this research approach can be used in investigations of the design or e-collaboration technologies and the impact of those technologies on people. This is followed by a discussion of key epistemological considerations, including that of whether action research can be conducted in a positivist manner. The chapter then summarizes two special issues of journals, on information systems action research, which provide scholarly illustrations of some of the arguments presented here. Finally, the chapter concludes with a discussion of how action research can be used by doctoral students investigating e-collaboration issues.

Action Research

According to most accounts, action research (AR) originated independently in the U.S. and England in the 1940s. In the U.S., AR emerged from the work of Kurt Lewin on a variety of topics, ranging from child welfare to group dynamics. Lewin was a German-born social psychologist whom many see as the "father" of AR. In England, AR's origins are not tied to a particular individual, but to an institution–the Tavistock Institute of Human Relations in London, where AR was used as a research method to both understand and treat socio-psychological disorders associated with war-related experiences.

To say that the range of areas and ways in which AR can be conducted is vast is an understatement. AR can be used in many general fields of inquiry such as bilingual education, clinical psychology, sociology, and information systems. It can be conducted in ways that are aligned with most epistemologies, including the positivist, interpretivist, and critical epistemologies. AR can have as its unit of analysis the individual, the small group, and even the entire organization. It can be used to address issues as varied as health concerns, environmental problems, engineering techniques, and business methods.

One of the key characteristics that distinguishes AR from most other research approaches, and also constitutes one of its main appeals, is that AR aims at both improving the subject of the study (often called "research client"), and generating knowledge, achieving both *at the same time*. While this characteristic may seem straightforward enough to easily differentiate AR from most other research approaches—such as experimental, survey, and case research—it is not.

Let us assume, for the sake of illustration, that a survey-based research project was conducted addressing the differential access to the Internet between two main income groups, one high (wealthy) and the other low (poor), in a particular city, where the reasons for the digital divide are unclear. Can that research be considered AR if a report based on it is used by the city's government to bridge the gap that characterizes the divide? The answer is "yes", if the research encompasses the city's actions, and possibly a follow-up survey assessment of the impact of those actions. The answer is "no", if the research ended with the analysis of the survey and the publication of the summary report.

Because of AR's dual goal, researchers employing it are said to have to satisfy two "masters" (Kock & Lau, 2001; Sommer, 1994)—the subject (or subjects) of the research, and the research community. Historically, one could argue that it has been harder to satisfy the latter, especially in fields of inquiry where AR has not traditionally been used—such as e-collaboration.

Action Research and E-Collaboration Inquiry

Research on e-collaboration has flourished worldwide, especially since the 1990s. This has been motivated by a number of factors, including the development of and experimentation with a variety of e-collaboration tools in the 1980s and 1990s (e.g., workflow coordination and group decision support systems), the emergence of the Internet in the early 1990s, and the explosion in the personal and commercial use of the Web in the mid 1990s (motivated by the development of the first Web browsers). The flourishing of e-collaboration research has generally coincided with the increasing use of AR in the study of technology-related issues, culminating with the publication of two related special issues dedicated to the discussion and illustration of the use of AR in information systems research (Baskerville & Myers, 2004; Kock & Lau, 2001).

In spite of the fact that e-collaboration research and AR have grown in importance together in the last 15 years or so, there is less AR applied to e-collaboration inquiry than could be expected. To be sure, there are examples of e-collaboration studies employing AR (see, e.g., DeLuca, 2003; Kock & Davison, 2003; Yoong & Gallupe, 2001). Nevertheless, the vast majority of the research on e-collaboration produced in the last 15 years has employed experimental research methods, followed by survey and case research methods. AR trails way behind, accounting for probably no more than 5 percent of the total e-collaboration research output. This situation mirrors a research-orientation trend discussed back in the early 1990s by Orlikowski and Baroudi (1991), when AR was found to account for less than 1 percent of the total information systems research output published in several major academic outlets.

While there is no "typical" e-collaboration AR study, previous research (Kock, 1999; 2001) suggests the existence of key elements that are likely to be shared by most e-collaboration studies employing AR, particularly studies following the positivist epistemological paradigm (this will be explored in more detail in the next section). Those key elements can be summarized as follows:

- **Research question(s):** This is the theory-based research question (or questions) that guides the data collection and analysis. Instead of a research question, the data collection and analysis may be guided by one or more hypotheses, but this is less commonly the case in AR than in other research approaches (e.g., experimental research). An example of research question is the following: does the use of a video-conferencing suite improve the quality of the outcomes generated by new product development teams whose members are geographically dispersed?
- **E-collaboration technology:** This is the technology whose impact on a research client is the main subject of the research. An example of e-collaboration technology is a video-conferencing suite.

- **Practical problem(s):** This is the problem (or problems) being faced by an individual, group or organization, which the e-collaboration AR study aims at solving, at least in part. Some prefer to refer to practical problems by using a more "benign" term, namely that of "opportunities for improvement". An example of practical problem is the following: new products need to be constantly developed by geographically dispersed teams, but the transportation and lodging costs associated with bringing team members together currently prevent more than two thirds of the needed teams from being conducted.
- **Research client:** This is the individual, group, or organization whose practical problem (or problems) is supposed to be solved by the e-collaboration AR study. An example of a research client would be an automobile manufacturer with several factories in the U.S. and overseas.

One of the most straightforward and efficient ways of conducting an e-collaboration AR study is to collect data using the same instrument (e.g., a questionnaire) at two key points in time, namely before and after the introduction of the e-collaboration technology. The technology introduction would more often than not have the goal of solving an important practical problem being faced by the research client. Usually, it is a good idea to collect quantitative as well as qualitative data before and after the technology introduction. The quantitative data can be used in simple non-parametric comparison of means analyses, whereas the qualitative data can be used to find explanations and underlying causes for the patterns observed in the data.

In spite of its simplicity, the type of research design discussed above is relatively rare in AR. It is much more common to see published examples of AR in which only qualitative data is collected, mostly during and after the AR intervention (e.g., e-collaboration technology introduction). Moreover, quite often AR studies are conducted through multiple iterations of Susman and Evered's (1978) AR cycle, rather than the "one shot," non-cyclical research design mentioned above. Susman and Evered's (1978) AR cycle involves the identification of practical problems, the solution of those problems, and reflection on the part of the researcher, which is then followed again by the identification and solution of problems, new reflection, and so on.

Some Epistemological Considerations

Epistemologies can be seen as systems of concepts, rules, and criteria that find acceptance among a community of researchers as a basis for the generation of what that community of researchers sees as valid knowledge. By far the most widely subscribed epistemology among e-collaboration researchers is positivism.

Research that conforms to positivist inquiry tenets usually departs from a set of theoretical propositions or hypotheses, and aims at testing those propositions or hypothesis through the analysis of empirical data. Also, in positivist research the data is usually (although not always) of a quantitative nature. The research methods employed in positivist studies often reflect those traditionally used by natural scientists.

One issue that has led to some debate among AR scholars in the past is whether AR can be conducted in ways that are consistent with different epistemologies, including the positivist epistemology. The debate has been motivated by the fact that AR has traditionally been used in research studies that do not conform very well with traditional positivist standards, and that are better aligned with what many would see as the interpretive and critical epistemologies (Audi, 2003). In fact, one could argue that today there is resistance in scholarly AR circles against the notion of positivist AR, and that resistance can be quite strong within specific AR communities (e.g., AR practitioners in Scandinavia).

The above scenario creates a problematic situation—what one could reasonably call a vicious circle. Since e-collaboration research is overwhelmingly positivist in nature, and there are practical reasons for this status quo, researchers who try to employ AR to study e-collaboration are hampered not only once but twice in their efforts. On one hand, they have to justify using AR in a positivist manner, which is likely to meet with opposition from AR scholars. On the other hand, they have to sell the notion that AR can be useful for e-collaboration research, which is likely to be seen with suspicion by established e-collaboration researchers.

This is an unfortunate state of affairs, because AR can address a key problem with past e-collaboration research, namely its lack of "real world appeal". In other words, since past e-collaboration research has been by and large based on laboratory experiments with students, it has been difficult for practicing managers and professionals to relate to many of the findings resulting from that research. Moreover, on a related note, research conducted in controlled laboratory settings arguably leads to findings that carry little external validity–which, interestingly, is often a criticism of AR studies as well (Kock, 2004).

Can AR be successfully employed in e-collaboration research? The answer to this question is certainly "yes", and there are several examples of that (Kock, 1999; 2004). Can that be done in a positivist way? Well, based on some recent examples (see, e.g., DeLuca, 2003), the answer to this follow-up question also seems to be "yes". The key here is perhaps to be creative so that certain characteristics of AR are used to add natural strengths to e-collaboration inquiry, rather than only natural threats for which "methodological antidotes" already exist (see, e.g., Kock, 2004, for a discussion of three such threats and related methodological antidotes).

A natural strength of AR comes from the observation that it exposes the researcher to significantly more (although relatively sparse) data than more focused research approaches (e.g., experimental and survey research). If one were to adopt Popper's (1992) view that exposure to a large body of data, whose analysis does not uncover evidence that contradicts a hypothesis, is in fact "evidence" in support of the hypothesis, then AR could be seen as quite adequate for positivist e-collaboration inquiry (see, e.g., Kock, 2001b, for a study that builds explicitly on this view).

Two Special Issues of Journals Worth Checking

E-collaboration researchers often identify themselves with broader research communities. One such community is that of information systems researchers. With that in mind, a couple of special issues on information systems AR are worth checking, as they provide exemplars of AR studies that can be used as a basis for e-collaboration researchers interested in employing AR. The first is the special issue on AR in information systems published in the journal *Information Technology & People* in 2001 (volume 14, number 1). The second is the special issue on AR in information systems published in the journal *MIS Quarterly* in 2004 (volume 28, number 3).

The special issue published in the journal *Information Technology & People* in 2001 was the first special issue ever on AR in information systems (Kock & Lau, 2001). The issue contained six articles. Three of those are conceptual, in the sense that they are aimed at providing insights on how to conduct information systems AR. The other three articles are empirical, in the sense that they discuss actual information systems AR studies and their results. Of the empirical articles, two addressed e-collaboration issues in the context of group support systems (Kock, 2005) investigations.

The special issue on AR in information systems published in the journal *MIS Quarterly* in 2004 was aimed at providing a set of exemplars of information systems AR studies of an empirical nature (Baskerville & Myers, 2004). As such, all of the six articles published in this special issue report on empirical studies that employed AR to investigate information systems phenomena. None of the articles seems to be aimed at squarely addressing e-collaboration issues, although at least two of the articles—Braa and colleagues' "Networks of Action", and Kohli and Kettinger's "Informating the Clan"—address issues that are likely to be relevant for e-collaboration researchers.

Doctoral Action Research on E-Collaboration

A great deal of the research output produced every year, and published in academic journals, is the direct result of doctoral research investigations. The field of e-collaboration is no exception to this general rule, so it is a good idea to contemplate the pros and cons of conducting doctoral research on e-collaboration issues employing AR.

Phillips and Pugh (2000) state, in their excellent book on how to successfully complete a doctoral program, that one of the best ways to get a doctoral degree is to test an existing theory. Conversely, the authors point out that it is not very wise to try to develop a new theory as part of one's doctoral research project. In spite of many doctoral students' propensity to think of their research projects as likely to lead to theoretical insights that will change the world in a major way, it is a good idea to heed Phillips and Pugh's (2000) advice. It is unlikely that doctoral students' ideas will have the same impact as Darwin's theory of evolution, or Einstein's theory of relativity (which were not developed as part of Darwin's or Einstein's doctoral work, by the way).

Conducting research aimed at testing an existing theory is quite likely to lead someone's research to fall into the general epistemological category called positivist research, discussed earlier. And, as previously argued, there is nothing wrong with conducting AR in a positivist manner. However, one problem may arise. Traditionally, AR has not been seen as the best approach for the conduct of positivist inquiry. In fact, AR has been widely viewed as an ideal approach to create new theories grounded in action-oriented projects, particularly in organizational settings.

So, what is a doctoral student to do when contemplating using AR to investigate e-collaboration issues? First, it would be advisable to have a look at examples of doctoral dissertations that accomplished this (see, e.g., DeLuca, 2003). Second, it is highly advisable to design the research in a positivist manner, following some of the suggestions provided earlier in this chapter. Finally, the student should make sure that the doctoral dissertation committee members are receptive to the idea of AR being conducted in a positivist manner. After all, those committee members are ultimately the ones that will decide whether the degree is granted or not. Those who employ and/or subscribe to the AR approach known as "canonical AR" are likely to be so inclined, and others who are not can be educated based on publications discussing canonical AR (see, e.g., Davison et al., 2004).

Nevertheless, a number of obstacles await those doctoral students who decide to employ AR to study e-collaboration issues. Those students who opt for studying e-collaboration effects in organizational settings will face the challenge of finding an organization or organizations willing to work with them. Even when organizational support is achieved, there is the danger that the support will be withdrawn before enough research data is collected. Finally, a multitude of political issues will have to be dealt with. For example, there may be suspicion and opposition by employees, if support is obtained from the organization's management first, without much grass-roots consultation. Dealing with such political issues is likely to ensure that the doctoral student employing AR will have to spend significantly more time and effort with the research project than doctoral students employing more traditional e-collaboration research approaches (e.g., experimental research).

Conclusion

This chapter discusses a number of issues in connection with the use of AR to conduct research on e-collaboration issues. It starts with a brief historical review of AR and its contemporaneous origins in the US and England. The chapter also discusses AR's more recent use in information systems, a field of inquiry that is often seen as related to that of e-collaboration. The chapter then goes on to discuss key elements that are likely to be shared by most e-collaboration studies employing AR.

Underlying much of the discussion presented in this chapter is the belief that AR can be conducted in ways that are closely aligned with the positivist epistemology. In fact, the chapter goes as far as arguing that there are certain advantages in conducting positivist AR in the context of e-collaboration inquiry. Among the reasons is that today the most widely subscribed epistemology (by far, it seems) among e-collaboration researchers is positivism.

The chapter provides a short review of two relatively recent special issues of journals, which are worth checking by those interested in conducting e-collaboration studies employing AR. It then concludes with a discussion on how one can successfully carry out a doctoral AR study addressing e-collaboration issues, as well as some of the difficulties that the doctoral student is likely to face.

References

Audi, R. (2003). *Epistemology: A contemporary introduction.* New York: Routledge.

Baskerville, R., & Myers, M.D. (2004). Special issue on action research in information systems: Making IS research relevant to practice. *MIS Quarterly*, *28*(3), 329-336.

Davison, R., Martinsons, M., & Kock, N. (2004). Principles of canonical action research. *Information Systems Journal*, *14*(1), 65-86.

DeLuca, D.C. (2003). *Business process improvement using asynchronous e-collaboration: Testing the compensatory adaptation model*. Doctoral dissertation. Philadelphia: Temple University.

Klein, H.K., & Myers, M.D. (1999). A set of principles for conducting and evaluating interpretive field studies in information systems. *MIS Quarterly*, *23*(1), 67-93.

Kock, N. (1999). *Process improvement and organizational learning: The role of collaboration technologies*. Hershey, PA: Idea Group Publishing.

Kock, N. (2001). Compensatory adaptation to a lean medium: An action research investigation of electronic communication in process improvement groups. *IEEE Transactions on Professional Communication*, *44*(4), 267-285.

Kock, N. (2001b). Changing the focus of business process redesign from activity flows to information flows: A defense acquisition application. *Acquisition Review Quarterly*, *8*(2), 93-110.

Kock, N. (2004). The three threats of action research: A discussion of methodological antidotes in the context of an information systems study. *Decision Support Systems*, *37*(2), 265-286.

Kock, N. (2005). What is e-collaboration? *International Journal of e-Collaboration*, *1*(1), i-vii.

Kock, N., & Davison, R. (2003). Can lean media support knowledge sharing? Investigating a hidden advantage of process improvement. *IEEE Transactions on Engineering Management*, *50*(2), 151-163.

Kock, N., & Lau, F. (2001). Information systems action research: Serving two demanding masters. *Information Technology & People* (Special Issue on Action Research in Information Systems), *14*(1), 6-12.

Orlikowski, W.J., & Baroudi, J.J. (1991). Studying information technology in organizations: Research approaches and assumptions. *Information Systems Research*, *2*(1), 1-28.

Phillips, E.M., & Pugh, D.S. (2000). *How to get a PhD: A handbook for students and their supervisors*. Philadelphia: Open University Press.

Popper, K.R. (1992). *Logic of scientific discovery*. New York: Routledge.

Sommer, R. (1994). Serving two masters. *The Journal of Consumer Affairs*, *28*(1), 170-187.

Susman G.I., & Evered, R.D. (1978). An assessment of the scientific merits of action research. *Administrative Science Quarterly*, *23*(4), 582-603.

Yoong, P., & Gallupe, B. (2001). Action learning and groupware: A case study in GSS facilitation research. *Information Technology & People*, *14*(1), 78-90.

Section II

Applied Research and Challenges

Chapter VI

The Role of Structured Conflict and Consensus Approaches in Virtual Team Strategic Decision Making

Jerry Fjermestad, New Jersey Institute of Technology, USA

Abstract

Do procedures that improve face-to-face decision meetings also improve virtual "meetings?" Might the effectiveness of such procedures improve with practice? This longitudinal experiment investigated the efficiency, effectiveness and group member perceptions of dialectical inquiry (DI) and constructive consensus (CC) approaches to strategic decision making in a virtual (distributed) computer-mediated-communications (CMC) environment. There were no differences between DI and CC groups in terms of decision effectiveness. However, this result has not been unusual in CMC research. DI groups had significantly higher perceived depth of evaluation than CC groups. CC groups reported greater decision acceptance and willingness to work together again than DI groups. The results are discussed in terms of their implications for group support systems research and design in the era of the World Wide Web.

Introduction

Increasingly, managers and professional information workers are communicating via the Internet and internal corporate networks, using "groupware" for both synchronous multi-media "meetings" and virtual (largely text-based, anytime/anywhere) discussions and project management. These are used both to support distributed task forces and project teams within existing organizations, and to create temporary or permanent "virtual organizations" to take advantage of new opportunities in electronic commerce (Hiltz & Wellman, 1997; Mowshowitz, 1997; Powell, Piccoli, & Ives, 2004). What kinds of structures, tools, and interaction processes work best with these new media? The availability of new technologies is outstripping our knowledge about how best to use them. We know that medium of communication does affect process and outcomes of group interaction (Daft & Lengel, 1986; Hiltz, Turoff, & Johnson, 1989; Priem, Harrison, & Muir, 1995; Rice, 1984). It is very likely that group procedures that have proven effective in face-to-face (FtF) decision-making and project meetings will not have the same effects in computer-mediated meetings, but without empirical comparisons, we do not know. Previous research on face-to-face groups indicates that groups that try to reach consensus on a choice decision without following any specific procedures often have impaired outcomes (process losses) relative to the efforts of others following specific procedures (Steiner, 1972). These include problems resulting from unequal participation, a failure to generate and explore alternative solutions before reaching a final choice, and a lack of critical examination of ideas.

Group interactions such as brainstorming and nominal group technique, and structured conflict procedures such as dialectical inquiry (DI) have been shown to decrease process losses and improve the outcomes of FtF decision making groups (Nunamaker, Dennis, Valacich, Vogel, & George, 1991; Schweiger, Sandberg, & Ragan, 1986; Schweiger, Sandberg, & Rechner, 1989). For example, several studies in the field of organizational strategic decision making have demonstrated that DI and similar structured conflict approaches, such as "devil's advocate" procedures, can improve decision quality [(Mason & Mitroff, 1981; Mitroff, Emshoff, & Kilmann, 1979, Schweiger, et al., 1986, 1989).

Unfortunately, researchers cannot confidently generalize these findings from studies of FtF groups to groups supported by computer based group support systems (GSS). This limitation is especially notable with respect to distributed or virtual (different time/different place) GSS computing environments. This is important given that organizations are migrating from traditional FtF communication and decision making to electronically mediated interactions, such as email and groupware (Powell et al., 2004). In addition, businesses are becoming more globally oriented, have flatter hierarchies, and are utilizing more cross functional teams, all of which is placing tremendous demands on decision makers' ability to coordinate dispersed activities and improve the effectiveness of the decisions (Chidambaram & Jones, 1993). The questions for decision makers are:

1. Can conflict generating techniques be effectively utilized in a virtual CMC environment? and
2. Will performance improve with experience?

This study is the first to examine the issue of whether structured conflict procedures are superior to consensus oriented procedures in a virtual communication environment. The study compares effectiveness of a structured conflict approach (DI) with a structured consensus approach (constructive consensus or CC), for strategic decision making tasks. To accomplish this we first gave groups a two-hour training session with a practice FtF task in order to familiarize the subjects with the GSS, the decision approaches (DI or CC) the experimental task type and their respective group members. Each group then worked on two different strategic decision tasks, each lasting for two weeks. A variable of secondary interest was the effect of "experience" on group performance. Several researchers (Chidambaram, 1989; Chidambaram, Bostrom, & Wynne, 1990) have found that in a decision room GSS computing environment, groups improved significantly with experience. We wanted to assess whether this relationship would hold for more extended distributed GSS situations. This question was addressed by comparing the performance of an initial two-week task with a second two-week task.

Background

Previous research in the field of organizational strategic decision making has demonstrated that structured conflict can improve the quality of decisions (Mason, 1969; Mason & Mitroff, 1981; Mitroff et al., 1979; Schweiger et al., 1986, 1989; Schwenk & Valacich, 1994; Tjosvold, 1982). However, these interventions have also been related to negative effects on both group perceptions and process outcomes (Rice, 1984; Schweiger et al., 1989; Turoff, 1991). The two basic structured conflict methods used in these studies are devil's advocacy (DA) and dialectical inquiry (DI). Schwenk's meta-analysis (Schwenk, 1989, 1990) indicates that while under some conditions DA is more effective than DI, in studies that focus on groups, DI has a slight advantage over DA. Thus, we chose DI for this study.

The Domain of this Study

DeSanctis and Gallupe (1987) first proposed a multidimensional contingency perspective taxonomy for GSS research consisting of group size (smaller, larger), member proximity (FtF, dispersed) and task type (McGrath's circumplex). Hiltz, Dufner, Holmes, and Poole (1991) enhanced the member proximity dimension to include virtual (different time conditions).

There are three contingency perspective dimensions consisting of place, time, and experience. The DeSanctis and Gallupe task dimension is nested with our experience dimension. This study and the studies conducted by Schweiger and associates (1986, 1989) and Tung and Heminger (1993) all use small size groups and thus, group size is not relevant. In comparison, they are in the same-place/same-time and experience with one session. Schweiger et al. (1989) adds a second session to the experience dimension. This study is in the different time /different place dimension for both sessions of the experience dimension. No previous studies have investigated these decision processes in a virtual CMC environment (Figure 1).

Figure 1. Domain of study

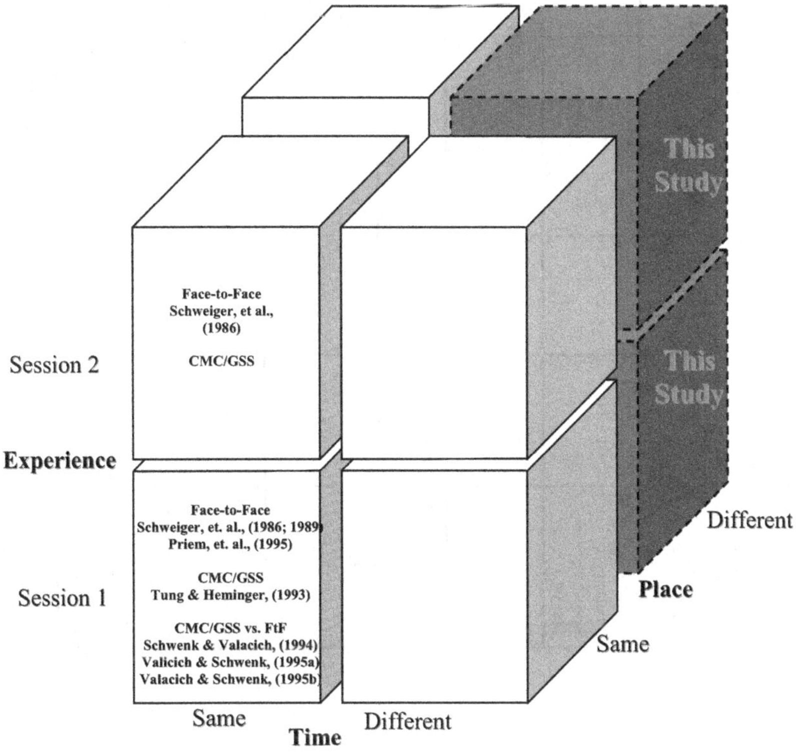

Table 1. A comparison of previous experimental outcomes

	Group Performance				Group Perceptions		
	Decision Time	Number of Comments	Decision Effectiveness	Depth of Analysis	Satisfaction/ Willingness	Perceived Depth of Analysis	Decision Acceptance
Face-to Face							
Schweiger, Sandberg, & Regan, (1986)	No measures	No measures	DA, DI > C*	DI > DA > C	C > DI > DA C> DA, DI*	DI > DA > C DI, DA > C*	C > DA > DI*
Schweiger, Sandberg, & Rechner, (1989) Session 1	C < DA < DI C < DI, DA*	No measures	DI > DA > C DA, DI >C*	DI >DA > C	C > DI > DA	DI > DA > C DA, DI > C*	C> DI > DA C > DI, DA*
Schweiger, Sandberg, & Rechner, (1995) Session 2	DI < DA < C S2 < S1*	No measures	DI > DA > C DA, DI > C*	DI > DA > C	C > Da > DI S2 > S1 *	DI > DA > C DI, DA > C* S1 > S2*	C > DI > DA C > DI, DA* S2 > S1*
Priem, Harrison, & Muir (1995)	No measures	No measures	C > DI	No measures	DI > C*	No measures	DI > C*
Decision Room							
Tung & Heminger (1993)	No measures	No measures	C > DI > DA	Assumptions: DI > DA, C DI > C*	DI > DA > C	DA > DI > C	DA > DI, C
Valacich & Schwenk (1995a)	Voting Rounds CMC > FtF * Decision Aid: DA > DI, E*	FtF > CMC*	FtF: DA > DI > E CMC: DA > E> DI Decision Aid: DA > DI, E*	FtF: DA > E > DI CMC: E > DA> DI Decision Aid: DA > DI, E*	Solution: DI > DA>E Process: E> DA > DI CMC > FtF *	No measures	No measures
Schwenk & Valacich (1995b)	No measures	No measures	DA > DI > E DA > DI, E*	DA > DI, E*	No measures	No measures	No measures
Valacich & Schwenk (1994)	No measures	FtF > CMC*	Objective DA > Carping DA*	Objective DA > Carping DA *	No measures	No measures	No measures

*Note: * Significant difference between treatments; CMC: Computer Mediated Communication; FtF: Face-to-Face; DA: Devil's Advocacy; DI: Dialectical Inquiry; C: Consensus; E: Expert; S1: Session 1; S2: Session 2*

Development of Hypotheses

Table 1 presents a comparison of the structured conflict experimental outcomes, all of which were conducted in FtF or same-time decision room environments. Hypotheses were developed by examining the weight of evidence for these studies and adopting the premise that the findings would be similar in a virtual environment. One could logically argue that since the communication mode was different, procedures that resulted in significant differences for groups meeting in the same room would not make any difference for different time/different place (virtual) groups. However, stating the null hypothesis as the expectation does not permit standard significance testing procedures.

Group Performance

Amount of Communication

The strategic decision making research generally has not addressed the issue of amount of communication. Connolly, Jessup, and Valacich (1990) suggest that this variable can have an important influence on the number of new ideas presented in a group. Experimental results utilizing GSS versus FtF for other types of tasks are mixed (Dubrovsky, Kiesler, & Sethna, 1991; Siegel, Dubrovsky, Kiesler, & McGuire, 1986; Smith & Vanecek, 1990). In the few studies addressing this issue, Valacich and Schwenk (1995a, 1995b) reported that FtF groups generate significantly more comments than CMC groups and that DI groups generate more comments (not significant) under either condition than DA or expert groups.

In addition, several studies have found that CMC groups become more efficient over time (Chidambaram et al., 1990; McGrath, 1993). Because DI is an unfamiliar procedure it is assumed that the first time a groups uses it more process related discussions will take place. Once a group becomes thoroughly familiar with DI, it is hypothesized that they will step through the procedure more quickly and with less discussion.

These findings led us to the following speculative hypotheses regarding the influence of the decision making approaches on group communication (number of comments):

H2.1: DI groups will communicate more than will CC groups.

H2.2: Communication will decrease with experience for both conditions.

H2.3: Communication for DI groups will decrease more than for CC groups.

Decision Effectiveness and Depth of Analysis

Decision effectiveness can be defined in terms of the quality of the group's assessment of a case or task, in relation to the business environment, resources, and situation. Steeb and Johnston (1981) define depth of evaluation (decision breadth) as a process where groups deliberate and consider a wide range of situational factors, opportunities, and constraint methods in developing potential solutions.

The primary conclusion drawn from the strategic decision making literature is that DI groups demonstrate superior performance in comparison to consensus groups (Schwenk, 1990). Schweiger et al. (1986, 1989) report that both DI and DA groups have significantly better decision quality and place a greater validity and importance on the assumptions than Consensus groups.

In the Schweiger et al. (1989) FtF study there is a significant effect for experience on decision effectiveness, and the validity and importance of assumptions. DI groups performed significantly better after both sessions than the CC groups. Also, there was a significant improvement in the validity and importance of the assumptions during the second session for DI groups. However, the difference in the overall number of assumptions between DI, DA, and CC was not significant.

The GSS research suggests that depth of analysis and decision effectiveness is improved via the technology (Dennis et al., 1988; Nunamaker et al., 1991). Chidambaram (1989) reports GSS groups generate significantly more alternatives than manual groups both overall and after sessions two, three and four. Pinsonneault and Kraemer (1989) suggest that GSS increases depth of analysis. Accordingly, many studies have found that GSS groups analyze more alternatives or analyze the same number in greater depth (Gallupe, DeSanctis & Dickson, 1988; Siegel et al., 1986; Tung & Heminger, 1993).

Depth of analysis and comments pertaining to an idea or solution fit this operational definition (Jessup et al., 1990; Jessup & Tansik, 1991). Mason and colleagues (Mason, 1969, Mason & Mitroff, 1981; Nelson & Mitroff, 1974) suggest that the key to effective high quality decisions is a critical evaluation process. The process stresses the evaluations of assumptions from diametrically opposed points of view (dialectical inquiry). The evaluation process has been operationalized by Schweiger et al. (1986, 1989) to include an assessment of the validity and importance of the assumption. In this study, depth of analysis is defined to be a composite of the number of facts and assumptions, and the sums of the validity and importance measure for both the facts and assumptions. These findings lead to the hypotheses related to effectiveness (quality of recommendation) and depth of analysis:

Effectiveness

H3.1: DI groups will be more effective than CC groups.

H3.2: Effectiveness levels will increase with experience for both conditions.

H3.3: Effectiveness levels for DI groups will increase more than CC groups.

Depth of Analysis

H4.1: DI groups will have a greater depth of analysis than CC groups.

H4.2: Depth of evaluation will increase with experience for both conditions.

H4.3: Depth of evaluation for DI groups will increase more than for CC groups.

Group Perceptions

Schweiger et al. (1986, 1989) found that FtF consensus approach yielded greater decision acceptance and more willingness to work together in the future than either the DI or DA approaches. Experiential effects showed that decision acceptance and willingness to work together in the future were significantly higher in the second session than in the first for all conditions. Perceived depth of analysis improved significantly as a result of experience only for the conflict approaches (Schweiger, et al., 1989). Tung and Heminger (1993) in a decision room GSS study found no difference in group perceptions after one experimental session. Valacich and Schwenk (1995a) report that there were no significant differences among DI and DA groups on solution and process satisfaction. However, CMC groups did have significantly higher levels of process satisfaction than FtF groups. The following hypotheses are offered on group perceptions:

Decision Acceptance

H5.1: CC groups will have higher levels of decision acceptance than DI groups.

H5.2: Decision acceptance will improve with experience for both conditions.

Perceived Depth of Analysis

H6.1: DI groups will have higher levels of perceived depth of evaluation than CC groups.

H6.2: Perceived depth of evaluation will improve with experience for both conditions.

Willingness to Work Together Again

H7.1: CC groups will have a greater willingness to work together again than DI groups.

H7.2: The willingness to work together again will improve with experience for both conditions.

Method

Experimental Design

The research design is a 2 × 2 factorial with repeated measures on session. The factors (Table 2) are decision approach (DI vs. CC) and experience (session 1 vs. session 2). There were 15 groups in CC condition and 16 groups in the DI condition.

Subjects

One hundred and sixty undergraduate and graduate students in computer science and management information systems at New Jersey Institute of Technology (NJIT) participated in this study. They all had some fluency with the use of E-mail and computers and were given course credit and a grade for participation. All subjects were assigned to groups based upon availability and scheduling constraints. The ideal a priori group size was six subjects per group, but due to the subjects' scheduling constraints the actual group sizes ranged from four to seven. Experimental conditions and task orders were randomly assigned to the groups and balanced across conditions.

Table 2. Asynchronous CMC 2 X 2 Repeated Measures Experimental Design

		CMC-Session (Within subjects factor)	
		Session 1	**Session 2**
Decision Approach	**Dialectical Inquiry (DI)**	**15 Groups**	**15 Groups**
(Between subjects factor)	**Constructive Consensus (CC)**	**16 Groups**	**16 Groups**

Cases

The cases for this study, developed by Chidambaram (1989), relate to an international winery, Palo Verde Vintners Incorporated. They present a series of problems facing the company and requiring the attention of the board of directors. The cases were modified and updated in order to reflect a virtual communications mode instead of a set of discrete FtF meetings. The "Threat of Takeover" case was used as a training task for all groups and the "Issue of Image" and "Product Line Expansion" were the experimental tasks. The cases were unstructured decision making tasks, with no right or wrong answers. This corresponds with McGrath's (1984) task circumplex as a type 4 task and fits Schweiger et al's (1986) requirements for strategic decision making. The order of presentation of the two cases was varied across groups and balanced across sessions. This helped control for possible contamination through task effects across sessions.

Facilities

Training was conducted in the Collaborative Systems (Co-Lab) at NJIT, a special computerized meeting room similar to that used in decision-room research (Dennis et al., 1988). The subjects in each group were seated at a U-shaped cluster of computer terminals (one for each subject). The Co-Lab was also equipped with a projector, two white boards and flip charts. The training session lasted approximately two hours. One hour was devoted to CMC training and the other hour integrated the CMC with the decision approach (DI or CC). Following the training, subjects were encouraged to use their own PC's to connect to the system from home or work, but could use Co-Lab or other NJIT facilities during their normal hours of operation. They were instructed not to communicate with each other except through the computer conferences. No examples of "unauthorized" out-of-CMC mode communication were reported by Co-Lab assistants in a post-experimental debriefing.

Software

The software was a modified version of the Electronic Information Exchange System (EIES 2), a computerized conferencing system that permits the user to participate in electronic conferences and to utilize decision tools such as "Question," "List," and "Vote" (Dufner, Hiltz, Johnson, & Czech, 1995). "Question" activities require each participant to enter their own response before seeing the responses of others (similar to Nominal Group Technique). "List" allows a group to compose a single common list of decision or action choices, and "Vote" provides a variety of voting options on such lists. EIES 2 can be considered to be a Level 2 GSS since it incorporates both communication and decision making features (DeSantics & Gallupe, 1987; Turoff, 1991).

Decision Approach Procedures

The Dialectical Inquiry Approach (DI)

The DI approach used is based upon the procedures developed by several researchers (Schweiger et al., 1986; Tung & Heminger, 1993), modified to support virtual communication and decision making. The DI groups were divided into two subgroups denoted as the Plan and Counter-plan subgroups. These groups were in separate conferences on the virtual CMC. All members of both groups were to initially develop an individual recommendation (including supporting facts and assumptions) within two business days and enter it in a List Activity in the CMC system. The Plan group then had two days to develop a single recommendation. Members read the individual case recommendations and then debated and discussed them in a "Question" Activity. When complete, the case leader organized and entered the subgroup's recommendation. This was then submitted to the Counter-plan sub-group, which had two days to negate the assumptions and develop a counter-plan.

The moderator then created a new conference for the full group and added the plan and counter-plan. The Full group's objective was to critically evaluate the plan and counter-plan through an electronic debate and discussion, and to develop a single final group recommendation. The List and Voting Activities ere available if the group chose to use them. The time limit for this task was four business days.

Constructive Consensus Approach (CC)

The CC approach followed the basic method developed by several researchers (Hall, 1971; Nemiroff, Pasmore, & Ford, 1976). The CC groups functioned as one group in a single conference for the entire task. Their objective was to reach consensus on a single final recommendation. Each individual group member had two days to develop an individual recommendation as a response to a "Question" Activity. The group then had eight business days to examine the case situations systematically and logically, in order to develop a final recommendation through debate and discussion. The "List" and "Vote" Activities were available if the group chose to use them.

Training Procedures

Training was divided into three sections: training in the software, training in the decision approach (DI or CC), and a practice task (The Threat of Takeover) which provided a synchronous walk through of the task and procedures the groups were to follow. The subjects upon entering the Co-Lab, were assigned randomly to a seat. The subjects were previously informed of the study objective and that they were required to complete a consent form and a background questionnaire. The subjects were first trained in the use of virtual CMC system and the decision tools, called "List," "Question," and "Vote." This portion of the training took approximately one hour to complete. Subjects then completed a questionnaire. Next, they were trained in their respective decision approaches (DI or CC). Immediately after this was completed, the trainer asked the group to select a leader. The leader was to be responsible for organizing the group's discussions and for entering the recommendation, at a minimum. The last training activity was the practice task, which took approximately one to one and one half hours to complete. The groups were given the Case background and task to read. They were asked to assume the role of the board of directors of the winery. When this was completed (approximately 15 minutes), the groups were instructed to use the software to complete the task following their assigned decision approach procedures. The groups then completed a set of questionnaires, were given the two case packets, and thanked for participating.

Experimental Procedures

The groups were given a "deadline" of 10 business days to complete each case, one case at a time; time extensions were given to groups that needed it. After each experimental case, the subjects completed a post-case questionnaire and then after the second case they also completed a post-experiment questionnaire. The subjects were informed that all work was to be performed in the conferences. To reinforce this and their role as board members, the subjects were told to assume that after the training session they were returning to their home cities and would not be able to contact the other members except through the CMC system. Group members who were delinquent in meeting the target dates for particular activities were called and/or messaged, as would usually occur in a corporate setting. Following the experiment the subjects were debriefed.

Dependent Measures

Group Performance

The performance measures were communication, decision effectiveness, and depth of analysis. Communication was the total number of comments that the group made in each case.

Decision effectiveness is a complex multidimensional variable that is difficult to measure. Several researchers (Chidambaram, 1989; Hirokawa & Poole, 1986) suggest that expert judges should be utilized to rate tasks that do not have a single correct solution. Because the tasks utilized in this study do not have a single correct solution, a panel of five expert judges was used to rate decision quality. The expert judges all had many years of prior business experience and a strong background in systems design and analysis. As described by Chidambaram (1989) the judges were given a two-hour training session with practice recommendations. The final recommendations (which included the assumption and fact sets) from each group were reformatted, coded to conceal the group or condition, and given to each judge.

Depth of analysis was a composite measure of the number, validity, and the importance of the facts of the case that each group was asked to provide with their final recommendation to each case (Rice, 1984). The expert judges independently rated the assumptions and facts on three dimensions:

1. The number of assumptions and facts brought to the surface by each group.
2. The validity of the assumptions and facts with respect to information provided in the task.
3. The importance of the assumptions and facts with respect to the recommendation made by the group.

Table 3. Inter-rater reliability cronbach's alpha coefficient

Dependent Measures	Alpha
Effectiveness	0.8740
Number of Assumptions	0.9355
Validity of Assumptions	0.7625
Importance of Assumptions	0.6819
Number of Facts	0.9477
Validity of Facts	0.7275
Importance of Facts	0.7471

The inter-rater reliabilities (Table 3) for effectiveness (0.87) and depth of analysis-assumptions, facts, both importance and validity (0.68 to 0.95) were reasonable for the type of decisions that were rated (Chidambaram, 1989; Schweiger et al., 1989).

Group Perception

Seven questionnaire items developed by Schweiger et al., (1986) were used to measure the group participants' perceptions. Group members evaluated the degree to which each statement described their feelings on a seven point scale (1, strongly agree; 4, neutral; 7, strongly disagree) on three instances (after the training case, after case one, and after case two) from the subjects participating in the study.

Results

Table 4 shows the means and standard deviations for the group performance and perception measures for each condition over the two tasks. Table 5 shows ANOVA for main effects.

Table 4. Means and standard deviations for the decision approaches

	Dialectical Inquiry (DI)				Constructive Consensus (CC)			
	Session 1		Session 2		Session 1		Session 2	
Variables	Means	Std.	Means	Std.	Means	Std.	Means	Std.
Group Performance								
Number of Comments	70.80	15.32	62.67	20.54	34.44	11.32	34.31	11.70
Decision Effectiveness	68.96	8.95	72.13	12.83	70.25	19.40	72.31	12.83
Depth of Analysis	267.39	44.47	278.19	49.48	233.08	111.74	271.16	86.63
Group Perceptions (The lower the score the greater the degree of agreement)								
Decision Acceptance	2.52	1.21	2.46	1.21	2.17	1.13	2.36	1.02
Perceived Depth of Analysis	3.05	1.26	3.15	1.38	3.29	1.38	3.47	1.32
Willingness to Work Together Again	2.80	1.44	2.51	1.28	2.32	1.16	2.39	1.17

Table 5. Analysis of variance

Group Performance			
Measure	Anova	F VALUES	Pr > F
Number of Comments	DI vs CC	70.74	0.0001
	S1 vs S2	1.10	0.2982
Decision Effectiveness	DI vs CC	0.05	0.8267
	S1 vs S2	0.59	0.4474
Depth of Analysis	DI vs CC	1.07	0.3060
	S1 vs S2	1.40	0.2421
Group Perceptions			
Perceived Depth of Analysis	DI vs CC	1.85	0.1844
	S1 vs S2	1.25	0.2731
	Interaction	2.15	0.0009
Decision Acceptance	DI vs CC	5.89	0.0217
	S1 vs S2	0.00	0.9814
Willingness	DI vs CC	2.67	0.1134
	S1 vs S2	1.70	0.2028
	Interaction	4.41	0.0445

Note: DI: Dialectical Inquiry, CC: Constructive Consensus, S1: Session 1,S2: Session 2
Interaction: Decision Approach crossed with Experience

Group Performance

Communication (Number of Comments): The DI groups were found to generate a significantly greater number of comments than were the CC groups, overall and during both tasks (F= 70.74, df= 1, 57, p = 0.0001). There were no significant effects for experience. A Duncan's Multiple Range Test indicated that there was a significant decrease (df= 57, alpha = 0.05) in the number of comments made during the second case for the DI groups.

Decision Effectiveness and Depth of Analysis: As shown in Tables 2 and 3, no significant effects for decision approach (DI or CC), experience or the interaction were found.

Group Perception

For decision acceptance there were no significant effects for condition or experience. However, DI groups had significantly greater perceived depth of analysis than CC groups (F= 3.98, df= 1, 62, p = 0.0471). There were no significant effects for experience.

The results for willingness to work together again revealed a significant effect for condition (F= 5.11, df= 1, 62, p = 0.0247), but not for experience. Least-squares means test revealed that CC groups had a significantly greater willingness to work together again than did the DI groups after task one and in total.

Discussion

The group performance and perception results and hypotheses are summarized in Table 4. There are five basic conclusions that can be derived from these results:

Table 6. Summary of group performance and perception results and hypotheses

	Condition	Experience	Session 1	Session 2	Improvement Between Sessions
Group Performance					
H2.0 Number Comments	DI > CC Supported	No Difference Not Supported	DI > CC	DI > CC	DI Decrease Supported
H3.0 Decision Effectiveness	No Difference Not Supported	No Difference Not Supported	No Difference	No Difference	No Difference Not Supported
H4.0 Depth of Analysis	No Difference Not Supported	No Difference Not Supported	No Difference	No Difference	No Difference Not Supported
Group Perception					
H6.0 Perceived Depth of Analysis	DI > CC Supported	No Difference Not Supported	No Difference	No Difference	No Difference Not Supported
H5.0 Decision Acceptance	CC > DI Supported	No Difference Not Supported	CC > DI	No Difference	No Difference Not Supported
H7.0 Willingness to Work Together Again	CC > DI Supported	No Difference Not Supported	CC > DI	No Difference	No Difference Not Supported

1. DI groups expended a greater effort than CC groups, as indicated by virtual meeting time and number of comments.
2. There was only one significant effect related to learning, (not shown in Table 4); an interaction between decision approach and experience. The number of comments decreased between session 1 and session 2, significantly more for the DI groups (duncan's multiple range test, alpha = 0.05).
3. DI groups tend to have greater depth of analysis. However, the differences as rated by expert judges were not significant. There was a significant perceived difference between these conditions.
4. CC groups have a greater willingness to work together again than the DI groups, especially after the first task. The CC groups tend to have stronger levels of decision acceptance than DI groups.
5. There were no significant differences between the processes in terms of the most important criterion, decision effectiveness. Given that the DI process requires more effort and that the participants were less accepting of it, this leads to the conclusion that in a virtual environment, DI is not worth the trouble.

In regard to conclusion 1, it may be that days to task completion was confounded in the study by the specific schedule of "due dates" implemented for the stages of the DI process. However, pilot studies indicated that it was not feasible for groups to complete the series of steps involved in DI in fewer days than the schedule provided. In any case, the total number of comments generated as a measure of time and effort spent on the process also showed significantly higher levels in DI than in the simpler consensus procedure.

Schweiger et al. (1989) reported that in FtF sessions, DI groups required more meeting time than CC groups, but only in the first session. They suggested that the DI groups gained procedural efficiency with experience. However, the results of this study suggest that in a CMC environment, where the medium is less "rich" (Daft & Lengel, 1986) than in a FtF environment, the efficiency gains for the DI groups (as rated by expert judges) are not significant, at least when extensive training takes place first, and not sufficient tot overcome the overhead of more extensive required communication procedures. The DI groups required significantly more virtual meeting time than CC groups over both tasks. DI groups generated almost twice as many comments in total across both tasks than did the CC groups. The DI groups did make significantly fewer comments during task two than they did in task one, suggesting that the groups did have modest procedural efficiency gains with experience.

The most compelling finding of this study is the absence of any significant differences between DI and CC with respect to decision effectiveness, in a distributed (virtual) environment. This is in contrast to the Schweiger et al. (1986 & 1989) studies of FtF groups, where the DI and the DA groups had significantly higher decision effectiveness than did CC groups. However, the mean absolute levels of decision effectiveness are high for both conditions (between 70 and 72). The scales were based on 0% to 100%, from very little effectiveness to very high at 100%. In comparison, Chidambaram (1989) reported that GSS groups were at 58.3% and 61.0% for sessions one and two, respectively, in a four session study.

This study used a composite measure for depth of evaluation which included the number of facts and assumptions, and their validity and importance. No significant differences were found resulting from the decision approach condition, experience over both tasks or as a result of the interaction.

One of the objectives of GSS is to improve and support the information exchange of groups (DeSantis & Gallupe, 1987). This is accomplished by promoting a positive interpersonal exchange of information. The greater the degree of change in communication (by providing opportunities to speed up, change the content, or change the direction of the messages) introduced by the technology, the more dramatic the impact on the decision process and outcomes. In the FtF conflict research the consensus groups had significantly lower performance than DI and DA groups, but had higher decision acceptance and willingness to work together again (Schweiger, et al., 1896, 1989). Based on Tung and Heminger's (1993) results and the findings reported here, it is suggested that the presence of decision support technology (GSS or CMC) equalized the consensus group's performance to that achieved by the conflict approaches. It is suggested that the communication technology helped accomplish this by promoting a positive interpersonal exchange of information. Thus, additional procedural structuring is not necessary in a computer-mediated environment.

In a typical FtF setting for consensus groups, perhaps all of the ideas do not get an equal "airing" (a process loss) thus, an incomplete interpretation is made, and perhaps all members do not participate equally (Dubrovsky et al. 1991). In contrast, the structured conflict groups, for DI in particular, work with smaller sets of information which the groups may feel they must defend because of the process. A richer medium (a FtF setting) may be required so that the members can get a "feeling" for an individual's position. We know from the literature that the conflict groups take longer and are less satisfied with the decision and the process (Schweiger, et al., 1896, 1989). This is further supported by this study; DI groups took about five days longer to develop the final recommendation and were less satisfied with the decision and process.

Conflict, in this study, did not produce more effective decisions. DI and CC groups produced equally effective decisions. DI groups had lower decision acceptance levels and were less willing to work together again. The results of this study suggest that CMC improves the performance of CC groups while maintaining the positive aspects of group development and harmony.

One of the main limitations of this study is the design of the DI CMC structure. The structure was designed for two separate sub-groups (each a separate conference) to work independently of each other. Each sub-group contained about one half of the total membership. The CC groups, on the other hand, were set up as one conference with full membership. Each group member could see when a member was active. The DI sub-groups could only see what was going on in their sub-group and could not communicate with the other sub-group during the Plan and Counter-plan phases. From observations and discussions with the DI group members, a better design may have been to have a single conference set up with two private sub-conferences, one for each of the sub-groups. DI members would then be able to communicate directly with the other sub-group and at the same time keep their phase of the dialectical process confidential. In this manner, then, the sub-group members would not "feel" as isolated as some reported.

Our results suggest that a computer-mediated-communication (CMC or GSS) environment can be an effective medium to support strategic decision making. Structured conflict techniques have proven superior to consensus and expert conditions in face-to-face situations. With the aid of computer-based decision technology, consensus decision approaches can be as effective as structured conflict. Thus, GSS equalizes consensus groups' performance to that of the dialectical inquiry groups without affecting decision and process satisfaction, and without the process losses that occur face-to-face.

This study was part of a series of experiments exploring the extent to which various types of decision processes and tools can help virtual groups to coordinate their interaction and improve their effectiveness. Generalizability is limited by the specific implementation of the DI and CC procedures used and the specific task and measures used (e.g., the quality of the expert judges and the sensitivity of the effectiveness rating procedures they employed). However, the conclusion that in the virtual CMC environment, procedural structuring makes little difference, is echoed by two related experiments. Dufner et. al., (1995) compared "parallel" and "sequential" (step-by-step) decision procedures, crossed with the presence or absence of the "List " and "Vote" tools for a preference type task. The tools made a significant positive difference, but decision structure did not. Ocker, Hiltz, Turoff, and Fjermestad (1996) compared the presence and absence of a decision structure based on IBIS task analysis crossed with communication mode, either FtF or CMC, for a software requirements task. CMC was significantly different from FtF in many respects, but the presence or absence of the decision process structuring made no difference. Thus, the weight of these three experiments supports the conclusion that in a virtual CMC medium, structuring of interaction through procedures that have been useful for FtF groups tends not to be helpful.

Additional investigations need to be conducted to ascertain the parameters of these findings. We have seen that work group cohesiveness and decision quality improvements in a decision room based GSS take time to develop. Structured conflict techniques also require sufficient time and practice before they become effective. Looking only at the first and second time increments does not equate to changes that may occur with ongoing use. Further studies should investigate the longitudinal relationships among group, tasks, technology, and decision approach.

Acknowledgments

This work has been partially supported by the National Science Foundation (Grant No. 9015236) and an SBR grant from NJIT.

References

Chidambaram, L. (1989). *An empirical investigation of the impact of computer support on group development and decision-making performance*. PhD dissertation, Indiana University.

Chidambaram, L., Bostrom, R.P., & Wynne, B.E. (1990). A longitudinal study of the impact of group decision support systems on group development. *Journal of Management Information Systems, 7*(3), 7-25.

Chidambaram, L., & Jones, B. (1993). Impact on communication medium and computer support on group perceptions and performance: A comparison of face-to-face and dispersed meetings. *MIS Quarterly, 17*(4), 465-491.

Connolly, T., Jessup, L., & Valacich, J.S. (1990). Effects of anonymity and evaluative tone on idea generation in computer-mediated groups. *Management Science, 36*(6), 689-703.

Daft, R.L., & Lengel, R.H. (1986). Organizational information requirements, media richness and structural design, *32*(5), 554-571.

Dennis, A.R., George, J.F. Jessup, L.M., Nunamaker, J.F., & Vogel, D.R. (1988). Information technology to support electronic meetings. *MIS Quarterly,* December, 591-618.

DeSanctis, G., & Gallupe, R.B. (1987). A Foundation for the study of group decision support systems. *Management Science, 33*(5), 589-609.

Dubrovsky, V.J., Kiesler, S., & Sethna, B.N. (1991). The equalization phenomenon: Status effects in computer-mediated and face-to-face decision making groups. *Human Computer Interaction, 6*, 119-146.

Dufner, D., Hiltz, S.R., Johnson, K., & Czech, R. (1995). Distributed group support: the effects of voting on group perceptions of media richness. *Group Decision and Negoiation, 4*(3), 235-250.

Gallupe, R.B., DeSanctis, G., & Dickson, G.W. (1988). Computer-based support for group problem-finding: An experimental investigation. *MIS Quarterly,* June, 277-296.

Hall, J. (1971). Decision, decisions, decisions. *Psychology Today, 5*, 51-54, 86, 88.

Hiltz, S.R., Dufner, D., Holmes, M., & Poole, M.S. (1991). Distributed group support systems: Social dynamics and design dilemmas. *Journal of Organizational Computing, 2*(1), 135-159.

Hiltz, S.R., Turoff, M., & Johnson, K. (1989). Experiments in group decision making, 3: Disinhibition, deindividuation, and group process in pen name and real name computer conferences. *Decision Support Systems, 5*, 217-232.

Hiltz, S.R., & Wellman, B. (1997). Asynchronous learning networks as a virtual classroom. *Communications of the ACM, 40*(9), 44-49.

Hirokawa, R., & Poole, M.S. (Eds.). (1986). *Communication and group decision making.* Beverly Hills, CA: Sage Publications.

Jessup, L.M., Connolly, T., & Galegher, J. (1990). The effects of anonymity on GDSS group process with an idea-generating task. *MIS Quarterly,* September, 313-321.

Jessup, L.M., & Tansik, D.A. (1991). Decision making in an automated environment: The effects of anonymity and proximity with a group decision support system. *Decision Sciences, 22*, 266-279.

McGrath, J.E. (1984). *Groups: Interaction and performance.* Englewood Cliffs, NJ: Prentice-Hall.

McGrath, J. (1993). Introduction: The JEMCO workshop-description of a longitudinal study. *Small Group Research, 24*(3), 285-306.

Mason, R.O. (1969). A dialectical approach to strategic planning. *Management Science, 15*(8), B403-B414.

Mason, R.O., & Mitroff, I.I. (1981). *Challenging strategic planning assumptions.* NY: John Wiley.

Mitroff, I.I., Emshoff, J.R., & Kilmann, R.H. (1979). Assumptional analysis: A methodology for strategic problem solving. *Management Science, 25*(6), 583-593.

Mowshowitz, A. (1997). Virtual organization. *Communications of the ACM, 40*(9), 30-37.

Nemiroff, P.M., Pasmore, W.A., & Ford, D.L. (1976). The effects of two normative structural interventions on established and ad hoc groups: Implications for improving decision making effectiveness. *Decision Sciences, 7*, 841-855.

Nelson, J.A., & Mitroff, I.I. (1974). An experiment in dialectical information systems. *Journal of the American Society for Information Science,* July-August, 252-262.

Nunamaker, J.F., Dennis, A. R., Valacich, J.S., Vogel, D.R., & George, J.F. (1991). Electronic meeting systems to support group work. *Communications of the ACM, 34*(7), 41-61.

Ocker, R., Hiltz, S.R., Turoff, M., & Fjermestad, J. (1996). The effects of distributed group support and process structuring on requirements development teams: Results on creativity and quality. *Journal of Management Information Systems, 12*(3), 127-153.

Pinsonneault, A., & Kraemer, K.L. (1989). The impact of technological support on groups: An assessment of the empirical research. *Decision Support Systems, 5,* 197-216.

Priem, R.L., Harrison, D.A., & Muir, N.K. (1995). Structured conflict and consensus outcomes in group decision making. *Journal of Management, 21*(4), 691-710.

Powell, A., Piccoli, G., & Ives, B. (2004). Virtual teams: A review of current literature and directions for future research. *The Data Base for Advances in Information Systems, 35*(1), 6-36.

Rice, R.E. (1984). *The new media.* Beverly Hills, CA: Sage Publications.

Schweiger, D.M., Sandberg, W.R., & Ragan, J.W. (1986). Group approaches for improving strategic decision making: A comparative analysis of dialectical inquiry, devil's advocacy, and consensus. *Academy of Management Journal, 29*(1), 51-71.

Schweiger, D.M., Sandberg, W.R., & Rechner, P.L. (1989). Experiential effects of dialectical inquiry, devil's advocacy, and consensus approaches to strategic decision making. *Academy of Management Journal, 32*(4), 745-772.

Schwenk, C. (1989). Research notes and communications: A meta-analysis on the comparative effectiveness of devil's advocacy and dialectical inquiry. *Strategic Management Journal, 10*, 303-306.

Schwenk, C.R. (1990). Effects of devil's advocacy and dialectical inquiry on decision making: A meta analysis. *Organizational Behavior and Human Decision Processes, 47*, 161-176.

Schwenk C., & Valacich, J.S. (1994). Effects of devil's advocacy and dialectical inquiry on individual versus groups. *Organizational Behavior and Human Decision Processes, 59*, 210-222.

Siegel, J., Dubrovsky, V., Kiesler, S., & McGuire, T.W. (1986). Group processes in computer-mediated communication. *Organizational Behavior and Human Decision Processes, 37*, 157-187.

Smith, J.Y., & Vanecek, M.T. (1990). Dispersed group decision making using nonsimultaneous computer conferencing: A report of research. *Journal of Management Information Systems, 7*(2), 71-92.

Steeb, R., & Johnston, S.C. (1981). A computer-based interactive system for group decision making. *IEEE Trans. Systems Man Cybernetics, 11*(8), 544-552.

Steiner, I.D. (1972). *Group processes and productivity.* New York: Academic Press.

Tjosvold, D. (1982). Effects of approach on superiors' incorporation of subordinates' information in decision making. *Journal of Applied Psychology*, *67*, 189-193.

Tung, L.L., & Heminger, A.R. (1993). The effects of dialectical inquiry, devil's advocacy, and consensus inquiry methods in a GSS environment. *Information & Management, 25*, 33-41.

Turoff, M. (1991). Computer-mediated requirements for group support. *Journal of Organizational Computing, 1*, 85-113.

Valacich, J.S., & Schwenk, C. (1995a). Devil's advocacy and dialectical inquiry effects on group decision making using computer-mediated group decision making. *Organizational Behavior and Human Decision Processes, 63*(2), 158-173.

Valacich, J.S., & Schwenk, C. (1995b). Structured conflict in individual, face-to-face, and computer-mediated group decision making: Carping versus objective devil's advocacy. *Decision Sciences, 26*(3), 369-393.

Chapter VII

E-Collaboration in Distributed Requirements Determination

Roberto Evaristo, University of Illinois at Chicago, USA
Mary Beth Watson-Manheim, University of Illinois at Chicago, USA
Jorge Audy, Pontifica Universidade Catolica at Porto Alegre, Brazil

Abstract

It is widely agreed that the trend toward distributed software development is growing. Although there are difficulties involved, this trend is here to stay, as organizations will continue to search for ways to develop software at lower cost but with same quality. Current research has focused primarily on the later stages of the software development life cycle, especially coding of software requirements. However, as organizations become more virtual, distributed development will become more apparent throughout the entire life cycle. In this study, we investigate distributed e-collaboration in requirements determination in software development. We report on results from a field experiment with two graduate level Information Systems classes, one located in Porto Alegre, Brazil and one in Chicago, U.S. The students in Brazil played the role of users whereas the students in Chicago role-played analysts. The Chicago-based students developed a requirements document for an information system by interviewing the Brazil students using an electronic discussion board. Our findings provide insight into the distributed analysis process and identify sources of potential problems.

Introduction

It is widely agreed that the trend toward distributed software development is growing (Herbsleb, Mockus, Finholt, & Grinter, 2001). Outsourcing of software development has become more common as organizations search for increased efficiency and lower costs. In particular, offshore outsourcing is attractive to organizations trying to take advantage of differential labor costs in other countries (Agarwal, 2003). Although there are difficulties involved as well, this trend is here to stay, as organizations will continue to search for ways to develop software at lower cost but with same quality.

At the same time, virtuality is increasingly common in organizations; more and more employees in different geographic locations are collaborating electronically. From a software development perspective, this means that users and stakeholders may be located in variety of different geographic locations, separated from each other and separated from systems analysts. Increasingly the trend toward distributed development will become more apparent throughout the entire life cycle, including analysis of software requirements in the early stages of the development life cycle.

Current research on distributed development has focused primarily on the latter stages of the life cycle, especially coding of requirements (e.g., Grinter, Herbsleb, & Perry, 1999). We believe our study is one of the first to address distributed analysis in software development. Our goal is to understand the distributed analysis process better and to identify sources of problems. In addition, we take a first step in the development of training for software developers to increase effectiveness in the distributed environment.

In this study, we report on results from an e-collaboration field experiment with two graduate level information systems classes, one located in Porto Alegre, Brazil and one in Chicago. The students in Brazil played the role of users whereas the students in Chicago role-played analysts. The Chicago-based students developed a requirements document for an information system by interviewing the Brazil students using an electronic discussion board.

The chapter is organized as follows: First, we review several different literature streams to establish the foundation for our research. Next we present the methodology used for our study. Finally we present the results and discuss the implication of the study for future research.

Background

In the following sections, we first explore the role of requirements determination in the analysis process. The prevailing assumption in the literature has been that requirements determination usually takes place in a face-to-face (FTF) setting. As there has been little research on distributed analysis, we turn to literature from distributed collaboration and cross-cultural relations to develop a foundation for our research.

Role of Requirements Determination in Distributed Analysis

Requirements determination is a critical part of the software development process, occurring early in the life cycle. Correct and complete requirements lead to a more efficient development process and increased quality and acceptance of the completed software product (Browne & Rogich, 2001). Brown and Rogich discuss requirements determination as a three-step process: (1) information gathering – eliciting requirements from users; (2) representation – modeling the elicited requirements in some physical fashion; and (3) verification – verifying with the user that the model of requirements is correct. We focus our study on the first step in the process, the initial elicitation of information from the user by the analyst.

Requirements determination, and especially information gathering, has long been a problematic area of software development (Browne & Rogich, 2001; Davis, 1982). Problems stem from a variety of sources, including human limitations, communication skills, and the complexity of the requirements determination task. Davis (1982) discusses the limitations of humans in specifying information requirements. Limited short-term memory, bias toward more recent or available information and the need to simplify complex information are some factors that contribute to incomplete user requirements.

In addition, the requirement definition task has "high dynamic complexity" (Briggs & Gruenbacher, 2002). This complexity stems from the evolutionary nature of the requirements, which are clarified only through multiple iterations of information gathering. Developing requirements is also dependent on input from a variety of different people using "same words to express very different concepts"(Briggs & Gruenbacher, 2002). The requirements task involves surfacing these differences where possible, and negotiating some consensus. Differences may not only be due to differences in interpretation and understanding (Urquhart, 1999) but also to differences in "vested interests" of the participants (Briggs & Gruenbacher, 2002) further increasing the complexity of the task.

Having a structure to think about a problem helps reduce the inherent complexity (Briggs & Gruenbacher, 2002). The development of a methodology for requirements elicitation provides such a structure. In a recent study, Browne and Rogich (Browne & Rogich, 2001) propose a task-level model of the requirements elicitation task. The model addresses both cognitive and communication problems in the requirements elicitation task. The model proposes that the user has an understanding, implicit and explicit, of the problem space that the information system will address. The analyst, through dialogue with the user, must develop understanding of the problem space. Using this information and information from other sources (e.g., documents and company policies), the analyst develops the representation of the requirements, i.e., the requirements document.

Communications skills are then crucial to effective requirements elicitation, and the development of a common understanding of the problem is a key objective. Furthermore, ineffective communication in this process is negatively correlated with project success (Urquhart, 1999). Although a number of other techniques have been proposed, interviews are the most commonly used requirements elicitation strategy (Dennis & Wixom, 2000). The assumption is that elicitation of user requirements will largely be based on synchronous FTF communication between the user and the analyst. In their popular textbook, Dennis and Wixom urge the analyst to establish rapport with the interviewee "so that he or she trusts you and is willing to tell you the whole truth" (p. 117). They provide tips on developing interpersonal skills important for interviewing, including a recommendation to "watch body language (yours and theirs)" (p. 118).

Explicit strategies and tactics for effective communication between the analyst and stakeholders have generally not been addressed (Urquhart, 1999). Beyond a discussion of interviewing techniques, communication skills training is largely ignored, there seems to be an implicit assumption that naturally occurring relationship development activities will take place in a FTF environment. In a distributed environment, however, FTF communication is often not feasible, and even synchronous electronic communication may become difficult.

Herbsleb and Mockus (2003) found evidence that software development work conducted across distributed sites takes longer to perform than similar work at collocated sites in part due to the change in patterns of communication, leading to reduced understanding of background information and context at distant sites. While this study does not focus specifically on the requirements elicitation task, the results provide evidence that distributed communication can have a negative effect on the development process.

The lack of explicit training and reliance on implicit strategies occurring in FTF interactions leaves requirements elicitation particularly vulnerable to negative consequences of distributing the development process. There is need for explicit training strategies for the elicitation task. As there has been little research on this question in the current literature on software development, we next turn to recent literature on communication-related consequences of distributed work.

Distributed Analysis as a Problem of Shared Understanding

Recent research has begun to address the difficulties in communication in a distributed environment from a mutual knowledge perspective (Cramton, 2001) or similarly, a shared mental model perspective (Hinds, 2000). Mutual knowledge is "knowledge that the communicating parties share in common and know they share" (Cramton, 2001). Hinds (2000) discusses the concept of "perspective taking"—a process whereby people interact with the goal of understanding the others' view—in developing a shared mental model. Both authors point out communication problems that occur as a consequence of working in a distributed environment and have significant effect on the development of shared understanding between communication partners. This view is especially relevant when examining distributed software analysis where the goal of the dialogue between analyst and user is to develop a shared understanding of the focal problem space. We next review some of the problems faced by dispersed collaborators.

Cramton (2001) found that geographically dispersed teams face significant problems maintaining mutual knowledge in collaborative endeavors. Dispersed team members in her study often did not discern which "features of their context and situation differed from the contexts and situation of remote partners and they did not communicate local information." While important to work across these differences to collaborate, her research suggests, "dispersed collaborators were not skilled at discovering and communicating such differences, and when differences were mentioned, remote partners sometimes failed to note or remember it."

In addition, the lack of shared context and mutual knowledge led to different interpretations of information. This had implications for development of trust, as problems were attributed to individuals rather than to situational misunderstandings. Cramton (2001) points out also that communicating and collaborating in a distributed environment is complicated by the difficulties in investigating and integrating information from multiple locations. For example, how does one interpret silence from a communication partner? Is it simply due to feedback lag, is the receiver having difficulty understanding information, is the receiver "slacking off"? Multiple interpretations must be weighed in the increasing complexity of the communication.

The heightened uncertainty of the computer-mediated environment increases the importance of trusting behaviors in effective communication (Jarvenpaa & Leidner, 1999). From the example above, a simple action such as timely message response may be interpreted as an indication of trust and increasing involvement between the communicators. The level of trust between communicators is important to developing the open dialogue important for software requirements elicitation. Jarvenpaa and Leidner (1999) found that teams high on trust were able to solve problems and resolve conflicts in a distributed environment where participants were limited to electronic communication.

Hinds (2000) also investigated consequences of communication and collaboration in a non-collocated environment. She found that distributed workers have less shared information, which remains unshared, and therefore develop different perspectives about the task. "Distributed workers have less overlap in their mental models of a task than do co-located workers, that context accounts for much of the discrepancy, and that distributed workers rarely discuss the contexts in which they are working.... Distributed teams may be less effective than co-located teams because they will be less able to understand their teammates' perspectives and will be less able to coordinate action." She discusses the need for ways to help team members "take teammates' perspective and develop a more shared image of the work."

Moreover, groups located in distant geographical locations are also likely to have different cultural make-ups. In this manuscript, we will adopt Hofstede's (Hofstede, 1984) cultural categorizations. Hofstede defined initially four cultural dimensions: power distance, individualism/collectivism, uncertainty avoidance, and femininity/masculinity. Later he added time horizon as a fifth dimension. The reader is referred to that source for a more detailed definition of the dimensions. In our case, the two sets of groups were over 5,000 miles apart and differed in culture.

Cross-Cultural Differences

For purposes of this study, it is interesting to compare the dimensions identified by Hofstede where U.S. individuals are different from Brazilians. Table 1 presents a summary of the scores for the four cultural dimensions he assigned (Hofstede, 1984).

Table 1. Summary of cultural scores (Hofstede, 1984)

	Brazil	U.S.
Power Distance	69	40
Individualism / Collect	38	91
Uncertainty Avoidance	76	46
Masculinity Femininity	49	62

U.S. individuals are considerably more individualistic as compared to the Brazilians. Individuals with higher scores on individualism will tend to value their own advancement more than they are interested on the group's advancement. Brazilians have a higher score than U.S. individuals on power distance, suggesting that they are more accepting of differences in power between subordinates and managers. Brazilians also tend to value quality of life more than the U.S. individuals based on their femininity/masculinity score compared to U.S. Finally, Brazilians are less likely to be willing to deal with uncertainty than U.S. individuals. Brazilians also have a longer time horizon attitude than U.S. individuals.

A priori, the differences in cultural scores suggest a set of differences in expectations of the respective groups. The most important would be Brazilians displaying a combination of higher interest in quality of life—and relationships—coupled with a higher valuation of group objectives.

Problem Statement

A common theme in the research we have examined is that the lack of shared context inherent in a dispersed environment creates additional problems for developing shared understanding between communication partners. Cramton (2001) points out that mutual knowledge is often referred to as "common ground" which is symbolic of the deeply engrained idea that mutual knowledge is dependent on co-presence. Similarly, Herbsleb et al. (2000) found: "collaborations over distance must contend with the loss of the rich, subtle interactions that collocated teams use to coordinate their work."

Partly due to such difficulties, most training for eliciting user requirements has been developed under the assumption that the elicitation of software requirements by the analyst takes place most efficiently in the FTF environment. Our goal is to develop a better understanding of distributed analysis and to develop a training approach for improving context sharing—or "common ground" in Cramton's words—and consequently the elicitation of requirements in this environment.

Methodology

The research setting was a graduate level information systems and organizations class at PUC/RS in Porto Alegre, Brazil, and a graduate level systems analysis and design (SAD) class at the University of Illinois, Chicago, taught by the first and last authors. Students in each class were assigned to groups of three to four members. There were three groups in each class. The students in the SAD class were "analysts" who were to interview the "users" from Brazil. The assignment for the analysts was to understand the requirements for the public voting system in Brazil and to develop an interface for the voting system. The interviews and discussions between the students took place entirely through the electronic discussion feature of the Blackboard system (web-based course instructional site at UIC). Students were instructed not to use e-mail or communication media other than the discussion board. Students were given 30 days to complete the assignment.

All groups also completed a "lessons learned" document. Questions the students were to address in the "lessons learned" document included:

a. Your perception of effort of each team (U.S. vs. Brazil).
b. What worked best?
c. What did not work?
d. Adequacy of the medium (discussion threads) to the task.
e. What were your concerns during the task?
f. What did you learn from this task?

In addition, the UIC students also turned in a description of the public voting system in Brazil. The students were informed that this project had dual objectives: (1) to give them experience in distributed analysis of software requirements and (2) the results would be used for research purposes. They were given the option of an alternative assignment, but no one chose this option.

Training

Selected groups from each class received training for collaboration in a non-collocated environment. This training had multiple objectives: (1) to raise awareness about miscommunication and lack of understanding in a distributed environment, (2) educate students about the underlying causes of this problem, in particular lack of mutual awareness of context, and (3) give students specific pointers for assessing how and when to share context. The training emphasized the importance of involvement of the communicator in understanding what contextual factors are important for the task being performed, e.g., time zone differences and expectations of task completion, and explicitly communicating this information. In addition, students were encouraged to help their communication partners to understand the importance of sharing context.

The instructor for each course trained randomly selected student groups. One Brazilian group was trained (Group A) and two U.S. groups trained (1, 2). Groups of users (A, B, C) and analysts (1, 2, 3) were paired. Groups at each university were not aware of which groups had been trained in the other university. Groups that were trained were asked not to discuss the training with groups who were not trained.

Data Analysis

We present data stemming from the reports submitted by the students on both universities. The U.S. reports, written from the perspective of a system analyst, had two sections: one, a description of the specifications for the electoral system in Brazil and the computerized interface; two, a "lessons learned" section. The Brazilian reports, written from the perspective of users, had only the lessons learned section. In this way, the report on lessons learned from group A, B and C (Brazil) will be compared with the report from group 1, 2 and 3 (U.S.). These reports are seen as the "perceived" status of the exchange, whereas the messages exchanged between the respective group dyads represent the actual exchanges. A careful qualitative analysis of the differences between perceived and real exchanges was performed based on the comparisons between the two "lessons learned" reports from the respective U.S. and Brazilian groups plus the complete collection of their written communication. We next present the results and then discuss conclusions from this analysis.

In general, differences in language did not seem to be a problem for any of the groups, although there were clearly small hiccups here and there. By and large, Brazilian students have been widely exposed to English by the time they enter college; moreover, some of the group members were working for different U.S. based multinationals where they were supposed to use English on a consistent basis to communicate with headquarters.

Groups A (Brazil) / 1 (U.S.)

Group 1 (score on the task of delivering specifications: 94) took to heart its training in context sharing. In fact, they were the only U.S. group that initiated the interaction. In their own words:

> *When asking questions, we tried to be very specific and describe in detail every concept we felt might be vague for Brazilians. We did not automatically assume our peers know what we mean by the personal identifier, such as Social Security Number, or by the rating scale. Conversely, sometime we needed to ask for further explanation on what Brazilian students submitted (e.g.: "...he receives its heading from voter and the voucher from voting..."). The main difficulty encountered in the project*

> *was the different context of the time pressure. For instance, our Brazilian counterparts did not share our sense of urgency, awareness of the tight schedule and excessive workload. Specifically, our context could be described as: "We only have several weeks for this project; we need to manage this efficiently. This is a cool and interesting experience but there are too many other assignments and exams to prepare for. We can't afford to spend more time than necessary on this." Conversely, the context for Brazilian students seemed to be: "Whatever this is about, it is an exciting exercise. We need to use this opportunity to exchange information with American students, to learn from them and promote ourselves.*

Their perceptions of the process were supported by the analysis of their emails to group A, the only group trained in Brazil. Members of Group 1 initiated the interviewing process by sending a rapid succession of emails (April 1st to April 4th) introducing everybody. In the next couple of days, the Brazilian group trickled in with introductory messages, member by member. In some cases, these were detailed messages including the URL for a personal home page. By April 7th, one of the members of the U.S. group sent a not-so-subtle message that they "meant business":

> *Hi! All, Thanks for such a nice introduction of u guys. hope u all had a nice weekend. As we are aware, we have not much time left lets get going with our ptoject. we all here in UIC are anxiously waiting for detailed information regarding the present voting system of Brazil and the requirement of the system. hope we get the required information very soon.take care.*

After another few exchanges fairly personal in tone from the Brazilian group, the U.S. group reiterated, on April 8th:

> *Alright guys, thank you very much for very cordial response!!! Looks like we all got to know each other, at least virtually. Now that we successfully carried out the introductory and social part, let's move on to the project. I'd suggest you brazilian guys start by introducing us to your voting system: anything you find important and interesting: physical interface (e.g. do you use touchscreen/keyboard?, is it interactive and easy to use even for the first-time user? is it time efficient, do you find the design of screens appealing? etc etc.) Each of you can submit your own experience and opinions, that would improve the objectivity. Then, I suggest, we will elaborate more on the parts of your report that will need further details.*

This message was followed almost immediately by a flurry of general information about Brazil, economy of the state where the Brazilian University is located, and a few more generalities. As a result, the U.S. group sent a long list of specific questions, which met with a short silence. When another U.S. group member sent a further set of questions before the previous ones were answered, the Brazilian group responded with a somewhat annoyed short note:

> *Guys, In the monday, we will be answering all its questions and sending bigger detailing of our politico system and as we make the election. You forgive the delay, and you have a little of patience. Thank you all very much and have a nice weekend.*

And as soon as a couple of answers came through, the U.S. students tried to give some positive reinforcement (somewhat misguided, as we will see below from the Brazilian students' reaction):

> *Hello Team, it seems that information has started to flow. Better late than never. Well I would like to mention one more thing that our team is lagging behind from other teams. This is what I felt after the discussion in the class yesterday.*

Group 1 went further in their report to explain that they were not sure how much the assignment was worth on the other side, and explicitly avoided sharing how much the assignment was worth on the U.S. side to avoid having the Brazilians decrease their involvement.

Although the report from Group 1 suggests that everything went very well ("All of us agreed that the Brazilian team was extremely pleasant to work with"), an analysis of Group A's report showed a completely different picture. Group A thought that the "immense" questionnaire just steamrolled their planned organization of efforts in sharing information with the "analysts"; Group A also expressed dissatisfaction with the collaboration technology, asserting that it was not appropriate to the task at hand because of the lack of synchronicity. Members felt that the site was not designed well, e.g., shared files were located in separate areas of the site from the discussion threads and it took too many clicks to access either area.

Most importantly, the Brazilians thought that their effort at providing what they considered to be context and background information was seem as irrelevant by the U.S. students—in fact, a waste of time which was a reason for complaints and insistent "prods." Their trust on their U.S. counterparts started very high, dropping when feedback was negative, and went up again at the end when the U.S. students showed high knowledge on the subject.

Very tellingly, the Brazilian students ended their report with the following comment:

> *They* [the U.S. students] *seemed to be direct and objective in their efforts, were more concerned with the task than with the interaction itself. For us the interaction, communication exchange was the main focus of the activity (non-technical aspects). ... In conclusion, it seems that the objectives of the two teams were not the same.*

Groups B (Brazil) / 2 (U.S.)

Group B (not trained) started the interaction with a short introduction. A small number of e-mails followed from both sides including a longish questionnaire sent by the U.S. students (Group 2), who had been trained in context sharing. In response, one Brazilian student e-mailed with a breakdown of which other Brazilian members would answer which question. Both groups liked using the discussion board, although the Brazilians longed for a richer media.

In Group 2's perspective (score on the task of delivering specifications: 87), the performance was good, and only had the risk of breaking down when the following happened, in the U.S. student's words:

> *For example when we asked about the "Blank" key, asking it in a manner like, "No one really told us what the "Blank" key definitively performs. We require additional details about this key"[it] would cause communication channels to actually deteriorate rather then improve them.*

The Brazilian students, all with prior system analyst training, disagreed. They noticed that the U.S. students were only interested in specific details about the electoral system, not about a more general background to base their analysis; as a consequence, there was no structure to the questions or requirements analysis. This was particularly evident in the fact that U.S. students sent a questionnaire before the background and domain were established. In their opinion, the U.S. group also failed to give feedback related to their understanding of what had been transmitted. As a result, they had doubts whether the U.S. students truly understood the system.

Further light on the matter can be gleaned from the U.S. report, where students say "we first wanted to obtain a general idea of their voting system." This is in stark opposition to what the Brazilian students perceived as total lack of interest in the generals of the situation.

The Brazilian students also showed disappointment in the fact that the U.S. students were not interested in a more personal involvement. In fact, from a total of 21 messages exchanged, only 4 originated in Chicago. Another source of disappointment for the Brazilians was the fact that the U.S. students summarily dismissed the structure the Brazilians created. Moreover, the perceived level of "stress and coldness" in the U.S. messages clearly left a bad taste in the Brazilian's minds. As a consequence, the high starting level of trust tended to fall continuously.

Groups C (Brazil) / 3 (U.S.)

In this case, neither group was trained in context sharing. The U.S. students (score on the task of delivering specifications: 95) seemed to enjoy using the discussion board, although pointing out the fact that threaded discussions were not ideal for certain tasks, e.g., data summarization. The Brazilian students were generally satisfied with the process, although unhappy with the following limitations. First, the U.S. students were too quick in sending out a list of questions, which somewhat threw the Brazilian students in a state of temporary confusion, since they had already planned to share certain pieces of background information. Second, most of the interaction was done with only one U.S. student, which limited the breadth of the interaction. On the other hand, this particular individual took the trouble to learn a few words in Portuguese and as a result was perceived as "committed" to relationship building. This may have affected their perceived trust level, which was very high during the whole period.

An interesting level of misunderstanding occurred when the Brazilians described the voting system as:

> *There is a small terminal (with some buttons and a screen) hard-wired to the electronic ballot box to validate the voting card number and to qualify the beginning of the voting process. The electronic ballot box is a type of device (a small box) with a screen, buttons of numbers (0-9) and three keyboard keys (Confirm, Correct, White).*

Eventually it was clarified that "white" was a literal translation of the Portuguese word "branco" which in fact should have been translated as "blank", since it means a vote that has been intentionally cast without any candidate written on it.

Data Discussion

The main objective of this study was to better understand of distributed analysis as well as to start developing a training approach for context sharing. The initial training program was designed to cover the main problems that had been identified under a relatively limited set of circumstances. This experiment proved to be a challenge to our training plan, and has in fact generated powerful suggestions for improvements. In the next few paragraphs, we will discuss what the data presented in the previous section. A summary of results is presented in Table 2.

At a first glance, it seems that the only group that was trained in Brazil took context sharing to mean something different than what was understood as context sharing by their U.S. counterparts. Brazilians tended to "contextualize" their understanding of context based on their cultural reality, and assumed that sharing general and personal background would do the trick. This was, however, seen by the U.S. group as mostly irrelevant and only delaying their completion of the task.

We speculate that cultural differences could have played a strong role in these differences. Brazilians are more likely to be collectivistic (as opposed to individualism, which runs very high in the U.S. culture, to borrow Hofstede's terms) and as a result more likely to value highly warm personal relationships. Nothing could be farther from the U.S. students' intentions. In fact, this observation was present in other groups as well, regardless of training or not in context sharing: the U.S. students' emphasis on task, versus the Brazilian students' emphasis on relationships.

Table 2. Summary of results

<table>
<tr><td>Group
A, B, C = Brazil
1, 2, 3 = US</td><td colspan="3">A1</td><td colspan="3">B2</td><td colspan="3">C3</td></tr>
<tr><td>Training (Y, N)</td><td colspan="3">A=Y, 1=Y</td><td colspan="3">B = N, 2 = Y</td><td colspan="3">C=N, 3=N</td></tr>
<tr><td>Score on Task[1]</td><td colspan="3">94</td><td colspan="3">87</td><td colspan="3">95</td></tr>
<tr><td>Perception of Performance[2]</td><td colspan="3">A = mixed
1 = mixed</td><td colspan="3">B = mixed
2 = good</td><td colspan="3">C= good
3 = good</td></tr>
<tr><td>Trust
(beginning, middle, and end of the project)</td><td>H</td><td>L</td><td>H</td><td>H</td><td>L</td><td>L</td><td>H</td><td>H</td><td>H</td></tr>
</table>

1. *Grade assigned by the professors on the reports prepared by the students.*
2. *Performance was defined as the quality of the interaction as perceived by the ability to reach ones' objectives.*

The experience of the other two groups (B/2 and C/3) was not as extreme. Group 2 was trained in context sharing. Their Brazilian counterparts were not very happy with their "relationship skills" and seriously doubted their technical knowledge. Finally, Group C/3 performed well and by and large bypassed all problems demonstrated by the other groups, even though neither had been trained in context sharing. In fact, this was the only group whose perception of performance correlated with the task scores.

Based on the limited amount of data available in this study, the training program in context sharing did not seem to clearly affect performance in distributed analysis. In fact, Table 2 shows that the only group that perceived performance to be good was the one not trained at all in either country. We believe that there may be reasons for such outcome. First, the number of groups involved is too small to generalize results; groups C/3, for instance, were the highest performing groups and intuitively may have done things prescribed in the context sharing training program (such as learning each other's words/metaphors/"language") even though they had not been trained for such. An analysis of the transcript of their communication does indeed show signs of that. Moreover, their level of trust continued to be high along the full process; that is one of the predictors of high performance in the literature. In fact, both other groups had at least mixed results on trust. Therefore, it could be that group differences are still the best predictor of performance. But the question remains: for competence-matched groups, would training in context sharing improve performance?

The data also showed some commonalities across all three groups. Their respective cultural makeup seemed to be one of the strongest predictors of the expectations in task performance and proportional interest in relationship building instead. In addition, another common issue across all groups included differences in how much uncertainty was tolerated in the determination of the requirements, something possible to be explained by cultural differences in the uncertainty avoidance scores (see Table 1). Other cultural differences related to Hofstede's dimensions were not responsible for much of the results.

In fact, a closer look shows that there were alternative explanations for such difference. The most likely is the difference in points devoted to the assignment: 5% of the total grade for U.S. students and 30% for Brazilian students. On a pure cost-effectiveness basis, the U.S. students may not have been to willing to spend more than the smallest amount of time possible in the assignment—or to "squeak by." Moreover, such difference could also explain the reason two of the U.S. groups seemed to be too eager to jump into actual long questionnaires instead of first gathering a more general situation analysis, even though that issue had been discussed in the systems analysis and design class a few weeks earlier in the context of gathering requirements. The Brazilian students, who all had very strong background in systems analysis and design due to their undergraduate coursework and in some cases even work experience, particularly noticed this shortcut attitude.

Naturally, it would be hard to eliminate the explanation of cultural differences as a potential partial cause for such differences in expectations. The learning gleaned from this fact is that the follow-up experiments should devise ways to eliminate confounds, either by using same weights on grades on all participants or conversely by eliminating the cultural difference.

Finally, alternative explanations for the results could also originate from the fact that the three U.S. groups had different levels of competence or effort spent in the assignment, something that was evident from the grade assigned by the professor to their respective reports.

Conclusion

We set out to improve our understanding of e-collaboration in distributed analysis with emphasis on the role of context sharing. We stopped short of conclusively showing that such training has a positive or negative influence on the quality of distributed analysis; however, we learned a lot about some of the issues associated with distributed analysis, particularly in a cross-cultural environment. Expectations about the role of task versus relationships may be one of the critical cultural differences—fortunately, something that can be at least brought into the open fairly easily by surfacing group assumptions before the work starts.

The fact that we had a very small sample of non-competence-matched student groups could have been the critical reason for lack of more conclusive results. However, we learned that context sharing can (and will) be perceived differently based on one's cultural context; that further studies should be more carefully matched on both group performance and on grade weights (the Brazilian students derived 30% of their final grade from their participation and reports, whereas the U.S. students only got 5% of their final grade the same way). The impact of culture on context sharing needs to be revised and appropriately dealt with as well. In addition to fixing such shortcomings, further studies should adapt the context sharing training based on current findings.

Acknowledgments

Professors Evaristo and Watson-Manheim gratefully acknowledge support from the Center for Research in Information Management at the University of Illinois, Chicago, in conducting this research. An earlier version of this work was published in the Proc. of the 37th Annual Hawaii International Conference on System Sciences, January 2004.

References

Agarwal, R. (2003). *Global outsourcing for IT.* SIM.

Briggs, R. O., & Gruenbacher, P. (2002). *Easy WinWin: Managing complexity in requirements negotiation with GSS.* Paper presented at the 35th Annual Hawaii International Conference on Systems Science.

Browne, G. J., & Rogich, M. B. (2001). An empirical investigation of user requirements elicitation: Comparing the effectiveness of prompting techniques. *Journal of Management Information Systems, 17*(4), 223-249.

Cramton, C. D. (2001). The mutual knowledge problem and its consequences for dispersed collaboration. *Organization Science, 12*(3), 346-371.

Davis, G. (1982). Strategies for information requirements determination. *IBM Systems Journal, 21*(1), 4-30.

Dennis, A., & Wixom, B. (2000). *Systems analysis and design.* New York: John Wiley & Sons.

Grinter, R., Herbsleb, J., & Perry, D. (1999). *The geography of coordination: Dealing with distance in R&D work.* Paper presented at the International ACM SIGGROUP Conference on Supporting Group Work, Phoenix, AZ.

Herbsleb, J., & Mockus, A. (2003). An empirical study of speed and communication in globally distributed software development. *IEEE Transactions on Software Engineering, 29*(6), 481-494.

Herbsleb, J., Mockus, A., Finholt, T., & Grinter, R. (2000). *Distances, dependencies and delay in a global collaboration.* Paper presented at the ACM Conference on Computer Supported Cooperative Work, Philadelphia.

Herbsleb, J., Mockus, A., Finholt, T., & Grinter, R. (2001). *An empirical study of global software development: Distance and speed.* Paper presented at the 23rd International Conference on Software Engineering.

Hinds, P. (2000). *Perspective taking among distributed workers: The effect of distance on shared mental models* (Working Paper # 6). Palo Alto: Stanford University.

Hofstede, G. (1984). *Culture consequences.* Newbury Park, CA: Sage.

Jarvenpaa, S., & Leidner, D. E. (1999). Communication and trust in global virtual teams. *Organization Science, 10*(6), 791-815.

Urquhart, C. (1999). Themes in early requirements gathering: The case of the analyst, the client, and the student assistance scheme. *Information, Technology and People, 12*(1), 44-70.

The chapter was previously published in the International Journal of e-Collaboration, 1(2), 40-56, April-June 2005.

Chapter VIII

Innovation Diffusion and E-Collaboration:
The Effects of Social Proximity on Social Information Processing

Shaila M. Miranda, University of Oklahoma, USA
Pamela E. Carter, Florida State University, USA

Abstract

Organizational arrangements such as telework are often believed to disrupt workers' social networks. This raises a concern regarding teleworkers' abilities to adjust to technological changes in organizations. Based on innovation diffusion theory, this chapter considers telework and interdependence as parallel dimensions of social proximity that may be expected to affect the diffusion of innovation in terms of users' social information processing (i.e., their technology beliefs, communication channels, and information sources). This proposition is investigated in a field-study conducted during the migration of a business unit to a new communications system. Technology users at the business unit were surveyed three times over a 12-week period—right before the conversion to the new system and at two six-week intervals following the conversion. These surveys assessed the impact of telework on respondents' beliefs toward the communication technology. Findings partially supported our hypotheses regarding the negative effect of remoteness on beliefs about technology. Users were then surveyed to investigate the media and sources they utilized to stay informed about the new technology. As anticipated, telework was related to an increased use of electronic media and of individual and authority information sources. Contrary to our expectations, though, results indicated a positive effect of telework on the use of collective sources and face-to-face media. Therefore, we conclude that teleworkers make a special effort to preserve their social networks.

Introduction

The effects of social proximity have been of concern to researchers and practitioners in regard to evolving organizational practices such as virtual teams and telework. Such practices have been found to impede collaboration, to compromise workers' identification with their organization, to engender feelings of isolation, and to constrict employees' long-term career potential (Baker & Aldrich, 1996; Cooper & Kurland, 2002; Frank & Lowe, 2003; Gerber, 1995; Kugelmass, 1996; Maznevski & Chudoba, 2000; Nilles, 1994). If such organizational practices that reduce social proximity in the workforce thus disrupt workers' social systems, how will they affect the diffusion of new technologies? This is the question addressed by this chapter.

Social systems have been viewed as critical to innovation diffusion. Individuals process information about innovations within the context of these social systems (Rogers, 1983). Information flows through social systems, facilitating learning and assimilation of the innovation and influencing individuals' beliefs about the innovation. Rogers reports on eight independent studies, all supporting the proposition that the interconnectedness within a social system has a positive impact on the diffusion of an innovation. He further proposes that relative advantage, an innovation characteristic, is "often the content of the network messages about an innovation" (Rogers, 1983). The number of linkages in a social network is believed to determine the extent of innovation diffusion (Abrahamson & Rosenkopf, 1997). Speaking more directly to diffusion of computer technology, Burkhardt (1994) found that a lack of direct contact with other users hurt users' perceptions of their self-efficacy with a new computer system, and self-efficacy has been shown to be an important predictor of technology diffusion (Compeau et al., 1999).

In a field study, we therefore explore this issue of social proximity and social information processing in a company undergoing a transition to a new communication system. Specifically, we studied the effects of telework and users' beliefs about a technological innovation at three time periods: prior to the changeover from the old technology to the new and twice following the changeover. We also explored the media and sources utilized by workers in seeking information and attempting to learn about the novel technology.

Antecedents of Innovation Diffusion

Central to the study of innovation diffusion is the understanding of diffusion as a process of social change entailing alteration to a social system in terms of its structures and functions (Rogers, 1995). Key aspects of the diffusion of innovation process are thus the *innovation* itself, the *social system* in which the innovation is introduced, the *communication channels* through which social system members learn about the innovation, and the *timing* of the process. Little attention has been paid, however, to how these four aspects of the innovation process come together. In Figure 1, we model the innovation in terms of users' beliefs about them. Together with communication channels and information sources, beliefs are viewed as dimensions of users' *social information processing* about the innovation. This social information processing is a critical precedent to innovation diffusion, as individuals within a social system are influenced by the opinions, information, and behaviors of salient others in the system (Fulk, 1993).

A key element of the social system that is relevant to the issue of innovation diffusion is *social proximity*. Such proximity facilitates the social information processing needed for diffusion to take place (Rice & Aydin, 1991). Other elements of the social system typically considered in the diffusion literature are *organizational interventions* such as championship (Kimberly & Evanisko, 1981), top management support (Sharma & Yetton, 2003), and training (Nelson & Cheney, 1987). However, given that our field study occurred within the context of a single organization within which organizational interventions did not vary across respondents, we limit the focus of our attention to the issue of social proximity within the social system. While not explicitly represented in our model, timing is a critical element, as information is processed over time and the effects of proximity on social information processing vary with time (Yoshioka & Athanasiou, 1971). This overview of the diffusion process and its antecedents are represented in Figure 1.

Social Proximity

Proximity is the "extent to which one could be exposed to social information in a given social system" (Rice & Aydin, 1991, p. 221). Proximity has been dem-

Figure 1. Antecedents of Innovation Diffusion

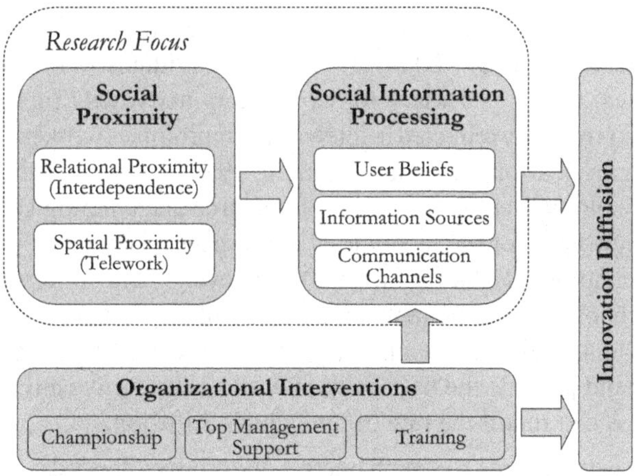

onstrated to have a significant impact on the diffusion of innovation in domains as diverse as agriculture (Hagerstrand, 1976) and biotechnology (Owen-Smith & Powell, 2004). There are three types of proximity: spatial, relational, and positional (Rice & Aydin, 1991). Spatial proximity reflects geographic distance, where individuals working close to each other increase the likelihood of exposure to social information processing and interaction. Relational proximity is reflected by communication proximity, the extent to which people interact directly and indirectly. Positional proximity reflects the structural proximity of individuals with regard to the extent to which individuals occupy the same roles. In this research, we focus on the first two forms of proximity. Spatial proximity is considered in relation to telework practices and relational proximity in terms of workers' interdependence. We treat spatial and relational proximity as two independent dimensions of social proximity, since communication technologies provide the connectivity necessary for interdependence in the case of teleworkers (Ramsower, 1985; Wellman, Salaff, Dimitrova, & Garton, 1996).

Telework is defined as work away from one's central office location in a variety of circumstances such as telecommuting, hoteling, mobile work, and supplemental at-home work (Raghuram, Wiesenfeld, & Garud, 1996; Venkatesh & Vitalari, 1992). Irrespective of the availability of technological support, remoteness strains organizational communication, information sharing, and relationship development (Davenport & Pearlson, 1998; Maruca, 1998). Communication is easier when individuals are proximate and can communicate directly with others (Shane, 1979). It enables impromptu face-to-face communication, which is suitable not only for conveying information, but also for beliefs and work-related concerns (Davenport & Pearlson, 1998). In the face of conflicting data, managers tend to rely more on visual than non-visual data, which can be problematic for teleworkers who are limited, therefore, in the information they process (Kulik & Ambrose, 1993). In contrast, geographic collocation facilitates the transfer of complex information and collective sense making (McGlynn et al., 2004). It enables individuals to develop a shared interpretive context that is necessary for exploratory activities (Zack, 1993). The absence of spatial proximity reflected in telework compromises workers' innovation-related modeling or vicarious learning (Bandura, 1977). Further, in the later stages of diffusion, technology users are frequently the source of technological innovation, as they initiate new uses for the technology and process changes to maximize the benefits of the technology (Orlikowski, 1996). However, if teleworkers lack comfort with existing technology or are unable to interact with coworkers in a creative and spontaneous fashion, they may be unable to develop technological or process innovations that could provide the organization with a competitive advantage. Thus, spatial remoteness can retard the rate of innovation diffusion.

Interdependence is the degree to which one's work product depends on inputs from coworkers (Thompson, 1967). As task interdependencies increase, so does relational proximity (i.e., the necessity for interaction). Relational proximity has been noted to be particularly significant in influencing workers' social information processing surrounding a technological innovation (Rice & Aydin, 1991).

Social Information Processing

Social information processing refers to the social construction of meaning surrounding the focal innovation (Fulk, 1993). We consider social information processing in terms of the beliefs held by users about the focal innovation and the media and sources utilized in their search for information about the innovation. Beliefs and attitudes about a target are inherently social constructions as individuals engage in collective interpretation of the target itself, the behaviors in relation to the target, and the effects of those behaviors (Salancik & Pfeffer, 1978). Thus, beliefs and attitudes are the focus of social information processing. Positive user beliefs about focal innovations facilitate their diffusion (Compeau et al., 1999; Davis et al., 1992; Venkatesh, 1999).

Social information processing thus entails social influences that occur through various communication channels or media, and reference various information sources (Fulk, 1993). Typically, media that are rich in social cues are believed to be most conducive to social information processing (i.e., the most influential), while leaner media impede such processing. Similarly, collective information sources (e.g., one's workgroup) have been noted to influence individuals' information processing about focal innovations (Fulk, 1993; Rice & Aydin, 1991).

Hypotheses Development

We now consider the manner in which the specific dimensions of social proximity modeled in Figure 1 (i.e., telework and interdependence) impact the three aspects of users' social information processing: technology beliefs, communication channels or media used to solicit information about the technology, and information sources utilized.

Technology Beliefs

In the technology diffusion literature, diffusion (the adoption of an innovation, the intention to use or the actual usage of an innovation) has been considered in terms of users' perceptions of the usefulness (or relative advantage) and ease-of-use (complexity) of the technology (Davis, Bagozzi, & Warshaw, 1989; Rogers, 1983). Perceived usefulness refers to the extent to which users believe that the technology contributes to their self-efficacy, and the perceived ease-of-use of an innovation is the degree to which users believe interacting with the technology is free of effort (Davis, 1989). Usefulness and ease-of-use have been found to have a strong positive impact on intentions to use the new technology, as well as reported current and projected future technology usage (Davis et al., 1989; Karahanna et al., 1999; Moore & Benbasat, 1991; Rogers, 1983; Venkatesh, 1999; Venkatesh, 2000).

Telework offers fewer opportunities for technology users to be exposed to the range of features and functionality of the novel technology. People adopt and subsequently use technologies when the perceived benefits from adoption and use exceed costs (Rogers, 1983; Tornatzky & Klein, 1992). Efforts to communicate features, functionality, and perceived benefits of new technologies through lean media are likely to be stymied as such media are ill-suited to communicating equivocal information (Dennis & Kinney, 1998). However, without this information it is unlikely that users will be able to adequately assess job relevance, output quality, and image considerations, which are all important factors in determining the perceived usefulness of a technology (Venkatesh & Davis, 1996).

In considering the effects of spatial proximity on user beliefs, it is also important to be attentive to the nature of the technology being implemented; viz., the communication system. A reliable technology infrastructure is critical to successful telework (Watad & DiSanzo, 2000), and a stable communication technology has been noted to have a positive impact on workers' perceptions of their productivity and performance as well as worker satisfaction (Belanger et al., 2001). In contrast, technology newness poses a liability for cooperative work (McGrath et al., 1993). Norms for cooperative work that depend on electronic communication are likely to be disrupted with a change in communication technology (Duarte & Snyder, 1999).

Thus, user beliefs about the usefulness of the new communication technology are likely to be negatively impacted by spatial proximity.

Coworkers can influence each others' perceptions of the technology directly with overt statements concerning the technology, and indirectly via vicarious learning (Fulk, Schmitz, & Steinfield, 1990). This influence provides external facilitating conditions, which make knowledge and resources available that can facilitate using the technology, and thereby also impact perceptions of ease-of-use (Taylor & Todd 1995; Venkatesh, 2000). However, to the extent that telework limits interactions through lean media, less social information processing of this sort can occur.

While both beliefs have been found to impact intentions to use a technology, the effect of perceived ease-of-use has been noted to be small and to decay more quickly over time than the effect of perceived usefulness (Davis et al., 1989; Karahanna et al., 1999). This is generally attributed to the fact that, over time, individuals gain experience with the technology, and with greater experience, the usefulness of the technology becomes more salient than the ease-of-use of the technology (Taylor & Todd 1995). In other words, perceived ease-of-use has been found to be less salient to the diffusion phenomenon. These arguments lead to the following hypotheses:

Hypothesis 1: Spatial and relational proximity will be related positively to perceived usefulness of a novel technology.

Hypothesis 2: Spatial and relational proximity will be related positively to perceived ease-of-use of a novel technology.

Hypothesis 3: Spatial and relational proximity will have a stronger and longer-term impact on perceived usefulness of a novel technology than on perceived ease-of-use.

Communication Channels

In regard to the medium through which innovations diffuse, interpersonal contact has been noted to be more effective than the use of mass communication channels in the diffusion of complex innovations (Rogers, 1983). We explored usage of three media in the solicitation of information about technology—e-mail, phone, and face-to-face conversations. Reliance on electronic communication results in the weakening of social ties, thus diminishing the ability of coworkers to influence each other (Kiesler, 1986).

Communicating information about an unfamiliar technology is an ambiguous and uncertain task. Users initially lack sufficient information about the various features of the technology and how they may be used effectively. Problems occur frequently and without warning. When problems or suggestions regarding the use of technology are communicated, these problems or suggestions may be interpreted differently, based on the recipient's level of expertise with the technology.

Rich media are more suitable than leaner media for ambiguous tasks, where necessary information is lacking, and the information available is subject to conflicting interpretations (Daft & Lengel, 1984). Rich media are required when the task involves a high occurrence of unexpected events, when there are no routinized procedures for dealing with such occurrences, and in communication across departments that are highly differentiated, for example, between corporate IT and other functional areas (Daft &Lengel, 1984).

Telework limits face-to-face interactions, making coworkers less physically available for face-to-face communication (Wiesenfeld, Garud & Raghuram, 1997). When the recipient of a message is potentially unavailable, utilizing leaner media, even in cases calling for richer media facilitates closure (Straub & Karahanna, 1998). Thus, teleworkers will need to resort to leaner media in order to reach closure. This leads to the following hypotheses:

Hypothesis 4: Spatial proximity will be related negatively to use of electronic media (e-mail and phone) to share information about a new technology.

Hypothesis 5: Spatial proximity will be related positively to use of the face-to-face medium to share information about a new technology.

Information Sources

Innovation decisions may be *optional* (i.e., made by individuals), *collective* (i.e., made by the group), or *authority* (i.e., made at the organizational level) (Rogers, 1983). While the initiator of a major technological innovation is frequently a legitimate authority, individuals and coworkers, too, can instigate the diffusion of an innovation. In fact, such self- and clan-based controls may be more effective in ambiguous situations than bureaucratic controls (Ouchi, 1979). As already seen, the introduction of a new technology can generate ambiguity and uncertainty in the workplace.

Teleworkers tend to be more self-sufficient than their peers and also more isolated from their workgroup and other members of the organization (Belanger & Collins, 1998). Therefore, authority and collective sources internal to the organization are less accessible to the teleworker. Since individuals tend to utilize the most accessible sources (Saunders & Jones, 1990), at first glance, it would appear that teleworkers are less likely to invoke authority and collective sources.

However, as a function of their sense of isolation, teleworkers are strongly motivated to overcome the strains of remoteness by staying in touch with their supervisors, channeling much of their organizational communication through them (Maruca, 1998). Teleworkers who received technical and emotional support from their supervisors were found to be more satisfied (Hartman, Stoner, & Arora, 1991). Teleworkers thus tend to be more dependent on their managers for a connection to the organization (Belanger & Collins, 1998) and tend to be concerned that their relationship with their managers may deteriorate over time (Reinsch, 1997). Teleworkers' insecurities and sense of isolation is likely to be particularly heightened with the deployment of a new communication technology. Under such circumstances, we therefore can expect increased teleworker contact with their supervisors in an effort to dispel the uncertainties surrounding the new technology and solicitation of information from these authority sources.

The informal workgroup has a strong impact on socialization, dispensing information about the work environment (Sherman, Smith, & Mansfield, 1986). However, telework reduces opportunities for such socialization (Ford & Butts, 1991), thereby limiting users' access to these collective sources. Furthermore, teleworkers are motivated to be as self-sufficient as possible and tend to perceive that their productivity and performance are negatively affected by their need for communicating with their coworkers (Belanger, Collins, & Cheney, 2001). Therefore, they are unlikely to rely on peers for information about the new technology.

Interdependence also is expected to impact the sources invoked by users in understanding the new technology. Under conditions of low workgroup attraction, authority sources have been found to be more salient; in contrast, when workers experience a high level of attraction to their workgroup, these collective sources become more salient to them (Fulk, 1993). Thus, when relational proximity is high, we can expect to see a heightened reliance on collective sources; when it is low, workers are more likely to invoke authority sources. We, therefore, propose the following:

Hypothesis 6: Spatial proximity will be related negatively to use of individual and authority information sources to learn about a new technology.

Hypothesis 7: Spatial proximity will be related positively to use of collective sources to learn about a new technology.

Hypothesis 8: Relational proximity will be related negatively to use of authority sources to learn about a new technology.

Hypothesis 9: Relational proximity will be related positively to use of collective sources to learn about a new technology.

Methods

The site of this investigation was a company in the broadcast industry with operations around the U.S. The study traced the conversion from one communications system to another at a single division in the firm. The firm initially used MS Mail, a DOS-based electronic communications system that consisted primarily of e-mail. The new electronic communications system was MS Exchange, which included not just enhanced e-mail facilities, but also various tools to support group work and organizational memory, and enhanced security and performance. Table 1 provides a comparison of some of the features and support provided by the MS Mail vs MS Exchange implementations.

The impact of telework on the diffusion of the new communications system was explored via a series of surveys in two stages. Stage 1 explored the changing worker beliefs toward their communication technology at three time periods: before the conversion to the new system and twice after conversion to the new system. In Stage 2 of the study, we surveyed users to determine media and source usage in their search for information regarding the new communications system.

The first survey at Stage 1 was conducted during a training session that marked the conversion point from the old system to the new. The training was conducted by the CIO and the systems manager. Each session lasted about three hours. Users attended these training sessions in groups of about 30 at an on-site training facility. The training was not hands-on, but rather an overview and demonstration of the features of the new communication system. The users also were provided with a manual containing documentation on the features of the new system. The CIO and the systems manager, along with the site support staff, were available for on-site support for a couple of days during the transition and training period.

Table 1. Comparison of communication systems

Tools	MS Mail	MS Exchange
Office support	▪ Basics (spell-check, attachments, etc.)	▪ Multiple profiles and mailboxes ▪ Automatic replying/forwarding without login
Organizational memory and workgroup support	▪ Limited shared folders (no user-control) ▪ Administrator-controlled distribution lists ▪ Individual schedules and contact lists	▪ Improved public folders allowing user-specified permissions ▪ User-controlled distribution lists ▪ Workgroup schedules and contact lists
Security and performance	▪ Separate logins for network access and e-mail ▪ Slow	▪ E-mail logins integrated with network access ▪ Digital signatures ▪ Higher speed ▪ More user-friendly

Users attending the training were required to respond to the pre-conversion survey, assessing their beliefs to the existing system, prior to arriving at the training session. Thus, the response rate at this time was 100%. A total of 159 responses were obtained at this time. The users were also surveyed at two time periods after the conversion to the new system: approximately six weeks after the conversion and another six weeks later. At these times, participants were given the option to respond to a paper version of the survey that was faxed to them, or an electronic version that was e-mailed to them. The second round of surveys yielded 57 responses, while the third round yielded 59 responses (51% and 54% percent of the sample, respectively[1]). This design is similar to the one used by Davis et al. (1989) to test their technology acceptance model, in that users were surveyed twice after being trained to use the technology. However, this study also included a baseline measure before the training and administered the first survey later in the study than was done in the Davis et al. (1989) study. This latter choice was made to allow the effect of telework to emerge, rather than measure immediate perceptions following the training session[2].

On the first three surveys, subjects responded to questions that assessed their work habits and perceptions of the technology. Relevant questions from the survey instrument appear in Appendix A. The fourth survey assessed subjects' information seeking behaviors. This survey was conducted approximately 14 weeks following the deployment of the new technology (and two weeks after the last technology beliefs survey). A total of 104 responses were obtained on this survey from people who had also completed the prior survey. The survey instrument used at this stage of the study is provided in Appendix B. All study variables, other than time, were assessed using self-report measures. Reliability of scales derived from all four surveys was determined using Cronbach's α.

Since all independent and dependent variables (except for time) at Stage 1 of the study were obtained from a single source, the possibility of shared variance between the independent and dependent variables being attributable to a common method variance should be addressed (Podsakoff & Organ, 1986). To this end, we conducted a single factor analysis for all the self-report items at this stage of the study, including responses obtained at all three time periods. The results of this factor analysis, with an extraction criteria of minimum eigenvalues of 1 and loadings from an oblique rotation required for establishing discriminant validity (Ford, MacCallum & Tait, 1986), are presented in Table 2. Two criteria are used as indicators of the presence of common method variance: (1) a single factor or an extremely dominant first factor (Podsakoff & Organ, 1986) and (2) the smallest correlation between latent factors (Lindell & Whitney, 2001). The measurement model in Table 2 is a multi-factor model, and the variance captured by the first factor in the model in Table 2 is not close to the total variance captured by all factors. The smallest correlation between the latent factors was found to be 0.021. These criteria indicate a minimal common method variance problem, if any, and, therefore, call for no further remedial measures. The absence of cross-loadings indicates the discriminant validity of the measurement model.

Independent Variables

Telework was assessed using a four-item, five-point scale developed for this study based on research by Venkatesh and Vitalari (1992). Subjects indicated the number of regular workday hours and supplemental hours they worked away from their office. The reliability of this measure was determined to be 0.82. For the analysis of Stage 1 data (viz., hypotheses regarding users' beliefs), the indicators of telework were scores reported on that survey. For the analysis of the Stage 2 data (viz., hypotheses regarding media and sources used), the telework scores used for the independent variable were a mean average of scores reported by users on the prior three surveys. This was done to accommodate constraints by management on the length of the survey administered. For hypothesis testing, telework was reverse-coded to yield the assessment of spatial proximity.

Interdependence or relational proximity was assessed using a four-item, five-point scale adopted from the Job Characteristics Index (Sims, Szilagyi, & Keller, 1976).

Table 2. Oblique factor loadings for stage 1 variables

Item	Usefulness	Ease-of-Use	Telework	Interdependence
Use1	0.836	-0.001	-0.004	-0.027
Use2	0.915	-0.026	0.034	-0.040
Use3	0.902	0.035	-0.059	-0.019
Use4	0.914	-0.045	-0.019	0.005
Use5	0.915	-0.018	-0.031	-0.013
Use6	0.699	0.258	0.011	0.091
Ease1	-0.088	0.867	0.018	-0.023
Ease2	0.151	0.712	0.100	-0.009
Ease3	0.056	0.801	0.039	-0.082
Ease4	0.223	0.617	-0.016	-0.042
Ease5	-0.080	0.851	-0.055	0.077
Ease6	-0.012	0.873	0.034	0.023
Interdependence1	0.044	-0.081	0.158	0.688
Interdependence2	0.014	0.117	-0.113	0.623
Interdependence3	0.071	-0.146	0.142	0.698
Interdependence4	-0.181	0.031	-0.088	0.636
Telework1	-0.062	0.090	0.774	-0.124
Telework2	0.052	-0.078	0.766	0.109
Telework3	-0.007	0.003	0.804	-0.028
Telework4	-0.040	0.035	0.819	0.092
Variance Explained	23.526%	20.054%	12.988%	9.296%

The reliability of this scale was determined to be 0.61. As with telework, assessments of interdependence for the analysis of beliefs were garnered from surveys 1-3. For the analysis of media and source usage, interdependence scores were computed as the mean average of scores from surveys 1-3.

Dependent Variables

Beliefs about the existing and the new e-mail system were assessed using the Davis (1989) measures. The reliability of the six-item, five-point perceived usefulness scale was determined to be 0.94, and the six-item, five-point perceived ease-of-use scale was 0.89.

Communication channels or media usage (i.e., usage of phone, e-mail, and face-to-face communication to learn about the new technology) were assessed using three-item, five-point scales. The reliabilities for the phone, e-mail, and face-to-face scales were 0.85, 0.90, and 0.86, respectively. Factor analysis, presented in Table 3, was conducted with an extraction criteria of minimum eigenvalues of 1 and an oblique rotation, and supports the discriminant validity of this measurement model.

Information source usage (i.e., use of individual, authority, and collective information sources) was assessed using five-point scales, with five, six, and six items, respectively. Individual sources identified were books/magazines/manuals and videos. The reliability of this scale was 0.92. Authority sources identified were the help desk and other IS staff. The reliability of this scale was 0.87. Collective sources were immediate coworkers and other business acquaintances. The reliability of this scale was 0.84. High scores on both scales indicated more frequent usage. Factor analysis

Table 3. Oblique factor loadings for communication channels used to seek information

Items	Phone	E-mail	Face-to-Face
Phone1	0.877	-0.129	-0.153
Phone2	0.942	0.134	0.115
Phone3	0.830	-0.095	0.098
E-mail1	0.088	-0.862	0.095
E-mail2	0.029	-0.866	0.061
E-mail3	-0.077	-0.883	0.103
FTF1	-0.064	-0.034	0.857
FTF2	0.078	-0.029	0.879
FTF3	0.049	0.002	0.916
Variance Explained	27.715%	26.408%	27.146%

Table 4. Oblique factor loadings for information sources used to seek information

Items	Individual	Authority	Collective
Individual1	-0.800	-0.153	-0.015
Individual2	-0.499	0.259	0.062
Individual3	-0.880	-0.043	-0.058
Individual4	-0.418	0.323	-0.022
Individual5	-0.943	-0.117	-0.051
Authority1	0.185	0.849	-0.153
Authority2	-0.106	0.554	0.126
Authority3	0.154	0.825	-0.045
Authority4	-0.153	0.669	0.170
Authority5	0.086	0.868	-0.056
Authority6	-0.158	0.714	0.045
Collective1	0.221	-0.044	0.898
Collective2	-0.308	0.220	0.408
Collective3	0.057	-0.110	0.878
Collective4	-0.310	0.216	0.491
Collective5	0.073	-0.072	0.877
Collective6	-0.340	0.163	0.523
Variance Explained	17.407%	21.908%	19.556%

Table 5. Descriptive statistics for Stage 1: Technology beliefs

Variables	Means (Standard Deviations)			Correlation (p-value)		
	Pre-Conversion (Baseline)	6-weeks Post-Conversion	12-weeks Post-Conversion	Inter-depend-ence	Ease-of-Use	Usefulness
Telework	1.76 (0.64)	1.82 (0.54)	1.63 (0.54)	0.029 (0.667)	0.090 (0.181)	0.004 (0.949)
Interdependence	3.87 (0.61)	2.19 (0.56)	2.17 (0.59)		-0.089 (0.185)	-0.065 (0.335)
Ease-of-Use	4.10 (0.55)	4.18 (0.64)	4.21 (0.59)			0.463 (0.000)
Usefulness	4.13 (0.69)	4.16 (0.85)	4.27 (0.72)			

Table 6. MANOVA for technology beliefs

Effects	Roy's Largest Root	F	(p)
Time*Spatial Proximity	0.047	3.243	0.023
Time*Relational Proximity	0.041	2.841	0.039

with an oblique rotation supporting the discriminant validity of this measurement model appears in Table 4[3]. Note that an extraction criterion limiting the model to three factors was applied to preclude the fragmenting of each of the three factors into two separate factors.

Results

Means and correlations for the study of users' beliefs toward the communication technology are presented in Table 5.

A multivariate analysis of variance was conducted to test the effects of the time period, interdependence, telework, and the appropriate interaction terms on perceived ease-of-use and perceived usefulness. Table 6 summarizes the MANOVA results for all dependent variables at this stage. The test criterion employed was Roy's Largest Root. This test has more power than the competing Wilks, Pillai, and Hotelling tests, and it is believed to be the most appropriate test when dependent variables are highly correlated (see Table 5) and when covariances are homogeneous (Box's M=4.308, F=0.708, p=0.644) (Hair et al., 1998).

Figure 2. Correlation of spatial and relational proximity with usefulness over time

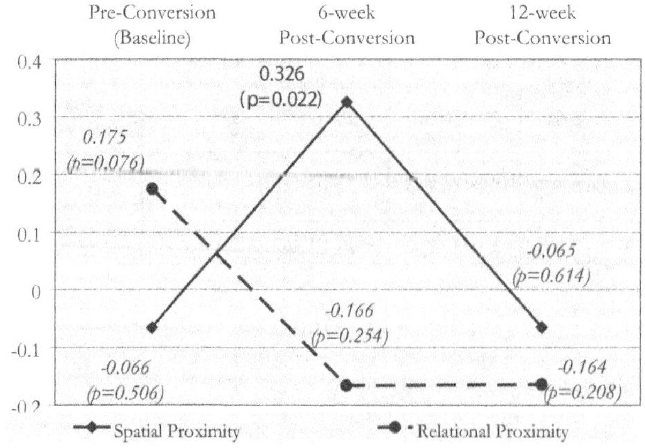

Table 7. Descriptive statistics for Stage 2: Communication channels and information sources

Variables	Means (Standard Deviations)	Correlation (p-value)						
		Telework	Individual	Authority	Collective	Phone	E-Mail	FTF
Inter-dependence	3.00 (0.26)	-0.029 (0.773)	0.075 (0.451)	0.236 (0.016)	-0.051 (0.611)	0.171 (0.084)	-0.063 (0.529)	-0.011 (0.910)
Telework	1.65 (0.36)		0.199 (0.044)	-0.010 (0.921)	0.241 (0.014)	0.172 (0.082)	0.262 (0.007)	0.173 (0.080)
Individual Source	1.40 (0.57)			0.290 (0.003)	0.330 (0.001)	0.365 (0.000)	0.317 (0.001)	0.199 (0.044)
Authority Source	2.16 (0.90)				0.205 (0.038)	0.533 (0.000)	0.211 (0.032)	0.031 (0.753)
Collective Source	2.20 (0.71)					0.396 (0.000)	0.331 (0.001)	0.578 (0.000)
Phone Medium	1.65 (0.82)						0.456 (0.000)	0.304 (0.002)
E-mail Medium	1.89 (0.89)							0.397 (0.000)
Face-to-Face Medium	2.22 (1.03)							

Further inspection of the interaction effects noted in the MANOVA via the individual ANOVAs indicated the effect held for perceived usefulness alone for both spatial proximity (F=3.232, p=0.023) and for relational proximity (F=2.836, p=0.039), not for perceived ease-of-use for either spatial proximity (F=0.880, p=0.452) or relational proximity (F=0.488, p=0.691). Further analysis, as depicted in Figure 2, indicates a significant positive correlation between spatial proximity and perceived usefulness at the six-week post-conversion point. All other correlations were insignificant. However, we note that this effect was observed only for perceived usefulness, not perceived ease-of-use, and then only briefly (i.e., at the six-week point alone, not

Table 8. MANOVAs for channels and sources used

Effects	**Roy's Largest Root**	**F**	**(p)**
Medium Usage			
Interdependence	0.058	1.882	0.138
Telework	0.083	2.713	0.049
Source Usage			
Interdependence	0.072	2.337	0.078
Telework	0.090	2.925	0.038

12-weeks after the implementation). Thus, hypothesis 1 was partially supported, but hypothesis 2 was not. Hypothesis 3 anticipating a stronger and more prolonged effect of telework on usefulness than on ease-of-use was also supported.

Means and correlations for the data from Stage 2 of the study—focusing on sources and media employed by users in learning the new system—are presented in Table 7.

Multivariate analyses of variance were conducted to test the effects of telework on media and sources used. Interdependence was retained as a control in this model. Table 8 summarizes the MANOVA results for all dependent variables at this stage. The test criterion employed was Roy's Largest Root. This test was deemed appropriate, since the dependent variables are highly correlated (see Table 7) and covariances are homogeneous (Box's $M_{(Source)}$=24.668, F=0.962, p=0.503; Box's $M_{(Medium)}$=27.244, F=1.062, p=0.388).

Further analysis of the effect of telework on media used revealed a significant increase in the use of e-mail with telework (F=7.316, p=0.008), and more marginal increases in the use of phone (F=3.350, p=0.070) and face-to-face communication (F=3.085, p=0.082). Thus, while hypothesis 4 was supported by the data, hypothesis 5 was not; in fact, the data indicate the opposite of the hypothesized effect to hold for the workers studied.

Table 9. Summary results of hypothesis testing

	Hypothesis	Finding
1.	Spatial and relational proximity will be related positively to perceived usefulness of a novel technology.	Partially supported
2.	Spatial and relational proximity will be related positively to perceived ease-of-use of a novel technology.	Not supported
3.	Spatial and relational proximity will have a stronger and longer-term impact on perceived usefulness of a novel technology than on perceived ease-of-use.	Supported
4.	Spatial proximity will be related negatively to use of electronic media (e-mail and phone) to share information about a new technology.	Supported
5.	Spatial proximity will be related positively to use of the face-to-face medium to share information about a new technology.	Not supported – reversed
6.	Spatial proximity will be related negatively to use of individual and authority information sources to learn about a new technology.	Supported
7.	Spatial proximity will be related positively to use of collective sources to learn about a new technology.	Not supported – reversed for collective sources
8.	Relational proximity will be related negatively to use of authority sources to learn about a new technology	Weakly supported
9.	Relational proximity will be related positively to use of collective sources to learn about a new technology	Not supported

Further inspection of the significant effect of telework on sources used indicated no difference in the use of authority sources ($F=0.001$, $p=0.975$), but significant increases in the use of individual ($F=4.238$, $p=0.042$) and collective ($F=6.117$, $p=0.015$) sources with increased telework. Thus, the data provide support for the effect of spatial proximity on use of individual sources as appears in hypothesis 6. There was no support for the hypothesized effect of telework on usage of authority sources, though. Contrary to our expectations for hypothesis 7, use of collective information sources increased with increases in telework.

The effects of interdependence on sources used was not significant at the conventional $\alpha=0.05$ level. However, since it was significant at $\alpha=0.10$, we considered the ANOVA effects for the three sources. The results indicate no differences in use of individual ($F=0.686$, $p=0.409$) and collective ($F=0.204$, $p=0.652$) sources with increased interdependence, but increases in the use of authority sources ($F=5.902$, $p=0.017$). Thus, the data provided weak support for hypothesis 8 and no support for hypothesis 9.

Discussion

The results of this study, reported in the preceding section, are summarized in Table 9. Next, we consider the effects of social proximity on each of the three aspects of social information processing.

Impact of Social Proximity on Beliefs

As anticipated, spatial proximity (i.e., low levels of telework) was found to have a significantly positive effect on perceived usefulness with the implementation of the new communication system. However, this effect was short-lived and did not hold for relational proximity. Nor was it visible in the case of users' beliefs about the perceived ease-of-use of the new technology.

One explanation for the absence of an effect for perceived ease-of-use may be the fact that teleworkers were simply less aware of the technical features offered by the new technology and, therefore, experienced no challenge in learning to use it. Given the very rudimentary capabilities of the old e-mail system, there was probably very little time required for users to replicate the functionality of the old system within the new system. The transition from a command-line system to one with a GUI interface probably also contributed to enhanced ease-of-use of the new technology, wiping out any noticeable impairment in perceived ease-of-use from remoteness.

A second explanation for this finding may lie in the fact that perceived ease-of-use historically has had only a weak and fleeting salience to the diffusion phenomenon (Davis, 1989). Therefore, it is possible that any noticeable impairment in these perceptions stemming from remoteness may have been experienced before the first post-conversion survey was conducted, thereby masking the effects of remoteness on these beliefs.

While the effect of spatial proximity on perceived usefulness increased significantly between the pre-conversion and the six-week post-conversion periods (r_0-r_1=-0.392, p=0.000), by 12 weeks after the conversion, the effect was insignificant and close to pre-conversion levels (r_0-r_2=-0.001, p=0.493). This suggests that spatial proximity provided only a brief advantage in the technology diffusion. This, too, may have been a function of the heightened functionality of the new system relative to the old and the training provided to the users, enabling all users—proximate or remote—to discover quickly the usefulness of the new technology. On-site training, in particular, has been noted to be beneficial to teleworkers (Watad & DiSanzo, 2000).

While the post-conversion effects of relational proximity on perceived ease-of-use were insignificant, an examination of the profile for the effects suggests a disruptive effect of relational proximity on perceived ease-of-use in the post-conversion periods. The drop in the nearly significant positive correlation between relational proximity and perceived usefulness between the pre-conversion and the six week post-conversion stage was highly significant (r_0-r_1=0.341, p=0.000). Unlike spatial proximity, the impact of relational proximity on perceived usefulness did not revert back to pre-conversion levels at 12-weeks past the conversion. Instead, the relationship was still significantly different from pre-conversions levels (r_0-r_2=0.339, p=0.000) and no different from levels at the six-week period (r_1-r_2=-0.002, p=0.486). Thus, the data provides some evidence that relational proximity actually may inhibit perceived usefulness of a novel technology. However, the nature of the focal technology (i.e., one that supported employee communication) may explain this finding. The initial e-mail system available to users had limited collaborative functionality, largely enabling only the transmission of messages among users. The new e-mail system introduced a range of collaborative tools such as shared contacts, calendars, and folders. These functions are particularly useful to highly interdependent workgroups. However, effective use of these functions requires users to develop shared norms regarding their use. The apparent disruption in the perceptions of usefulness of the technology among highly interdependent workers is, therefore, attributable to the absence of such shared norms, precluding effective use of the advanced collaboration functions of the new technology. In contrast, more independent workers relied more on features that did not require such consensus on norms of use (e.g., automatic forwarding and replying and integrated logins),and, therefore, perceived the new technology to be more useful than did their more interdependent counterparts.

Impacts of Social Proximity on Communication Channels Used

As anticipated, low spatial proximity (i.e., telework) was associated with an increased use of e-mail in soliciting information about the novel technology. The increased usage of telephone queries with telework was more marginal. Contrary to our expectations, however, lower spatial proximity was not associated with a decreased use of face-to-face communication. Rather, the more individuals teleworked, the more they appeared to rely on face-to-face communication to learn about the new technology. This finding may be a function of the fact that few of the people in our sample appeared to telework for much more than half of their regular work week. They, therefore, took the opportunity to learn more about the technology when they could interact personally with their coworkers. Prior researchers have termed this effect "compensatory adaptation," where individuals work to offset deficiencies in their available communication medium (Kock, 2001). Again, this finding is consistent with earlier research on telework, which suggests that teleworkers make every effort to preserve their ties with members of their organization (Belanger & Collins, 1998).

Impacts of Social Proximity on Information Sources Used

Our expectation was that spatial remoteness would encourage workers to seek information from individual and authority sources; in contrast, spatial proximity was expected to be positively related to use of collective sources. The data only supports our expectations with regard to individual sources. No relationship between spatial proximity and use of authority sources was observed, and, contrary to our expectations, spatial remoteness was related also to the use of collective sources.

Again, the somewhat limited extent of telework within the organization studied may shed light on the unexpected findings with regard to sources invoked. Since workers were able to connect with their peers for at least half of the work week, they were unlikely to experience the disconnectedness from their work group that typically results in the over-reliance on those in authority (Belanger & Collins, 1998; Fulk, 1993; Maruca, 1998). Furthermore, the periodic accessibility of collective sources permitted workers to leverage them to learn about the novel technology (Saunders & Jones, 1990). Here, too, compensatory adaptation may have played a role.

Our data supported the anticipated negative effect of relational proximity on use of authority sources. Thus, disconnectedness from one's workgroup does prompt a reliance on authority figures, as suggested by the communication literature (Fulk, 1993). However, the data provided no support for the anticipated increased reliance on collective sources with relational proximity. This suggests that perhaps workers with high spatial proximity avail themselves of the range of information sources that are accessible to them (Saunders & Jones, 1990).

Reconsidering the Social Nature of Information Processing

At first glance, the findings of this study appear to conflict with Granovetter's (1973) theory of weak ties. Granovetter suggested that weak, rather than strong, ties were instrumental in diffusion. However, our findings point to reliance on strong ties, as reflected in the popularity of face-to-face interaction and collective sources. Perhaps considering the stages of diffusion will help us reconcile our apparently contradictory findings.

Rogers (1983) observed several stages in the diffusion of an innovation. Notably, he observed that awareness of an innovation precedes its evaluation, trial, and adoption. Granovetter's work on weak ties addresses the awareness stage. This is true also of Burt's (1995) more recent work on structural holes. Here, too, we see that weak ties that span groups are beneficial in making individuals competitively aware of information. However, once individuals are aware of an innovation, they may rely on stronger ties in assisting them in making further decisions on its adoption and use. Support for this perspective comes from Marsden's work on discussion networks. Marsden (1987) found that Americans tend to rely on small, dense, and homogeneous networks for discussing matters important to them. Thus, while weak ties may be helpful in facilitating initial awareness, strong ties may be necessary in facilitating innovation evaluation and use.

Implications and Suggestions for Future Research

The findings of this study are reassuring for managers and workers in telework environments. They demonstrate that telework need not retard the diffusion of an innovation. More importantly, they suggest that teleworkers can and do invest an effort in preserving their ties to their organization. As noted earlier, this has been a frequent concern with teleworker environments, as well as with other alternate work arrangements.

The reliance of remote workers on face-to-face interaction and collective sources may suggest the need for richer electronic technologies such as videoconferencing. Management and worker strategies that facilitate face-to-face worker interactions, despite the nature of the work arrangement, also may be helpful in providing teleworkers with the interaction necessary for them to successfully complete their work and preserve their social networks.

Our research considered telework and interdependence in terms of spatial and relational proximity. While this represents a contribution to the telework literature, our design did not permit us to investigate the third type of proximity: positional proximity. Future research would do well to consider the effects of this form of proximity on social information processing. As with earlier research, our study highlights the fact that users' beliefs about the ease-of-use of the innovation cease to be salient fairly early in the diffusion process. Future research, therefore, should assess beliefs earlier in the diffusion process.

Problems endemic to field studies prevented us from (1) studying the downstream effects of social information processing on diffusion and (2) contrasting the diffusion of an innovation that was also a critical communication channel with the diffusion of a different type of technology[4]. These are important design issues that would greatly extend our understanding of the effects of proximity on innovation diffusion. Future research should also investigate the effects of more extensive telework. None of the workers in our sample indicated that they worked away from the office for more than 30 hours per week. We may notice different effects on diffusion and social networks with more extensive or with exclusive telework.

References

Abrahamson, E., & Rosenkopf, L. (1997). Social network effects on the extent of iInnovation diffusion: A Computer simulation. *Organization Science*, *8*(3), 289-309.

Baker, T., & Aldrich, H.E. (1996). Prometheus stretches: Building identity and cumulative knowledge in multi-employer careers. In M. Arthur & D. Rousseau (Eds.), *The boundaryless career* (pp. 123-149). Oxford: Oxford University Press.

Bandura, A. (1977). Self-efficacy: Toward a unifying theory of behavioral change. *Psychological Review*, *84*, 191-215.

Belanger, F., & Collins, R.W. (1998). Distributed work arrangements: A research framework. *The Information Society*, *14*, 137-152.

Belanger, F., Collins, R.W., & Cheney, P.H. (2001). Technology requirements and work group communication for telecommuters. *Information Systems Research*, *12*(2), 155-176.

Bhattacherjee, A., & Premkumar, G. (2004). Understanding changes in belief and attitude toward information technology usage: A theoretical model and longitudinal test. *MIS Quarterly*, *28*(2), 229-254.

Burkhardt, M.E. (1994). Social interaction effects following a technological change: A longitudinal investigation. *Academy of Management Journal*, *37*(4), 869-898.

Burt, R. (1995). *Structural holes: The social structure of competition.* Cambridge, MA: Harvard University Press.

Compeau, D.R., Higgins, C.A., & Huff, S.L. (1999). Social cognitive theory and individual reactions to computing technology: A longitudinal study. *MIS Quarterly, 23*(2), 145-158.

Cooper, C.D., & Kurland, N.B. (2002). Telecommuting, professional isolation, and employee development in public and private organizations. *Journal of Organization Behavior, 23*(4), 511-531.

Daft, R.L., & Lengel, R.H. (1986). Organizational information requirements, media richness, and structural design. *Management Science, 32*(5), 554-571.

Davenport, T.H., & Pearlson, K. (1998). Two cheers for the virtual office. *Sloan Management Review, 39*(4), 51-65.

Davis, F.D. (1989). Perceived usefulness, perceived ease of use, and user acceptance of information technology. *MIS Quarterly, 13*(3), 318-340.

Davis, F.D., Bagozzi, R.P., & Warshaw, P.R. (1992). Extrinsic and intrinsic motivation to use computers in the workplace. *Journal of Applied Social Psychology, 22*(14), 1111-1132.

Davis, F.D., Bagozzi, R.P., & Warshaw, P.R. (1989). User acceptance of computer technology: A comparison of two theoretical models. *Management Science, 35*(8), 982-1003.

Duarte, D., & Snyder, N. (1999). *Mastering virtual teams: Strategies, tools and techniques that succeed.* San Francisco: Jossey-Bass.

Festinger, L. (1957). *A theory of cognitive dissonance.* Evanston, IL: Row, Peterson.

Festinger, L., Schachter, S., & Back, K.W. (1950). *Social pressure in informal groups.* New York: Harper.

Ford, R.C., & Butts, M.A. (1991). Is your organization ready for telecommuting? *S.A.M. Advanced Management Journal, 56*(4), 19-23.

Frank, K.E., & Lowe, D.J. (2003). An examination of alternative work arrangements in private accounting practice. *Accounting Horizons, 17*(2), 139-151.

Fulk, J. (1993). Social construction of communication technology. *Academy of Management Journal, 36*(5), 921-950.

Fulk, J., Schmitz, J., & Steinfield, C.W. (1990). A social influence model of technology use. In J. Fulk & C. Steinfield (Eds.), *Organizations and communication technology* (pp. 117-141). Newbury Park, CA: Sage.

Galup, S., Saunders, C., Nelson, R., & Cerveny, R. (1997). The use of temporary staff and managers in a local government environment. *Communication Research, 24*(6), 698-730.

Gerber, B. (1995, April). Virtual teams. *Training*, 36-40.

Granovetter, M. (1973). The strength of weak ties. *American Journal of Sociology*, *78*(6), 1360-1380.

Hagerstrand, T. (1976). *Innovation as a spatial process.* Chicago: University of Chicago Press.

Hair, J.F., Anderson, R.E., Tatham, R.L., & Black, W.C. (1998). *Multivariate data analysis*. Upper Saddle River, NJ: Prentice Hall.

Hartman, R.I., Stoner, C.R., & Arora, R. (1991). An investigation of selected variables affecting telecommuting productivity and satisfaction. *Journal of Business and Psychology*, *6*(2), 207-225.

Hightower, R., & Sayeed, L. (1996). Effects of communication mode and prediscussion information distribution characteristics on information exchange in groups. *Information Systems Research*, *7*(4), 451-465.

Hollingshead, A.B. (1996). The rank-order effect in group decision making. *Organizational Behavior and Human Decision Processes*, *68*(3), 181-193.

Karahanna, E., Straub, D.W., & Chervany, N.L. (1999). Information technology adoption across time: A cross-sectional comparison of pre-adoption and post-adoption beliefs. *MIS Quarterly*, *23*(2), 183-213.

Kiesler, S. (1986, January-February). Thinking ahead: The hidden messages in computer networks. *Harvard Business Review*, 46-59.

Kimberly, J.R., & Evanisko, M.J. (1981). Organizational innovation: The influence of individual, organizational, and contextual factors on hospital adoption and technical and administrative innovations. *Academy of Management Journal*, *24*(4), 689-713.

Kock, N. (2001) Compensatory adaptation to a lean medium: An action research investigation of electronic communication in process improvement groups. *IEEE Transactions on Professional Communication*, *44*(4), 267-285.

Kraut, R.E., Rice, R.E., Cool, C., & Fish, R.S. (1998). Varieties of social influence: The role of utility and norms in the success of a new communication medium. *Organization Science*, *9*(4), 437-453.

Kugelmass, J. (1996). *Telecommuting: A manager's guide to flexible work arrangements*. New York: Lexington Books.

Lee, A.S. (1994). Electronic mail as a medium for rich communication: An empirical investigation using hermeneutic interpretation. *MIS Quarterly*, *18*, 143-157.

Markus, M.L. (1994). Electronic mail as the medium of managerial choice. *Organization Science*, *5*(4), 502-527.

Marsden, P.V. (1987). Core discussion networks of Americans. *American Sociological Review*, *52*, 122-131.

Maruca, R.F. (1998, July-August). How do you manage an off-site team? *Harvard Business Review*, 22-35.

Maznevski, M.L., & Chudoba, K.M. (2000). Bridging space over time: Global virtual team dynamics and effectiveness. *Organization Science*, *11*(5), 473-492.

McGrath, J.E., Arrow, H., Gruenfeld, D.H., Hollingshead, A.B., & O'Connor, K.M. (1993). Groups, tasks, and technology: The effects of experience and change. *Small Group Research*, *24*(3), 406-420.

Moore, G.C., & Benbasat, I. (1991). Development of an iInstrument to measure the pPerceptions of adoptiong an information technology innovation. *Information Systems Research*, *2*(3), 192-222.

Nelson, R.E. (1986). Social networks and organizational intervention: Insights from an area-wide labor-management committee. *Journal of Applied Behavioral Science*, *22*, 65-76.

Nelson, R.R., & Cheney, P.H. (1987). Training end users: An exploratory study. *MIS Quarterly*, *11*(4), 547-559.

Nilles, J.M. (1994). *Making telecommuting happen. A guide for telemanagers and telecommuters*. New York: Van Nostrand Reinhold.

Orlikowski, W. (1996). Improvising organizational transformation over time: A situated change perspective. *Information Systems Research*, *7*(1), 63-92.

Ouchi, W.G. (1979). A conceptual framework for the design of organizational control mechanisms. *Management Science*, *25*(9), 833-848.

Owen-Smith, J., & Powell, W.W. (2004). Knowledge networks as channels and conduits: the effects of spillovers in the Boston biotechnology community. *Organization Science*, *15*(1), 5-21

Raghuram, S., Wiesenfeld, B., & Garud, R. (1996). Distance and propinquity: A new way to conceptualize work. *Proceedings of Telecommuting '96*, Jacksonville, Florida.

Ramsower, R. (1985). *Telecommuting: The organizational and behavioral effects of working at home*. Ann Arbor, MI: UMI Research Press.

Reinsch, N.L. (1997). Relationships between telecommuting workers and their managers: An exploratory study. *The Journal of Business Communication*, *34*(4), 343-369.

Rice, R.E., & Aydin, C. (1991). Attitudes toward new organizational technology: Network proximity as a mechanism for social information processing. *Administrative Science Quarterly*, *36*(2), 219-244.

Rogers, E.W. (1983). *Diffusion of innovationsI.* New York: The Free Press.

Rogers, E.W. (1995). *Diffusion of innovationsI.* New York: The Free Press.

Salancik, G.R., & Pfeffer, J. (1978). A social information processing approach to job attitudes and task design. *Administrative Science Quarterly, 23*(2), 224-253.

Saunders, C.S., & Jones, J.W. (1990). Temporal sequences in information acquisition for decision-making: A focus on source and medium. *Academy of Management Review, 15*(1), 29-46.

Schepp, D., & Schepp, B. (1995). *The telecommuter's handbook.* New York: McGraw-Hill.

Sherman, J.D., Smith, H.L., & Mansfield, E.R. (1986). The impact of emergent network structure on organizational socialization. *Journal of Applied Behavioral Science, 22*(1), 53-63.

Sims, H.P., Szilagyi, A.D., & Keller, R.T. (1976). The measurement of job characteristics. *Academy of Management Journal, 19*, 195-212.

Straub, D., & Karahanna, E. (1998). Knowledge worker communications and recipient availability: Toward a task closure explanation of media choice. *Organization Science, 9*(2), 160-175.

Taylor, S., & Todd, P.A. (1995). Assessing IT usage: The role of prior experience. *MIS Quarterly, 19*(4), 561-570.

Tornatzky, L.G., & Klein, K.J. (1992). Innovation characteristics and innovation adoption implementation: A meta-analysis of findings. *IEEE Transactions on Engineering Management, 29*, 28-45.

Venkatesh, A., & Vitalari, N.P. (1992). An emerging distributed work arrangement: An investigation of computer-based supplemental work at home. *Management Science, 38*(12), 1687-1706.

Venkatesh, V. (1999). Creation of favorable user perceptions: Exploring the role of intrinsic motivation. *MIS Quarterly, 23*(2), 239-260.

Venkatesh, V. (2000). Determinants of perceived ease of use: Integrating control, intrinsic motivation, and emotion into the technology acceptance model. *Information Systems Research, 11*(4), 342-365.

Watad, M.M., & DiSanzo, F.J. (2000). Case study: The synergism of telecommuting and office automation. *Sloan Management Review, 41*(2), 85-96.

Weisenfeld, B., Garud, R., & Raghuram, S. (1997). Communication modes as determinants of organizational identification in a virtual organization. *Proceedings of the Academy of Management Conference*, Boston, Massachusetts.

Wellman, B., Salaff, J., Dimitrina, D., & Garton, L. (1996). Computer networks as social networks: Collaborative work, telework, and virtual community. *Annual Review of Sociology.*

Yoshioka, G.A., & Athanasiou, R. (1971). Effect of site plan and social status variables on distance to friends' home. *American Psychological Association Proceedings, 6*, 273-274.

Endnotes

[1] A survey of 17 non-respondents on surveys 2 and 3 of Stage 1 indicated that 41% didn't complete the surveys because they lacked time, 18% misplaced the surveys, 18% claimed they hadn't received them, and 23% said they had completed them, but they probably hadn't reached the researcher due to some administrative problems.

[2] Since the training was not hands-on, immediate perceptions could not be expected to have any basis in the respondents' experience and were, therefore, not solicited.

[3] One item was dropped for cross-loading

[4] The participating company sold the division that was the focus of this study before we could investigate a second innovation, as was initially planned. Other research constraints included questionnaire length (i.e., limited to one page) and the kinds of questions that could be asked (i.e., precluded from asking specific questions regarding organizational position, etc.).

Appendix A: Stage 1 Questionnaire

We are interested in tracking your communication needs and comfort level using e-mail, now and throughout our conversion to the new system. Please use the scales provided to respond to the following questions.

PERCEIVED USEFULNESS QUESTIONS

Strongly Agree 1	Agree 2	Neutral 3	Disagree 4	Strongly Disagree 5

_____ Using e-mail in my job enables me to accomplish tasks more quickly.
_____ Using e-mail increases my productivity.
_____ Using e-mail enhances my effectiveness on the job.
_____ Using e-mail improves my job performance.
_____ Using e-mail makes it easier to do my job.
_____ I find e-mail useful in my job.

PERCEIVED EASE-OF-USE QUESTIONS

Not at all	A little	A moderate amount	To a great extent	To a very great extent
1	2	3	4	5

_____ Learning to use our e-mail system was easy for me.
_____ I find it easy to get e-mail to do what I want it to do.
_____ My interaction with our e-mail system is clear and understandable.
_____ I find our e-mail system to be flexible to interact with.
_____ It was easy for me to become skillful at using our e-mail system.
_____ I find our e-mail system easy to use.

INTERDEPENDENCE QUESTIONS

Strongly Agree	Agree	Neutral	Disagree	Strongly Disagree
1	2	3	4	5

_____ How much of your job depends upon your ability to work with others?
_____ To what extent do you complete work that has been started by another employee?
_____ To what extent is dealing with other people a part of your job?
_____ How much feedback do you receive from individuals other than your manager?

TELEWORK QUESTIONS

None	1-15 hours	16-30 hours	31-45 hours	>45 hours
1	2	3	4	5

_____ How many hours per week do you work away from your office location *during* your regular work hours?
_____ How many hours per week do you work away from your office location *outside* your regular work hours?
_____ How much time do you spend during the regular work day away from your office location *on work that you would normally do at your office*?

_____ How much time do you spend after-hours each week away from your office location *on work that you would normally do at your office?*

Appendix B: Stage 2 Questionnaire

E-MAIL SURVEY

We would like to understand how you have continued to learn about the new e-mail system since the initial training session. Please take a few moments and use the scale below to respond to the following three questions.

Never 1	Rarely 2	Sometimes 3	Often 4	Always 5

1. When I have a problem with e-mail, I look for a solution:

_____ in books, magazines, or manuals (SOURCE USAGE: INDIVIDUAL).
_____ from the help desk (SOURCE USAGE: AUTHORITY).
_____ from other IS staff (SOURCE USAGE: AUTHORITY).
_____ from coworkers (SOURCE USAGE: COLLECTIVE).
_____ from other business acquaintances (SOURCE USAGE: COLLECTIVE).
_____ in training videos (SOURCE USAGE: INDIVIDUAL).
_____ by talking with people over the phone (MEDIA USAGE: PHONE).
_____ by interacting with people via e-mail (MEDIA USAGE: E-MAIL).
_____ by talking with people face-to-face (MEDIA USAGE: FACE-TO-FACE).

2. I learn about new e-mail features:

_____ from books, magazines, or manuals (SOURCE USAGE: INDIVIDUAL).
_____ from the help desk (SOURCE USAGE: AUTHORITY).
_____ from other IS staff (SOURCE USAGE: AUTHORITY).
_____ from coworkers (SOURCE USAGE: COLLECTIVE).
_____ from other business acquaintances (SOURCE USAGE: COLLECTIVE).
_____ in training videos (SOURCE USAGE: INDIVIDUAL).

_____ by talking with people over the phone (MEDIA USAGE: PHONE).
_____ by interacting with people via e-mail (MEDIA USAGE: E-MAIL).
_____ by talking with people face-to-face (MEDIA USAGE: FACE-TO-FACE).

3. I learn about new ways to use e-mail on my job:
_____ from books, magazines, or manuals (SOURCE USAGE: INDIVIDUAL).
_____ from the help desk (SOURCE USAGE: AUTHORITY).
_____ from other IS staff (SOURCE USAGE: AUTHORITY).
_____ from coworkers (SOURCE USAGE: COLLECTIVE).
_____ from other business acquaintances (SOURCE USAGE: COLLECTIVE).
_____ in training videos (SOURCE USAGE: INDIVIDUAL).
_____ by talking with people over the phone (MEDIA USAGE: PHONE).
_____ by interacting with people via e-mail (MEDIA USAGE: E-MAIL).
_____ by talking with people face-to-face (MEDIA USAGE: FACE-TO-FACE).

The chapter was previously published in the International Journal of e-Collaboration, 1(3), 35-57, July-September 2005.

Chapter IX

Internet-Based Customer Collaboration: Dyadic and Community-Based Modes of Co-Production

Ulrike Schultze, Southern Methodist University, USA

Anita D. Bhappu, Southern Methodist University, USA

Abstract

Co-production, which is the generation of value through the direct involvement of customers in the creation of a service context and in the design, delivery, and marketing of goods and services that they themselves consume, implies customer-firm collaboration. The nature of this collaboration, however, is highly dependent on the organization's service design, which increasingly includes Internet technology, as well as customer communities. Whereas dyadic co-production implies a single customer's involvement with a firm, community-based co-production implies multiple customers simultaneously engaged in value-adding activities with a firm. In order to build a theoretical understanding of these modes of customer collaboration and to explore the role and implications of Internet technologies within them, we develop a contingency theory of customer co-production designs. We then use cases of Internet-based services to highlight the benefits and challenges of relying on Internet technology to implement customer co-production.

Introduction

E-collaboration, which entails collaboration among individuals using electronic technologies to complete a common task (Kock, 2005), is prevalent in today's service sector, where it frequently takes the form of customer co-production enabled by Internet technologies. As the image of the customer as passive audience and consumer is being replaced by one of the customer as an active co-creator of value (Prahalad & Ramaswamy, 2000), organizations increasingly view their customers as resources that contribute both knowledge and labor to the production process (Larsson & Bowen, 1989). This form of customer collaboration (or co-laboring) is not only evident in business-to-business (B2B) service delivery, where organizations' supply chains are becoming vertically integrated (e.g., Walmart shares daily sales information with Procter & Gamble), but also in business-to-customer (B2C) service environments where customers' actions not only trigger but also complete a transaction (e.g., customers assembling their IKEA furniture themselves) (Normann & Ramirez, 1993).

Internet technologies (e.g., e-mail, interactive Web sites, self-service applications) create new opportunities for customer co-production. For instance, customers increasingly purchase travel services, books and other products online. They do online research about their medical symptoms before they see a health service provider (e.g., Hogg et al., 2003), and they increasingly check their bank balance or the status of a delivery online instead of calling a customer service representative. As such, customers are increasingly co-laboring in the production of the goods and services that they themselves consume.

Customer co-production, however, is not limited to situations in which Internet technology is used to facilitate the dyadic interaction between an individual customer and a firm. Instead, collaborative Internet technologies (e.g., listservs, discussion boards and wikis) have created new opportunities for community-based forms of customer co-production. For instance, online gamers rely on a community of players to create the entertainment value of a collaborative game. The medical information that patients consult is frequently generated by a community of people who have had first-hand experience with a given condition. eBay would not exist if not for its community of buyers and sellers that create its dynamic and eclectic marketplace. Similarly, personal network services such as MySpace and LinkedIn also rely on a community of customers to co-produce the value of their services.

Internet technologies present both opportunities and challenges for the design and delivery of services in general (Bitner, Ostrom, & Meuter, 2002), and customer co-production in particular. This is because the Internet facilitates a "shift in the role of the customer – from isolated to connected, from unaware to informed, from passive to active" (Prahalad & Ramaswamy, 2005: 2). For instance, by providing access to information in a cost-effective way (Malone, Yates, & Benjamin, 1987), Internet technologies erode the information asymmetry that has traditionally characterized many customer-firm interfaces (Kulkarni, 2000). This can create significant challenges for service providers.

For example, Hogg et al.'s (2003) report that the healthcare consultation process changed significantly as customers increasingly went online to learn about medical conditions and treatment options. Whereas the consultation process used to be one in which the health care provider acted as the primary source of information, advice, and decision-making, in the Internet-enabled service environment, the health care provider acts as interpreter and evaluator of information that patients gather from multiple online sources. Thus, as patients became more active co-creators of their own treatment, the interaction and power dynamics of the dyadic patient-provider relationship changed.

Furthermore, using Internet technology in community-based modes of co-production presents numerous opportunities and challenges for firms. Von Hippel (2005) cites many examples of customer-led innovations such as the open source movement, which would have been very difficult to achieve without the Internet. However, the lack of physical controls and social presence online proves especially challenging in community-based modes of co-production. For instance, even though eBay was founded on the beliefs that people were essentially 'good,' meaning that participants would transact business in an honorable manner and that the community could police itself through a reputation rating system, over time, eBay has had to implement a number of safeguards to protect its participants from fraud. These safeguards include insurance, an escrow service, policing of posting (to prevent illegal items from being offered), and taking disciplinary actions against violators. Thus, one key challenge in the community-based model of co-production is the policing of inappropriate and even illegal behavior on the part of customers.

In this book chapter, we seek to explore the opportunities and challenges surrounding the dyadic and community-based modes of Internet-based customer co-production. To this end, we will develop a multi-dimensional definition of customer co-production,which we distinguish between the dyadic and community-based modes. In order to develop an understanding of the role and implications of Internet technology in customer co-production, we then present a framework for classifying different co-production designs. Next, we describe and analyze three cases in which Internet technology was used to instantiate a co-production design. We identify some of the opportunities and challenges that Internet technology creates in each of these cases. We close with suggestions for future research.

Customer Co-Production

The notion of co-production has a substantial history in the public sector. As city and state governments struggle with limited resources, they typically look to citizens to volunteer their time and to assist public-sector service providers with labor and information. In the public administration literature, co-production is thus defined as "direct citizen involvement in the design and delivery of city services with professional service agents" (Brudney & England, 1983), and "the degree of overlap between two sets of participants—regular producers and consumers" (Brudney & England, 1983). Co-production, therefore, implies collaboration (or co-laboring) between customers and service providers[1].

Co-production is generally associated with services rather than goods (Bowen & Jones, 1986; Larsson & Bowen, 1989). This is because services are intangible and need to be consumed at the time of production lest their value be lost (Mills & Margulies, 1980). Thus, the utility of a service depends on the customer who completes the service by consuming it (Ramirez, 1999). For instance, performing a play to an empty house or flying an empty plane is value lost. Also, the consumption of services typically relies on customers interacting with service providers. Indeed, the service production function is considered to be relational (Bell, 1976), which implies that value, in the form of customer experience, for instance, is created at the point of interaction between the customer and the firm (Prahalad & Ramaswamy, 2004). Lastly, human services such as medical care, education, and psychiatric counseling, which seek to affect the personal transformation of the consumer, require customers to actively participate in the generation of value, e.g., eating less to losing weight (Dellande, Gilly, & Graham, 2004) or studying to learn a new skill.

This does not mean, however, that co-production is confined to service industries, e.g., banking, retail, transportation, insurance, health care, and education. Instead, as Normann and Ramirez's (1993) description of IKEA's co-production strategy highlights, the distinction between goods and services tends to be equivocal and fluid (Gershuny, 1978; Vargo & Lusch, 2004). By unbundling the assembly service from the finished good, IKEA invites its customers to co-produce the value of their (unassembled) furniture. In contrast, most furniture manufacturers subsume the service of assembly in the finished, tangible good. This highlights not only the equivocality of the boundary between goods and services, but also that co-production is not limited to services.

Whitaker (1980) defines co-production in terms of three dimensions: (i) requesting assistance, (ii) cooperation, and (iii) mutual adjustment. This categorization scheme provides us with a starting point for developing a multi-dimensional definition of co-production. The different dimensions of co-production in our framework, Figure 1, are activity, mode of cooperation, and type of interdependence. The activity dimension describes *what* customers do to co-produce value, whereas the coop-

Figure 1. Multi-dimensional definition of customer co-production

Dimensions	Elements			
Activity	Organizational Citizenship Behaving Appropriately	Design Determining Requirements; Making Custom Request	Delivery Completing / Producing Good or Service	Marketing Recommending and Referring
Mode of Cooperation	Customer Motivation Voluntary vs Involuntary (Compliant)		Customer Participation Active vs Passive	
Type of Interdependence (customer-provider and customer-customer)	Sequential Planned Coordination	Pooled Standardized Coordination	Reciprocal Mutual Adjustment	

eration and interdependence dimensions describe *how* customers co-produce, i.e., their motivation for co-producing and the nature of the customer-provider and/or customer-customer interdependence.

Activity

Engaging in *organizational citizenship* behavior, i.e., behaving appropriately and in a way that creates a congenial social context (Lengnick-Hall, Claycomb, & Inks, 2000), is especially important when the service takes place in a social setting. For instance, travelers on a flight co-produce a safe flight by obeying the orders of the crew, e.g., fastening seatbelts and clearing the aisles.

When customers develop a clearer understanding of their needs and make a request for service (either custom or standard), they are engaged in the *design* activity. Von Hippel's (2005) research on customer-led innovation provides numerous examples of customers engaged in co-design. However, according to Whitaker's (1980), the simple act of requesting assistance is also an example of a design activity. The degree of customer involvement in design depends on the input uncertainty relating to the service (Argote, 1982). For instance, when service options are well defined and customers have a clear understanding of their needs (low input uncertainty), the act of requesting assistance merely triggers a service. However, when the information required to determine the features of products or services is highly equivocal (high input uncertainty), the task of requesting assistance becomes more complex and more difficult to structure. Also, to the extent that service organizations treat customers' requests for assistance as feedback on their extant services, requesting assistance shapes the design of both current and future goods and services.

Delivery, on the other hand, consists of the customer's completion of or participation in the production of goods and services. The degree of customer involvement in delivery varies depending on the performance ambiguity associated with the product being consumed (Bowen & Jones, 1986; Siehl, Bowen, & Pearson, 1992). For instance, when it is difficult to assess service quality or attribute service outcomes to provider performance, services are characterized by high performance ambiguity. Examples of services with high performance ambiguity include fitness training and weight loss programs, where it is difficult to fault the trainer or program counselor if a client does not lose weight. This is because successful outcomes are also dependent on customers' active participation in the production process (e.g., exercise and eat healthier foods).

The *marketing* activities that customers engage in remain largely invisible to providers and firms (Chervonnaya, 2003). Therefore, they are frequently omitted from definitions of co-production. Nevertheless, marketing is not only beneficial to the provider firm (e.g., word of mouth advertising), but also to the customer, especially if the product or service in question is subject to network effects (e.g., fax machines and instant messaging become more valuable to the individual when more people use it.

Mode of Cooperation

To cooperate means to work jointly or to unite to produce an effect. The cooperation dimension applies equally to dyadic and community-based modes of co-production. For instance, a customer might work with a provider to develop the custom specifications of a piece of software. Alternatively, the customer might collaborate with other software developers to write an open-source version of an application (von Hippel, 2005).

Based on Brudney and England's (1983) work, we conceptualize cooperation as a mode, that is, the how and why of a customer's participation in value creation. For instance, Brudney and England (1983) point out that, ideally, customers should cooperate voluntarily in co-production activities, but that there is a fine line between *voluntary and involuntary (or compliant)* cooperation in the public sector. For instance, for effective sanitation, residents are expected to move their trash to the curb on a given day of the week. Failure to comply with these rules of co-production typically results in fines, suggesting that customer behavior is motivated by compliance rather than voluntary cooperation.

Brudney and England (1983) also distinguish between *active and passive* cooperation. Active cooperation implies that customers purposefully engage in design, delivery or marketing activities. Passive cooperation implies that customers refrain from disruptive behavior and thereby enable other producers to do their work. For instance, by posting only legitimate and legal sales items on eBay, a seller co-produces an efficient and effective online marketplace.

Even though Brudney and England (1983) maintain that, in theory, co-production should be limited to voluntary and active cooperation, they acknowledge that, in practice, it is difficult to determine when behavior is motivated by voluntary or involuntary cooperation. Furthermore, passive cooperation tends to be invisible (Chervonnaya, 2003), suggesting that firms are unlikely to consider it in their co-production design until, for instance, consumers actively engage in disruptive behavior or stop behaving in the same, taken-for-granted manner.

Type of Interdependence

Our third dimension of co-production encompasses Whitaker's (1980) notion of mutual adjustment. Mutual adjustment occurs when participants in either a customer-customer or a customer-provider relationship, base their actions on their joint consideration of the issues. This is accomplished through considerable communication and the reciprocal modification of each party's expectations and actions. In personal or human services, where the goal is to transform the customer (particularly his/her behavior), developing an understanding of the customer's problems, needs and/or wishes requires mutual adjustment throughout the design and delivery process, and it may even call for mutual transformation (e.g., the teacher learning from students, and students learning from each other).

According to Thompson (1967), mutual adjustment is the most appropriate coordination mechanism in situations where participants' actions are *reciprocally interdependent.* For instance, a psychologist's ability to help patients is dependent on the patient's ability and willingness to trust him/her. Unless patients voluntarily share their hopes, fears and dreams with the psychologist, it is unlikely that the psychologist can adjust his/her treatment to their needs. In contrast, when participants are *sequentially interdependent*, the most effective coordination mechanism is planning. For instance, organizations forecast what their stock levels or service capacities need to be in order to satisfy consumers' demands. In situations of *pooled interdependence*, coordination is best achieved through standardization. For instance, collaborative filtering technologies, on which recommendation systems like the one used by Amazon.com are built, rely on a pool (or data warehouse) of customers' ratings of books and music. To make these diverse ratings available for analysis, they have to be in a standardized format. We include all three forms of interdependence and their related coordination mechanisms in our definition of co-production as Larsson and Bowen (1989) highlight that all three are manifest in co-production.

In summary, our multi-dimensional definition of co-production suggests that customers are valuable resources in the creation of a service context and in the design, delivery, and marketing of goods and services because they add vaule with their knowledge, skill, and labor. Depending on the specific combination of activity, mode of cooperation, and type of interdependence, co-production can take different forms. For instance, co-production can be as limited as a customer voluntarily requesting assistance to set up telephone service, which triggers a sequentially interdependent service delivery process that is relatively devoid of customer involvement (see Figure 2a). Alternatively, co-production can be as extensive as a cancer patient repeatedly interacting with his/her oncologist, compliantly undergoing a series of radiation treatments that require the patient to actively take medications, and keeping the oncologist informed of symptoms after each treatment (see Figure 2b). As such, our multi-dimensional definition of co-production can be represented as a cube, which defines a specific service. Each side of the cube represents one of the dimensions in Figure 1. By specifying all three of the dimensions in our 'co-production cube,' we can assess the degree of customer co-production in different service environments.

Figure 2. 'Co-production cube'

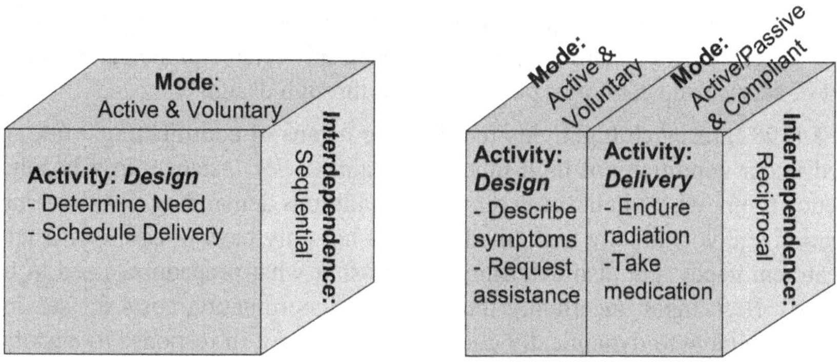

Figure 2a:

Requesting Phone Service

Figure 2b:

Undergoing Cancer Treatment

A Contingency Framework of Co-Production Designs

Similar to prior research on organizational design, we take a contingency approach to specifying the most effective forms of co-production in different service environments. While it is not always clear what the important design contingencies are and how they relate to organizational forms (Argote, 1982), there is considerable consensus that uncertainty is a contingency central to organizational design (Galbraith, 1973). In the context of service design, *input uncertainty* is a key contingency (Siehl et al., 1992) because it describes a firm's lack of information about the overall composition of customer inputs. Input uncertainty "is expressed as a function of the number of choices or alternatives in a given situation, e.g., patient conditions [encountered by a hospital emergency room], and of the probability of various alternatives occurring" (Argote, 1982). Larsson and Bowen (1989) define input uncertainty as incomplete information about the what, when, where, and how of the customer's input.

Input uncertainty can be expressed in terms of the amount and equivocality of information needed from the customer. We consider information equivocality the more crucial design contingency because organizations can reduce the amount of information they need by limiting their service offerings, thereby reducing input uncertainty through design. Equivocality describes whether information is of doubtful significance and whether it can be interpreted in different ways. For example, a request for something "hot" to eat could be interpreted as meaning "warm" or "spicy." Therefore, information equivocality is closely related to the nature of the product or service and cannot be easily reduced through design.

Argote's (1982) research highlights that flexible means of coordinating work are required under conditions of high input uncertainty. For instance, in a hospital emergency room, where both the diversity of conditions demanding treatment and information equivocality are high, medical staff not only have to carefully establish treatment needs, but also determine on-the-spot what procedures need to be performed. High input uncertainty thus increases coordination costs for service providers who have to dynamically coordinate their work in response to customers' equivocal requests for assistance. A scripted repertoire of responses cannot be developed in such situations, and programmed coordination mechanisms such as rules and authority structures are not the most effective means of coordinating (Argote, 1982).

Performance ambiguity is another key design contingency highlighted in the service literature (Siehl et al., 1992; Bowen & Jones, 1986). As mentioned earlier, performance ambiguity refers to the difficulty of assessing service or product quality (Ouchi, 1980). It is related to the intangibility of the object being exchanged and its complexity, i.e., the difficulty of establishing the role and value of each component's contribution to the quality of the good or service. For example, performance ambiguity is relatively high in education because it is difficult to assess students' knowledge before the commencement and after the completion of an educational program. Furthermore, even if one could assess students' learning, it would be difficult to attribute success or failure to the educational program due to the ambiguity of the cause-effect relationships in the learning process. Given the reciprocal interdependence in most human service settings, assessing the value of contributions made by individual resources is problematic (Bowen & Jones, 1986). This is especially true when co-production is community-based rather than dyadic in nature.

Performance ambiguity is a design contingency frequently applied in transaction cost economics (Ouchi, 1980), a theory concerned with the boundary of firms (Williamson, 1975). High performance ambiguity implies high transaction costs because the product or service being exchanged is not completely contractible, which makes it difficult to assess whether the exchange was equitable. For instance, when a service provider is highly dependent on a customer for the successful delivery of a service, it is difficult to establish the value contributed by the service provider (Ouchi, 1980). Therefore, parties to the exchange must actively monitor the service delivery process to ensure equity. Such monitoring implies high transaction costs for the firm, especially if co-production is community based rather than dyadic

When transaction costs are high, goods or services should be produced within the firm so that it can rely on its employment relations and, ultimately, fiat to manage incomplete contracts (Williamson, 1991). Where performance ambiguity is high, hierarchical organizational designs are the most effective. If performance ambiguity is low, however, exchange participants can establish complete and enforceable contracts to govern the exchange. Thus transaction costs are relatively low, and markets are the most effective way of managing the exchange.

The literature on service design (e.g., Bowen & Jones, 1986; Jones, 1987) relies on transaction cost economics to determine whether to locate customers inside or outside the firm. In this research, customers are referred to as "partial" (Mills & Morris, 1986) or "transient" (Namasivayam, 2003) employees, and service designs based on long-term customer-provider relationships are labeled "hierarchies" (Bowen & Jones, 1986; Jones, 1987). Given Williamson's (1991) later work, however, organizational forms that are characterized by long-term customer-provider relationships should be called "hybrids" – or "networks" (Thompson, 2003) – rather than "hierarchies," as they reside between the two discrete structural alternatives of markets and hierarchies. The label "hierarchy" should be reserved for organizational designs characterized by a legally recognized organizational boundary. Furthermore, the notion of customers becoming part of the firm is foreign to transaction cost economics because contracts with employees are very different from those with customers (Williamson, 1991).

Figure 3. Co-production design framework

		Performance Ambiguity	
		Low	High
Input Uncertainty	Low	*Quadrant I* **Scripted Market** - Booking airline tickets - Virtual trading (e.g., Marketocracy)	*Quadrant II* **Scripted Relationship** - Buying IKEA furniture - Weight-loss program
	High	*Quadrant III* **Personalized Market** - Hospital emergency rooms - Book recommendations (eg., Amazon)	*Quadrant IV* **Personalized Relationship** - Post-Graduate education - Citizen newspaper (e.g., Bayosphere)

In our contingency framework of co-production designs (see Figure 3), we call the two structural alternatives for exchange relations between providers and customers "markets" and "relationships." Markets are most effective under conditions of low performance ambiguity, whereas relationships are most effective under conditions of high performance ambiguity. Similarly, we label the two methods of coordination co-production activities as "scripted" and "personalized." Scripted modes of coordination are most effective under conditions of low input uncertainty, whereas personalized modes of coordination are most effective under conditions of high input uncertainty. The four resulting co-production designs (quadrants) are: Scripted Market, Scripted Relationship, Personalized Market, and Personalized Relationship.

Quadrant I. Scripted Market

The scripted market bears much resemblance to Mills and Margulies' (1980) *maintenance interactive service organization* and Larsson and Bowen's (1989) *sequential standardized service design*. The customer-firm interface is characterized by low information equivocality and programmed decisions on the part of service providers. Customer requests are limited to an established set of service options, leaving little room for customers to influence service design. By standardizing service options and scripting the customer-firm interface, firms can program their service delivery process. For these same reasons, individual service providers are interchangeable, preventing customers and employees from forming interpersonal ties. Performance ambiguity is low due to the tangibility of the product and/or the low complexity of the service production process.

According to Mills and Margulies (1980), this form of co-production is particularly prevalent in consumer banking. Bank tellers, for example, typically handle a predetermined set of customer service requests, which are associated with standardized processes that require the bank tellers to make routine decisions. By scripting the customer-firm interface and programming service delivery processes, banks can offer low-cost (Larsson & Bowen, 1989) yet reliable (Mills & Margulies, 1980) banking services to customers. However, because the bank and its customers are sequentially interdependent, the customer must actively request assistance in order to initiate the delivery of standardized banking services.

Virtual trading services, like those supported Marketocracy.com, represent an example of community-based co-production. Marketocracy is an investment management firm, which runs a league of 70,000 virtual traders. It then takes a lead from the best-performing virtual portfolios to shape its investment strategy for its real mutual fund. While the virtual trading part of Marketocracy's service is indicative of both low information equivocality (i.e., traders know what stocks they are buying and selling), and low performance ambiguity (i.e., traders are responsible for their portfolio's yield), the service related to Marketocracy's 'real' mutual fund seems to reflect higher performance ambiguity. This is due to the firm's reliance on its virtual traders, who may also be their customers, for its investment decisions. Marketocracy's 'real' investment service, therefore falls into the scripted relationship quadrant, which will be discussed next.

Quadrant II. Scripted Relationship

Neither Mills and Margulies (1980) nor Larsson and Bowen (1989) identify a service design that closely resembles the scripted relationship. However, Bowen and Jones (1986) do identify an *impersonal hierarchy service design* that bears some resemblance to the scripted relationship. They suggest that standardized, hierarchical exchanges will only take place when organizations, such as monopolistic service providers (e.g., utility companies), can impose agreements unilaterally on their captive customers. Another example of an impersonal hierarchy is the penitentiary, where the process of rehabilitation is located within the prison's organizational boundaries, and inmates' participation is coerced through rules and authority structures. Bowen and Jones (1986) highlight that—in the face of high performance ambiguity—customers would be willing to become partial employees in a highly structured production process only under such supra-normal conditions.

The main difference between our conceptualization of the scripted relationship and Bowen and Jones' (1986) impersonal hierarchy is that we do not regard organizational forms, which require high customer participation throughout the delivery process, as hierarchies. In our framework, the customers remain outside of the organization's boundaries even as they form and sustain close, long-term relationships with their service providers.

An example of a scripted relationship is the co-production design at IKEA (Normann & Ramirez, 1993) where customers purchase unassembled furniture, transport it themselves, and then assemble it at home. By voluntarily doing some of the work in an otherwise sequentially interdependent production process, customers are able to purchase furniture at IKEA for lower prices. Information equivocality in this setting is relatively low. Not only is furniture tangible and can be described in precise terms (e.g., size, type of wood), but customers can also see and touch the assembled furniture in the IKEA store before they purchase it. The tangibility of the product also implies that there are a finite number of ways in which the furniture can be assembled. Thus, the process of furniture assembly can be scripted and compiled into a set of instructions.

However, performance ambiguity is relatively high as IKEA's service delivery process relies on customers to complete the production process. Thus, the respective contributions of and the causal relationships between resources (furniture pieces, assembly instructions, customer) and outcomes (assembled furniture) are ambiguous. What if the assembled furniture wobbles or is misaligned? Who is responsible for this ostensible failure —the furniture designer or the customer? IKEA's generous return policy seems to acknowledge this high performance ambiguity, as the organization relies on trust to manage the incomplete contract with its customers. For instance, IKEA seems to trust customers to put forward their best effort to comply with the furniture assembly instructions, and customers appear to trust IKEA to only sell furniture that they can indeed assemble on their own.

Quadrant III. Personalized Market

The personalized market bears much resemblance to Mills and Margulies' (1980) *task interactive service organization* and Larsson and Bowen's (1989) *sequential customized service design* where customers' task specifications precede providers' production of goods and services. The customer-firm interface is focused on task accomplishment based on customers' personal specifications. In the personalized market, performance ambiguity is low due to the tangibility and/or low complexity of the good or service. However, information equivocality is high in the personalized market, implying that the identification of the customers' requirements and expectations is challenging and that the decisions that service providers have to make are non-routine. Furthermore, the uniqueness of each customer's request means that the coordination of production activities cannot be programmed, but must remain flexible and adaptable.

An example of a personalized market is a hospital emergency room where the range of customers' medical needs is difficult to anticipate. Treatment activities are therefore defined and dynamically coordinated in response to an incoming patient's symptoms and conditions. Diagnostic decisions are complex because health care providers have to accurately evaluate test data in combination with equivocal information from the patient about his/her condition, which may also be difficult to elicit, especially if the patient is unconscious or in trauma. Therefore, input uncertainty is high. However, performance ambiguity is relatively low because stabilizing the patient's condition is the responsibility of the medical staff on call and the patient's participation is limited to requesting medical care and responding to questions about his/her condition.

The Amazon book recommendation service is a community-based co-production example of the personalized market design. However, as this case will be discussed in detail in the next section, we will not elaborate on it here.

Quadrant IV. Personalized Relationship

Personalized relationships bear close resemblance to Mills and Margulies' (1980) *personal interactive service organization*, whose primary objective is to provide services that transform the individual customer through non-programmed coordination and monitoring. Examples include education and counseling. Personalized relationships also reflect characteristics of Larsson and Bowen's (1989) *reciprocal service design*, which is marked by reciprocal interdependence and mutual adjustment between service provider and customer. Customer input is required throughout the delivery process to ensure that the final outcome (good or service) is aligned with customers' needs and expectations.

Performance ambiguity in the personalized relationship is high. To manage this ambiguity, organizations rely on social attachment (Mills & Margulies, 1980) and embedded relationships (Uzzi, 1999) between customers and service providers. Service provider interchangeability is therefore low (Mills & Margulies, 1980). These embedded relationships engender norms of reciprocity and trust, which are key to motivating customers to actively participate in value co-creation.

A good example of personalized relationships is post-graduate education, where performance ambiguity is high due to the intangibility of the product and the high degree of reciprocal interdependence between faculty and graduate students. For instance, students typically generate a lot of new ideas, which faculty then help them refine. In this way, students learn skills and gain a better understanding of a topic area. At the same time, faculty rely on their students' ideas and labor to further their own careers, for instance, by staying up-to-date with topics and by writing joint publications with their students.

Information equivocality at both the design and delivery stage is high. For instance, it is difficult for students to articulate what they mean by and expect from a "good education" and where their research interests lie. When it then comes to writing the thesis, information equivocality is again high. Ideas, literature reviews and experiments that the candidate believes are moving him/her toward the completion of the thesis, might be interpreted very differently by the thesis committee.

Given the high input uncertainty and high performance ambiguity, both faculty and student tend to rely on long-term relationships and the social capital inherent in it (e.g., sense of obligation and reciprocity) to manage the exchange. Thus, thesis advisors allow their students to graduate even though they may believe that the thesis could have been improved still, and graduate students might put their advisors' names on publications based on their dissertation, even though their advisor may not have assisted in writing the specific paper.

Citizen newspapers, such as Bayosphere.com (a Bay Area online newspaper that folded in early 2006), are an example of community-based co-production. The success of a community-based local newspaper—online or not—is dependent on its customers for an engaged readership that actively contributes content. In the online world, blogs play an increasing role in this form of value co-creation. However, as a publisher, the newspaper is also responsible for filtering contributions and for highlighting or promoting certain content. Given the interdependent nature of content production (both customer-customer and customer-firm interdependence), performance ambiguity is high. Similarly, information equivocality is high as the meaning of an 'interesting' or 'locally relevant' piece, is relatively open to interpretation.

Examples of Internet-Enabled Co-Production

Having outlined our contingency framework of co-production designs, we now turn our attention to three examples of Internet-enabled service environments. Our purpose in analyzing these cases is to gain insights into the conditions under which reliance on Internet technologies affect changes in customer co-production. In particular, we are interested in understanding how Internet technologies impact the co-production designs in the different quadrants differently, and how it affects the exogenous variables on which these designs are contingent, i.e., input uncertainty and performance ambiguity. Furthermore, we will highlight some of the unintended consequences generated by the incorporation of Internet technologies.

Booking an Airline Ticket Online

When customers want to book an airline ticket online, they are typically confronted with a highly scripted interface into which they enter information about their travel needs, e.g., departure and arrival cities, dates of travel, number of passengers, etc.

With this unequivocal request for assistance, the online booking system then offers the customer available flights sorted either by price or schedule. Some systems give customers the option of looking for a cheaper flight, provided their search parameters (e.g., travel days, number of stops) are somewhat flexible. If one of these options meets the customer's needs, then s/he must enter personal contact and/or billing information to place the reservation on hold or purchase the ticket.

The co-production design instantiated in this example reflects the scripted market. The customer-firm interface is characterized by low input uncertainty because information about flights is relatively unequivocal. Although the customer has a wide variety of options in the form of search parameters, these are all standard and pre-defined, thus limiting customer requests to an established set of options. Neither the flight schedule, nor the functionality of the Web site is generated in response to a specific customer's request for service. This low input uncertainty also makes the airline's delivery process highly programmable.

Comparing the Internet-enabled booking scenario with one in which a customer service representative assists that customer (see Figure 4), we see that performance ambiguity in the online setting is even lower than in the provider-based setting. This is because the information regarding the flights is more transparent to the customer, and because the task of matching customer needs to the available flights is left completely to the customer. By disintermediating the service provider, the SST allows the customer to interact directly with the firm's automated back-office operations. This makes it relatively easy to trace who is to blame if a mistake is made. For instance, the airline holds the customer responsible for errors. If customers inadvertently purchase a ticket that does not meet their needs (e.g., wrong dates of travel), they have to pay a change fee to remedy the situation. Nevertheless, it is in the airline's interest to minimize the likelihood of customers making mistakes

Figure 4: Booking an airline ticket

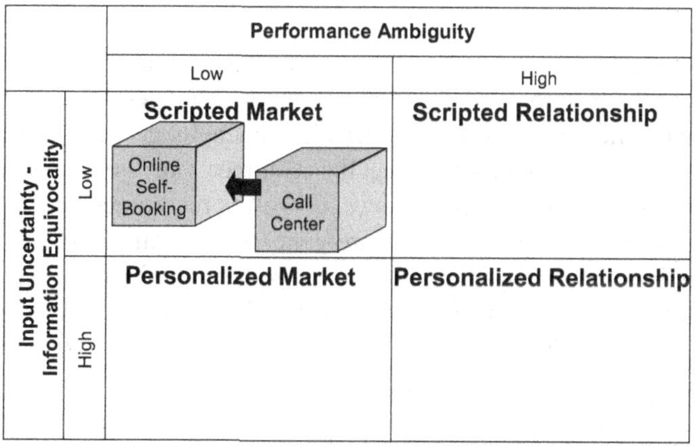

during bookings. For this reason, the design of the SST is such that customers are repeatedly asked to confirm their flight selections, thus giving them opportunities to uncover mistakes themselves.

One unintended consequence of having customers interact with a highly scripted system is that it severely restricts customer input. As highlighted by Whitaker (1980), customers' requests for assistance shape both current and future service offerings. In provider-mediated service environments, where service providers match customer needs with available service options, the customer-firm interface is less scripted than in the Internet- enabled service environments and customers may request services that fall outside of the predetermined options. By paying attention to such requests, firms may be able to detect emerging customer requirements and/or expectations, and respond to them by designing new service offerings.

Book Recommendations at Amazon.com

The main difference between the scripted and the personalized market design is the degree of input uncertainty. Experiential goods like books, music and movies, which highlight the ambiguous distinction between goods and services, provide a good illustration of how different levels of input uncertainty can be associated with one object. As a good, a book is a product whose characteristics (e.g., title, author, binding) can be readily described, thus making it suitable for a scripted market design. As a service, that is, the learning or entertainment value that it renders, however, the book is highly equivocal. Thus, if a customer is looking for a good cookbook, input uncertainty is relatively high. In order to respond to the request for a good cookbook, a service provider would have to gather copious information about the customer, e.g., his/her tastes in cookbooks, before recommending a suitable book. Therefore, the service of recommending books is an example of a personalized market co-production design.

On the surface, it appears that Amazon.com's recommendation system is an example of a personalized market design as it bases book recommendations on a customer's personal specifications and tastes, even though these may be implicitly derived. Taking the example of a customer searching for a good cookbook, we see the Amazon customer entering search terms into a single, general-purpose search box. In addition to listing books that meet the customer's keyword search, Amazon also makes available readers' book reviews, as well as recommendations for other, similar books. These recommendations are generated by Amazon's collaborative filtering technology, which builds a profile of customers' preferences to personalize its book recommendations. Thus the options offered customers are not scripted, but dynamically assembled in response to a customer's request for assistance. These book reviews represent community-based co-production within a service design of dyadic co-production.

Figure 5. Book recommendation

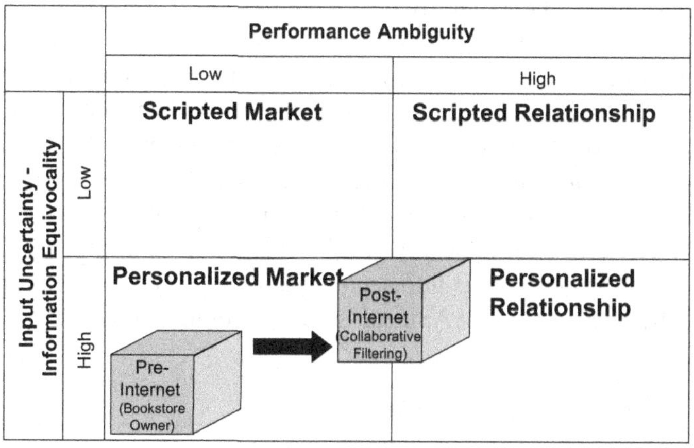

However, the dynamic assembly of these recommendations is highly programmed through the collaborative filtering technology. Amazon creates an implicit profile for each customer based on past purchases. By comparing the purchases of customers with similar profiles (i.e., "neighbors"), Amazon then recommends books to a customer based on the books that his/her neighbors bought. Therefore, Amazon's co-production design relies on the pooling of customer information (pooled interdependence), as well as the sequential ordering of customer requests and recommendation responses (sequential interdependence). Through its reliance on pooled customer information, the performance ambiguity inherent in Amazon's recommendation service increases (see Figure 5).

In order to determine what mode of cooperation is reflected in Amazon's recommendation system, we need to separate between the two profiles on which the recommendations are based. Amazon relies on both implicit and explicit profiles. Implicit profiles are derived from customers' purchases. To develop these, Amazon requires neither voluntary nor active cooperation from customers. In contrast, explicit profiles, which are based on customers' intentional ratings, do require both active and voluntary customer cooperation. For instance, for every book that customers have purchased from Amazon, they can indicate whether they "loved" or "hated" it, and whether it should be included in their personal profile. Books purchased as gifts do not necessarily reflect the customer's personal taste in books. Thus, explicit profiles refine and improve the accuracy of implicit profiles, and therefore increase Amazon's ability to create value through recommendations.

It is the involuntary and inactive mode of customer cooperation underlying Amazon's book recommendation service that potentially gives rise to unintended consequences. Unless customers voluntarily and actively refine their implicit profiles through explicit ratings, the accuracy of Amazon's recommendations is likely to deteriorate. For instance, if customers do not identify which books were purchased for themselves and which were purchased as gifts, the customer's profile remains vague. Since there are currently few incentives for customers to explicitly rate their past purchases, it is not clear that the implicit ratings, on which Amazon's system currently relies for the majority of its recommendations, can be readily augmented by customer's active and voluntary cooperation. Furthermore, there is nothing preventing customers from submitting explicit ratings that are not truthful, which is a challenge associated with community-based co-production. To the extent that Amazon's recommendation system takes explicit ratings into account at all, such inaccurate ratings could compromise the effectiveness of Amazon's book recommendation service.

Insurance Brokering at WebGA

Since relationship-based modes of organizing tend to be more prevalent in B-to-B than in B-to-C settings (Anderson, Hakansson, & Johanson, 1994), we take our SST example from the B-to-B realm. WebGA (a pseudonym) is a "general agent"[2] in the small group health insurance market (a detailed description of this case can be found in Schultze (2003) and Schultze and Orlikowski (2004)). As a general agent, WebGA mediates between independent insurance brokers and insurance carriers by providing brokers with "proposals" or "quotes" for health insurance plans from multiple carriers, as well as help with selling, e.g., accompanying brokers on sales calls and providing brokers with sales advice and materials such as enrollment forms and benefits packages.

WebGA's revenues consist of an "override," a commission paid by the insurance carrier for insurance policies sold through a general agent. This means that there is a high degree of reciprocal interdependence between WebGA and its the customers. While WebGA relies on brokers' sales success for its income, brokers rely on WebGA for information (both public and privileged) and assistance with selling. Furthermore, the input uncertainty is this realm is high. For instance, what is meant by "the best health plan" is equivocal. Thus, WebGA's service reflects the conditions of the personalized relationship co-production design.

Given the reciprocal interdependence and the performance ambiguity surrounding the delivery of health insurance sales and service, WebGA has traditionally relied on embedded relationships as a means of coordinating the co-production between its sales reps and its broker customers. However, in 1999, WebGA complemented its relationship-based customer-firm interface with an Internet-based self-service technology (SST), which allows customers to generate their own insurance quotes. The logic underlying this design of relationship-SST complementarity was that the structured activities associated with *quoting* (i.e., matching the needs of the group seeking insurance with available plans) could be automated, thus freeing the WebGA reps up to engage in *consulting* activities. These consulting activities include less structured tasks such as gathering market intelligence from brokers, and providing them, in turn, with advice and privileged information, as well as hands-on assistance such as accompanying the broker on sales calls. Mutual adjustment is the primarily mode of coordinating consulting activities.

Prior to the introduction of the online quoting system, quoting and consulting activities were inextricably intertwined as WebGA reps exchanged privileged information with their broker customers as part of quoting. In the new SST-enabled interaction, quoting and consulting are separated in space and time. Nevertheless, WebGA reps are alerted via e-mail every time one of their brokers runs an online quote. This alert prompts the WebGA rep to follow up with the broker through a personal phone call or an e-mail. In this way, the WebGA reps try to build or maintain their embedded relationships with their brokers. However, some brokers resist these attempts at relationship building by refusing to answer the WebGA rep's calls or e-mails. Such acts of non-cooperation and non-compliance eventually result in the customer having his/her access to the online quoting system revoked. However, "cutting off" the customer in this manner represents a measure of last resort for WebGA.

Since the challenges that this SST-enhanced co-production design generated for both WebGA sales reps and their customers have previously been described in detail (Schultze, 2003; Schultze & Orlikowski, 2004), we will merely highlight here some of the unintended consequences that the technology generated. In the case of WebGA, there was considerable tension between the Internet-based and the representative-based customer interfaces. For instance, the quoting engine included insurance plans that some of the WebGA reps could not endorse in good conscience. When brokers presented these plans to their clients and maybe even sold them, the WebGA reps had to resolve the conflict between the SST's quoting results and their own consulting recommendations. Such inconsistencies between the two service channels undermined the customer-provider relationship.

Furthermore, as brokers relied increasingly on the online system to do their quoting, the reps' opportunities to personally interact with them declined, making it more difficult to build the rapport and trust needed to add value through consulting activities. This was because the reps relied on their customers for intelligence from the field. Additionally, as brokers used the SST channel more than they did their WebGA rep, they also began to feel less beholden to their rep and less obliged to write their cases through WebGA. Thus, the weakening of the embedded relationships between customers and providers threatened WebGA's ability to ensure customer cooperation when it came to submitting cases. Indeed, the introduction of the online quoting system highlighted just how much WebGA relied on these relationships—and the social capital and rules of reciprocity inherent in them—to ensure that brokers complied with the unenforceable agreement that they write through WebGA those cases that had benefited from its quoting and consulting services.

Figure 6. WebGA

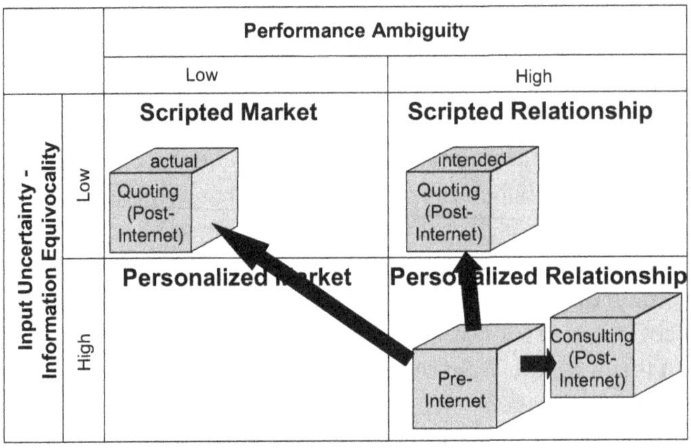

Relating the WebGA case back to our contingency framework, we can see that prior to the introduction of its online quoting technology, the firm's co-production design reflected the personalized relationship (see Figure 6). Quoting and consulting activities were offered only as a bundle and through personal contact between a broker customer and his/her WebGA representative. The introduction of the online SST meant that quoting and consulting were separated. While the consulting activity remained in the personalized relationship quadrant, the quoting activity was expected to migrate into the scripted relationship quadrant. Indeed, WebGA wanted the relationship between its customers and its reps to remain intact, and therefore sought to maintain virtual integration between quoting and consulting. Every time a customer quoted online, their WebGA sales rep was alerted and was expected to follow up with the customer.

However, the lack of seamless integration between WebGA's provider- and Internet-based channels began to undermine the customer-provider relationship, suggesting that some of WebGA's customers regarded WebGA's quoting service in terms of a scripted market design, which is instantiated through arm's-length relationships. This presented a problem for WebGA, however, as it did not price its quoting services separately from its consulting services.

Concluding Remarks

Co-production implies collaboration between firms and their customers in the creation of a social context and in the design, delivery, and marketing of goods or co-generation of value through the services that customers consume. Internet technology facilitates new opportunities for customer co-production and the co-creation of value (Prahalad & Ramaswamy, 2004). In this paper, we developed a multi-dimensional definition of co-production, noting that there are both dyadic and community-based modes of customer co-production. We also developed a contingency framework of co-production designs based on the exogenous variables of input uncertainty and performance ambiguity. Using three examples of Internet-enabled services, we then generated insights into the implications of relying on Internet technologies for the different co-production designs and into the unintended consequences that these technologies can generate. We now focus on Internet technology's impact on the two exogenous variables that constitute the design contingencies in our framework, i.e., input uncertainty and performance ambiguity.

The performance ambiguity of a service is affected by the Internet's support for the unbundling of goods and services. For instance, in the Internet-enabled environment, goods become increasingly digital, which allows them to be unbundled them from their physical storage and distribution mechanisms (Altinkemer & Bandyopadhyay, 2000). Thus the sale of music in the form of a physical CD or tape is challenged by the availability of sound files that are distributed over the Internet (e.g., iTunes). Similarly, the Internet creates the possibility that business processes that typically define a corporation, e.g., customer management, product innovation and infrastructure management, can be distributed across multiple outsourcers whose operations are nevertheless so tightly integrated that the boundaries between the service providers are virtually imperceptible (Hagel & Singer, 1999). This is indicative of Malone et al.'s (1987) *electronic integration effect*, i.e., the use of technology to create joint, interpenetrating processes between exchange partners.

As we saw from the WebGA case, the commercialization of the Internet allowed the firm to unbundle its service and separate it into quoting (moderate performance ambiguity) and consulting (high performance ambiguity). By separating quoting from consulting, WebGA effectively reduced the performance ambiguity of its overall service offerings, as only consulting could now be considered high in performance ambiguity. Thus, similar to Malone et al. (1987), we would suggest that there is an overall expansion of market-based service arrangements as low-ambiguity activities are increasingly unbundled from medium- to high-ambiguity activities and then migrated to the Internet.

Input uncertainty is also affected by the introduction of Internet technology. As our discussion of the Amazon.com recommendation system showed, high information equivocality can be managed through technologies such as collaborative filtering and natural language search engines. Thus, with increased technological sophistication, it becomes increasingly possible to automate the matching of customers' needs and expectations with extant service options, especially if these are offered by a range of specialized service providers, who each face less input uncertainty. Furthermore, as Malone et al (1987) highlight, the Internet facilitates the creation of online brokers who match buyers and sellers, i.e., the *electronic brokerage effect*. These brokers create value by absorbing the input uncertainty that individual firms would otherwise have had to deal with (Anderson & Anderson, 2002). Thus, we anticipate that Internet technology—in part through its facilitation of community-based co-production—renders environments that were previously considered high in input uncertainty less so. In this way, more opportunities for programmed means of coordination are created.

It is also important to note that the Internet increases transparency (Sinha, 2000). Not only does the technology make it easier for customers to do price comparisons across multiple online firms, but it is also easier for online firms to observe customers' behavior. For instance, online firms can collect data on what items the customer purchased, but also on what items the customer considered during his/her purchase decision. To the extent that online firms collect customers' online behavior and use it in their decision making, they are leveraging the co-production opportunities that the Internet offers. However, this form of co-production is largely passive and involuntary (e.g., Amazon's implicit profiling). The long-term implications of this type of co-production especially with respect to consumers' rights, for instance, represent an important area of research.

In light of these Internet-enabled shifts, another opportunity for future research is to identify empirical evidence of these shifts. In the interest of taking the IT artifact seriously (Orlikowski & Iacono, 2001), such research should examine how the features of the Internet-based technologies in their social context of use affect each of the co-production dimensions (i.e., activity, mode of cooperation and type of interdependence). Particular attention should be paid to the unintended consequences of these technologies. As is evident from the WebGA case, even though the electronic integration effect ensures that no key operational information is lost when customers use Internet-based SST to generate their own quotes, tensions resulting from the lack of integration between the Internet- and the provider-based channel were apparent. Such situated, practice-based insights are necessary to provide guidelines for the design of both dyadic and community-based modes of co-production.

Despite the challenges highlighted in the WebGA case, it is noteworthy that, on some measures, the deployment of Internet-based SST has been successful. For instance, two reasons why organizations invest in SST are reducing costs, e.g., wages of customer service representatives, and enhancing customer service, e.g., giving customers 24x7 access to service and information (Meuter, Ostrom, Rountree, & Bitner, 2000). Thus, reports that Southwest Airline was able to close three of its call centers at the end of 2003, in part because more and more customers were booking their flights online, suggests that the implementation of SST has been successful in the scripted market co-production design quadrant. Furthermore, Amazon's success as an online retailer, evidenced by the fact that in February 2004 it earned the highest customer satisfaction index score ever recorded by the American Society for Quality (Michigan State University), suggests that the deployment of SST for services located in the personalized market has been effective.

Nevertheless, it appears that we have fewer examples of SST and Internet technology deployments, their success and their impacts on customer co-production in situations of high performance ambiguity, i.e., in the scripted and personal relationship quadrant. While some online auction services like eBay stand out as shining examples of successful community-based customer co-production, much hallowed citizen newspapers like Bayosphere.com, have fallen short of their promise. Future research should therefore focus particularly on the co-production designs characterized by high performance ambiguity.

References

Altinkemer, K., & Bandyopadhyay, S. (2000). Bundling and the distribution of digitized music over the Internet. *Journal of Organizational Computing and Electronic Commerce, 10*(3), 209-224.

Anderson, J. C., Hakansson, H., & Johanson, J. (1994). Dyadic business relationships within a business network context. *Journal of Marketing, 58*(4), 1-15.

Anderson, P., & Anderson, E. (2002). The new e-commerce intermediaries. *MIT Sloan Management Review, 43*(4), 53-62.

Argote, L. (1982). Input uncertainty and organizational coordination in hospital emergency units. *Administrative Science Quarterly, 27*(3), 420-434.

Bell, D. (1976). *The coming of post-industrial society: A venture in social forecasting*. New York: Basic Books.

Bitner, M. J., Ostrom, A. L., & Meuter, M. L. (2002). Implementing successful self-service technologies. *Academy of Management Executive, 16*(4), 96-108.

Bowen, D. E., & Jones, G. R. (1986). Transaction cost analysis of service organization-customer exchange. *Academy of Management Review, 11*(2), 428-441.

Brudney, J. L., & England, R. E. (1983). Toward a definition of the coproduction concept. *Public Administration Review, 43*(1), 59-65.

Chervonnaya, O. (2003). Customer role and skill trajectories in services. *International Journal of Service Industry Management, 14*(3/4), 347-363.

Dellande, S., Gilly, M. C., & Graham, J. L. (2004). Gaining compliance and losing weight: The role of the service provider in health care services. *Journal of Marketing, 68*(7), 78-91.

Galbraith, J. R. (1973). *Designing complex organizations*. Reading, MA: Addison Wesley.

Gershuny, J. (1978). *After industrial society? The emerging self-service economy.* Atlantic Highlands, NJ: Humanities Press.

Hagel, J., & Singer, M. (1999). Unbundling the corporation. *Harvard Business Review, 77*(2), 133-141.

Jones, G. R. (1987). Organization-client transactions and organizational governance structures. *Academy of Management Journal, 30*(2), 197-218.

Kock, N. (2005). What is e-collaboration? *International Journal of E-Collaboration, 1*(1).

Kulkarni, S. P. (2000). The influence of information technology on information asymmetry in product markets. *Journal of Business & Economic Studies, 6*(1), 55-72.

Larsson, R., & Bowen, D. E. (1989). Organization and customer: Managing design and coordination of service. *Academy of Management Review, 14*(2), 213-233.

Lengnick-Hall, C. A., Claycomb, V., & Inks, L. W. (2000). From recipient to contributor: Examining customer roles and experienced outcomes. *European Journal of Marketing, 34*(3/4), 359-383.

Malone, T. W., Yates, J., & Benjamin, R. I. (1987). Electronic Markets and electronic hierarchies. *Communications of the ACM, 30*(6), 484-497.

Meuter, M. L., Ostrom, A. L., Rountree, R. I., & Bitner, M. J. (2000). Self-service technologies: Understanding customer satisfaction with technology-based service encounters. *Journal of Marketing, 64*(July), 50-64.

Mills, P. K., & Margulies, N. (1980). Toward a core typology of service organizations. *Academy of Management Review, 5*(2), 255-265.

Mills, P. K., & Morris, J. H. (1986). Clients as "partial" employess of service organziations: Role Development in client participation. *Academy of Management Review, 11*(4), 726-735.

Namasivayam, K. (2003). The consumer as "transient employee": Consumer satisfaction through the lens of job-performance models. *International Journal of Service Industry Management, 14*(3/4), 420-435.

Normann, R., & Ramirez, R. (1993). From value chain to value constellation: Designing interactive strategy. *Harvard Business Review, 71*(4), 65-77.

Orlikowski, W. J., & Iacono, C. S. (2001). Research commentary: Desperately seeking the "IT" in IT research—A call to theorizing the IT artifact. *Information Systems Research, 12*(2), 121-134.

Ouchi, W. G. (1980). Markets, bureaucracy and clans. *Administrative Science Quarterly, 25*(1), 129-142.

Prahalad, C. K., & Ramaswamy, V. (2000). Co-opting customer competence. *Harvard Business Review, 78*(1), 79-87.

Prahalad, C. K., & Ramaswamy, V. (2004). *The future of competition: Co-creating value with customers*. Boston: Harvard Business School Press.

Ramirez, R. (1999). Value co-production: Intellectual origins and implications for practice and research. *Strategic Management Journal, 20*(1), 49-65.

Schultze, U. (2003). Complementing self-serve technology with service relationships: The customer perspective. *Electronic Services Journal, 3*(1), 7-31.

Schultze, U., & Orlikowski, W. J. (2004). A practice perspective on technology-mediated network relations: The use of internet-based self-serve technologies. *Information Systems Research, 15*(1), 87-106.

Selnes, F., & Hansen, H. (2001). The potential hazard of self-service in developing customer loyalty. *Journal of Service Research, 4*(2), 79-90.

Siehl, C., Bowen, D. E., & Pearson, C. M. (1992). Service encounters as rites of integration: An information processing model. *Organization Science, 3*(4), 537-555.

Sinha, I. (2000). Cost transparency: The net's real threat to prices and brands. *Harvard Business Review, 78*(2), 43-50.

Thompson, G. F. (2003). *Between hierarchies & markets: The logic and limits of network forms of organization*. New York: Oxford University Press.

Thompson, J. D. (1967). *Organizations in action: Social science bases of administrative theory*. New York: McGraw-Hill.

Uzzi, B. (1999). Embeddedness in the making of financial capital: How social relations and networking benefit firms seeking financing. *American Sociological Review, 64*(August), 481-505.

Vargo, S. L., & Lusch, R. F. (2004). Evolving to a new dominant logic for marketing. *Journal of Marketing, 68*(1), 1-17.

von Hippel, E. (2005). *Democratizing Innovation*. Cambridge, MA: MIT Press.

Whitaker, G. P. (1980). Coproduction: Citizen participation in service delivery. *Public Administration Review, 40*(3), 240-246.

Williamson, O. E. (1975). *Markets and Hierarchies*. Englewood Cliffs, NJ: Prentice Hall.

Williamson, O. E. (1991). Comparative economic organization: The analysis of discrete structural alternatives. *Administrative Science Quarterly, 36*(2), 269-296.

Endnotes

1 In the strategy literature on co-production, the customer is regarded as supplier (Normann & Ramirez, 1993; Prahalad & Ramaswamy, 2000), while the organizational literature refers to the customers as partial employee (Mills & Morris, 1986). In the public administration literature, in turn, customers are referred to as consumer-producers (Brudney & England, 1983).

2 Double quotes signify emic or industry-specific terms.

Chapter X

Patterns in Electronic Brainstorming: The Effects of Synergy, Social Loafing, and Time on Group Idea Generation

Alan R. Dennis, Indiana University, USA
Alain Pinsonneault, McGill University, Canada
Kelly McNamara Hilmer, University of Tampa, USA
Henri Barki, HEC Montréal, Canada
Brent Gallupe, Queen's University, Canada
Mark Huber, University of Georgia, USA
François Bellavance, HEC Montréal, Canada

Abstract

Previous research has shown that some groups using electronic brainstorming generate more unique ideas than groups using nominal group brainstorming, while others do not. This study examined two factors through which group size may affect brainstorming performance: synergy and social loafing. Groups brainstormed using three techniques to manipulate synergy and two group sizes to manipulate social loafing. We found no social loafing effects. There were significant differences in synergy, but not the ones we had theorized. Instead, we found a time effect: nominal brainstorming groups that received no synergy from the ideas of others produced more ideas than electronic groups in the first time period and fewer ideas in the last time period. We conclude that synergy from the ideas of others is only important when groups brainstorm for longer time periods and may have a harder time generating ideas. We also conclude that electronic brainstorming groups, whether in the field or in the research laboratory, should be given at least 30 minutes to work on tasks or else they will be unlikely to develop synergy.

Introduction

The idea of using brainstorming has been around for almost 50 years (Osborn, 1957). Yet traditional group brainstorming, where group members verbally share their ideas, has not been found to be a very productive idea generation technique when compared to other brainstorming techniques (Mullen, Johnson, & Salas, 1991). A controversy has surfaced recently regarding two other forms of brainstorming—nominal group brainstorming and electronic brainstorming.[1] Both of these techniques have been found to be more productive than traditional verbal brainstorming but the question remains as to which one is more productive—nominal or electronic brainstorming. Some studies in the early 1990's found that electronic groups generated more ideas than nominal groups (Dennis & Valacich, 1993; Valacich, Dennis, & Connolly, 1994) but a recent study has cast doubt on these findings and claimed that the productivity of electronic brainstorming may be an illusion (Pinsonneault et al., 1999a). This is the subject of debate, with some researchers arguing that group size plays an important role: large electronic groups outperform large nominal groups but small nominal groups outperform small electronic groups (Dennis & Valacich, 1999; Pinsonneault et al., 1999b).

The purpose of this paper is to investigate two underlying theoretical factors that may influence the relative productivity of small and large nominal and electronic brainstorming groups: synergy and social loafing. Large electronic brainstorming groups may experience more synergy (and thus produce more ideas) than small groups on a per person basis because they have more potential sources of synergy. However, these same large brainstorming groups may also experience more social loafing (and thus produce fewer ideas) than small groups on a per person basis because members are more likely to perceive their contributions to be less needed. In this paper, we attempt to separate these competing factors to better understand how group size may affect brainstorming performance.

Previous Research

Group creativity and brainstorming have long been the subject of academic research. The general conclusion of this body of research is that people generate fewer ideas when they work together in verbally interacting groups than when they work in nominal groups—i.e., when they work separately and later pool their ideas (Mullen et al., 1991; Paulus, Larey, & Ortega, 1995). Reasons for this are mainly due to production blocking and evaluation apprehension that prevail in verbal communication, but do not exist in nominal groups. Production blocking refers to the need to take turns speaking in verbal communication (Diehl & Stroebe, 1987). When participants are prevented from contributing an idea when they first think of it, they may forget it or suppress it because the idea later seems less relevant or original. If they try to retain the idea, they must focus on remembering it, which prevents them from generating new ideas or attending to the ideas of others (Diehl & Stroebe, 1991). Evaluation apprehension may cause participants in verbal brainstorming to withhold ideas because they fear a negative reaction from others (Diehl & Stroebe, 1987; Lamm & Trommsdorff, 1973).

Over the last decade a new form of brainstorming—called electronic brainstorming—has emerged. With electronic brainstorming, participants interact via computers. They type their ideas into their computers simultaneously. These ideas are shared via the computers by allowing each member to read on their computer screen the ideas others in the group have generated. Electronic brainstorming does not improve the productivity of small groups but may improve the productivity of large groups (Dennis & Valacich, 1999). There have been conflicting results in comparing nominal brainstorming to electronic brainstorming (Pinsonneault et al., 1999a).

Much of the prior electronic brainstorming research has been guided by the process gains and losses framework (Steiner, 1972; Hill, 1982). Simply put, communication among group members introduces factors into the brainstorming process that improve performance (process gains) and factors that impair performance (process losses) relative to group members who work separately without communicating but later pool ideas (nominal groups). Several dozens of plausible sources of process losses and gains in verbal and electronic brainstorming have been proposed (see Camacho & Paulus, 1995; Mullen et al., 1991; Pinsonneault et al., 1999a). The traditionally important process losses of production blocking and evaluation apprehension have been essentially eliminated in electronic brainstorming because participants need not wait to contribute ideas and because ideas can be contributed anonymously. Nominal groups do not exhibit these losses (Pinsonneault et al., 1999a).

Three key differences between electronic brainstorming and nominal group brainstorming that have the potential to change with group size are synergy (a potential process gain), cognitive interference (a potential process loss), and social loafing (another potential loss) (Dennis & Valacich, 1999; Pinsonneault et al., 1999a; Pinsonneault et al., 1999b).

Synergy and Cognitive Interference

Synergy is the ability of an idea from one participant to trigger a new idea in another participant—an idea that would otherwise not have been produced (Dennis & Valacich, 1993; Lamm & Trommsdorff, 1973). Synergy—or the "assembly bonus"—is perhaps the most fundamental potential source of process gains. Synergy is caused by the ideas that group members exchange. Osborn's (1957) advice to "piggyback" on the ideas of others strives to increase the synergy that participants derive by building on the ideas of others. Ideas from others can serve both to stimulate ideas within one category or line of thought, as well as providing additional topic categories that would otherwise have been overlooked (Paulus, 2000). That is, the ideas of others can stimulate both idea fluency and idea flexibility (Guilford, 1975).

Synergy is likely to increase as participants are exposed to more ideas because there are more sources from which to draw inspiration in triggering a new idea (up to some limit, beyond which more ideas simply creates information overload) (Dennis & Valacich, 1993; Gallupe et al., 1992; Valacich, Dennis, & Connolly, 1994). Thus as the number of ideas a participant receives increases, so too should the number of ideas a participant generates—again, up to some limit (Dennis & Valacich, 1999).

As group size increases, the number of ideas that participants receive from others should increase and thus synergy should increase, which is why large electronic brainstorming groups have generally produced more ideas than small electronic brainstorming groups (Dennis & Valacich, 1993; Dennis & Williams, 2005). Because nominal groups are unable to draw on the ideas of others, they experience no synergy and thus produce fewer ideas than large electronic brainstorming groups.

This argument rests on the presumption that the ideas received by a participant can be used by that participant to trigger new ideas. That is, synergy is only possible if the ideas received from others have some value and do not simply repeat ideas that participant already has considered. If ideas repeat ideas already considered, they have little potential to induce synergy.

Likewise, if the participant is capable of generating ideas with no external stimulation, there is little value to be gained from synergy. That is, synergy only increases the number of ideas produced if the participant has "run out" of ideas and cannot generate more without help. If participants are capable of producing ideas for the length of time available by themselves, receiving ideas from others will not result in more ideas. In fact, this may actually decrease the number of ideas produced due to cognitive interference.

Cognitive interference is in many ways the inverse of synergy. Cognitive interference occurs when the ideas generated by other participants interfere with an individual's own idea generation activities (Pinsonneault et al., 1999a; Straus, 1996). Attention must be diverted away from the generation of ideas to the understanding of the ideas from other group members and thus fewer attention resources are devoted to producing ideas.

Cognitive interference may also be due to the content of the ideas contributed by others, because ideas from others serve to stimulate cognitive activity in one area, while limiting the flexibility of idea production in other areas (Nijstad, Diehl, & Stroebe, 2003). That is, ideas from others may narrow one's conception of the idea space and focus idea generation on only one aspect of the task (Dennis & Valacich, 1993; Pinsonneault et al., 1999a).

In summary, there is a tension in the balance of potential process gains from synergy and the potential process losses from cognitive interference. Nominal groups do not benefit from synergy and do not suffer from cognitive interference. Electronic brainstorming groups have the potential to benefit from synergy and suffer from cognitive interference. Synergy and cognitive interference are two sides of the same coin: the ideas of others can both stimulate new ideas and interfere with the production of one's own ideas. Based on prior research (Dennis & Valacich, 1999), we believe that the potential gains from synergy exceed the potential losses from cognitive interference. Therefore, we hypothesize:

H1: The number of ideas produced per person will be higher in groups whose members receive more ideas from others.

Social Loafing

Social loafing (also called free riding) is the tendency for individuals to expend less effort when working in a group than when working individually (Karau & Williams, 1993; Kerr & Bruun, 1983; Weldon & Mustari, 1988). Social loafing may arise because participants believe their contributions to be dispensable and not needed for success and/or because responsibility for is diffused among many participants (Chapman, Arenson, Carrigan, & Gryckiewiz, 1999; Harkins & Petty, 1982; Karau & Williams, 1993; Latane, Williams, & Harkins, 1979).

Social loafing is reduced when participants believe they are being evaluated as individuals, rather than collectively as a group (Karau & Williams 1993) and thus differences in performance become more noticeable when members of nominal groups believe themselves to be working as individuals, not as members of groups. Performance differences are reduced when members of nominal groups believe themselves to be working as members of groups[2].

Social loafing can be expected to increase as group size increases because perceived dispensability and diffusion of responsibility increase as the number of participants increases. As social loafing increases with group size, the number of ideas generated should decrease.

Historically, the effects of social loafing on idea production have been difficult to separate from the effects of synergy/cognitive interference, because both synergy/cognitive interference and social loafing tend to increase with group size. As group size increases, synergy increases and more ideas are produced. However, as group size increases, social loafing increases, resulting in fewer ideas. In this study, we manipulate social loafing separately from synergy in order to better understand their individual effects on the productivity of idea generation. We hypothesize that as participants perceive themselves to be in larger groups, they will have a greater tendency to engage in social loafing and produce fewer ideas. Therefore:

H2: The number of ideas produce per person will decrease as group size increases.

Method

A laboratory experiment with a 2x3 research design with repeated measures on one condition was used. The first condition was group size (small vs. large) intended to manipulate social loafing. The second condition (the repeated condition) was the idea generation technique intended to manipulate synergy (nominal group brainstorming intended to produce no synergy, electronic brainstorming with a small idea pool size intended to produce modest synergy, and electronic brainstorming with a large idea pool size intended to produce high synergy).

In traditional brainstorming experiments, it is difficult to separate the social loafing effects due to group size from its likely effects on synergy, because larger groups typically generate more total ideas than smaller groups. It is also difficult to control the ideas received by individuals because each group is different and individual group members are influenced by the actions of the other members of their group. Therefore, to provide a tightly controlled experimental manipulation in which we could manipulate social loafing and synergy separately, we used a groupware simulator, not a true electronic brainstorming system. A groupware simulator is designed to look and feel like a true electronic brainstorming system but instead of sharing ideas among group members, the simulator simply presents ideas from a prepared script as the ideas from "other group members." Simulators have been used successfully in prior electronic brainstorming and other groupware research (e.g., Garfield et al., 2001; Hilmer & Dennis, 2001; Satzinger, Garfield, & Nagasundaram, 1999).

Subjects

A sample of 216 sophomore, junior, and senior business students at a large state university received course credit for participating in the study. Subjects were randomly assigned into either a small or large group size, resulting in ten 6-member groups and thirteen 12-member groups. All subjects within a group generated ideas with each technique, but the order of the techniques differed using a fully blocked experimental design.

Tasks

All subjects performed three idea generation tasks similar to those in prior research. One task asked subjects to generate ideas to improve the environment. Another task sought ideas to increase the amount of tourism in the United States. The third task asked for ideas to improve public safety in the United States[3]. All subjects completed all three tasks, but the order in which the tasks were presented differed using a fully blocked experimental design. Subjects were given 12 minutes to perform each task. This time was chosen so as not to unduly fatigue subjects in performing three tasks and because similar lengths of time (e.g., 10-15 minutes) have been used in prior brainstorming research (e.g., Diehl & Stroebe, 1987; Dennis & Valacich, 1993; Gallupe et al., 1992; Harkins & Petty, 1982; Paulus & Dzindolet, 1993).

Independent Variables

The first independent variable was group size designed to induce shifts in social loafing. It is difficult to make compelling arguments for the choice of one specific size of group over another. Prior empirical research suggests that there is an important point of inflection in electronic brainstorming versus nominal group performance around eight or nine member groups (Dennis & Valacich, 1999), so we wanted to choose one group size below this point and one size above this point. Therefore, we chose to use groups of 6 and 12 members. These sizes have been commonly used for small and large groups in prior research (Pinsonneault et al., 1999a).

To reinforce the group size manipulation, the groupware simulator prominently displayed the size of the group in which the subject was working (even though subjects could look around and count the number of members in their group). The simulator also displayed a counter of the total number of ideas purportedly generated by all members of the group. This idea counter increased from zero to a predetermined end number during each experimental time period following a typical group productivity pattern (an initial burst of ideas, followed by a slight lull, and then gradually increasing again). The end number for the counters was chosen based on a typical productivity rate of about one (potentially redundant) idea per person per minute[4] (c.f., Gallupe et al., 1992). This consistent per-person level of idea production was also chosen to control any potential "matching," whereby group members attempt to produce ideas at the same rate as others (Camacho & Paulus, 1995). For groups of size 12, the end numbers were 146, 153, and 154 (remember that each group performed three separate idea generation tasks). For groups of size 6, the end numbers were 74, 78, and 79.

The second independent variable was the idea generation technique designed to induce different amounts of synergy. In all treatments, participants typed their ideas into the groupware simulator. In the electronic brainstorming treatments, instead of exchanging those ideas with other participants, the simulator presented participants with ideas that appeared to be from other group members but in fact were drawn from a script written by the researchers. The ideas displayed in the simulator came from ideas generated in prior experiments using these tasks.

Subjects were informed that they would receive some, but not all the ideas produced by the other members of their group. Subjects generated ideas for all tasks using a computer, but the number of ideas "from other group members" that they saw varied for each treatment. In the nominal group brainstorming treatment, subjects only saw their own ideas being displayed (i.e., the size of the idea pool was zero); no ideas "from others" were displayed. The small idea pool treatment was designed to be representative of the number of ideas produced by a small group and consisted of 28 ideas shown (but, of course, idea pool size was manipulated separately from group size). In this treatment, a small amount of ideas was displayed with the subject's own ideas intermixed with the ideas "from others." In the third treatment, a large pool of ideas was displayed (again intermixed with the subject's own ideas). The large idea pool treatment was intended to be representative of a large group and displayed 56 ideas.

Procedures

Subjects were randomly assigned to groups of 6 or 12 within a session and sessions were randomly assigned to a particular sequence of techniques and tasks used. Subjects first completed a consent form that also asked for age and gender. Consistent with prior research, we gave the standard brainstorming instructions to all groups in all treatments, which were included with the consent form and repeated on each task sheet (see Appendix A). Next, subjects were shown how to use the groupware simulator. Because the simulator was straightforward to use, subjects did not have a practice session. Subjects then used the simulator to generate ideas on one task using one of the three techniques (nominal group, electronic-small idea pool, electronic-large idea pool). After generating ideas, subjects filled out a questionnaire which assessed satisfaction with the process. They then received a second task, generated ideas using a different technique and completed the questionnaire again. Subjects then received the third task, generated ideas using a different technique and completed the questionnaire again. Finally, the subjects were debriefed and released.

Dependent Variables

Productivity was measured by the average number of unique ideas generated per participant in a group. For each task, the output of all group members was combined into one file. The number of unique ideas generated by each group in each treatment was then counted according to the procedure described in Bouchard and Hare (1970) and Cooper et al. (1993) and then divided by the number of group members. The transcripts of the group and simulator ideas were evaluated by one coder by following a detailed guide that explained how to identify redundant ideas and to calculate the number of unique ideas. Another coder using the same coding rules independently coded a random subset of the transcripts. Inter-rater reliability was acceptable ($r = .96$).

The group process satisfaction measure is shown in Appendix B. The items were drawn from previous research (Dennis & Valacich, 1993) and had adequate reliability (α=.86).

Statistical Analysis

The data were analyzed with a linear model for repeated measures that took into account the incidental effect of the time period (order) in which the three techniques were assigned to the groups of subjects (Keppel & Wickens, 2004). Therefore, the following parameters were included in the statistical model: the main effect of group size, the main effect of technique, the main effect of period, and the two-way and three-way interactions between these effects. Statistical significance was set at the 5% level. The Bonferroni method was used for post hoc multiple comparisons and computation of 95% confidence intervals (C.I.) for differences between means. The unit of analysis was the group for the average number of unique ideas generated and the subject for the satisfaction measure. All statistical analyses were conducted using SAS statistical software for Windows, release 8.02.

Results

Table 1 presents the mean number of unique ideas generated per individual and the standard deviation according to group size and technique. Table 2 presents the results of the analysis of variance for the main effects and for all terms representing two-way and three-way interactions.

As can been seen from Table 2, the technique and period main effects as well as the technique-period interaction were significant. Thus the different techniques appeared to provide different levels of synergy/cognitive interference leading to different performance, but the effects interacted with the time period in which the technique was used. Figure 1 illustrates the cell-level means for the technique by period interaction. The data suggest that the no-synergy nominal groups performed better in the first two time periods but that the electronic brainstorming groups with

Table 1. Mean number of unique ideas per individual by group size and technique

Group Size	Technique	N	Mean	Standard Deviation
6	No Synergy (Nominal Groups)	10	9.3	1.1
6	Modest Synergy (Electronic-Small Idea Pool)	10	8.6	1.9
6	High Synergy (Electronic-Large Idea Pool)	10	8.3	2.4
12	No Synergy (Nominal Groups)	13	10.7	1.7
12	Modest Synergy (Electronic-Small Idea Pool)	13	9.6	1.7
12	High Synergy (Electronic-Large Idea Pool)	13	8.7	1.5

Table 2. Statistical results for average number of ideas

Main Effect or Interaction	DF	F	p-value
Group Size	(1, 21)	2.92	.102
Period	(2, 30)	10.28	<.001
Group Size * Period	(2, 30)	2.09	.141
Technique	(2, 30)	3.56	.041
Group Size * Technique	(2, 30)	.92	.408
Period * Technique	(4, 30)	3.32	.023
Group Size * Period * Technique	(4, 30)	1.10	.373

a small idea pool produced more ideas in the last time period. Overall, the two electronic brainstorming technologies seem to follow a similar pattern. Groups using electronic brainstorming techniques in period 3 produced significantly more unique ideas per individual than groups using the same electronic brainstorming technique in period 1 (Electronic-Small Idea Pool: Bonferroni's adjusted $p < .005$ and the 95% C.I. for the difference: 2.83 ± 2.21; Electronic-Large Idea Pool: Bonferroni's adjusted $p <.019$ and the 95% C.I. for the difference: 2.74 ± 2.43). In contrast, the productivity of groups using nominal brainstorming was not significantly different from period 1 to 3 (Bonferroni's adjusted p-values for the comparisons between periods 1 and 2, 1 and 3, and 2 and 3, were all over the 5% level).

Table 2 also shows that, contrary to expectations, group size and its interactions were not statistically significant, indicating that there were no differences in individual performance when subjects believed themselves to be in groups of 6 versus groups of 12. That is, there were no social loafing effects on performance.

Analysis of subjects' satisfaction (see Table 3) showed that subjects were more satisfied in the second and third time periods than in the first time period ($p<.001$)[5]. Less important in terms of magnitude of effects but also statistically significant, there were also a main effect of technique ($p= .034$), time period by group size and time period by technique interactions ($p=.024$, and $p=.025$, respectively).

Figure 1. The Technique-period interaction for the average number of ideas

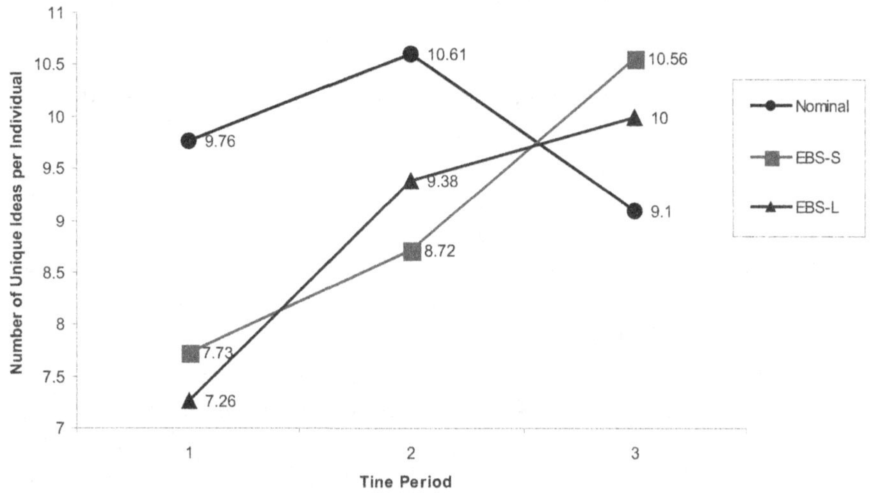

Table 3. Statistical results for satisfaction

Main Effect or Interaction	DF	F	p-value
Group Size	(1, 214)	0.35	.552
Period	(2, 416)	69.96	<.001
Group Size * Period	(2, 416)	3.77	.024
Technique	(2, 416)	3.40	.034
Group Size * Technique	(2, 416)	1.50	.225
Period * Technique	(4, 416)	2.82	.025
Group Size * Period * Technique	(4, 416)	0.51	.726

Discussion

We hypothesized that the productivity of electronic brainstorming might be influenced by two competing factors: 1) synergy from reading the ideas of others (net of cognitive interference), which would increase as the size of the idea pool increased; and 2) social loafing from the perceived dispensability of one's effort, which would increase as the size of the group increased. We found no evidence of increased social loafing due to group size. Individuals produced the same number of ideas on average whether they believed themselves to be a part of a small 6-member group that produced about 52 ideas in the 12-minute time period or a larger 12-member group that produced about 118 ideas in the 12-minute time period.

We found significant synergy effects due to the idea pool size[6], but not the ones we hypothesized. In the first time period, the electronic brainstorming groups who received the ideas of others (either a small or large idea pool) produced fewer ideas than nominal groups who received no ideas from others (no idea pool). In the second time period, nominal groups produced more ideas than the electronic brainstorming groups who received a small idea pool from others. In the final time period, the situation was reversed: electronic brainstorming groups with a small idea pool produced more ideas than nominal groups.

We therefore conclude that time plays a critical role in influencing the relative value of electronic brainstorming versus nominal group brainstorming. While several factors have been advanced as important factors influencing the relative benefit of these two techniques (e.g., Dennis, & Valacich, 1999; Pinsonneault, et al., 1999a; 1999b) we do not believe that the impact of time has been adequately explored.

At least three, probably not entirely mutually exclusive, explanations can be provided for the time-based pattern observed here. First, the experimental session required participants to generate ideas on three different 12-minute tasks sequentially for a total of 36 minutes of idea generation, interspersed by short breaks answering questionnaires. By the time they reached the third idea generation task, subjects may have been tired or have been more likely to run out of ideas and thus relied more on ideas of others. Thus perhaps subjects' internal cognitive reservoir of ideas was drained, and they required more external stimulation to produce ideas. While electronic brainstorming groups could take advantage of the ideas "from others" to trigger their ideas, nominal groups could not do this. In so doing, electronic brainstorming groups with a small idea pool in period 3 were able to generate more ideas than nominal groups and more ideas than electronic brainstorming groups in previous periods. Even though fatigue may have set in, it did not cause less satisfaction. On the contrary, satisfaction increased over time.

Second, as previously argued, electronic brainstorming entails a more complex idea generation process than nominal brainstorming. Electronic brainstorming groups need to read ideas generated by other group members, understand and interpret them, and generate new ideas themselves (Pinsonneault et al., 1999a, 1999b). In nominal brainstorming, members concentrate exclusively on the cognitively simpler task of generating ideas by themselves. It is possible that learning how to effectively use electronic brainstorming to generate ideas took longer than with nominal brainstorming. Since subjects were only shown how to use the software and did not have a chance to practice using it before the experiment began, the low performance for electronic brainstorming groups in period 1 may be due to a learning effect. A possible learning curve can be seen for both electronic brainstorming treatments in Figure 1. This would explain why electronic brainstorming groups generated fewer unique ideas in period 1 than in period 3 and why nominal groups outperformed electronic brainstorming groups in period 1.

Finally, the first ideas received from others may have had a constraining effect on the production of subsequent ideas (Smith, 2003). That is, when individuals in electronic brainstorming groups see the first ideas from other group members, the interaction may either open up or constrain the possible idea space. When these first few ideas from others tend to focus on one area, it may serve to constrain the perceived idea space. Individuals may focus their attention and idea generation on the initial theme(s) of other group members, thereby leading to cognitive inertia and decreasing the number of possible ideas generated (Nijstad, Diehl, & Stroebe, 2003).

We selected the ideas presented by the simulator over time to be somewhat related, rather than jumping all over the idea space. We did this to make the simulator ideas appear more realistic to the subjects (we reasoned that ideas coming from many different topic areas might make some subjects suspect the ideas were coming from a database). In hindsight, this may have been a mistake, because the selected focus of the ideas could have had a constraining effect (particularly in period 1 when subjects were just learning to use the software and unsure of social norms for use). Prior research has shown that using software with multiple windows devoted to different idea themes can reduce this constraining effect and significantly increase the number of ideas produced (Dennis et al., 1996, 1997). In all prior studies in which electronic brainstorming groups produced more ideas than nominal groups, the software provided multiple windows devoted to different themes. Our study, however, did not use multiple windows, and thus may have heightened the constraining effect of cognitive inertia.

We reviewed prior research in search of evidence that might tend to support or refute our learning effects and cognitive fatigue interpretations. Most but not all prior electronic brainstorming experiments included some training on the use of the electronic brainstorming software (Straus, 1996; Dennis & Valacich, 1993; Valacich, Dennis, & Connolly, 1994). We see no pattern of results to suggest a learning effect; we believe this interpretation remains plausible, but unsupported. There is, however, some support for our cognitive fatigue interpretation. Previous electronic brainstorming experiments have used time periods ranging from 10 minutes to 30 minutes. Prior studies that have found electronic brainstorming to produce more ideas than nominal group brainstorming have typically used time periods of 30 minutes (e.g., Dennis & Valacich, 1993), while those finding the reverse have typically used shorter time periods of 15 minutes (e.g., Gallupe et al., 1994).

Thus we conclude that time is an important moderating factor in understanding the effects of synergy on electronic brainstorming performance. For some short time period (e.g., 10-20 minutes), participants produce more ideas working in nominal groups without synergy from the ideas of others. They have sufficient ideation resources to produce ideas from their own knowledge and thoughts, and the ideas of others provide at least as much cognitive interference as they do synergy. After that point, however, participants exhaust their own private ideation resources and perform better if they can use the ideas of others to stimulate their own ideas.

We conclude that electronic brainstorming only enables synergy leading to increased production of ideas when participants have problems producing ideas on their own. When time periods available for brainstorming are short (e.g., 15 minutes or less) and participants are fresh, then electronic brainstorming appears to add little value. Electronic brainstorming appears to be most beneficial when individuals have trouble producing ideas (e.g., fatigue) and are given sufficient time to enable them to take advantage of the synergy from reading other's ideas.

This study suffers from the normal limitations of experimental laboratory research. We used ad hoc groups of undergraduate business students working for a short time on a task for which they had no vested interest in the outcome. The simulator used a interface common to many CMC tools (upper window to read others' comments and lower window to type comments), but it is possible that use of commercial tools (e.g., NetMeeting, Instant Messenger, Groove) might have produced different results. For example, it is possible that the ideas in the simulator prevented participants from contributing ideas because the simulator presented an idea that the participant had just thought of, but had not had time to type. Nonetheless, we believe that this study has several implications for future research and practice.

We believe that our results have implications for future research. Perhaps the most important implication is the need for more studies to understand the effects of time on brainstorming. We believe that our results, when combined with those of prior research, indicate that there are important—and to date under-articulated—effects due to time, but we can offer no direct empirical results. We did not set out to test this question and thus cannot answer it directly.

Our results suggest that electronic brainstorming might be particularly helpful when group creativity is limited. In the early stages of our experimental sessions, group members were able to generate ideas without the help of external stimuli. However, after a while, generating ideas became more difficult and electronic brainstorming helped groups to be more creative. This might be indicative of an "S" shape pattern. An "S" shape pattern would mean that the synergy effect of electronic brainstorming is minimal early in the idea generation task (when group members can easily generate ideas without external stimuli). However, after a certain period of time, group members find it more difficult to generate ideas and the synergy offered by electronic brainstorming becomes a key catalyst to idea generation, thereby increasing the productivity of electronic brainstorming groups over time. This effect may last for a certain period of time, after which it levels off, as does productivity.

Our results also suggest that electronic brainstorming may not be appropriate for all groups. For instance, groups that are already productive working for short time periods may not gain any synergy benefit from receiving the ideas from others provided by electronic brainstorming. On the other hand, electronic brainstorming might help boost the creativity of less productive groups or those working for longer periods of time. As a practical matter, we believe that our results suggest that electronic brainstorming sessions should be longer than 15 minutes; we recommend 30 minute sessions, whether it is used in the field or in the research laboratory. We believe that groups will be unable to gain much synergy from using electronic brainstorming for shorter time periods than this.

It also seems that different brainstorming approaches may be best suited for different stages of brainstorming. For example, our results suggest that a better performance may be obtained by combining techniques, and using nominal brainstorming first followed by electronic brainstorming in the later part of a brainstorming session, when productivity slows down, much like the nominal group technique (Delbecq & Van de Ven, 1974; Van de Ven & Delbecq, 1971). That is, participants should first generate ideas individually, without accessing the ideas of others. Then, after some time has elapsed (e.g., 10-15 minutes) and participants have begun to "run out" of ideas, they should be given access to the ideas of others to help trigger new ideas.

We conclude that electronic brainstorming (and other techniques that enable participants to see the ideas of others) produces synergy and triggers more ideas only when participants have difficulty generating ideas on their own (e.g., when they are tired). For those tasks in which ideas come simply or whose time is constrained such that participants will not run out of ideas before time expires, electronic brainstorming will likely not improve performance. Electronic brainstorming is likely to be of most value for tasks for which participants have sufficient time to contribute their own ideas and then pause to consider the ideas of others and to use those ideas to trigger new ideas.

References

Bouchard, T. J., & Hare, M. (1970). Size, performance, and potential in brainstorming groups. *Journal of Applied Psychology, 54* , 51-55.

Camacho, L. M., & Paulus, P. B. (1995). The role of social anxiousness in group brainstorming. *Journal of Personality and Social Psychology, 68*, 1071-1080.

Chapman, J. G., Arenson, S., Carrigan, M. H., & Gryckiewiz, J. (1993). Motivational loss in small task groups: Free riding on a cognitive task. *Genetic, Social, and General Psychology Monographs, 119*, 57-73.

Cooper, W. H., Bastianutti, L., Young, V., McCallum, L., Anderson, L., & Gallupe, R. B. (1993). *A manual for coding brainstorming*. School of Business, Queen's University, Kingston, Ontario, Canada,.

Delbecq, A. L., & Van de Ven, A. H. (1974). Effectiveness of nominal, delphi, and interacting group decision making processes. *Academy of Management Journal, 17*, 605-621.

Dennis, A. R., & Valacich, J. S. (1993). Computer brainstorms: More heads are better than one. *Journal of Applied Psychology, 78*, 531-537.

Dennis, A. R., & Valacich, J. S. (1999). Electronic brainstorming: Illusions and patterns of productivity," *Information Systems Research, 10*, 375-377.

Dennis, A. R., Valacich, J. S., Carte, T. A., Garfield, M. J., Haley, B. J., & Aronson, J.E. (1997). The effectiveness of multiple dialogues in electronic brainstorming. *Information Systems Research, 8*, 203-211.

Dennis, A. R., Valacich, J. S., Connolly, T., & Wynne, B. (1996). Process structuring in group brainstorming. *Information Systems Research, 7*, 268-277.

Dennis, A. R., & Williams, M.L. (2005). A meta-analysis of group size effects in electronic brainstorming: More heads are better than one. *International Journal of E-Collaboration, 1*(1), 24-42.

Diehl, M., & Stroebe, W. (1987). Productivity loss in brainstorming groups: Toward the solution of a riddle," *Journal of Personality and Social Psychology, 53*, 497-509.

Diehl, M., & Stroebe W. (1991). Productivity loss in idea-generating groups: Tracking down the blocking effect. *Journal of Personality and Social Psychology, 61*, 392-403.

Gallupe, R. B., Cooper, W. H., Grise, M. L., & Bastianutti, L. M. (1994). Blocking electronic brainstorms. *Journal of Applied Psychology, 79*, 77-86.

Gallupe, R. B., Dennis, A. R., Cooper, W. H., Valacich, J. S., Bastianutti, L. M., & Nunamaker, J. F. (1992). Electronic brainstorming and group size. *Academy of Management Journal, 35*, 350-369.

Garfield, M. J. Taylor, N. J., Dennis, A. R. & Satzinger, J. W. (2001). Modifying paradigms: Individual differences, creativity techniques and exposure to ideas in group idea generation. *Information Systems Research, 12*, 323-333.

Guilford, J. P. (1975). Creativity: A quarter century of progress. In I. A. Taylor & J. W. Getzels (Eds.), *Perspectives in creativity* (pp. 37-59). Aldine, Chicago.

Harkins S. G., & Petty, R. E. (1982). Effects of task difficulty and task uniqueness on social loafing. *Journal of Personality and Social Psychology, 43*, 1214-1229.

Hill, G. W. (1982). Group versus individual performance: Are N + 1 heads better than one? *Psychology Bulletin, 91*, 517-539.

Hilmer, K. M., & Dennis, A. R. (2001). Stimulating thinking in decision making: Cultivating better decisions with groupware one individual at a time. *Journal of Management Information Systems, 17*(3), 93-114.

Karau, S. J., & Williams, K. D. (1993). Social loafing: A meta-analytic review and theoretical integration. *Journal of Personality & Social Psychology, 65*, 681-706.

Keppel, G., & Wickens, T.D. (2004). *Design and analysis: A researcher's handbook* (4th ed.). NJ: Pearson Prentice Hall.

Kerr, N. L., & Bruun, S. E. (1983). Dispensability of member effort and group motivation losses: Free rider effects. *Journal of Personality and Social Psychology, 44*, 78-94.

Lamm, H., & Trommsdorff, G. (1973). Group versus individual performance on tasks requiring ideational proficiency (brainstorming): A review. *European Journal of Social Psychology, 3*, 361-388.

Latane, B., Williams, K., & Harkins, S. (1979). Many hands make light work: The causes and consequences of social loafing. *Journal of Personality and Social Psychology*, *37*, 822-832.

Mullen, B., Johnson, C., & Salas, E. (1991). Productivity loss in brainstorming groups: A meta-analytic integration. *Basic and Applied Social Psychology*, *12*, 3-23.

Nijstad, B. A., Diehl, M. & Stroebe, W. (2003). Cognitive stimulation and interference in idea-generating groups. In P. B. Paulus & B. A. Nijstad (Eds.). *Group creativity: Innovation through collaboration* (pp. 137-159). Oxford University Press.

Osborn, A. F. (1957). *Applied imagination* (rev. ed.). Scribner, New York.

Paulus, P. B. (2000). Groups, teams, and creativity: The creative potential of idea-generating groups. *Applied Psychology, 49*, 237-262.

Paulus, P. B. & Dzindolet, M. T. (1993). Social influence processes in group brainstorming. *Journal of Personality and Social Psychology*, *64*, 575-586.

Paulus, P. B., Larey, T. S., & Ortega, A. H. (1995). Performance and perception of brainstormers in an organizational setting. *Basic and Applied Social Psychology, 17*), 249-265.

Pinsonneault, A., Barki, H., Gallupe, R. B., & Hoppen, N. (1999a). Electronic brainstorming: The illusion of productivity. *Information Systems Research*, *10*, 110-133.

Pinsonneault, A., Barki, H., Gallupe, R. B., & Hoppen, N. (1999b). The illusion of electronic brainstorming productivity: Theoretical and empirical issues. *Information Systems Research, 10*, 378-380.

Satzinger, J. W., Garfield, M. J., & Nagasundaram, M. (1999). The creative process: The effects of group memory on individual idea generation. *Journal of Management Information Systems*, *15*(4), 143-160.

Smith, S. (2003). The constraining effects of initial ideas. In P. B. Paulus & B. A. Nijstad (Eds.),*Group creativity: Innovation through collaboration* (pp. 13-31). Oxford University Press.

Steiner, I. D. (1972). *Group process and productivity.* NJ: Academic Press.

Straus, S. G. (1996). Getting a clue: The effects of communication media and information dispersion on participation and performance in computer-mediated and face-to-face groups. *Small Group Research*, *57*, 448-467.

Valacich, J. S., Dennis, A. R., & Connolly, T. (1994). Idea generation in computer-based groups: A new ending to an old story. *Organizational Behavior and Human Decision Processes*, *57*, 448-467.

Van de Ven, A. H., & Delbecq, A. L. (1971). A group process model for problem identification and program planning. *The Journal of Applied Behavioral Science, 7*, 466-474.

Weldon, E. & Mustari, E. L. (1988). Felt dispensability in groups of coactors: The effects of shared responsibility and explicit anonymity on cognitive effort. *Organizational Behavior and Human Decision Processes, 41*, 330-351.

Endnotes

1 With nominal group brainstorming, individual group members generate ideas independently without communicating with others and then later combine their ideas with those of the rest of their group. With electronic brainstorming, networked computers with brainstorming software are used to enable group members to exchange ideas with other group members as they generate their own ideas.

2 For equal comparisons to electronic brainstorming groups, subjects in nominal groups in our study were told that their ideas would be assessed together as a group, not individually.

3 The data were collected prior to September 11, 2001.

4 Our participants averaged about one idea per person per minute before eliminating redundant ideas.

5 The means are 3.93, 5.20, and 5.27 with significant differences being Period 1 < Period 2 (95% C.I.: 1.27 ± 0.30) and Period 1 < Period 3 (95% C.I.: 1.34 ± 0.30).

6 Post-hoc tests without Bonferroni's adjustments found these differences significant at .05. After the Bonferroni's correction, the differences between nominal and EBS-L in period 1 and between nominal and EBS-S in period 2 were significant at the 10% level.

Appendix A

Brainstorming Instructions

This is a study of group idea generation using a technique called electronic brainstorming. The procedure is relatively straightforward. You will work as a part of group to generate ideas on three separate tasks. You will type your ideas into your computer and click a button to send them to other members of your group. Sometimes (not always) you will be able to read some (but not all) of the ideas typed by your group members on your screen.

Electronic Brainstorming uses five rules:

1. The goal is to generate as many ideas as you can. The greater the number of ideas the better.
2. Type each idea as briefly as you can and move onto the next idea.
3. Do not talk with others or look at their computers (because they may see a slightly different set of the group's ideas).
4. Do not criticize the ideas contributed by other members of your group.
5. Do not be afraid of contributing silly, wild, or unusual ideas. Wild ideas often prompt other people to think of new ideas. It is easier to change a wild idea into a useful idea than it is to think up a new idea.

Appendix B

Questionnaire Measures

How do you feel about the process by which you generated ideas?

Not Satisfying					Very Satisfying	
1	2	3	4	5	6	7

How satisfied are you with the idea generation process you used?

Not Satisfied					Very Satisfied	
1	2	3	4	5	6	7

How comfortable did you feel with the idea generation process you used?

Not Comfortable						Very Comfortable
1	2	3	4	5	6	7

I feel satisfied with the computer-based process my group used to discuss this problem.

Strongly Disagree						Strongly Agree
1	2	3	4	5	6	7

The chapter was previously published in the International Journal of e-Collaboration, 1(4), 38-57, October-December 2005.

Section II

Research Syntheses and Debate

Chapter XI

Are We Genetically Maladapted for E-Collaboration?

Ned Kock, Texas A&M International University, USA
Donald Hantula, Temple University, USA

Abstract

Do we have e-collaboration genes, that is, genes that code for biological adaptations that are well aligned with the demands posed by e-collaboration? A look at our ancestral past through an evolutionary psychology lens generally suggests a negative answer to this question. It seems that our biological communication apparatus, which includes several brain modules, is in fact designed to excel in co-located communication involving face-to-face interaction. Our biological apparatus appears to be ill adapted for e-collaboration, especially in situations where text-intensive and asynchronous interaction technologies (e.g., e-mail) are used for communication. Implications for research and practice of these conclusions are discussed, particularly as they refer to the explanatory and predictive power of the conclusions.

Evolutionary Psychology

Long before Darwin (1859) proposed his theory of evolution by natural selection there has been debate about how much of our behavior is influenced by our "nature" (or our genes), and what types of behavior are particularly affected by our genetic makeup. Behaviors that are strongly influenced by our genes, and that thus are assumed to be more closely related to our biological structure than our cultural backgrounds, are often referred to as "instinctive" behaviors. Thus, from this perspective it makes sense to say that the compulsion that many of us feel to eat more candy than we need is in fact an instinct, most likely motivated by the scarcity of food containing high-calorie sugars in the ancestral environments in which we evolved, from Australopithecus to Homo sapiens.

On one extreme of the debate of how much of our behavior is influenced by our genes are those sometimes referred to as biological determinists, who believe that nearly all of our behavior is determined by our genes, often ignoring evidence to the contrary. On the other extreme, are those who subscribe to the notion that our genetic makeup influences virtually none of our behavior, ignoring the many striking similarities in behavior across markedly different cultures, as well as the many studies that show key similarities between identical twins raised separately.

Most serious human evolution researchers today adopt a more balanced view than the ones that characterize the extremes discussed above. There is a general belief, among most human evolution researchers, that behavioral traits are defined in part by "nature" and in part by "nurture." Moreover, most human evolution researchers today subscribe to the epigenetic view (see, e.g., Kuper, 1994; Lickliter & Honeycutt, 2003; Wilson, 2000) that most biological traits, even those believed to be largely inherited through our genes, are the result from an intricate interplay between genetic and environmental influences. This view essentially assumes that only a few biological traits are innate (e.g., blood type), with the majority of those traits being defined by both the genetic structure of the individual and environmental circumstances surrounding that individual (e.g., height, body fat percentage).

Research on the evolution of human instincts is one of the primary subjects of the field of evolutionary psychology (Buss, 1999; Miller, 2000; Tooby & Cosmides, 1992). Two of the general assumptions underlying the current work of evolutionary psychologists are that: (a) the human brain is functionally identical across different individuals, and (b) the current human brain is made up of functional modules that incorporate adaptations that maximized survival and/or reproductive capacity in our ancestral past. In other words, even though it is undeniable that different individuals have different brains, evolutionary psychologists generally assume that all human brains have essentially the same functional modules. And, it is also assumed that the human brain incorporates a number of adaptations to survival and mating problems that hominids have faced in the evolutionary path that led to Homosapiens.

The Ape that Uses E-Mail

E-collaboration has gone from science fiction speculation to a daily reality for most workers, in what could be seen as "a second in a lifetime" in evolutionary terms. Given this, the following questions could be posed. Have we evolved adaptations aimed at making us excel at e-collaboration? If not, have we evolved adaptations that are somewhat conducive to e-collaboration, even if not closely matched with it? These questions are relevant because today many of us, especially those employed in knowledge-intensive fields, probably conduct most of our work-related communication electronically. Moreover, current workplace trends in connection with virtual work and communication technologies dissemination suggest that the amount of work-related electronic communication is likely to increase in the future.

When we look at our evolutionary past in order to answer the above questions, the evidence that is presented to us leads to one inevitable conclusion—we likely have genes that code specifically for co-located communication adaptations. During over 99 percent of our evolutionary cycle we communicated either face-to-face or across the short distances that voice and noise can be conveyed, simply because no other form of communication had been available to us during that period. Conversely, most of today's successful e-collaboration technologies support geographically distributed interaction, and rely heavily on text, which is a form of pictorial communication that employs written symbols (e.g., letters and ideograms).

The first forms of cave paintings date as far back as 40 thousand years ago, but most of the evidence in connection with prehistoric cave paintings (as well as other forms of prehistoric art) suggests that they were not used for pictorial communication, at least in the most literal sense of the word. For example, cave paintings were not generally used as maps, to indicate the location of food or water reserves. Instead, it seems that most cave paintings and other forms of prehistoric art were used as a basis for rituals, or produced as part of rituals (Chauvet et al., 1996; Gombrich, 1995; Janson, 1997).

Even if cave paintings had been used for pictorial communication, two notions would have to be accepted for us to conclude that our brain is somehow designed to excel in the use of today's text-intensive e-collaboration technologies. Firstly, we would have to accept the notion that, in the 40 thousand years since the emergence of the first cave paintings, the ability to produce pictorial representations (and understand what they were trying to convey) conferred a significant survival and/or reproductive advantage to the individuals who possessed that ability. Secondly, we would have to accept the notion that 40 thousand years of evolution was enough to erase the likely adaptations for non-pictorial, co-located communication that have taken place in the previous 3.5 million years or so since the emergence of the first hominids—the Australopithecines, of which the most famous example is perhaps "Lucy" (see, e.g., Boaz and Almquist, 1997).

While the two notions above may be possible, most of the evidence in connection with human evolution suggests that they are unlikely. The most likely scenario is that our brain has been primarily designed to excel in co-located communication, especially where face-to-face interaction takes place, and is ill adapted for text-intensive e-collaboration involving geographically distributed individuals. A substantial amount of empirical research evidence provides support for this scenario (Kock, 2004). This scenario somehow brings to mind the idea that Homo sapiens is in fact "the ape that uses e-mail".

So What?

Many people are fascinated by evolutionary arguments. We include ourselves in that category, especially regarding arguments that try to explain human behavior toward technology. Nevertheless, it is important to address the "so what" issue. That is, so what if our brain is not particularly designed to use communication media that suppress elements normally present in co-located communication, as most e-collaboration media do? It is still undeniable that the human brain is also among the most plastic of all animal brains, a characteristic that allows us to learn how to use unnatural e-collaboration media through practice to the point that those media become virtually "second nature" to us.

Our answer to the above "so what" question has two facets. One of the facets refers to the predictive power of the evolutionary perspective explored here, which allows us to infer certain causal relationships linking the naturalness of an e-collaboration medium and the amount of mental effort experienced by the individuals using that medium to accomplish a collaborative task. The other facet refers to the explanatory power of the evolutionary perspective explored in this chapter, which we believe allows us to provide a scientific basis for certain notions purported by a widely cited and much criticized theory generally known as "media richness theory" (Daft & Lengel, 1986).

The predictive power of the perspective explored here. The meaning of the statement that "our brain is ill adapted to the use of text-intensive e-collaboration technologies" is essentially that the circuitry in our brain, or the neural networks that make up our brain, are not particularly designed for the use of those e-collaboration technologies. Or, in other words, those neural networks are designed for co-located communication, the most natural form of human communication (simply because this was the form of communication used during most of the human evolutionary journey). However, what geographically distributed electronic communication may have in common with more ancestral forms of communication is the fact that in both distributed electronic communication and in non face-to-face but co-located communication without any support of any technology (such as yelling across an expanse of forest), we may not be able to see one another and pick up on visual cues available, but we can still communicate and accomplish certain tasks successfully. So, there may be some vestigial remnants to build on. Nevertheless, the use of e-collaboration technologies generally requires users to adapt by altering their behavior to fit the new situation because the evolved or "hardwired" brain circuitry is not "in place" for e-collaborative work.

The above discussion allows us to predict with some certainty that e-collaboration technologies that create communication media which are too different from the form of co-located communication used by our hominid ancestors will generally require more brain effort, or "mental effort" (a more widely used term), to be used. Indeed, it may be easily understood that face-to-face communication is the easiest and most natural form of communication, followed by co-located but non face-to-face communication. The more different the communication medium created is from the face-to-face medium, the more mental effort will be required, a claim that can be substantiated easily by reflection on one's own experiences in working and communicating across a field or other expanse.

However, additional mental effort may not be a big problem in certain types of collaborative tasks. Say, a group of people trying to develop a new product, and interacting mostly electronically, will probably feel more mental fatigue after a 5-hour e-collaboration session than if they were interacting face-to-face. Yet, that may have an insignificant impact on the quality of the design of the new product they are developing. People adapt by altering their behavior, and as such may work harder to accomplish such a task. We may also expect that their affective reaction to the extra effort expended may be less positive than if they were working face-to-face.

In other types of collaborative tasks, such as tasks that involve business-to-consumer interaction (e.g., a business representative helping a customer perform a financial transaction online), extra mental effort may prompt the customer to go to a competitor who provides a more natural interface for communication. Again, people tend to adapt by altering their behavior, and may do so by seeking out an "easier" Web-based provider of goods or services (see DiClemente & Hantula, 2003; Smith & Hantula, 2003 for an evolutionary account of this behavior based on foraging theory). Some companies that operate as Web-based facilitators of business-to-consumer interaction have been banking on this notion for a few years already (Gilbert, 1999).

The explanatory power of the perspective explored here. The above discussion may prompt some – particularly those who are familiar with media richness theory – to argue that what was said above is basically a restatement of the main tenets of that theory. Hopefully the next few paragraphs will make it very clear that this is not the case, and that the evolutionary perspective explored in this chapter differs substantially from that espoused by media richness theorists.

Media richness theory (Daft & Lengel, 1986) argues that different communication media possess different degrees of "richness". This numerical attribute is correlated with the degree to which a medium supports several communication elements; notably the degree of support for the use of non-verbal cues (e.g., tone of voice and body language), and the degree of feedback immediacy afforded by the medium (i.e., fast back-and-forth interaction). Even though media richness theory was devised nearly 20 years ago, it is still contemporarily used as a basis for empirical research published in prestigious journals (Kahai & Cooper, 2003).

Media richness theory has never presented a scientific reason why human beings should prefer communication media with a high degree of support for the use of non-verbal cues and for feedback immediacy. The Darwinian perspective explored in this chapter does provide a scientific reason for a preference toward a specific benchmark, namely co-located face-to-face communication. It does not rely on medium attributes per se, which could arguably make that benchmark less important, and in consequence weaken the main theoretical pillars that underlie this Darwinian perspective.

Support for the use of non-verbal cues can be enhanced beyond what is available in face-to-face interaction through virtual reality media. The evolutionary perspective taken here would lead us to assume that those artificially enhanced media would also be unnatural, and thus lead to increased mental effort. That would be most likely due to another phenomenon generally known as "information overload", which can be seen as something like the opposite of the non-verbal cue suppression phenomenon associated with the use of certain text-intensive e-collaboration technologies such as e-mail.

Media richness theory, in its original form, also argued that individuals would generally avoid media of low levels of richness for complex and knowledge-intensive tasks (generally called "equivocal" tasks, in media richness parlance). When those users could not exercise that choice (e.g., in situations where their media choice was limited to one single medium of low richness, like e-mail) media richness theory predicts that the quality of the final outcome of their collaborative task would suffer.

There is plenty of empirical research evidence showing beyond much doubt that individuals may purposely choose media of low levels of richness for complex and knowledge-intensive tasks, and that such choice can lead to even better quality outcomes than outcomes generated through the use of the face-to-face medium (see, e.g., DeRosa et al, 2004, Kock, 1998 & 2001). That evidence usually comes together with evidence that the choice of communication media that suppresses many of the elements found in face-to-face interaction leads to a perception that the communication medium is "difficult to use" and "not very user-friendly". While this combined body of evidence is incompatible with media richness theory predictions, it does indeed appear to fit well with the evolutionary perspective explored here.

In most tasks, whether they are collaborative or not, quantify of effort does not necessarily define outcome quality. And this is true for mental effort as well. Let us assume that one individual is asked to build a spear out of a tree branch using one hand only (and a sharp tool, used for wood shaping), whereas another individual is asked to accomplish the same task with the same tool, but using both hands. While it is quite possible that significantly more effort (and time) will be required from the individual using only one hand, that does not mean that the spear produced by the individual using both hands will be of better quality. In fact, the opposite may happen, if the individual using both hands is somehow more sloppy at completing the task, which may be motivated by the fact that he or she does not have to spend as much effort as the individual using only one hand. Less effort may lead to less of a sense of commitment toward completing the task successfully, or use of only one hand may spur additional adaptation in the form of careful checking of the work, again resulting in a superior spear.

This discussion also points out an important cautionary note in the selection and interpretation of dependent variables in e-collaboration research. Media choice, mental effort, individual satisfaction with group/process/results, quality and quantity of performance are all separate and distinct entities. At different times they may or may not correlate with one another, however they are not suitable proxies for one another. Adaptation requires effort, especially early on, and a concomitant decrease in satisfaction with process may not necessarily extend to a similar affective reaction to one or more attributes of the results. Individual affective reaction or media choice may be independent of performance. There has been an unfortunate nudge-nudge wink-wink tradition within psychology of subtly substituting attitudes for behaviors, affective reactions for performance outcomes and the like, much to the long-term detriment of theory and methodology. As we begin to take seriously the implications of an evolutionary analysis of e-collaboration it is critical that reductions of mental effort on the part of researchers do not supersede proper and rigorous research design and analysis.

The Quick Information Exchange Paradox

Let us look at the following scenario. Two people, a man and a woman, have agreed to meet at a later date on a particular address, where the house in which the woman lives is located. The woman needs to communicate to the man her home address. Let us also assume that both work in offices that are a short walk from each other. In this situation, would not it be arguably less mentally demanding for both the woman and the man if she e-mailed him her home address, rather than walking to him and conveying that information face-to-face? The answer is probably "yes", which begs a follow-up question: is this answer consistent with the evolutionary perspective presented in this chapter? The appearance here is that the answer to this last question is "no", which characterizes what we refer to here as the "quick information exchange paradox".

Giving a "no" answer to the latter question above would be consistent with the intuitive notion that e-mail makes quick information exchanges such as the one illustrated above easier, but would also bring us back to "square one" in terms of the evolutionary perspective explored here. Giving a "yes" answer does not, but requires some explaining. The following paragraphs take the second path, and argue that the apparent paradox does not really exist.

The mental effort alluded to in the previous section is that associated with the communicative act, not with any non-communicative act that may be directly or indirectly related to the communicative act. For example, if two people are located in different cities, and they want to communicate face-to-face, it is reasonable to assume that a certain (possibly sizeable) amount of mental effort will have to be spent in the act of traveling to a common location. The evolutionary perspective explored here, which refers specifically to the mental effort associated with communication interactions, has nothing to say in connection with the travel-related mental effort. That effort is simply outside the scope of the perspective, and is covered by other theoretical perspectives (see, e.g., Trevino et al., 1990). In other words, the additional mental effort involved in traveling (e.g., driving a car for hundreds of miles, buying plane tickets over the Web) is not included in our evolutionary perspective's assessment of the total amount of mental effort involved in the communication interaction.

Communicating to someone a home address, in the scenario used to illustrate the quick information exchange paradox, is not the only thing that the woman did when she sent the man an e-mail message with the information about her home address. She also provided that information to him in such a way that it was already recorded on a non-volatile medium for his future reference, and, most likely, printing. In a face-to-face interaction, the recording of the information by the man on some kind of non-volatile medium (e.g., a piece of paper) would have normally followed the communication of the home address information, so that he would remember the address later. The additional recording of the information is an activity that itself requires some degree of mental effort. That activity would have to be carried out together with the communication of the information. The additional recording activity is essentially what makes the use of the face-to-face medium to appear more cumbersome than the use of the e-mail medium in the quick information exchange scenario used to illustrate the paradox—which, as it can be seen, is not a "true" paradox after all.

A similar paradoxical scenario is that of three individuals (the number of individuals could be higher) who have to e-collaborate in order to accomplish a common task, namely the task of writing a report about an audit that they performed on an organization's financial records. Each of the three individuals writes a set of sections of the report, and the sets of sections that each of them write make up three independent parts of the report. The question is: would not it be easier for the individuals to write the report collaboratively using e-mail (with attachments) than face-to-face? The answer is, most likely, "yes". Is this compatible with the evolutionary perspective discussed in this chapter? The answer is also "yes", and the explanation is analogous to the one provided in the previous paragraphs. Essentially, there was little or no communication involved in the e-collaborative task of putting the audit report together. The e-collaboration technology in question (e-mail with attachments) was quite appropriate for the e-collaborative task, which required some manipulation of sections of text produced independently by the three writers, and very little communication.

Conclusion

This chapter presents and discusses a Darwinian perspective on electronic communication behavior that suggests that we humans are essentially intelligent primates that use e-collaboration technologies. This statement is not, of course, meant to be shocking or offensive to anyone. It incorporates the notion that our biological communication apparatus is in many ways designed for forms of communication that have been used over millions of years by our ancestors, some of which (e.g., Australopithecus afarensis) would be perceived by many today as looking more like apes than modern human beings.

This chapter is premised on the belief that it is useful for us to understand certain instincts that have been endowed on us by evolution. Many of those instincts make us less adapted to life in urban society, because the developments that have led to urban society occurred too fast (in evolutionary time) to lead to major changes in our genetic makeup. Among those instincts is aggression, which underlies a vast array of behaviors that go from "road rage" to wars. Other examples are the instincts that compel us to consume more fatty foods and salt than we need, which were generally scarce and difficult to obtain in our evolutionary past, but plentiful and easy to acquire in urban society. Clogged arteries and high blood pressure are often the result of these instincts, which can be seen as maladaptations to modern urban life.

Some of the e-collaboration-related instincts that we discussed in this chapter are not in the same category as those mentioned above in terms of how bad they are for our health (at least that seems to be the case so far). Nevertheless, those instincts reflect the same general situation in which all of us human beings find ourselves today. Unfortunately, most of our species-wide adaptations are better aligned with the demands of pre-historic life than they are with the demands of life in today's cities.

References

Boaz, N.T., & Almquist, A.J. (1997). *Biological anthropology: A synthetic approach to human evolution*. Upper Saddle River, NJ: Prentice Hall.

Buss, D.M. (1999). *Evolutionary psychology: The new science of the mind*. Needham Heights, MA: Allyn & Bacon.

Chauvet, J.M., Deschamps, E.B., & Hillaire, C. (1996). *Dawn of art: The chauvet cave*. New York: Harry N. Abrams.

Daft, R.L., & Lengel, R.H. (1986). Organizational information requirements, media richness and structural design. *Management Science, 32*(5), 554-571.

Darwin, C. (1859). *On the origin of species by means of natural selection*. Cambridge, MA: Harvard University Press.

DeRosa, D.M., Hantula, D.A., Kock, N. & D'Arcy, J.P. (2004). Communication, trust, and leadership in virtual teams: A media naturalness perspective. *Human Resources Management* Journal, *34*(2), 219-232.

Gilbert, J. (1999). LivePerson focuses on the human touch. *Advertising Age, 70*(23), 62.

Gombrich, E.H. (1995). *The story of art*. London: Pheidon Press.

Janson, H.W. (1997). *History of art*. Upper Saddle River, NJ: Prentice Hall.

Kahai, S.S., & Cooper, R.B. (2003). Exploring the core concepts of media richness theory: The impact of cue multiplicity and feedback immediacy on decision quality. *Journal of Management Information Systems. 20*(1), 263-281.

Kock, N. (1998). Can communication medium limitations foster better group outcomes? An action research study. *Information & Management, 34*(5), 295-305.

Kock, N. (2001). Compensatory Adaptation to a lean medium: An action research investigation of electronic communication in process improvement groups. *IEEE Transactions on Professional Communication, 44*(4), 267-285.

Kock, N. (2004). The psychobiological model: Toward a new theory of computer-mediated communication based on Darwinian Evolution. *Organization Science, 15*(3), 327-348.

Kuper, A. (1994). *The chosen primate: Human nature and cultural diversity*. Cambridge, MA: Harvard University Press.

Lickliter, R., & Honeycutt, H. (2003). Developmental dynamics: Toward a biologically plausible evolutionary psychology. *Psychological Bulletin, 129*(6), 819-835.

Miller, G.F. (2000). *The mating mind: How sexual choice shaped the evolution of human nature*. NY: Doubleday.

Tooby, J., & Cosmides, L. (1992). The psychological foundation of culture. In J.H. Barkow, L. Cosmides, & J. Tooby (Eds.), *The adapted mind: Evolutionary psychology and the generation of culture* (pp. 19-136). NY: Oxford University Press.

Trevino, L. K., Daft, R. L., & Lengel, R. H. (1990). Understanding manager's media choices: A symbolic interactionist perspective. In J. Fulk & C. Steinfield (Eds.), *Organizations and communication technology* (pp. 71-94). Newbury Park, CA: Sage..

Wang, H., & Zhang, L. (2004). Linear generalization probe samples for face recognition. *Pattern Recognition Letters, 25*(8), 829-840.

Wilson, E.O. (2000). *Sociobiology: The new synthesis*. Cambridge, MA: Harvard University Press.

Chapter XII

Propositions for Cognitive Support of E-Collaboration

C.A.P. Smith, Colorado State University, USA
Stephen C. Hayne, Colorado State University, USA

Abstract

Recent research has proposed that groupware performance may be affected by two factors, the strongest of which is the fit between the task and the groupware structures selected for use. We suggest that the link is deeper; there needs to be a fit between the task and the group's cognitive structures as mapped to the groupware structures. In this paper we address this shortcoming by integrating recent theories of cognition (distributed cognition, transactive memory and template theory) from the perspective of electronic collaboration. We refine the concept of cognitive fit as applied to group work and offer propositions for further study. We show that template core data are used during situation assessment and that slot data refine response selection. Finally, we propose several techniques by which the group cognitive effort can be minimized, thereby leaving more capacity for the collective task. This approach is especially applicable to naturalistic group decision situations.

Introduction

An emerging theme in today's workplace is the pressure to do more with less. For example, the U.S. economy continues to expand even though the numbers of people employed remains fairly static: resulting in remarkable productivity gains (Bureau of Labor Statistics, 2004). In the public sector, schools, universities, governments, police, hospitals, and firemen are all under pressure to reduce their overhead while maintaining levels of service. The military is not immune to these trends, retention and recruitment are serious issues for the military at a time when major operations are taking place in several areas of the world. This pressure to increase productivity creates a stressful work environment for employees, and places a premium on the ability to discover ways to work more effectively.

Most work involves some kind of group activity rather than individual activity (Thompson & Fine, 1999). Work groups have many forms, including project teams, boards of directors, management teams, planning teams, juries, and committees of various types. Most important economic, political, legal, scientific, cultural, and military decisions are made by groups, not individuals (Keltner, 1989).

As the pace of work continues to increase, many work groups must face situations that routinely have high stakes, time-pressure, and uncertainty. In this challenging task environment, group members are often pushed to their limits of performance. Humans have limited cognitive resources of memory, attention and perception; availability of these resources directly impacts our task performance (Wickens, 1984).

To address some of these limitations, tools have been developed to support specific cognitive strategies for individual decision makers (Kaempf, Klein, & Wolf, 1996). Performance has been shown to improve when there is a good cognitive fit between the task and the tool (Dunn & Grabski, 2001; Vessey, 1991). Software support for group decision-making has been a central research area of information systems in the last 30 years (for reviews, see Dennis & Williams, 2005; DeSanctis & Gallupe, 1987; Jessup & Valacich, 1993; McGrath & Hollingshead, 1994; Nunamaker, 1997). This electronic collaboration (e-collaboration) can be broadly defined as collaboration among individuals engaged in a common task using electronic technologies. While some meta-analyses have shown mixed results (Benbasat & Lim, 1993; McLeod, 1992; Pinsonneault & Kraemer, 1990), many studies have shown that e-collaborative teams can outperform face-to-face teams (Schmidt, Montoya-Weiss, & Massey, 2001 as merely one example). However, within the large body of literature on e-collaboration, we are not aware of any software that is specifically designed to optimize the utilization of human cognitive resources in collaborative situations. Most systems have addressed behavioral issues associated with human interaction or have implemented algorithms designed to increase decision or communication efficiency.

Most recently, Dennis, Wixon, and Vandenberg (2001) have suggested that groupware performance may be affected by two factors, the strongest of which is the fit between the task and the groupware structures selected for use. We suggest that the link is deeper; there needs to be a fit between the task and the group's cognitive structures as mapped to the groupware structures. In this paper we address this shortcoming by integrating recent cognitive theory with collaboration and put forward several propositions for further study.

Theoretical Foundation

Groups can accomplish larger and more complex tasks than individuals. Yet, there are many factors affecting group effectiveness that have been categorized into process losses and process gains (Jessup & Valacich, 1993; Nunamaker, 1997). While this simple model has an intuitive appeal, it begs the question, "how does one maximize gain or minimize loss?" From the perspective of cognition, we believe the answer to this question requires the integration of at least three broad areas of study:

- Individual cognitive psychology, including abilities and limitations,
- Groups and social interactions, including communications and motivations, and
- The role of software artifacts as stimulating structures for human interactions.

A complete review of any one of these topics is beyond the scope of this paper, so we will limit our review to a subset of these topics that apply most directly to collaboration and cognition. For our purposes, we assume that each group member understands their role in the group, and the roles of the other group members. We assume that the members are motivated to achieve the stated objectives of the group. We restrict ourselves to decision domains having high stakes, time pressure, and some uncertainty. And, finally, we presume that the group has some kind of e-collaboration or groupware support, e.g., a shared workspace.

There are many tasks that fit within the limitations of our assumptions: tasks having a sufficiently large scope to require group effort, and presenting a significant cognitive challenge. Consider the case of a financial services firm seeking to choose investments for their clients' retirement portfolios. One such financial services firm, TIAA-CREF (2004) has stated that one of their three key investment philosophies is "collaborative expertise". Each type of investment requires different kinds of experts and decisions must be made quickly in the marketplace. For example, decisions about what kinds of bonds to purchase for fixed-income portfolios depend on the work of credit analysts, sector analysts, acquisition specialists, portfolio managers and quantitative managers. In a nutshell, their collective task is to identify stocks to purchase, to decide how much to weight them in the portfolio and when to make the trades. To be successful, these different kinds of investment professionals must work together in a way that makes the most of each skill set, and their firm wants this to happen not just within an asset class, but also throughout their entire organization. Firms like TIAA-CREF may manage as much as U.S. $100 billion; we suggest that collaborative portfolio management involves high-stakes, time pressure and some uncertainty. We will use this example throughout the paper.

In the following sub-sections, we review the limitations of individual cognition, theories of group-level cognition related to transactive memory, shared mental models, and distributed cognition as integrated with template theory. Each topic is summarized with a group cognitive proposition.

Model Human Processor

Our goal is to specify a set of prescriptions for designers of collaborative systems that will provide mechanisms to improve group performance by reducing the cognitive effort required to perform group tasks. The importance of reducing cognitive effort stems from the notion that humans have limited cognitive resources. The capacity or resource models (e.g., Kahneman, 1973; Navon & Gopher, 1979; Wickens, 1984) view the human system as having a limited reservoir of resources that are quantifiable, divisible, allocatable, and scarce. To the extent that the cognitive effort to perform some task can be reduced, then people will be likely to make fewer errors, and to have more residual effort available for other task-related activities; in our case, group oriented tasks.

Multiple resource theory proposes that there are separate and finite reservoirs of cognitive resource (Wickens, 1984, 2002), some of which are potentially available simultaneously for different purposes. Figure 1 shows the model human processor proposed by Card, Moran, and Newell (1986). The model shows various cognitive resources, including different types of memory (long-term and separate working memory stores for visual and auditory working memory), separate processors for perception, motor control, and an executive "cognitive" processor. Working memory refers to temporary or "short-term" memory that humans use to buffer our recent perceptions, or to gather our recollections from "long-term" memory.

It requires some cognitive effort to retrieve memories from long-term storage. Once those long-term memories are "active" in short-term memory, it also takes some ongoing effort to keep them active. These efforts are expended by the cognitive processor, and are generally referred to as "attention." Humans have a finite amount of attention resource, which can be consciously directed to a variety of tasks, such

Figure 1. Model of the human information processor (Card, Moran, & Newell, 1986).

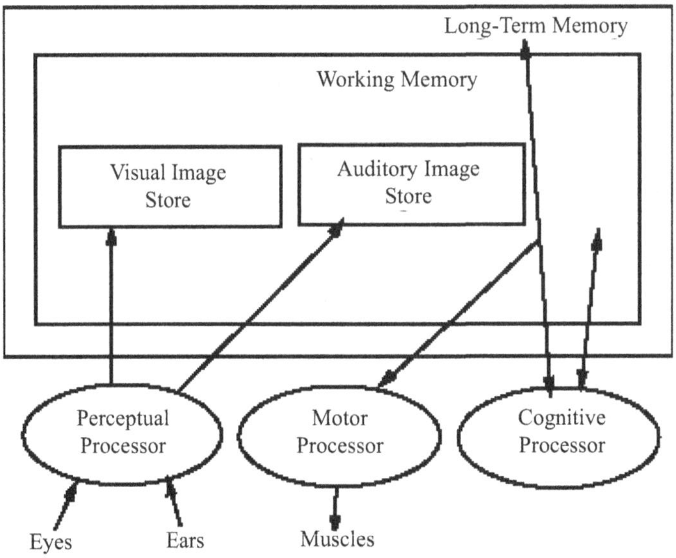

as retrieving memories from long-term storage, maintaining memories in short-term storage, directing sensory activities (e.g., looking or listening carefully), and controlling motor processes. We have difficulty dividing attention among several tasks, or attending to all the information provided by the senses (Broadbent, 1958; Treisman 1969). As a result, we often do not perceive most of the information that is available to us (Lavie, 1995). As Nobel Laureate Herb Simon has said, "a wealth of information creates a poverty of attention (Varian, 1995)." The "perceptual" and "motor" processors also have limitations, i.e., the eyes and ears can detect a limited range of light and sound.

Short-term memory is limited to two separate stores of relatively small capacity (see Figure 1). The presence of separate memory stores has received significant recent support (Baddeley, 1992, 1998; Baddeley, Chincotta, & Adlam, 2001; Wickens, 2002; Wickens & Liu, 1988; Winn, 1990). Baddeley's (1992) terminology has been generally adopted as the standard; he refers to these separate resources as "visio-spatial" and "articulatory-loop" memory. While Chase and Simon (1973a, 1973b) adopted Miller's (1956) estimate for the size of each short-term memory store as about 7 ± 2 items, more recently, the size of the visio-spatial store has been estimated as a maximum of 4 items (Zhang & Simon, 1985; Gobet & Clarkson, 2004; Gobet & Simon, 2000). These limitations are additive; it is possible to simultaneously hold about four items in visio-spatial memory while holding approximately seven items in articulatory-loop memory.

Up to this point, we have described the construct of "cognitive effort" as it applies to individual persons rather than groups of persons. In the next sections, we assimilate Hutchins (1991) construct of distributed cognition, and Wegner's (1987) theory of transactive memory which allow us to bridge the unit of analysis from individuals to groups.

Distributed Cognition

Not only do individuals have cognitive limitations, groups are also limited in their capacity to remember everything required to accomplish the task. Hutchins (1991) introduced distributed cognition as a mechanism to explain how high-performing teams create a distributed socio-technical system. Socio-technical systems refer to groups of people, and the technologies they use to interact. Hutchins asserts that a distributed socio-technical system engages in two kinds of cognitive work: the cognition that is the task, and the cognition that governs the coordination of the elements of the task. The cognitive properties of this socio-technical system are produced by an interaction between the structures internal to individuals and structures external to individuals.

The technologies used by a socio-technical system may be as simple as paper and pencil, or as complex as a jet cockpit. Hutchins (1995) describes the complex process by which a commercial jet aircraft transitions from cruise flight to landing: there are several steps, each requiring careful consideration of aircraft weight, speed, and configuration of airfoils. The task requires the crew to perform complex computational tasks while simultaneously monitoring the performance of the aircraft, as well as remembering the appropriate sequence of actions that result in a safe landing. The task creates a high cognitive load, and is prone to errors. Aircraft systems designers have found that placing a "bug" on the airspeed indicator (an external representation) reduces cognitive effort.

Distributed cognition allows us to consider that cognitive effort can be distributed among group members and external representations. That is, elements of a task might be represented in the external environment, and be available to the group for inspection. By making a representation "public", the group can share it. External representations (at the least) serve to expand the amount of available memory for the group (see Figure 2).

Proposition 1: External representations increase the memory available to the group.

Group memory, in this case, could be defined as:

$$(N * (4 + 7)) + i + j - (N * k)$$

where N is the group size, 4 and 7 being the established estimates for the capacity of the separate channels of short term memory, i is the number of visio-spatial external representations and j is the number of articulatory-loop external representations and k is a function of the amount of attention each team member has. Attention is a scarce resource and impacts the ability to maintain items in short-term memory. Note that these external representations can be technical artifacts that extend the memory (and cognitive) capacity of socio-technical systems, without directly affecting the communications (behaviors) of the group members.

In our TIAA-CREF example, if the team is supported with a shared workspace, the quantitative manager could display the expected risk characteristics (beta) of a particular portfolio. This would be the external representation and could take the form of an electronic "post-it" note, or symbol. All the other group members could refer to that representation as they conduct their analyses and thus not have to store this data in their memory.

Transactive Memory

Group memory may now be larger, but not everyone in the group has access to it. For these memories (including external representations) to be available to the group, one or more members of the group must remember where to find the information they need. In order to achieve the benefits of collective recall, the individual group members will require a system for encoding, storing, retrieving, and communicating their own and other's representations. This system has been called a transactive memory system (Wegner, 1987) and includes the cognitive abilities of the individuals as well as meta-memory, that is, the beliefs that the members have about their memories. Members of a group have access to the collective memory by virtue of knowing which person remembers which information (see Figure 3).

By having a shared awareness of who knows what information, cognitive load is reduced because each individual only has to remember "who knows what" in the

Figure 2. Distributed cognition increases the size of group memory

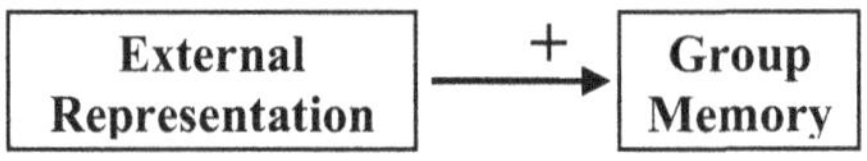

Figure 3. Transactive Memory increases the size of group memory

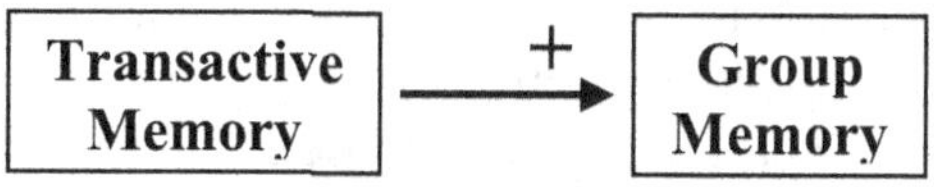

group and not the information itself. Greater access to expertise can be achieved, and there is less redundancy of effort (Wegner, Erber, & Raymond, 1991). Mohammed and Dumville (2001) point out that developing a transactive memory system reduces the rehashing of shared information and allows for the pooling of unshared information. Moreland (1999) also showed that transactive memory systems improved performance and that training people together allowed for the development of such a system. It is not yet clear if communication is essential for building transactive memory. Hollingshead and Brandon (2003) argue that group memory is increased when there is communication and is better when the communication conditions are the same at the time of learning and at recall than when they are different. Moreland and Myaskovsky (2000), however, showed that communication itself was not responsible for improved performance; groups that had handouts of each other's skills, yet did not communicate with each other, performed as well as the members of the group who were trained together. Perhaps external representations of transactive memory can suffice when the decision environment is static.

Recently, Brandon and Hollingshead (2004) suggest that transactive memory can be defined as an explicit portrait of relationships between task, expertise and people, or "TEP" units. A TEP unit relates a conception of a task to hierarchically organized domains of knowledge (expertise), and then to a person(s) (location). Complete TEP units are quite useful because we can use them to directly access the distributed knowledge. A TEP unit provides a guide for "who knows what". Partial TEP units—units missing T, E, or P information—is less useful because we now have a broader subset to search for the knowledge.

To integrate distributed cognition with transactive memory, the group socio-technical system must develop incorporate TEP units. And, if TEP units are placed into the external environment, the effort required recalling "who knows what" is reduced, thus increasing the groups' cognitive processing capacity.

Proposition 2: Transactive memory systems increase the cognitive capacity of groups.

The difficulty of maintaining an accurate transactive memory increases linearly with the size of the group. To illustrate this point, we make the assumption that each group member has a reasonably accurate representation of "what the whole group knows," and a similarly accurate knowledge of "what I know." Maintaining an accurate map of "who knows what" requires remembering the TEP units for at least (N-2) group members, where there are N members in the group. As the group grows in size, the task of maintaining an accurate transactive memory map increases linearly. Thus, transactive memory increases the collective cognitive resources available to the group, but there is also an increasing burden on those collective resources related to maintaining the group transactive memory. By implication, there is some optimum size for any task-group, such that the group has the benefit of its collective wisdom, without expending all its efforts on maintaining awareness of one another.

Returning to the financial management example, the skill sets and sector responsibilities of the sector analysts (and all other group members) should be made publicly available. When a new or existing group member wishes to know the forecast profile for a particular company, if they don't find it as an external representation, they can search the transactive memory system, to find out who to ask. The group would not have to build or hold this knowledge in their memories.

Stimulating Structures and Coordination

Public representations have been studied before in other contexts. Grassé (1959) coined the term stigmergy, referring to a class of mechanisms, or stimulating structures, that mediate animal-animal interactions. The concept has been used to explain the emergence, regulation, and control of collective activities of social insects (Susi & Ziemke, 2001). Social insects exhibit a coordination paradox: they seem to be cooperating in an organized way. However, when looking at any individual insect, they appear to be working independently as though they were not involved in any collective task. The explanation of the paradox provided by stigmergy is that the insects interact indirectly by placing stimulating structures in their environments. These stimulating structures trigger specific actions in other individuals (Theraulaz & Bonabeau, 1999). Stigmergy appears to be the ultimate example of reduction of cognitive effort because social insects, having essentially no cognitive capability, are able to perform complex collaborative tasks.

We suggest that this concept can be applied to human teams, i.e., when a stimulating structure is placed in the external environment by an individual, other team members can interpret it and take appropriate action, without the need for specific communication or coordination (see Figure 4). Stigmergy in its current form is complementary to distributed cognition, because the stimulating structure may or may not have any cognitive properties. However, we suggest that if a stimulating structure (artifact) is mapped to a cognitive memory construct (chunk or template as discussed later), the cognitive effort required for coordination and collaboration can be significantly reduced (Hayne, Smith, & Vijayasarathy, 2005a).

Figure 4. Stimulating structures improve team coordination

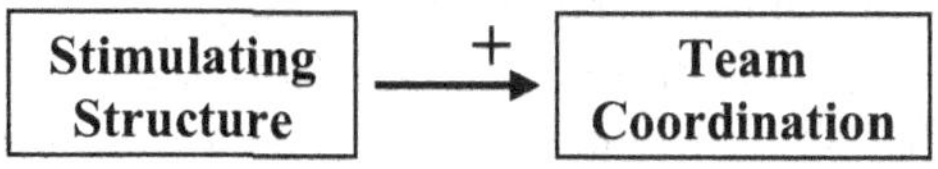

Proposition 3: Stimulating structures reduce the effort required for cognition that governs the group's coordination on the elements of a task.

In a group of size N, it may be necessary for each member to coordinate their activities with every other member. In this extreme case, the amount of dyadic coordination required will be N*(N-1). That is, the maximum amount of coordination required will increase as the square of the number of members in the group. Thus, the amount of cognitive effort required for coordinating activities will quickly exceed the available collective cognitive resources as the group size increases. A potential benefit of the stigmergy strategy is that it removes the requirement for every group member to explicitly coordinate with every other member. Stigmergy can extend the maximum useful size of a group, at least to the limits that are imposed by transactive memory as discussed earlier.

Continuing with our TIAA-CREF example, acquisition specialists would display a "recommend buy at X" for a particular stock on the shared workspace. Once this stimulating structure is represented on the screen, portfolio and quantitative managers would immediately take whatever action they deemed appropriate without the need for further coordination or communication. We will recommend a format for display of this information in the next section.

Template Theory and Memory Chunks

While we have shown that various types of external representations are important, we suggest it is critical that they be mapped directly to the right cognitive memory construct, chunks or more specifically, templates. Experts in various domains vastly outperform novices in the recall of meaningful material coming from their domain of expertise. To account for this result, Chase and Simon (1973a, 1973b) proposed that experts acquire a vast database of chunks, containing, as a first estimate, 50,000 chunks. When presented with material from their domain of expertise, experts recognize chunks and place a pointer to them in short-term memory. These chunks, each of which contains several elements that novices see as units, allow experts to recall information well beyond what non-experts can recall (Simon, 1974).

However, recent intensive research in skilled memory has shown that parts of the original chunking model must be incorrect. For example, in contrast to the usual assumptions about short-term memory, chess masters are relatively insensitive to interference tasks (Charness, 1976; Frey & Adesman, 1976) and can recall several boards that have been presented successively (Cooke, Atlas, Lane, & Berger, 1993; Gobet & Simon, 1996a). In addition, Chase and Ericsson (1982) and Staszewski (1990) have shown that highly trained subjects can memorize up to 100 digits dictated at a brisk rate (1 second per digit). Experts can also increase the size of their chunks based on new information; effectively increasing short-term memory (Gobet & Simon, 1998). Because an explanation of this performance based on chunking requires learning far too many chunks, Chase, Ericsson and Staszewski proposed that these subjects have developed structures ("retrieval structures") that allow them to encode information rapidly into long-term memory (LTM). Such structures have been used at least since classical times, when rhetoricians would link parts of a speech to a well-known architectural feature of the hall in which the speech was to take place, to facilitate recall (Yates, 1966). Retrieval structures are an essential aid to expert memory performance. Gobet and Simon (1996b) went on to demonstrate that the time required to encode and retrieve chunks is much shorter than previously believed. These results lead to the development of template theory.

Template theory assumes that many chunks develop into more complex structures (templates), having a "core" of data to represent a known pattern of information, and slots for variable data to enhance the core (Gobet and Simon, 1996a; Gobet and Simon, 2000). Templates have been referred to by various other names in other non-cognitive domains, i.e. schemas (Bartlett, 1932), frames (Minsky, 1977), prototypes (Goldin, 1978; Hartston & Wason, 1983), etc. In the domain of chess, templates allow rapid encoding and retrieval from long-term memory of more data than chunks (10-15 items as opposed to 4-5 items). For example, when a chess position pattern is recognized (say, as a King's Indian defense), the corresponding stored representation of the chess board provides specific information about the location of a number of core pieces (perhaps a dozen) together with slot data which may possess default values ("usual" placements in that opening) that may be quickly revised. Templates are cued by salient characteristics of the position, and are retrieved from long-term memory in a fraction of the time than other memory structures.

If a template can be retrieved from long-term memory in essentially the same time as other constructs from short-term memory, the team can significantly increase memory capacity by representing templates in the external environment, for all to see, attend to and retrieve (see Figure 5).

Figure 5: The use of templates expands the capacity of short-term memory

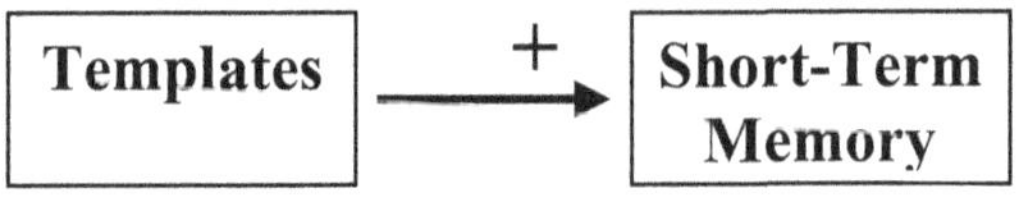

Proposition 4: Templates increase the effective size of group short term memory.

Framed in our financial services example, we suggest that the "buy" simulating structure from the previous section be displayed in a form that matches the memory structure in which the group has been trained. This might be some kind of icon in the shared workspace, with a ticker symbol and limit price embedded within the icon. The icon serves as an external representation of the "buy" template. The core data about the firm will be retrieved from the individual's memory and the slot memory for limit price will be overwritten by the data on the screen. Group members do not have to keep all this information in short-term memory because it can be so effortlessly retrieved when needed.

The network of templates is grown by two learning mechanisms, familiarization and discrimination. When a new object is presented, it is sorted through a hierarchical discrimination net. When a template node in the discrimination net is reached, the new object is compared with the image at the node. If the existing image under-represents the new object, features are added to the stored image (familiarization). If the information in the existing image and the new object differ on some feature, the new object is stored as a new node in the discrimination net (discrimination). Gobet and Jackson (2002) have demonstrated this process with complete novice subjects when learning chess.

Thus, template theory offers a major advantage over previous representations of short-term memory. Template theory offers the possibility that we may discover ways to improve human performance by taking advantage of the distinctions between the cognitive structures of core and slot memory.

Situation Assessment, Response Selection and Template Core/Slot

While template theory describes an innovative way to retrieve memories, we need decision theory to act upon them. Klein (1993) developed the theory of recognition-primed decision making (RPD) to describe how individual experts make decisions in naturalistic environments and suggested that experts make decisions by recognizing patterns in a developing situation. According to RPD, tactical decision makers recognize the current situation in so far as it is similar to some recalled and similar situation stored in their memory. This situation assessment, and its associated plan of action (or response selection), is retrieved from memory for use in the current situation. RPD has been validated by Kaempf, Klein, and Wolf (1996) when they found that experts make almost 90% of their decisions by "feature matching" between the current situation and one from prior experience. Experts spent most of their time scanning the environment and developing their situation assessments.

Relatively little time was spent selecting and implementing responses. Because of the similar results from the domain of chess (Gobet, 1997; Gobet & Simon 1998; Gobet & Simon, 2000), we argue that from a cognitive perspective, experts build discrimination nets of templates to enable this feature matching.

It is at this point where template theory provides insight to the cognitive mechanisms behind situation assessment and response selection for individuals. As a decision maker scans their environment they are directing attention to their perceptual processes. The information they perceive is sorted through their template discrimination net, and when core items are noticed, the appropriate templates are retrieved. In other words, core data items activate recognition of familiar patterns, thus creating situation awareness (see Figure 6a). As templates are retrieved, the slot data are made available in short-term memory. These slot data provide additional information to the decision maker regarding variants of the patterns, and potential strategies for action. In other words, the slot data provide the key to successful responses (see Figure 6b).

Evidence suggests that teams perform essentially the same steps as individual experts, with some additional executive functions (Hayne, Smith, & Turk, 2003; Hayne, Smith, & Vijayasarathy, 2005a). Similar to individual experts, teams assess the situation and perform "feature-matching" tasks which trigger recall of similar situations from their collective memory. The "core" of the template appears to be retrieved first by team members (Hayne, Smith, & Vijayasarathy, 2005b). Then, teams select a response by adapting a strategy from their previous experience and slot data is used to refine the response.

Proposition 5: Template core data enables group situation assessment.

Proposition 6: Template slot data enables group response selection.

In our final portfolio management example, when the "buy" icon is displayed on the shared workspace, all team members who attend to this stimulating structure, retrieve the core data associated with the "buy" template. This retrieval is effortless, and the team members know exactly what response is appropriate. While this significantly increases e-collaboration, we suggest that if slot data is also represented, i.e. the date/time by which a trade needs to be completed, a more detailed response can be motivated in the other group members.

Figure 6a. Template core data improves situation awareness

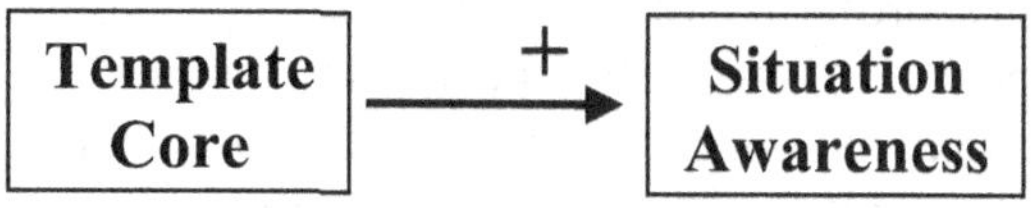

Figure 6b. Template slot data improves response selection

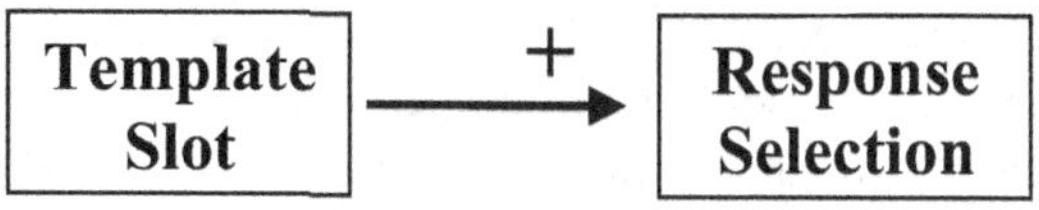

Cognitive Strategies

In the previous sections we have described the general limitations of cognitive capacity for attention, perception, and memory. We have explained in some detail the mechanisms that facilitate individual and group recall and how they impact e-collaboration. Based on these fundamental properties of cognition, we now put forward three strategies that can be applied to any task. These global strategies should reduce individual cognitive effort and thus improve group work.

Minimize the Net Cognitive Effort Required for a Collaborative Task

Remember, the total cognitive effort required for collaboration is comprised of two components, one associated with task-related cognition, and another associated with coordination-related cognition. These separate efforts draw from the same pool of available cognitive resources. Thus effort expended on coordination activities reduces the cognitive effort available for task-related activities.

Keeping an item "active" in short-term memory requires effort from our cognitive processor. The cognitive processor also directs attention to perceptual processes and activates motor processes. In socio-technical systems, the cognitive processor for each group member must devote some available effort to coordination-cognition. Coordination cognition may include reserving some perceptual capacity for intra-group communications, some short-term memory for the current status of other group members' activities, and some cognitive processor capacity for noticing when coordination actions are required. So, for groups engaged in e-collaboration, the members' cognitive processors must perform several tasks: maintaining information active in short-term memory, retrieving-from and storing-to long-term memory, directing perceptual processes, and activating motor responses. If a cognitive processor becomes overloaded, there may be insufficient attention resources available to maintain information active in short-term memory. In other words, we may forget things because we are busy, rather than because the demands on our short-term memory are excessive. Strictly speaking, this is not a failure of short-term memory. Rather it represents a limitation of the collective cognitive resources available for perception, attention, and memory. This distinction is important. In order to make a task easier, we must understand why it is hard. Collaboration tasks are especially difficult, because each group member must reserve some cognitive capacity for coordination-cognition, leaving less available for task-cognition.

We propose that e-collaboration systems should seek to minimize the net cognitive effort required by a group in the performance of a task. The system should promote load-sharing so that any member of the group is not forced to exceed their individual limitations for attention, memory, or perception. The net cognitive effort includes the efforts expended by group members to coordinate their actions. We have discussed how the stigmergy strategy can reduce the cognitive effort required for coordination. Every collaborative task is likely to have some optimum amount of coordination which permits the group members to achieve their collective goals without expending unnecessary effort on the coordination process.

Beyond these basic prescriptions for reducing effort, we offer an additional insight. As mentioned earlier, most naturalistic tasks involve situation assessment and response selection (Kaempf, Klein, & Wolf, 1996). Templates are discriminated by their core data items; retrieval of matching templates provides the initial options for situation assessment. Response selection is based primarily on the slot data: once a pattern is recognized by virtue of the core data, the response depends on the state of the ancillary information. This provides an opportunity to reduce cognitive effort by tailoring e-collaboration tools for the task: situation assessment or response selection. During situation assessment, core data items should be perceptually salient. Furthermore, if different templates share some core items but not others, then the discrimination task can be made less effortful by drawing the users' attention to the non-shared core items. In other words, draw the users' attention to the core items that are most diagnostic of the situation. When situation assessment has been completed, the information presentation can be altered to make the slot data items more salient, as an aid to response selection.

Transform Computational Tasks to Perceptual Tasks to Increase Performance

In the example of the "airspeed bug" on the airspeed indicator (above), the crew transforms an effortful cognitive task into a simple perceptual task (see Figure 7): when the airspeed needle points at the bug, the pilots perform the next action in their landing procedure. The airspeed bug provides a simple visual cue to the current state of the landing procedure. The external representation frees up short-term memory and cognitive capability in the crew members.

For humans, stigmergy is especially effective under conditions of time pressure. The limitations of short-term memory are exacerbated by the stress of time pressure: it has been shown that stress causes the release of a cortical steroid that interferes with memory (de Quervain, Roozendaal, Nitsch, McGaugh, & Hock, 2000; Kirschbaum, Wolf, & Hellhammer, 1996). In complex multi-tasking environments, it is not uncommon for decision groups to be interrupted in the middle of a process. After dealing with the interruption, the group may find it difficult to resume the process. Often, this results in restarting from the beginning. Using stigmergy, systems designers can provide stimulating structures (perceptual cues) to the point in a process at which execution was interrupted. Transforming the effortful task of remembering where to resume to a simple perceptual task can reduce errors and save time. This is especially useful under time pressure, when saving time is critical and the stress of time pressure further degrades our already limited memory capacity.

Transform Task Modality to Reduce Effort

When the demands of a task exceed the capacity of either short-term memory store (visio-spatial or articulatory-loop), task performance degrades. Thus the mode by which information is presented can affect task performance. Consider an e-collaboration system that presents information to a group in the performance of their task: if the task is visually intensive, presentation of any additional information in visual form may exceed the capacity of the members' visio-spatial stores. However, in the same visually intensive task, if additional information is presented aurally,

Figure 7. Cognitive task type transformation improves performance

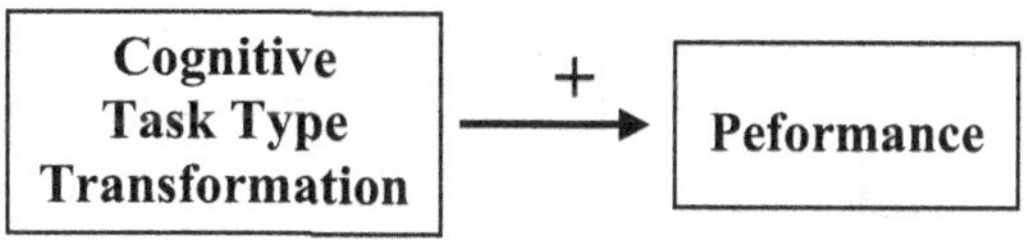

then the additional information may be maintained in the members' articulatory-loop memory, and not interfere with their task performance. For optimal performance, we suggest that each group member's cognitive load be balanced between both visio-spatial and articulatory-loop. Tasks should be transformed between task modes as necessary (see Figure 8) to accomplish this goal.

In summary, balancing the load between visio-spatial and articulatory-loop memory is an effective strategy for improving task performance.

Implications for Practitioners

There are several benefits that may result from the approach described here. We expect that it is possible to:

1. Reduce the amount of overt supervision and coordinating actions required for groups engaged in complex collaborative tasks,
2. Improve organizational memory for "who knows what,"
3. Make decisions faster, and
4. Reduce errors of situation assessment.

To illustrate these advantages, we refer to a recent article by Talbot (2004) which describes military operations in Afghanistan. Talbot describes an operation that occurred in the fall of 2001 in which an insurgent convoy was detected, surveilled, and interdicted. What makes the example unusual is that the forces involved were collaborating outside their formal chains of command in an ad-hoc team:

> *The scene was a cold night in 2001... A U.S. Air force pilot en route from Uzbekistan noticed flashing lights in the mountains below, near the Pakistan border... he radioed his observation to the webmaster. The webmaster relayed the message across a secure network accessible to special forces in the region. One team replied that it was near the position and would investigate. The team identified a convoy of trucks*

Figure 8. Cognitive task mode transformation improves performance

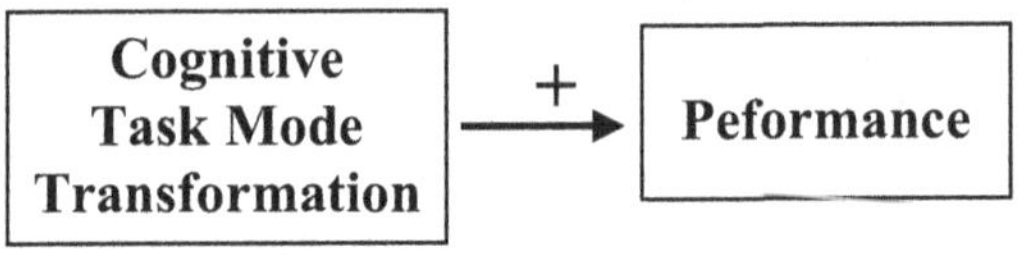

> *carrying Taliban fighters and got on the radio to ask if any bombers were in range. One U.S. Navy plane was not far off. Within minutes, the plane bombed the front and rear of the convoy, sealing off the possibility of escape. Not long after, a gunship arrived and destroyed the crippled Taliban column.* (Talbot, p. 44)

The example above illustrates the advantages of a distributed socio-technical system having access to the cognitive aids described in this article. In this case, the operation was triggered by the application of good transactive memory: the pilot of the first aircraft notices something unusual, and he knows "who needs to know this?" The webmaster uses a technical artifact to place a stimulating structure on a publicly available external representation: he posts the observation on a web page. All the special forces in the area are scanning their environment—they notice the stimulating structure placed on the public representation. Without requiring any external supervision, the nearest special forces team immediately understands the implication of the stimulating structure. In contrast, other teams in the region also know that the stimulating structure has no relevance to their missions. Thus the stimulating structure has made it possible to reduce the effort expended for coordination. This example also illustrates the reductions in time-to-decision that can be achieved by minimizing the degree of overt supervision. Furthermore, by virtue of having the nearest team make a visual identification of the convoy, the possibility of a tragic mistake is minimized.

While this example is in the military domain, we believe the benefits are equally applicable to other complex collaborative tasks. For example, the collaboration by multiple public agencies in their responses to natural disasters such as hurricanes or earthquakes could be improved through application of the principles outlined in this article. On a more mundane scale, many businesses charge their employees to work on cross-functional teams for projects ranging from strategic planning to employee parking. Achieving these outcomes in less time and with less overt coordination would be beneficial.

Conclusion

We have integrated recent cognitive theory of individual decision-making and applied it to collaboration. Vessey (1991) coined the term "cognitive fit" to describe individual enhanced performance when there is a good match between the information emphasized in the representation type and that required by the task type. We offer an extension to Vessey's findings and give propositions for further study. We have proposed several techniques by which collective cognitive effort may be minimized.

We believe that our prescriptions, grounded in cognition, have wide applicability and offer significant opportunities to improve group performance.

Acknowledgment

This research is supported by Dr. Mike Letsky at the Office of Naval Research, Grant #N00014-02-1-0371.

References

Baddeley, A. (1992). Working memory. *Science, 255*(5044), 556-559.

Baddeley, A. (1998). Recent developments in working memory. *Current Opinion in Neurobiology, 8*(2), 234-238.

Baddeley, A., Chincotta, D., & Adlam, A. (2001). Working memory and the control of action: Evidence from task switching. *Journal of Experimental Psychology: General, 130,* 641-657.

Bartlett, F. C. (1932). *Remembering.* Cambridge: Cambridge University Press.

Benbasat, I., & Lim, L. (1993) The effects of group, task context and technology variables on the usefulness of group support systems: A meta-analysis of experimental studies. *Small Group Research, 24*(4), 430-462.

Brandon, D., & Hollingshead, A. (2004). Transactive memory systems in organizations: Matching tasks, expertise, and people. *Organization Science, 15*(6), 633-644.

Broadbent, D. E. (1958). *Perception and communication.* London: Pergammon Press.

Card, S. K., Moran, T. P., & Newell, A. (1986). The model human processor: An engineering model of human performance. In K. R. Boff, L. Kaufman, & J. P. Thomas (Eds.), *Handbook of perception and human performance 2* (Chap. 45). New York: Wiley & Sons.

Charness, N. (1976). Memory for chess positions: Resistance to interference. *Journal of Experimental Psychology: Human Learning and Memory, 2,* 641-653.

Chase, W. G., & Ericsson, K. A. (1982). Skill and working memory. In G. H. Bower (Ed.), *The psychology of learning and motivation* (Vol. 16, pp. 1-58). New York: Academic Press.

Chase, W. G., & Simon, H. A. (1973a). Perception in chess. *Cognitive Psychology, 4,* 55-81.

Chase, W. G., & Simon, H. A. (1973b). The mind's eye in chess. In W. G. Chase (Ed.), *Visual information processing* (Chap. 5). New York: Academic Press.

Cooke, N.J., Atlas, R.S., Lane, D.M., & Berger, R.C. (1993). Role of high-level knowledge in memory for chess positions. *American Journal of Psychology, 106,* 321-351.

Dennis, A., Wixom, B., & Vandenberg, R. (2001). Understanding fit and appropriation effects in group support systems via meta-analysis. *MIS Quarterly, 25*(2), 167-193.

Dennis, A. R., & M. L. Williams, (2005). A meta analysis of group size effects in electronic brainstorming: More heads are better than one. *International Journal of e-Collaboration* (in press).

de Quervain, D. J.-F., Roozendaal, B., Nitsch, R.M., McGaugh, J. L., & Hock, C. (2000, April). Acute cortisone administration impairs retrieval of long-term declarative memory in healthy human subjects. *Nature Neuroscience, 3*(4).

Desanctis, G., & Gallupe, R. (1987). A foundation for the study of group decision support systems. *Management Science, 33,* 589-609.

Dunn, C., & Grabski, S. (2001). An investigation of localization as an element of cognitive fit in accounting model representations. *Decision Sciences, 32*(10), 55-94.

Frey, P.W., & Adesman, P. (1976). Recall memory for visually presented chess positions. *Memory and Cognition, 4,* 541-547.

Gobet, F. (1997). A pattern-recognition theory of search in expert problem solving. *Thinking and Reasoning, 3,* 291-313.

Gobet, F., & Clarkson, G. (in press). Chunks in expert memory: Evidence for the magical number four… or is it two? *Memory, 12*(6), 732-747

Gobet, F., & Jackson, S. (2002). In search of templates. *Cognitive Systems Research, 3*, 35-44.

Gobet, F., & Simon, H.A. (1996a). Templates in chess memory: A mechanism for recalling several boards. *Cognitive Psychology, 31,* 1-40.

Gobet, F., & Simon, H.A. (1996b). Recall of rapidly presented random chess positions is a function of skill. *Psychonomic Bulletin & Review, 3,* 159-163.

Gobet, F., & Simon, H. A. (1998). Expert chess memory: Revisiting the chunking hypothesis. *Memory, 6,* 225-255.

Gobet, F., & Simon, H. A. (2000). Five seconds or sixty? Presentation time in expert memory. *Cognitive Science, 24*(4), 651-682.

Goldin, S. E. (1978). Memory for the ordinary: Typicality effects in chess memory. *Journal of Experimental Psychology: Human Learning and Memory, 4*, 605-616.

Grassé, P. (1959). La Reconstruction du Nid et les Coordinations Inter-Individuelles Chez Bellicositermes Natalensis et Cubitermes sp. La théorie de la Stigmergie: Essai d'interprétation du Comportement des Termites Constructeurs. *Insectes Sociaux, 6*, 41-81.

Hayne, S., Smith, C.A.P., & Turk, D. (2003). The effectiveness of groups recognizing patterns. *International Journal of Human Computer Studies, 59*, 523-543.

Hayne, S., Smith, C.A.P., & Vijayasarathy, L. (2005a). The use of pattern-communication tools and team pattern recognition. *IEEE Transactions on Professional Communication, 48*(4), 377-390.

Hayne, S., Smith, C.A.P., & Vijayasarathy, L. (2005b). Pattern recognition: Sharing cognitive chunks under time pressure. In *Proceedings of Hawaii International Conference on System Sciences* (pp. 30b-40b).

Hartston, W. R., & Wason, P. C. (1983). *The psychology of chess.* London: Batsford.

Hollingshead, A., & Brandon, D. (2003). Transactive memory systems in organizations: Matching tasks, expertise, and people. *Human Communication Research, 29*(4), 607-615.

Hutchins, E. (1991). The social organization of distributed cognition. In L. Resnick, J. Levine, & S. Teasdale (Eds.), *Perspectives on socially shared cognition* (pp. 283-307). Washington, DC: American Psychological Association.

Hutchins, E., (1995). How a cockpit remembers its speeds. *Cognitive Science, 19*, 265-288.

Jessup, L., & Valacich, J. (1993) Group support systems: A new frontier. New York: MacMillan.

Kaempf, G., Klein, G., & S. Wolf, (1996). Decision making in complex naval command-and-control environments. *Human Factors, 38*(2), 220-231.

Kahneman, D. (1973). *Attention and effort.* Englewood Cliffs, NJ: Prentice-Hall.

Keltner, J.S. (1989). Facilitation: Catalyst for group problem-solving. *Management Communication Quarterly, 3*(1), 8-31.

Kirschbaum, C., Wolf, O. T., & Hellhammer, D. H. (1996). Stress- and treatment-induced elevations of cortisol levels associated impaired declarative memory in healthy adults. *Life Sciences, 58*(17), 1475-1483.

Klein, G. (1993). A recognition-primed decision (RPD) model of rapid decision making. In G. A. Klein, J. Orasanu, R. Calderwood, & C. E. Zsambok (Eds.), *Decision making in action: Models and methods.* Norwood, NJ: Ablex.

Lavie, N. (1995). Perceptual load as a necessary condition for selective attention. *Experimental Psychology: Perception and Performance, 21(3)*, 451-468.

McGrath, J. E., & Hollingshead (1994). *Groups: Interacting with technology.* Thousand Oaks, CA: Sage.

McLeod, P. (1992). An assessment of the experimental literature on electronic support of group work: Results of a meta-analysis. *Human-Computer Interaction, 7*(3), 257-280.

Miller, G. A. (1956). The magical number seven, plus or minus two: Some limits on our capacity for processing information. *The Psychological Review, 63,* 81-97.

Minsky, M. (1977). Frame-system theory. In P. N. Johnson-Laird & P. C. Wason (Eds.), *Thinking: Readings in cognitive science.* Cambridge: Cambridge University Press.

Mohammed, S., & Dumville, B. C. (2001). Team mental models in a team knowledge framework: Expanding theory and measurement across disciplinary boundaries. *Journal of Organizational Behavior, 22*, 89-106.

Moreland, R. (1999). Transactive memory and job performance: Helping workers learn who knows what, in J. Levine, L. Thompson, & D Messick (Eds.), *Shared cognition in organizations: The management of knowledge* (pp. 3-32). Mahwah, NJ: Lawrence Erlbaum Associates.

Moreland, R. L., & Myaskovsky, L. (2000). Exploring the performance benefits of group training: Transactive memory or improved communication? *Organizational behavior and human decision processes, 82*, 117-133.

Navon, D., & Gopher, D. (1979). On the economy of the human processing system. *Psychological Review, 86*, 214-253.

Nunamaker, J.F. (1997). Future research in group support systems: Needs, some question, and possible directions. *International Journal of Human-Computer Studies, 47*(3), 357-385.

Pinsonneault, A., & Kraemer, K. (1990). The effects of electronic meetings on group processes and outcomes: An assessment of the empirical research. *European Journal of Operational Research, 46*(2), 143-161.

Schmidt, J., Montoya-Weiss, M., & Massey, A. (2001). New product development decision-making effectiveness: Comparing individuals, face-to-face teams, and virtual teams. *Decision Sciences, 32*(4), 575-600.

Simon, H.A. (1974). How big is a chunk? *Science, 183*, 482-488.

Staszewski, J. (1990). Exceptional memory: The influence of practice and knowledge on the development of elaborative encoding strategies. In F. E. Weinert & W. Schneider (Eds.), *Interactions among aptitudes, strategies, and knowledge in cognitive performance* (pp. 252-285). New York: Springer.

Susi, T., & Ziemke, T. (2001). Social cognition, artefacts, and stigmergy: A cooperative analysis of theoretical frameworks for the understanding of artefact-mediated collaborative activity. *Journal of Cognitive Systems Research, 2,* 273-290.

Talbot, D. (2004). How technology failed in Iraq. *Technology Review*, November, 36-45.

Theraulaz, G., & Bonabeau, E. (1999). A brief history of stigmergy. *Artificial Life, 5*, 97-116.

Thompson, L., & Fine, G. A. (1999). Socially shared cognition, affect, and behavior: A review and integration. *Personality and Social Psychology Review, 3*(4), 278-302.

TIAA-CREF. (2004). Performance in concert: The keys to TIAA-CREF's investment philosophy. *Advance,* Fall, 12-15.

Treisman, A. M. (1969). Strategies and models of selective attention. *Psychological Review, 76*, 282-299.

U.S. Bureau of Labor Statisitics. (2004). *Productivity and costs*. Retrieved November 5, 2004, from Unitied States Department of Labor, Bureau of Labor Statistics, Archived Productivity and Costs: ftp://ftp.bls.gov/pub/news.release/History/prod2.09022004.news

Varian, H. (1995). The information economy: How much will two bits be worth in the digital marketplace? *Scientific American*, 200-201.

Vessey, I. (1991). Cognitive fit: A theory-based analysis of the graphs versus tables literature. D*ecision Sciences, 22*(2) 219-240.

Wegner, D. M. (1987). Transactive memory: A contemporary analysis of the group mind. In B. Mullen & G. R. Goethals (Eds.), *Theories of group behavior* (pp. 185-208). New York: Springer.

Wegner, D. M., Erber, R., & Raymond, P. (1991). Transactive memory in close relationships. *Journal of Personality and Social Psychology, 61*(6), 923-929.

Wickens, C. D. (1984). *Processing resources in attention.* In R. Parasuraman & R. Davies (Eds.), Varieties of attention (pp. 63-101). Orlando, FL: Academic Press.

Wickens, C. D. (2002). Multiple resources and performance prediction. *Theoretical Issues in Ergonomic Science, 3*, 159-177.

Wickens, C. D., & Liu, Y. (1988). Codes and modalities in multiple resources: A success and qualification. *Human Factors, 30*, 599-616.

Winn, W. (1990). Encoding and retrieval of information in maps and diagrams. *IEEE Transactions On Professional Communication, 33*(3), 103-107.

Yates, F. (1966) *The art of memory*. Chicago: University of Chicago Press.

Zhang, G., & Simon, H.A. (1985). STM capacity for Chinese works and idioms: Chunking and acoustical loop hypotheses. *Memory and Cognition, 13*, 193-201.

Chapter XIII

A Meta-Analysis of Group Size Effects in Electronic Brainstorming: More Heads are Better than One

Alan R. Dennis, Indiana University, USA
Michael L. Williams, Pepperdine University, USA

Abstract

Electronic brainstorming (EBS) has been a focus of academic research since the 1980s. The results suggest that in most—but not all—cases, groups using EBS produce more ideas than groups using verbal brainstorming. In contrast, the results comparing groups using EBS to groups using nominal group brainstorming have been mixed: sometimes EBS group produce more ideas, while in other cases, nominal groups produce more. This article examines the effects of group size on EBS, verbal brainstorming, and nominal group brainstorming. We found that group size is a significant factor in predicting the performance of EBS relative to verbal brainstorming, and nominal group brainstorming. As group size increases, the relative benefit of EBS increases. EBS groups outperform verbal groups when group size reaches four people. EBS groups outperform nominal groups when group size reaches 10 people.

Introduction

Communication is a fundamental element of group creativity. Researchers have long considered how to improve communication to improve group creativity, but unfortunately the general conclusion of this research is that, people generate fewer ideas when they work together in groups than when they work separately and later pool their ideas (i.e., nominal groups) (Mullen, Johnson, & Salas, 1991; Paulus, Larey, & Ortega, 1995).

Electronic brainstorming (EBS) was introduced in the 1980s, with the hope of using computer-mediated electronic communication to improve group creativity. With EBS, group members communicate by exchanging typed messages, instead of speaking verbally. Initial research on EBS suggested that EBS groups could generate more ideas than verbal brainstorming groups (e.g., Gallupe, Dennis, Cooper, Valacich, Bastianutti, & Nunamaker, 1992) and as many or more ideas as nominal groups who work in the presence of each other but do not exchange ideas (e.g., Dennis & Valacich, 1993). Recent research has challenged these early studies, suggesting that productivity gains compared to nominal groups are an "illusion" (Pinsonneault, Barki, Gallupe, & Hoppen, 1999). This challenge has sparked a new debate over the "illusion" or "pattern" of EBS productivity compared to other approaches, a debate that has led different researchers to different conclusions (cf. Dennis & Valacich, 1999; Pinsonneault & Barki, 1999).

The goal of this article is to integrate the previous research on EBS using meta-analysis to draw conclusions about the effects of EBS relative to verbal brainstorming and nominal group brainstorming. We begin by examining the important theoretical underpinnings of EBS and then examine each of the important ways in which EBS may change traditional approaches to creativity, and how group size affects the impacts of these factors. We then present the methods and results of our meta-analyses. We close with a discussion of these results and draw implications for future research and practice.

Process Gains and Losses from EBS

Much of the prior EBS research was guided by the processes gains and losses framework (Hill, 1982; Steiner, 1972). Simply put, communication among group members introduces factors into the brainstorming process that act to improve performance (process gains) and to impair performance (process losses) relative to individuals who work separately without communicating but later pool ideas (referred to as nominal groups). Several dozen plausible process losses and gains in verbal brainstorming and EBS have been proposed (see Camacho & Paulus, 1995;

Table 1. Potential processes gains and losses

	Nominal Group Brainstorming	Verbal Brainstorming	Electronic Brainstorming
Process Gains			
• Synergy	None	Increases as the size of the group increases	Increases as the size of the group increases
• Social Facilitation	Depends upon group structure	Some effect	Some effect
Process Losses			
• Production Blocking	None	Increases as the size of the group increases	None
• Evaluation Apprehension	None	Increases as the size of the group increases	None
• Social Loafing	Depends upon group structure	Increases as the size of the group increases	Increases as the size of the group increases
• Cognitive Interference	None	Increases as the size of the group increases	Some effect
• Communication Speed	Some Effect	None	Some Effect

Mullen et al., 1991; Pinsonneault et al., 1999). Two process gains (synergy, social facilitation) and five process losses (production blocking, social loafing, evaluation apprehension, cognitive interference and communication speed) have received the most research attention and are the ones that we believe are most important (Dennis & Valacich, 1999; Diehl & Stroebe, 1987; Pinsonneault & Barki, 1999; Pinsonneault et al., 1999). See Table 1.

Potential Process Gains

Synergy is the ability of an idea from one participant to trigger a new idea in another participant, an idea that would otherwise not have been produced (Dennis & Valacich, 1993; Lamm & Trommsdorff, 1973). Synergy—or the "assembly bonus" (Collins & Guetzkow, 1964)—is perhaps the most fundamental potential source of process gains. Osborn's (1957) advice to "piggyback" on the ideas of others strives to increase the synergy that participants derive by building on the ideas of others. Synergy will increase as the size of the group increases because there is likely to be a greater range of ideas with the potential to trigger new ideas (Dennis & Valacich, 1993; Gallupe et al., 1992; Valacich, Dennis, & Connolly, 1994). It should be noted that there is not a necessary, direct relationship between group size and synergy.

Two important variables have been shown to effect the development of synergy in group creativity: diversity and attention. The diversity of team membership has been shown to be related to higher-quality team decision making (Gruenfeld, 1995; Jackson, 1992), and group creativity (Bantal & Jackson, 1989; Jackson, May, & Whitney, 1995; Williams & O'Reilly, 1998). Diversity seems to have some effects on synergy, but the exact nature of the effect is still unclear. The second variable that affects synergy is attention to ideas. Recent research indicates that even small EBS groups can experiences process gains from synergy when participants receive instructions to focus their attention and memory on the ideas presented by others (Dugosh, Paulus, Roland, & Yang, 2000; Paulus & Yang, 2000). Each of these studies serves to emphasize the value of synergy in EBS while simultaneously suggesting additional moderating variables on the effect of group size on synergy.

Social facilitation is the ability of the presence of others to affect one's performance (Allport, 1920; Levine, Resnick, & Higgins, 1993; Zajonc, 1965). If individuals are experienced in performing a task, or expect that they can perform the task well, working in the presence of others improves performance (Robinson-Staveley & Cooper, 1990; Sanna, 1992). However, if individuals have low expectations about performance, working in the presence of others has been shown to impair performance (Robinson-Staveley & Cooper, 1990; Sanna, 1992). For relatively simple tasks such as those commonly used in brainstorming, social facilitation is typically seen as a potential process gain (Pinsonneault et al., 1999) but one with only a small effect (Bond & Titus, 1983). Social facilitation may also exist in nominal groups if participants work in the presence of each other even if they do not communicate, so it is best considered a process gain of group structure, not of group communication. Because it does not depend upon whether participants can communicate or not (but rather on how they sit), we do not view social facilitation as a true process gain that can be attributed to group interaction, but one that potentially flows to even nominal groups that work in the same room but do not communicate.

Potential Process Losses

Production blocking refers to the need to take turns speaking in verbal brainstorming (Diehl & Stroebe, 1987). When participants are prevented from contributing an idea when they first think of it, they may forget it or suppress it because the idea later seems less relevant or original. If they try to retain the idea, they must focus on remembering it, which prevents them from generating new ideas or attending to the ideas of others (Diehl & Stroebe, 1991).

Production blocking is the single most important source of process losses in verbal brainstorming groups (Diehl & Stroebe, 1987; Gallupe, Cooper, Grise, & Bastianutti, 1994; Valacich et al., 1994). Production blocking in verbal brainstorming groups increases as the size of the group increases, because the probability of occurrence increases directly with the number of participants and because more participants are blocked as size increases (Dennis & Valacich, 1993; Gallupe et al., 1992; Valacich et al., 1994). Production blocking is non-existent in nominal groups because group members do not communicate while generating ideas. Production blocking is essentially non-existent in EBS groups because all participants can contribute ideas simultaneously (Dennis & Valacich, 1993; Pinsonneault et al., 1999; Valacich et al., 1994).

Evaluation apprehension may cause participants in verbal brainstorming to withhold ideas because they fear a negative reaction from other participants (Diehl & Stroebe, 1987; Lamm & Trommsdorff, 1973). Osborn's (1957) advice to withhold criticism tries to reduce evaluation apprehension. Evaluation apprehension should be minimal in nominal groups because participants do not share ideas; when ideas are pooled they are usually anonymous. Evaluation apprehension in verbal brainstorming should increase as group size increases because there are more participants who might criticize an idea (Gallupe et al., 1992). EBS can be designed so that participants contribute ideas anonymously which should reduce or eliminate evaluation apprehension (Cooper, Gallupe, Pollard, & Cadsby, 1998; Dennis & Valacich, 1993).

Anonymity has been shown to effect behavior in several studies (Diener, 1979; Diener, Fraser, Beaman, & Kelem, 1976; Saks & Ostrom, 1973; Siegel, Dubrovsky, Kiesler, & McGuire, 1986; Zimbardo, 1969). Frequently, anonymity is seen to produce a deindividuating cover for behavior that would not otherwise occur (Diener, 1979). These deindividuating behaviors induce participants to share ideas that might otherwise be withheld due to evaluative apprehension. There is some evidence that participants in anonymous conditions contribute more controversial and non-redundant ideas than those in non-anonymous conditions (Cooper et al., 1998).

Prior research on anonymity is equivocal. Many laboratory experiments have examined the effects of anonymity on idea generation performance but virtually none have found any effects due to anonymity (Cooper et al., 1998; Dennis & Valacich, 1993). Prior studies on anonymity in EBS show no effects on inhibition (George, Easton, Nunamaker, & Northcraft, 1990; Hiltz, Turoff, & Johnson, 1989; Lea & Spears, 1991), group communication (Siegel et al., 1986) or group performance (George et al., 1990; Jessup, Connolly, & Galegher, 1990; Prentice-Dunn & Rogers, 1982). But anonymity does effect criticalness (Connolly, Jessup, & Valacich, 1990; Jessup et al., 1990; Lea & Spears, 1991; Postmes & Lea, 2000; Prentice-Dunn & Rogers, 1982) and can produce more conservative decisions (Hiltz et al., 1989).

In contrast to the findings from laboratory experiments with undergraduate students, there is significant anecdotal evidence from field studies that anonymity can have significant effects (c.f. Nunamaker, Dennis, Valacich, Vogel, George, 1991). There are also strong theoretical arguments to suggest that anonymity can be important in some situations (Diener, 1979; Diener et al., 1976; Saks & Ostrom, 1973; Siegel et al., 1986; Zimbardo, 1969). We believe—but cannot prove—that anonymity is important in some organizational situations but has little effect on undergraduate students working in ad hoc groups in laboratory settings. Such settings may foster fewer inhibitions than corporate settings with employees.

Social loafing (or free riding) is the tendency for individuals to expend less effort when working in a group than when working individually (Karau & Williams, 1993). Social loafing may arise because participants believe their contributions to be dispensable and not needed for group success and/or because responsibility for completing the task is diffused among many participants (Harkins & Petty, 1982; Karau & Williams, 1993; Latane, Williams, & Harkins, 1979). Social loafing is reduced when participants believe they are being evaluated as individuals, rather than collectively as a group (Karau & Williams, 1993). Therefore, differences in social loafing become more noticeable when members of nominal groups believe themselves to be working as individuals, not as members of groups. As with production blocking, social loafing can be expected to increase as group size increases because perceived dispensability and diffusion of responsibility increase as the number of participants increases. Social loafing is also made stronger when anonymity is provided in EBS. Anonymity was one of the manipulations of early social loafing studies (Bartis, Szymanski, & Harkins, 1988; Karau & Williams, 1993).

Cognitive interference is in many ways the inverse of synergy. Cognitive interference occurs when the ideas generated by other participants interfere with an individual's own idea generation activities (Pinsonneault & Barki, 1999; Straus, 1996). Cognitive interference may be due to the need to attend to ideas presented by others as they appear (e.g., in verbal brainstorming, a spoken idea disappears as soon as it is uttered so a missed idea is a lost idea). Cognitive interference may also be due to the content of the ideas contributed by others because ideas from others serve to stimulate cognitive activity in one area while limiting the flexibility of idea production (Ziegler, Diehl, & Zijlstra, 2000). That is, brainstorming may suffer from cognitive inertia by focusing idea generation on only one aspect of the overall task (Dennis & Valacich, 1993; Pinsonneault & Barki, 1999). The effect of cognitive inertia is strengthened by social influence processes and social convergence (Festinger, 1954; Larey & Paulus, 1999). As members compare behavior across the group, they tend to converge at a similar level, and when there is not a strong performance incentive, they tends to be at the level of the least productive members (Camacho & Paulus, 1995; Larey & Paulus, 1995; Paulus & Dzindolet, 1993).

Cognitive interference in verbal brainstorming groups should increase with group size, because more people are contributing more ideas which increase potential interference. EBS is less susceptible to cognitive interference because ideas are stored in the system as they are contributed so participants need not attend to them as they arrive, but instead can generate ideas as they choose and only interrupt their individual idea generation process when they desire the stimulation from other's ideas. While EBS may still suffer from cognitive inertia, the ability to provide for—or to intentionally induce –multiple simultaneous dialogues or threads of conversation means that it is quite unusual for groups to focus on one narrow set of ideas (Dennis, Valacich, Carte, Garfield, Haley, & Aronson, 1997; Dennis, Valacich, Connolly, & Wynne, 1996). In other words, EBS allows group members to carry on multiple, potentially unrelated conversations concurrently; they are thus to choose when and if they participate in each conversation. The ability of EBS to structure participants' cognitive focus may be one of its most powerful contributions (Dennis, Aronson, Heninger, & Walker, 1999; Dennis et al., 1997).

Communication speed is another potential process loss that is found in EBS and to some extent in nominal group brainstorming. Communication speed is influenced by the need to type or write rather than speak. For most people, speaking is faster than typing or writing (Williams & Karau, 1991) so the need to type may inhibit idea generation by slowing down communication (Nunamaker et al., 1991). To date, no studies have examined this potential process loss of EBS in detail. It should be noted that in prior studies, sometimes members of nominal groups have written their ideas, sometime they have typed their ideas, and sometimes they have spoken their ideas. Members of EBS groups can either type or speak their ideas, although in practice all research studies have required participants to type their ideas.

The Role of Group Size

One of the important factors in understanding the potential effects of EBS use is group size, because the balance of process gains and losses changes dramatically depending upon the size of the group. Although previous research indicates that dyads perform as well as nominal groups (Diehl & Stroebe, 1987; Mullen et al., 1991), size effects are clear in larger groups.

Verbal brainstorming groups, for example, should experience process gains of synergy and social facilitation as group size increases. But they also are expected to suffer from process losses that increase with the size of the group due to production blocking, social loafing, evaluation apprehension, and cognitive interference. Nominal group brainstorming experiences process gains from social facilitation but no gains from synergy. Likewise, if nominal groups anonymously sum the product of their work, they may experience some social loafing and communication speed problems, but no production blocking, evaluation apprehension, or cognitive interference. EBS groups should experience synergy that increases with group size, as well as some social facilitation effects. EBS groups are also likely to suffer from cognitive interference, lower communications speed, and social loafing that increases with group size.

Figure 1 offers a shorthand summary of these patterns. The figure does not attempt to display the detailed effects of individual process gains and losses on brainstorming methods, but merely indicates the overall trend effects for each method and the effects of group size. For example, overall process gains for both verbal and EBS groups should increase with group size to some threshold level where the value of adding another participant will be only minimally positive. Process losses in verbal brainstorming groups should increase fairly quickly as the size of group increases; previous research suggests that losses increase more quickly than gains, because nominal groups have outperformed verbal brainstorming groups. It should be noted, however, that some of the process losses incurred by verbal brainstorming groups will not follow a linear trend. For instance, although the effect of evaluative apprehension should increase with group size, social impact theory (Latane, 1981) suggests that this effect will level off when the group reaches a threshold size. Additionally, the effect of production blocking by a single participant in a small group (e.g., 3-5) will have a larger proportional effect than in a large group (e.g., 25+). That is not to suggest an eventual decrease in process losses, but a curvilinear relationship. In contrast, process losses for EBS groups start higher (because of communications speed problems and the inherent loss of typing versus speaking) but increase much more slowly with group size. The primary message of Figure 1 is the indication that at some point, process gains should exceed process losses, and EBS groups should outperform nominal groups.

Figure 1 suggests two conclusions. First, for verbal vs. EBS groups, we would expect large EBS groups to generate more ideas than similarly sized verbally brainstorming groups. Our expectations for smaller groups are less clear. EBS introduces a fixed communication speed process loss due to the need to type regardless of the size of group. Conversely, small verbal groups suffer few production blocking losses, and—depending upon on the group—would also likely suffer few losses due to evaluation apprehension. We believe that for most small groups, the losses introduced in EBS due to the need to type, would exceed the losses introduced in verbal brainstorming from production blocking, and evaluation apprehension. Therefore, small verbal brainstorming groups should generate more ideas than similarly sized EBS groups. The pattern of gains and losses in EBS versus verbal brainstorming (see Figure 1) suggest that there should be a curvilinear relationship between size and the relative performance differences between EBS and verbal brainstorming groups.

Our second set of conclusions pertains to nominal vs. EBS groups. Nominal groups experience gains only from social facilitation, the same gains we could logically expect for EBS groups. EBS groups, however, experience synergy that increases with group size. Both nominal and EBS groups can be expected to experience similar losses due to social loafing (modest), production blocking (none), and evaluation apprehension (none). EBS groups may suffer from cognitive interference. EBS groups may suffer more from communications speed effects because they must type while nominal groups can write which may be faster. Once again, the use of EBS imposes an initial fixed cost which may be overcome as group size increases. Thus we expect that small nominal brainstorming groups should generate more ideas than small EBS groups. Conversely, large EBS groups should generate more

Figure 1. Process gains and losses

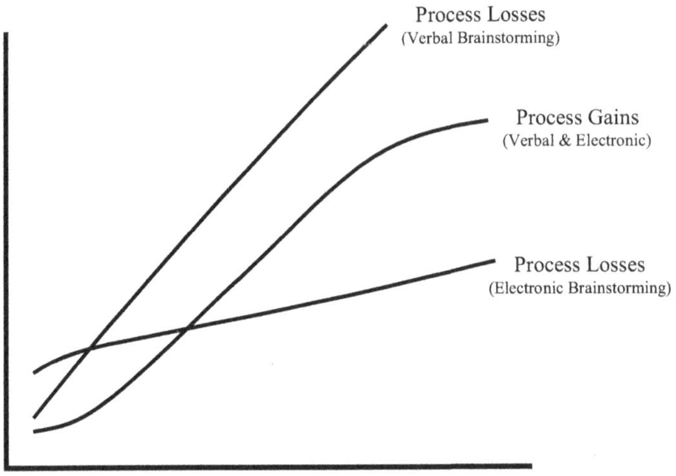

ideas than large nominal brainstorming groups. The pattern of gains and losses in EBS versus nominal group brainstorming (see Figure 1) suggest that there should be a curvilinear relationship between size and the relative performance differences between EBS and nominal groups.

Method

Selection of Studies

To locate studies, we performed computer searches on 11 databases, did manual searches through likely MIS, psychology and management journals and conference proceedings, and read previous literature reviews[1]. We focused only on published refereed papers, including journal articles and conference papers but omitting dissertations and working papers. We also omitted studies of e-mail and "chat" software. We selected all papers that reported the results of a test of a treatment group (EBS use) to a control group (verbal or nominal group brainstorming) and provided means and standard deviations (or other statistics) for the number of ideas produced.

This resulted in 21 articles. Studies containing several experiments or multiple conditions with different group sizes were disaggregated and treated as separate data points (Hunter & Schmidt, 1990). For example, Gallupe, et al. (1992) reported the comparison between EBS and verbal brainstorming groups for five levels of group size. Since individuals were randomly assigned to conditions, we treated the five levels of group size as independent studies for the analyses. This procedure resulted in a data set with 22 usable data points for the EBS versus verbal brainstorming comparison and 14 usable data points for the EBS versus nominal group brainstorming comparison.

Analysis Technique

It is beyond the scope of this article to describe in detail the statistical algorithm underlying a meta-analysis (see Hunter & Schmidt, 1990). In short, the mean number of ideas for the verbal brainstorming groups (or nominal brainstorming groups) is subtracted from the mean number of ideas for the EBS groups, and this difference is divided by the pooled standard deviation from both conditions to produce a weighted average effect size for each study. A positive effect size means that the EBS groups generated more ideas while a negative effect size means that the verbal or nominal groups generated more ideas.

We then analyzed the data using two separate regressions, one for the EBS versus verbal brainstorming comparison, and one for the EBS versus nominal brainstorming comparison. We used group size as the independent variable and the effect size as the dependent variable. Because we theorized a curvilinear relationship, the regression equation had four terms:

$$\text{EffectSize} = \text{constant} + \beta_1 * \text{GroupSize} + \beta_2 * \text{GroupSize}^2 + \beta_3 * \text{GroupSize}^3$$

Results

EBS vs. Verbal Brainstorming

Table 2 shows the results from the EBS versus verbal brainstorming regression. All three beta terms were statistically significant. The model had an adjusted R^2 of 43.7%, suggesting a good fit.

Table 2. EBS versus verbal brainstorming regression results

Parameter	Estimate	t	p
Intercept	-6.220	-2.45	0.026
Group size	3.440	2.59	0.019
Group size^2	-0.502	-2.36	0.030
Group size^3	0.024	2.32	0.033

Table 3. EBS versus nominal brainstorming group regression results

Parameter	Estimate	t	p
Intercept	2.031	1.36	0.191
Group size	-1.289	-2.49	0.023
Group size^2	0.174	3.21	0.005
Group size^3	-0.006	-3.30	0.004

EBS vs. Nominal Group Brainstorming

Table 3 shows the results from the EBS versus nominal group brainstorming regression. All three beta terms were statistically significant. The model had an adjusted R^2 of 77.3%, suggesting a good fit.

Discussion

We argued that group size would play an important role in affecting the process gains and losses in EBS relative to those in verbal brainstorming groups and nominal groups. The results show a clear pattern: group size is a significant factor in explaining the performance differences between EBS and verbal groups. Simply put, size matters; it explains almost half of the differences relative to verbal groups and about three quarters of the differences relative to nominal groups.

The data support our arguments that there is a curvilinear relationship between size and relative benefits, but the patterns are different between the verbal brainstorming and nominal group brainstorming. Figure 2 shows a plot of the predicted performance differences between EBS and verbal and nominal groups, using the coefficients from the two regression models to produce the curves. We plotted the

Figure 2. Predicted performance difference curves

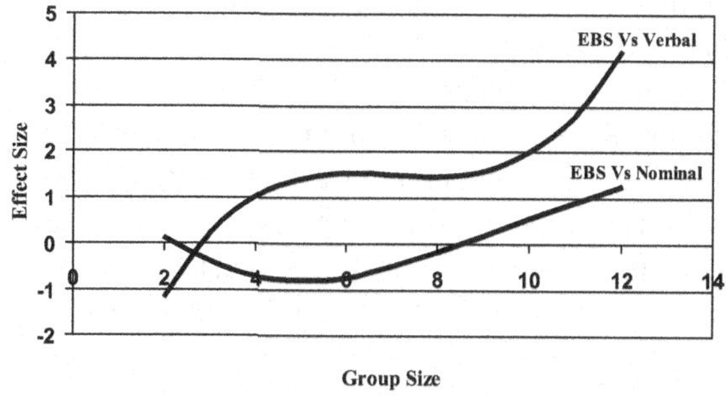

curves in this figure over the range of group sizes for which we had the most data (2-12 member groups).

From Figure 2, we can see that for very small groups (2-3 members), verbal brainstorming is better. In verbal groups of these sizes, there are few process losses, while the need to type introduces noticeable losses in the EBS groups. However, once group size reaches four members, EBS groups produce more ideas than verbal groups. The effect size in this size range is about 1.5, which is a very large effect size (Cohen (1988) labels an effects size of 0.8 as "large"). The relative performance differences remain at about this level until group size reaches 10 members, whereupon the differences begin to dramatically rise again.

The pattern in Figure 2 for EBS versus nominal group brainstorming is slightly different. Two-member EBS and nominal groups produce about the same number of ideas, but as size increases (from 3-8 members), EBS groups produce fewer ideas (a medium effect size of about -0.4 to -0.8, average about -0.6). As group size increases, the performance differences begin to reverse and EBS gradually starts to outperform nominal groups, so that with 10-12 member groups, EBS produces increasingly more ideas (an effect size of about 1.0).

Although the two curves are shaped differently, they suggest the same basic conclusion: EBS groups underperform verbal and nominal brainstorming groups initially, with a gradual increase in performance as group size increases. For verbal brainstorming, the break-even point comes quickly, so that EBS groups produce more ideas in groups with just four members. For nominal group brainstorming, the break-even point comes later; it is not until group size hits about 10 members that EBS groups begin to produce more ideas than nominal groups.

These results generally support our arguments that EBS can be a useful technique. EBS can reduce important sources of process losses while still enabling synergy to occur. While EBS appears to mitigate many of the process losses that increase with group size (e.g., production blocking, evaluation apprehension) it also appears to impose some initial fixed cost, which may be attributed to the need to type.

Interestingly, performance benefits to relative nominal groups appear to drop as size reaches three members and then gradually improve at the 7-8 person range. We see a similar plateau in this range relative to verbal groups. We speculate that this decrease in performance can be attributed primarily to cognitive interference from conducting dual tasks. Members of nominal groups, interact with no other participants. Their task is to solely generate ideas, uninterrupted by outside events. EBS groups, however, must generate ideas and also attend to ideas from other participants. This may introduce some dual task cognitive interference because participants must perform two tasks: generating ideas and reading ideas of others. Dual task interference is a well-known, well-studied phenomenon typically focusing on elementary tasks (e.g., measuring the millisecond delays in pressing buttons in response to seeing different lights or hearing different sounds that occur near simultaneously) (Pashler, 1994). For more complex tasks, individuals can choose to allocate their attention to one task or the other in a sequential manner (or in a near simultaneous manner) that effectively enables both tasks to be performed in a given time period with some degradation in overall performance (Garcia-Larrea, Perchet, Perrin, & Amenedo, 2001; Sarno & Wickens, 1995).

We believe that dual task interference is a plausible explanation which suggests that the cost of monitoring ideas from others initially exceeds the benefits from synergy from reading those ideas; that is, in small groups it costs more time and cognitive effort to attend to the small number of ideas (which keeps participants from thinking of their own ideas) than there are offsetting gains in triggering new ideas from the ideas of others. At some point, however, as group size increases there are enough incoming ideas from others that a critical mass of source ideas is created that begins to produce synergy. In other words, at a large enough group size there are enough new and different ideas coming from other participants that attending to them becomes worthwhile and triggers new ideas that would otherwise not have been produced.

Implications

We believe that the use of EBS can play a key role in enhancing group creativity, particularly for larger groups that suffer from the process losses inherent in verbally interacting groups. Several conclusions can be drawn from EBS research. First, it is clear that EBS can improve group creativity in certain situations. The advantages of synergy and social facilitation as well as the ability to bridge time and space make EBS an invaluable tool for many groups. We recommend that large groups (e.g., >8) seeking to generate ideas choose first to work together using EBS brainstorming, either in special-purpose meeting rooms equipped with computers or over the Internet using Web-based brainstorming tools or simply via electronic mail. For smaller groups, the use of nominal groups, brainwriting (Paulus & Yang, 2000), or their organizational cousin, Nominal Group Technique (Delbecq, Van de Ven, & Gustafson, 1975; Van de Ven & Delbecq, 1971) still seems appropriate. However, given the ubiquitous use of computing technology in modern organizations, most nominal groups will most likely use computer-based tools to record ideas thus making the sharing of ideas very simple using EBS tools or electronic mail.

Second, it appears that group size is the critical factor in determining the effectiveness of EBS to support productive group creativity. As group size increases, the benefits of synergy and reduced production blocking and cognitive interference are more noticeable. Smaller groups however (especially those with 2-3 members) will receive fewer benefits from using EBS over verbal or nominal techniques.

Finally, with the rise of the Internet, EBS tools are increasingly ubiquitous. As tools like Instant messenger, Web boards and others are diffused throughout society, people become more accustomed to using the computer as a tool for communication. This familiarity should allow them to use EBS tools more effectively.

While we believe our conclusions are reasonable and appropriate, there are also clear needs for future research. One area that we believe is most promising, both for theoretical and applied research is the development of new tools. Most current EBS software tools simply automate existing techniques. However, computer technology enables the creation of a variety of new ways to interact that would not be possible without the computer. For example, Dennis et al. (1999) investigated the impact of a very simple dialogue structure: participants were simultaneously given three separate windows in which to enter ideas, each focusing on a different aspect of the problem. This structure enabled participants to contribute ideas on different aspects of the problem simultaneously; something not possible in verbal brainstorming where every participant must listen to every other participant. This simple structure improved performance by about 50%.

The use of EBS enables the development and testing of a variety of far more complex structures which may have greater or lesser impacts on performance. We need additional research to develop and test new ways in which groups can work together to generate ideas.

While this article has focused on group creativity, the implications of EBS and their impact on creativity goes beyond simple idea generation (Dennis and Reinicke, 2004). The essence of creativity is the development and exchange of ideas that ultimately find their way into later stages of organization processes such as decision making or planning. EBS can play an important role in improving performance in these stages as well (Dennis, Wixom, & Vandenberg, 2001), by improving the sharing of information during group discussions (Dennis, 1996). Continued research into the use and usefulness of EBS will provide a richer understanding of how technology can enable more efficient and effective group processes and creativity.

References

Allport, F. H. (1920). The influence of the group upon association and thought. *Journal of Experimental Psychology, 3*(3), 159-182.

Bantal, K. A., & Jackson, S. E. (1989). Top management and innovations in banking: Does the composition of the top team make a difference. *Strategic Management Journal, 10*, 107-124.

Bartis, S., Szymanski, K., & Harkins, S. (1988). Evaluation and performance: A 2-edged knife. *Personality and Social Psychology Bulletin, 14*(2), 242-251.

Bond, C. F., & Titus, L. J. (1983). Social facilitation: A meta-analysis of 241 studies. *Psychology Bulletin, 94*, 265-292.

Camacho, L. M., & Paulus, P. B. (1995). The role of social anxiousness in group brainstorming. *Journal of Personality and Social Psychology, 68*, 1071-1080.

Collins, B. E., & Guetzkow, H. (1964). *A social psychology of group processes for decision-making*. New York: Wiley.

Cohen, J. (1988). *Statistical power analysis for the behavioral sciences* (2nd ed.). Hillsdale, NJ: Lawrence Earlbaum Associates.

Cooper, W. H., Gallupe, R. B., Pollard, S., & Cadsby, J. (1998). Some liberating effects of anonymous electronic brainstorming. *Small Group Research, 29*(2), 147-178.

Delbecq, A., Van de Ven, A. H., & Gustafson, D. H. (1975). *Group techniques for program planning*. Chicago: Scott Foresman and Co.

Dennis, A. R. (1996). Information exchange and use in group decision making: You can lead a group to information but you can't make it think. *MIS Quarterly, 20*(3), 433-455.

Dennis, A. R., Aronson, J. E., Heninger, W. G., & Walker II, E. (1999). Structuring time and task in electronic brainstorming. *MIS Quarterly, 23*(1), 95-108.

Dennis, A.R., & Reinicke, B.A. (2004). Beta versus VHS and the acceptance of electronic brainstorming technology. *MIS Quarterly, 28*(1), 1-20.

Dennis, A. R., & Valacich, J. S. (1993). Computer brainstorms: More heads are better than one. *Journal of Applied Psychology, 78*(4), 531-537.

Dennis, A. R., & Valacich, J. S. (1999). Electronic brainstorming: Illusions and patterns of productivity. *Information Systems Research, 10*.

Dennis, A. R., Valacich, J. S., Carte, T. A., Garfield, M. J., Haley, B. J., & Aronson, J. E. (1997). The effectiveness of multiple dialogues in electronic brainstorming. *Information Systems Research, 8*(2), 203-211.

Dennis, A. R., Valacich, J. S., Connolly, T., & Wynne, B. (1996). Process structuring in group brainstorming. *Information Systems Research, 7*(3), 268-277.

Dennis, A. R., Wixom, B. H., & Vandenberg, R. J. (2001). Understanding fit and appropriation effects in group support systems via meta-analysis. *MIS Quarterly, 25*(2), 167-194.

Diehl, M., & Stroebe, W. (1987). Productivity loss in brainstorming groups: Toward the solution of a riddle. *Journal of Personality and Social Psychology, 53*, 497-509.

Diehl, M., & Stroebe, W. (1991). Productivity loss in idea-generating groups: Tracking down the blocking effect. *Journal of Personality and Social Psychology, 61*, 392-403.

Diener, S. C. (1979). Deindividuation, self-awareness, end disinhibition. *Journal of Personality and Social Psychology, 37*, 1160-1171.

Diener, S. C., Fraser, E., Beaman, A. L., & Kelem, R. T. (1976). Effects of deindividuation variables on stealing among Halloween trick-or-treaters. *Journal of Personality and Social Psychology, 33*, 178-183.

Dugosh, K. L., Paulus, P. B., Roland, E. J., & Yang, H. C. (2000). Cognitive stimulation in brainstorming. *Journal of Personality and Social Psychology 79*(5), 722-735.

Festinger, L. (1954). A theory of social comparison processes. *Human Relations, 7*, 117-140.

Gallupe, R. B., Cooper, W. H., Grise, M. L., & Bastianutti, L. (1994). Blocking electronic brainstorms. *Journal of Applied Psychology, 79*(1), 77-86.

Gallupe, R. B., Dennis, A. R., Cooper, W. H., Valacich, J. S., Bastianutti, L., & Nunamaker, J. F. (1992). Electronic brainstorming and group size. *Academy of Management Journal, 35*, 350-369.

Garcia-Larrea, L., Perchet, C., Perrin, F., & Amenedo, E. (2001). Interference of cellular phone conversations with visumotor tasks: An ERP study. *Journal of Psychophysiology, 15*(1), 14-21.

George, J. F., Easton, G. K., Nunamaker, J. F., & Northcraft, G. B. (1990). A study of collaborative group work with and without computer based support. *Information Systems Research, 1*(4), 394-415.

Gruenfeld, D. (1995). Status, ideology and integrative complexity on the U.S. Supreme Court: Rethinking the politics of political decision making. *Journal of Personality and Social Psychology, 68*, 5-20.

Harkins, S., & Petty, R. E. (1982). Effects of task difficulty and task uniqueness on social loafing. *Journal of Personality and Social Psychology, 16*, 457-462.

Hill, G. W. (1982). Group versus individual performance: Are N + 1 heads better than one? *Psychology Bulletin, 91(*3), 517-539.

Hiltz, S. R., Turoff, M., & Johnson, K. (1989). Disinhibition, deindividuation, and group process: An approach to improving the effectiveness of groups. *Decision Support Systems, 5*(2), 217-232.

Hunter, J.E., & Schmidt, F.L. (1990). *Methods of meta-analysis: Correcting error and bias in research findings*. Newbury Park: Sage Publications.

Jackson, S. E. (1992). Team composition in organizations. In S. Worchel, W. Wood, & J. Simpson (Eds.), *Group process and productivity* (pp. 138-173). UK: Sage.

Jackson, S. E., May, K. E., & Whitney, K. (1995). Understanding the dynamics of diversity in decision making teams. In R. A. Guzzo & E. Salas (Eds.), *Team effectiveness and decision making in organizations* (pp. 204-226). San Francisco: Jossey-Bass.

Jessup, L. M., Connolly, T., & Galegher, J. (1990). The effects of anonymity on group process in automated group problem solving. *MIS Quarterly 14*(3), 313-321.

Karau, S. J., & Williams, K. (1993). Social loafing: A meta-analytic review and theoretical integration. *Journal of Personality and Social Psychology, 65*, 681-706.

Lamm, H., & Trommsdorff, G. (1973). Group versus individual performance on tasks requiring identical proficiency (brainstorming): A review. *European Journal of Social Psychology, 3*, 361-388.

Larey, T. S., & Paulus, P. B. (1995). Individual and group goal setting in brainstorming groups. *Journal of Applied Psychology, 25*, 1579-1596.

Larey, T. S., & Paulus, P. B. (1999). Group preference and convergent tendencies in small groups: A content analysis of group brainstorming performance. *Creativity Research Journal, 12*(3) 175-185.

Latane, B. (1981). The psychology of social impact. *American Psychologist, 36*, 343-356.

Latane, B., Williams, K., & Harkins, S. (1979). Many hands make light the work: The causes and consequences of social loafing. *Journal of Personality and Social Psychology, 37*, 823-832.

Lea, M., & Spears, R. (1991). Computer-mediated communication, de-individuation and group decision-making. *International Journal of Man-Machine Studies, 34*, 283-301.

Levine, D., Resnick, L. B., & Higgins, E. T. (1993). Social foundations of cognition. *Annual Review of Psychology, 44*, 585-612.

Mullen, B., Johnson, C., & Salas, E. (1991). Productivity loss in brainstorming groups: A meta-analytic integration. *Basic and Applied Social Psychology, 12*, 3-23.

Nunamaker, J. F., Dennis, A. R., Valacich, J. S., Vogel, D. R., & George, J. F. (1991). Electronic meeting systems to support group work. *Communications of the ACM, 34*(7), 41-61.

Osborn, A. F. (1957). *Applied imagination*. New York: Scribner.

Pashler, H. (1994). Dual-task interference in simple tasks: Data and theory. *Psychological Bulletin, 116*(2), 220-244.

Paulus, P. B., & Dzindolet, M. T. (1993). Social influence processes in group brainstorming. *Journal of Personality and Social Psychology, 64*, 575-586.

Paulus, P. B., Larey, T. S., & Ortega, A. H. (1995). Performance and perceptions of brainstormers in an organizational setting. *Basic and Applied Social Psychology, 17*, 249-265.

Paulus, P. B., & Yang, H. C. (2000). Idea generation in groups: A basis for creativity in organizations. *Organization Behavior and Human Decision Processes, 82*(1), 76-87.

Pinsonneault, A., & Barki, H. (1999). The illusion of electronic brainstorming productivity: Theoretical and empirical issues. *Information Systems Research, 10*(4), 378-382.

Pinsonneault, A., Barki, H., Gallupe, R. B., & Hoppen, N. (1999). Electronic brainstorming: The illusion of productivity. *Information Systems Research, 10*, 110-133.

Postmes, T., & Lea, M. (2000). Social processes and group decision making: Anonymity in group decision support systems. *Ergonomics, 43*(8), 1252-1274.

Prentice-Dunn, S., & Rogers, R. W. (1982). Effects of public and private self-awareness on deindividuation and aggression. *Journal of Personality and Social Psychology, 43*(3), 503-513.

Robinson-Staveley, K., & Cooper, J. (1990). Mere presence, gender, and reactions to computers: Studying human computer interaction in the social-context. *Journal of Experimental Social Psychology, 26*(2), 168-183.

Saks, M. J., & Ostrom, T. M. (1973). Anonymity in letters to the editor. *Public Opinion Quarterly, 37*, 417-422.

Sanna, L. J. (1992). Self-efficacy theory: Implications for social facilitation and social loafing. *Journal of Personality and Social Psychology, 62*(5), 774-786.

Sarno, K. J., & Wickens, C. D. (1995) Role of multiple resources in predicting time-sharing efficiency: Evaluation of three workload models in a multiple-task setting. *The International Journal of Aviation Psychology, 5*(1), 105-130.

Siegel, J., Dubrovsky, V., Kiesler, S., & McGuire, T. (1986). Group processes in computer-mediated communication. *Organization Behavior and Human Decision Processes, 17*, 157-187.

Steiner, I. D. (1972). *Group process and productivity.* San Diego: Academic Press.

Straus, S. G. (1996). Getting a clue: The effects of communication media and information dispersion on participation and performance in computer-mediated and face-to-face groups. *Small Group Research, 57*(3), 448-467.

Valacich, J. S., Dennis, A. R., & Connolly, T. (1994). Idea generation in computer-based groups: A new ending to an old story. *Organization Behavior and Human Decision Processes, 57*, 448-467.

Valacich, J. S., & Schwenk, C. (1985). Devil's advocacy and dialectical inquiry effects on group decision making using computer-mediated versus verbal communication. *Organization Behavior and Human Decision Processes, 63*(2), 158-173.

Van de Ven, A. H., & Delbecq, A. (1971). Nominal and interacting group process for committee decision-making effectiveness. *Academy of Management Journal, 14*(2).

Williams, K., & O'Reilly, C. (1998). Demography and diversity in organizations: A review of 40 years of research. *Research in Organizational Behavior, 20*, 77-140.

Williams, K. D., & Karau, S. J. (1991). Social loafing and social compensation: The effects of expectations of coworker performance. *Journal of Personality and Social Psychology, 61*, 570-581.

Zajonc, R. B. (1965). Social facilitation. *Science, 149*, 269-274.

Ziegler, R., Diehl, M., & Zijlstra, G. (2000). Idea production in nominal and virtual groups: Does computer-mediated communication improve group brainstorming? *Group Processes & Intergroup Relations, 3*(2), 141-159.

Zimbardo. (1969). The human choice: Individuation, reason and order versus deindividuation, impulse and chaos. In W. J. Arnold & D. Levine (Eds.), *Nebraska symposium on motivation* (pp. 237-307). Lincoln: University of Nebraska Press.

Endnote

[1] The 11 databases were ABI Inform, Computer and Information Systems Abstracts, Academic Press Journals, Current Contents, Lexis-Nexis' Academic Universe, Social Sciences Abstracts, ERIC, PsycINFO, SocioAbs, and Web of Science, plus one created by Prof. Jerry Fjermestad of the New Jersey Institute of Technology. The hand-searched journals and conference proceedings were *MIS Quarterly, Information Systems Research, Journal of Management Information Systems, Journal of Applied Psychology, Small Group Research, ICIS* and *HICSS.*

The chapter was previously published in the International Journal of e-Collaboration, 1(1), 24-42, January-March 2005.

Chapter XIV

Virtual Teams: What We Know, What We Don't Know

Alain Pinsonneault, McGill University, Canada
Olivier Caya, McGIll University, Canada

Abstract

This chapter reviews the extant empirical literature on virtual teams and presents what we know and what we don't know about them. Drawing upon the literature from both Organization Behavior and IS, we propose a framework that integrates the most important variables affecting virtual teams. The framework is then used to assess the effects of virtual teamwork on group processes and outcomes. The paper also discusses the challenges facing researchers studying virtual teams and presents an agenda for future research.

Introduction

Throughout the last decade, virtual teams (VT) have gained a significant interest from both IS academic and managerial communities. Due to recent breakthroughs in telecommunication and information technologies, organizations are no longer constrained by geographical distance or time zone differences, enabling managers to access previously unavailable expertise, enhance cross-functional interactions necessary to deal with today's highly dynamic business environment, and form the best possible groups (Griffith, Sawyer & Neale, 2003; Powell, Piccoli & Ives, 2004; Sole & Edmondson, 2002; Townsend, deMarie, & Hendrickson, 1998). While many researchers claim that we still know little about the idiosyncratic nature of virtual teamwork (Maznevski & Chudoba, 2000; Lurey & Raisinghani, 2001), the recent research efforts on this topic have generated a significant body of knowledge that needs to be synthesized and assessed.

The objective of this paper is twofold. First, it aims at synthesizing the extant empirical evidence on virtual teams. Second, it develops an agenda for future research on virtual teams. The paper is organized into three sections and a conclusion. The first section presents a conceptual framework that integrates the OB and IS literature and serves as the basis for assessing the empirical literature. The second section describes the method used to conduct our review and the third section presents the results of our assessment. The paper concludes by discussing the findings and suggesting an agenda for future research.

Framework of Virtual Team Research

Virtual Teams: A Definition

In this paper, we adopt Hinds and Bailey's (2003) conceptualization of virtual teams: in virtual teams (1) members are separated by distance and (2) are forced to rely on technologies to mediate their communication and to coordinate their work. Virtual teams can be culturally distributed (Jarvenpaa, Knoll & Leidner., 1998; Kayworth & Leidner, 2001-2002), spread across multiple time zones (Massey, Montoya-Weiss, & Hung, 2003; Piccoli & Ives, 2003), functionally distributed (Malhotra, Majchrzak, Carman, & Lott; Zolin, Hinds, Fruchter, & Levitt, 2004), organizationally distributed (Majchrzak, Rice, Malhotra, & King, 2000), or present combinations of these distribution modes (Maznevski & Chuduba, 2000). These team arrangements are also referred to as geographically dispersed teams, geographically distributed teams, and dispersed teams.

Framework For Analysis

The framework we propose is based upon the "input-process-output" model (see Figure 1) traditionally adopted in research on groups (Guzzo & Shea, 1992). This general conceptualization has been widely used in research on traditional groups (Littlepage, 1995) and in GSS (Pinsonneault & Kreamer, 1990; Powell et al., 2004), and has the potential to serve as a way to organize the variables of virtual team research that have been studied over the years. The fundamental logic underlying this framework is that properties of the group, its members, and the context (input variables) influence how the work is executed within a group (group process variables), which, in turn, influences the results or outcomes of the group (output variables).

Input Variables

Input variables refer to the general work conditions under which virtual teams co-workers operate as well as the main characteristics of the group. Based upon the research of Pinsonneault and Kraemer (1990), we have identified five main categories of input variables relevant for virtual team research: (1) personal factors (characteristics of the group members including traits such as personality, roles, and other elements relevant to individuals within the virtual groups); (2) situational factors (elements of the environment and the broader work setting); (3) task characteristics (attributes of the task(s) performed by the group); (4) group structure (the nature of the relationships among group members); and (5) technology support (main characteristics and functions of the technological media used by the virtual team members).Group process variables represent the interactions occurring within the group once it begins working. These variables capture the main characteristics of the group dynamics experienced by virtual team co-workers. There are five main categories of group process variables: (1) group dynamics (group-level constructs that emerge from the interactions among co-workers); (2) interpersonal behaviors (specific types of behavior acted out by virtual team members); (3) interpersonal conflicts and conflict management (the intensity and/or type of conflicts experienced within virtual teams, and the different strategies undertaken to deal with these conflicts); (4) communication and information exchange (characteristics of the communication process and attributes of the information exchanged); and (5) coordination and control (activities aimed at regulating and organizing group members' resources and actions).

Figure 1. Framework of Virtual Teams Research

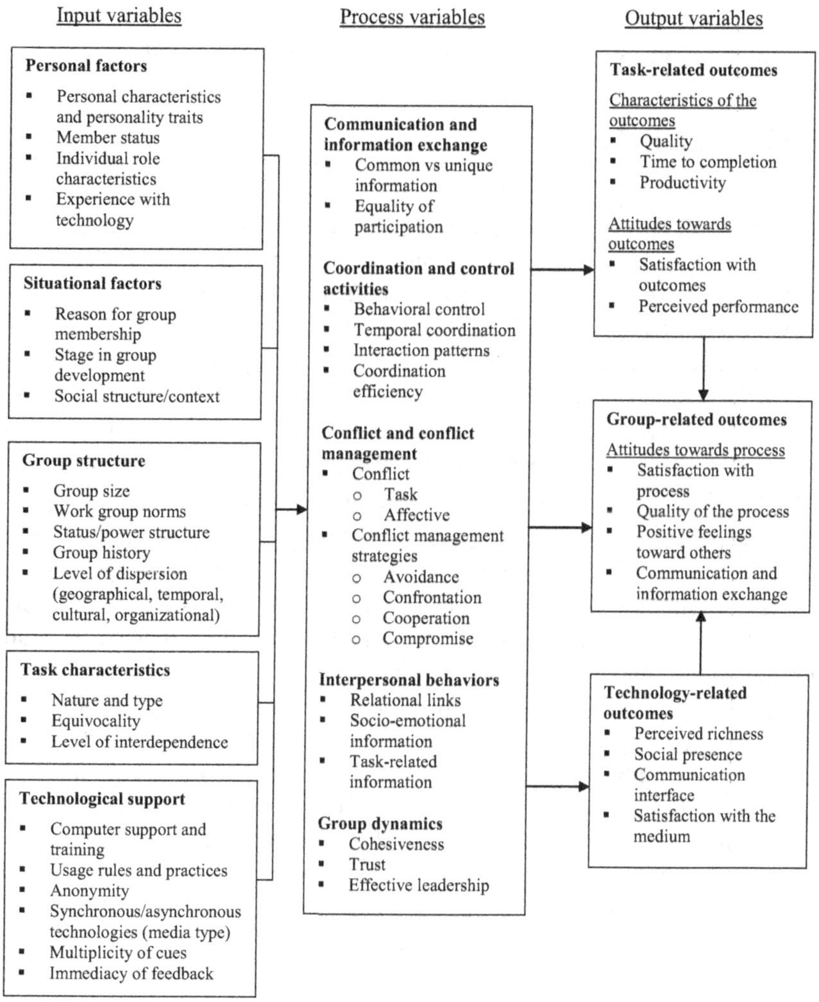

Output

Output variables represent the various group outcomes that result from the work conducted by virtual teams. As can be seen in figure 1, we have grouped the output variables into three distinct categories: (1) task-related outcomes (performance measures related specifically to the task); (2) group-related outcomes (attitudes and perceptions toward group processes); and (3) technology-related outcomes (attitudes toward and perceptions of the technology used).

Method

Our assessment follows Webster and Watson's (2002) recommendations.

Identifying the Relevant Literature

The first step of our review was to find and select all relevant research articles related to the topic of virtual teams. To do this, we performed a series of queries on ABI/INFORMS and reviewed other targeted publications and conference proceedings that were susceptible to including research on virtual teams. Using the online databases (scholarly referred articles/proceedings only), we queried for the following keywords in the title and abstract fields: virtual team(s), virtual group(s), distributed team(s), distributed group(s), dispersed team(s), dispersed group(s), group(s) and communication technology. This search resulted in 135 papers. Fifty-two conceptual papers were excluded, leaving a sample of 83 empirical papers.

The second step consisted in ensuring that each empirical study did in fact focus upon virtual teams and not other forms of group settings. To structure this process, we used the idiosyncratic characteristics of a virtual team suggested by Hinds and Bailey (2003). For the first criterion, members geographically dispersed, all studies that reported the smallest level of geographical dispersion possible (i.e., group members at the same site but in different rooms/workspaces) were included. Although this criterion might sound permissive, it actually provided us with a large variance in the geographical dispersion of teams and allowed us to study its effect on process and outcome variables. For the second criterion, reliance on technology to communicate and coordinate, we identified the technological medium(s) used by virtual team members to perform their task/project. Using these two criteria, a final sample of 62 empirical studies published in 29 academic journals was obtained (see Appendix 1 for the list of articles and journals).

Structuring the Review

To structure our review, we created a concept matrix which mapped all input, process, and output variables studied in past research. According to Webster and Watson (2002), this "concept-centric" approach is appropriate for assessing the behavior of a given research variable across several studies. To do this, we created an electronic spreadsheet that includes all the input, process, and outcome variables identified in Figure 1. Every vertical entry (column) of the spreadsheet corresponds to a unique concept (variables in Figure 1) and each horizontal entry (line) represents an empirical study (author(s) and year of publication). We then entered the details of each study by assigning specific codes to each variable (independent, moderating, mediating, and dependent) studied. For instance, when a study provided evidence of an increase in the level of a specific concept, a positive sign (+) was inserted in the corresponding cell. For a decrease in the level of a concept, a negative sign was used (-). When no significant change was observed for a concept, we entered a 0 in the appropriate cell. This routine was performed for all process and output variables assessed for each of the 62 papers.

Input variables were treated as antecedents of process and outcome variables. We therefore decided to more precisely identify the input variables as being manipulated, controlled, or not controlled[1]. We also gathered detailed data about the technologies/media used, the nature of the dispersion (geographical, cultural, temporal), and the characteristics of the task at hand. Finally, for each paper, we collected information about the objective, research strategy, theoretical foundations, and the attributes of the groups studied (group size, number of controlled groups and number of experimental groups).[2]

Assessment of the Findings

Three main steps were followed in order to assess how the virtual environment affects group processes and outcomes. First, we evaluated the consistency of results across studies for a given variable. For example, we compiled all findings relative to the variable "quality of output" to determine whether or not they converged. Second, we determined whether or not some of the input variables (manipulated, controlled, or not controlled) or other elements of the research context could provide alternative explanations for the findings observed or could offer insights to resolve inconsistencies. For example: Have laboratory studies and field studies found the same effects relative to a given variable such as "quality of output"? Are divergent findings due to differences in the nature of the tasks used across studies? Third, we assessed the finding consistency across variables. For example, are the results regarding quality of outcomes consistent with the findings on perceived performance?

Findings

Group Process

Group Dynamics

Trust

The concept of trust is one of the most important process variables in virtual team research. This is due to the fact that trustworthy relationships help to compensate for the lack of proximity between group members and also affect the way dispersed coworkers manage the uncertainty and complexity of the virtual environment (Jarvenpaa & Leidner, 1999). Three main findings emerge from research on trust in virtual teams. First, initial interactions seem critical for establishing trust in virtual teams. Jarvenpaa and colleagues (1998, 1999) found that virtual teams tend to develop "swift trust" based upon group members' initial impressions each other. These impressions are typically formed after the first electronic communication episodes. The importance of initial interactions is also emphasized by Zolin et al. (2004) who show that cross-functional virtual team members constantly rely upon early impressions of perceived trustworthiness and perceived follow-through in order to evaluate their distant partners' reliability. Second, research indicates that the antecedents of trust are dynamic and change over the life cycle of a virtual team. Jarvenpaa et al. (1998) found that perceptions of other members' ability and integrity initially act as antecedents of trust in virtual teams, while perceived benevolence becomes an important determinant of trust over time. They also found that the communication behaviors and actions necessary to develop trust early on in the life of a virtual team are different from those required to maintain trust later on (Jarvenpaa and Leidner, 1999). Third, we found evidence that moderate use of process structure mechanisms helps develop and maintain trust in virtual teams. Jarvenpaa et al.'s (1998) study indicates that taking part in a team building activity is helpful for stimulating the antecedents of trust (ability, benevolence, integrity). Similarly, Warkentin and Beranek (1999) report that, over time, dispersed team members who receive communication training eventually reach a superior degree of trust compared to those who do not receive such training. The importance of process structure activities is also reported by Tan et al. (2000), who show that teams using a "dialogue technique" (i.e., a three-stage technique that facilitates shared understanding in virtual teams) consistently report a higher level of trust than those teams who do not use this communication mechanism. However, some structural mechanisms can also hinder the formation of trust. In fact, Piccoli and Ives (2003) observed that behavioral control diminished the level of interpersonal trust among virtual team members because it increased their vigilance and, consequently, the likelihood that reneging and incongruence incidents are detected.

Cohesiveness

Group cohesion has been positively associated with performance measures in both traditional and computer-supported groups (Chidambaram, 1996; Lurey & Raisinghani, 2001; Maznevski & Chudoba, 2000). Two main results can be observed. First, virtual teams need to engage in more communication episodes than traditional teams in order to develop the same degree of cohesiveness. While Warkentin et al. (1997) found that dispersed groups using asynchronous computer-mediated communication systems (CMCS) failed to develop an overall level of cohesiveness that matched that of their face-to-face counterparts, other studies suggest that, over time, this discrepancy tends to disappear as dispersed coworkers become adept at exchanging enough personal information to generate increasing levels of cohesiveness (Burke & Aytes, 1998; Walther, 1995). Despite the fact that Warkentin et al. (1997) found the virtual context to have a negative effect on cohesiveness, they also found a positive association between CMCS usage and cohesion within virtual teams. This suggests that a higher number of communication episodes may help establish cohesion in the virtual setting. Second, process structure mechanisms help develop cohesiveness within virtual teams. Consistent with previous findings on trust, three studies found a positive relationship between process structure mechanisms (i.e., promoting communication training early in the team's lifecycle, using a "dialogue technique", and using a GSS with an embedded goal setting structure) and group cohesiveness in virtual teams (Huang et al., 2003; Tan et al., 2000; Warketin & Beranek, 1999).

Interpersonal Behaviors

Socio-Emotional vs. Task Oriented Information

Mixed findings are obtained in terms of the amount of socio-emotional and task-related information exchanged when virtual groups are compared to collocated teams. First, it seems that virtual teams are more task-oriented than face-to-face teams. Galegher and Kraut (1994) found that members of face-to-face groups engage in more social communications than their virtual team counterparts and Warkentin et al. (1997) observed that virtual teams had fewer relational links than traditional groups. However, a second group of studies indicates that over time, virtual teams reduce their task-focus and tend to increase socio-emotional communications (Burke & Aytes, 1998; Walther 1995, 1997; Walther et al., 1994). The difference in these two findings seems to be explained by the fact that studies in the first group did not consider the effect of time on communication patterns. When temporal development and group development are taken into account, the communication patterns of virtual teams appear to be similar to those observed in traditional groups (Burke & Aytes, 1998; Walther et al., 1994). Over time, virtual teams can achieve high levels of immediacy, affection, similarity, and relaxation (Walther 1995, 1997) and may even become more socially-oriented than face-to-face teams (Walther, 1995).

Overall, these two groups of studies suggest that, under certain conditions, virtual team members can develop strong relational ties that approximate and sometimes exceed those of relationships forged in collocated teams (Burke & Aytes, 1998; Chidambaram, 1996; Walther & Burgoon, 1992; Walther 1995; Walther, 1997).

Interpersonal Conflicts and Conflict Management

Two main findings emerge from the empirical evidence. First, virtual teams do not differ from traditional teams in terms of the overall level of conflict experienced by their members (Mortensen & Hinds, 2001; O'Connor et al., 1993). In fact, both Mortensen and Hinds (2001) and O'Connor (1993) found no significant effect of the virtual context on either task or affective conflict. Interestingly, Mortensen and Hinds (2001) provide evidence of a positive relationship between the percentage of computer-mediated communication and task conflicts. Second, interpersonal conflicts are detrimental for virtual team outcomes. In fact, research shows that both task and affective conflicts are negatively related with performance (Mortensen & Hinds, 2001; O'Connor, 1993) and liking toward one another (O'Connor, 1993).

Communication and Information Exchange

Common vs. Unique Information Exchanged

The balance of unique and common information exchanged is of paramount importance in distributed teams due to the fact that sharing uniquely held information (i.e., exchange of information owned by only one member of the group) reflects expertise sharing, one of the most touted benefikts of virtual teams (Hinds & Bailey, 2003; Sole & Edmondson, 2002). Research on information sharing in virtual teams indicates that virtual teams exchange less unique information than do traditional teams. Smith and Vanecek (1990) and Hightower and Sayeed (1996) show that virtual team members using asynchronous media exchange less unique information than their collocated counterparts. Similarly, Warkentin et al. (1997) found that face-to-face teams exchanged more unique information in one meeting than virtual teams did in three weeks of online interactions. Finally, the uneven distribution of unique information was recently identified by Crampton (2001) as an important communication problem inherent in distributed work arrangements. Overall, these results provide support for a negative effect of virtual setting on the exchange of unique information.

Equality of Participation

Past research on technology-supported communication suggests that telecommunication technologies tend to equalize participation in groups and reduce domination by certain members during interpersonal exchanges (Pinsonneault & Kreamer,

1990). The studies we analyzed provide no support for this argument as virtual team members do not participate more equally than their face-to-face counterparts. For example, Galegher and Kraut (1994) observed that virtual team members experienced lower perceived fairness in the distribution of labor compared to their face-to-face counterparts. In a series of three experiments, Weisband et al. (1995) found that computer-mediated communication was either not correlated or negatively correlated with equality of participation. Aiken and Vanjani (1997) found that members of hybrid virtual teams (part of the team is in one room and the rest is in another workspace) reported higher level of perceived equality of participation than did their face-to-face counterparts.

Coordination and Control Activities

Coordination and control activities refer to the efforts of team members to manage collective resources, clarify individual roles and responsibilities, and structure the interactions within the group (McGrath, 1991). Because virtual teams cannot rely on traditional forms of social control such as direct supervision, physical proximity, and shared experiences, they must use new ways to coordinate their efforts (Massey et al., 2003; Montoya-Weiss, 2001). We observed two main outcomes relative to coordination and control activities in virtual teams. First, coordination activities are more difficult to conduct in virtual teams than in collocated teams. Early work by Galegher and Kraut (1994) shows that virtual teams experienced lower coordination efficiency when compared to traditional teams. They also found that coordination efficiency decreases over time in virtual teams, while the opposite occurs in face-to-face teams. Temporal coordination mechanisms (i.e. a process structure imposed to intervene and direct the pattern, timing, and content of communication within a group) have been found to alleviate the negative effects of virtual teams on coordination efficiency (McGrath, 1991; Massey et al., 2003; Montoya-Weiss et al., 2001; Ocker et al., 1995-1996; Yoo & Alavi, 2004). It is important to note that the usage of coordination and control mechanisms can also decrease trust in virtual teams (Piccoli & Ives, 2003). Overall, the empirical evidence suggests that a moderate level of coordination and control can be beneficial for regulating interactions in virtual teams.

Task Outcomes

Quality

The majority of empirical studies, found no difference between the quality of outcomes of collocated teams and virtual teams (Aiken & Vanjani, 1997; Chidambaram & Jones, 1993; Dennis & Kinney, 1998; Galegher & Kraut, 1994; Gallupe & McKeen, 1990; Ocker et al., 1995-96; Smith & Vanacek, 1990; Warkentin & Beranek, 1999). Other researchers found that under certain circumstances, virtual teams produced better quality outcomes than did collocated teams (Baker, 2002; Burke & Chidambaram, 1999; Ocker et al., 1998; Schmidt et al., 2001; Sharda et al., 1988). Among the factors that have the potential to facilitate the production of high quality outcomes in virtual teams, we note the integration of multiple sources of knowledge and expertise (Balthazard et al., 2004; Majchrzack et al., 2000; Sole & Edmondson, 2002; Yoo & Kanawattanacha, 2000), the use of temporal coordination mechanisms and predictable interaction patterns (Massey et al., 2003; Montoyas-Weiss et al., 2001), and the combination of various communication media (Aiken & Vanjani, 1997; Baker, 2002; Dennis & Kinney, 1998; Majchrzack et al., 2000; Malhotra et al., 2001; Maznevski & Chudoba, 2000; Ocker et al., 1998).

Time to Completion

In general, past empirical studies suggest that compared to traditional groups, virtual teams take more time to complete their task (Gallupe & McKeen, 1990; Hightower & Sayeed, 1996; Sharda, 1988; Warkentin & Beranek, 1999; Thompson & Coovert, 2003). Interestingly, Dennis and Kinney (1998) noted that groups who combined audio and video communication devices were able to perform their task faster than groups using text-based media only. Overall, these findings indicate that virtual teams take longer to complete their tasks than traditional teams.

Satisfaction with Outcomes and Perceived Performance

Mixed findings are reported from studies that assessed members' satisfaction toward outcomes and their perceptions of group performance. While some studies found no effect of the virtual context on satisfaction with outcomes (Aiken & Vanjani, 1997; Cass et al., 1992) and perceived performance (Gallupe & McKeen, 1990; Sharda et al., 1988), others found that virtual team members perceived their performance to be inferior to that of their face-to-face counterparts (Cass et al., 1992; Galegher & Kraut, 1994; Warkentin et al., 1997). Interestingly, a combination of virtual and traditional team meetings seems to be the optimal arrangement. In fact, Ocker et al. (1998) found that groups interacting both face-to-face and in asynchronous dispersed setting express more satisfaction towards outcomes than either face-to-face only groups, or asynchronous only groups. Furthermore, some factors have been found to affect perceived performance. Tan et al. (2000) found that virtual teams relying upon a dialogue technique reported higher levels of perceived performance and satisfaction with outcomes when compared to teams that did not receive such treatment. Finally, recent work by Balthazard (2004) indicates that adopting a constructive interaction style is associated with increasing perceptions of performance within virtual teams.

Group Outcomes

Satisfaction with Process and Positive Feelings Toward Others

Here again, mixed findings are found when we review the effect of the virtual context on member satisfaction with the process. A recognizable number of studies indicate that the level of process satisfaction of virtual team members does not differ from that of members of traditional teams (Aiken & Vanjani, 1997; Andres, 2002; Burke & Aytes, 1998; Cass et al., 1992; Dennis & Kinney, 1998; Hollingshead et al., 1993; Ocker et al., 1998; Smith & Vanecek, 1990; Straus & McGrath, 1994). Interestingly, most of the distributed groups in these studies interacted through a combination of various media (Burke & Aytes, 1998; Dennis & Kinney, 1998) or combined virtual interactions with occasional face-to-face meetings (Aiken & Vanjani, 1997; Maznevski & Chudoba, 2000; Ocker et al., 1998). In contrast, studies that reported a negative association between communication technology usage and process satisfaction relied upon a single technology and never interacted face-to-face (Gallupe & McKeen, 1990; Thompson & Coovert, 2002, 2003). Taken together, these two results suggest that virtual teams relying on multiple communication media express more satisfaction with the process than virtual teams using only one communication medium. In regard to the concept of members' appreciation of one another, we found evidence that the virtual environment negatively influences the extent to which group members have positive feeling toward others (Andres, 2002; Galegher & Kraut, 1994; Weisband & Atwater, 1999). These findings seem consistent with previous results on task versus socio-emotional exchanges particularly as the three studies that found an inferior level of liking toward others were conducted over relatively short periods of time (from 3 hours to 2 weeks). The limited number of communication episodes resulting from this time constraint may explain why virtual team members failed to develop strong relational links.

Communication and Information Exchange Effectiveness

The vast majority of studies provide evidence of a lower level of perceived communication and information exchange effectiveness in virtual teams when compared to traditional teams (Chidambaram & Jones, 1993; Galegher & Kraut, 1994; Hightower & Sayeed, 1996; Smith & Vanecek, 1990; Straus & McGrath, 1994; Thompson an&d Coovert, 2002; 2003). Among the factors that can help teams achieve higher levels of communication effectiveness, we note the presence of a leader (Kayworth & Leidner, 2000, 2001-2002; Yoo & Alavi, 2004), the development of a shared social context/structure (Crampton, 2001; Sole & Edmondson, 2002; Zack & McKenney, 1995), reliance on process structure mechanisms (Huang et al., 2002; Jarvenpaa et al., 1998, 1999; Tan et al., 2000), and predicable, frequent, and timely interaction (Kayworth & Leidner, 2001-2002; Massey et al., 2003; Maznevski & Chuduba, 2000; Orlikowski & Yates, 1994).

Discussion

The present review attempts to extend our knowledge of the effects of the virtual teams on group processes and outcomes. With regard to group process variables, our review indicates that, compared with traditional team co-workers, virtual team members (1) need more communication episodes to develop cohesiveness, (2) tend to be task-oriented in early stages of the group's lifecycle, (3) but develop the same strength of relational links over time, (4) experience the same level of interpersonal conflicts, (5) exchange less unique information, (6) participate less equally, and (7) express more difficulties in coordinating their efforts. Where output variables were concerned, we found evidence that virtual teams (1) do not differ from traditional teams in terms of quality of outcomes, (2) take more time to complete their task, (3) communicate less effectively, and (4) that their members develop less appreciation toward each other. These findings are discussed in further detail in the following paragraphs.

Our review indicates that virtual teams seem to experience difficulties in communicating and exchanging information. This is consistent with Crampton's (2001) study in which she presents five broad types of information problems that are derived from the virtual environment. The virtual context seems to inhibit the exchange of unique information, which leads to uneven distribution of information, and unequal participation. This is in line with the coordination difficulties experienced in virtual teams (Galegher & Kraut, 1994). Finally, these findings are consistent with the fact that the perceived communication and information exchange effectiveness seems to be lower in virtual teams than in face-to-face teams. More research is needed to identify the factors that facilitate the dissemination of uniquely held information in virtual teams and to improve the coordination among dispersed team members.

The empirical evidence regarding the effects of the virtual context on task-related outcomes is also interesting. Despite several communication difficulties, virtual team members seem to be able to adjust their work practices and achieve a performance level (i.e., quality, perceived performance, satisfaction with outcomes) that matches that of their face-to-face counterparts. This is also consistent with Crampton's study, who reported "no obvious direct relationship between the incidence and severity of particular information problems and performance" (Crampton, 2001 p. 361). Previous work on adaptation in virtual teams (Majchrzack et al., 2000; Malhotra et al., 2001) provides support for this argument and demonstrates that dispersed members are able to modify their technology, group, and organizational structures to match their informational needs and ultimately generate outcomes that meet and even exceed previous standards of quality.

Two mechanisms appear to be particularly powerful in alleviating the process losses of virtual teams: (1) the reliance on process structure mechanisms and (2) the combination of multiple communication media. The first mechanism, process structure mechanisms, was found to foster group cohesiveness (Huang et al., 2003; Tan et al., 2000; Warkentin & Beranek, 1999), facilitate the establishment of trust (Jarvenpaa et al., 1998; Tan et al., 2000; Warkentin & Beranek, 1999), and improve communication and information exchange effectiveness (Huang et al., 2003; Tan et al., 2000). We found evidence that the second strategy, when virtual teams relied on multiple media instead of a single communication tool, led to greater satisfaction with the process (Burke & Aytes, 1998; Dennis & Kinney, 1998; Maznevski & Chudoba, 2000; Ocker et al., 1998), equalization of participation (Aiken & Vanjani, 1997), and higher quality of outcomes (Dennis & Kinney, 1998; Majchrzack et al., 2000; Malhotra et al., 2001; Ocker et al., 1998). Multiple communication media offer more opportunities for exchanging diverse types of information and appear to provide the necessary flexibility for dealing with the various information processing requirements that characterize the virtual work environment. Together, these two strategies offer support for the research framework suggested by Zack and McKenney (1995, p. 399) on social context and interaction patterns in computer-supported groups. According to the authors, the social context includes the culture, distribution of power, and the social norms, habits, practices, expectations, and preferences held by a group regarding its present and past interaction (Zack & McKenney, 1995 p. 396). Our review indicates that, when relying on process structure mechanisms, virtual team members implicitly define some components of the social context which later influences their pattern of interactions. Facilitated by multiple communication media, these patterns of interaction are more easily sustained, resulting in an increasing level of perceived of communication effectiveness and high quality outcomes. In summary, the two strategies discussed above appear to act as catalysts for building a shared social context within virtual teams and facilitate, maintain, and improve communication in such groups.

An Agenda for Future Research

While virtual teams seem to be able to overcome group communications inefficiencies, the fact that their performance does not surpass that of face-to-face teams is intriguing and surprising, especially given their greater access to a larger pool of expertise and knowledge. More research is needed to identify factors that might help virtual teams overcome communication inefficiencies and better exploit their larger knowledge pool. Our review identified four research avenues along that line.

First, research is needed on factors that facilitate and inhibit knowledge and expertise sharing in virtual teams. Although this is thought to constitute one of the most important benefits of virtual teams, we found very few studies that empirically assessed the challenges related to knowledge and expertise sharing in virtual teams.

Moreover, the present review indicates that expertise sharing might be more limited than expected.

A second research avenue concerns the various distribution attributes often used to characterize virtual teams. Although it is said that virtual teams may be distributed geographically, temporally, culturally, organizationally, or functionally, rare are the studies that have been able to isolate the effects of each specific structural dimension on group processes and outcomes. For example, it is unclear if knowledge and information exchange is affected by temporal dispersion, technology usage, functional diversity, cultural heterogeneity, or by a combination of these factors. Because dispersion can occur on single attributes (e.g., variation in geographical dispersion, variation in temporal dispersion) and on a combination of attributes (e.g., variation in geographical and temporal dispersion), we may also expect different virtual team configurations to emerge from the combination of theses structural characteristics, each having their own set of potential opportunities, risks, and managerial challenges (see O'Leary & Cummings, 2002). To better understand the nature of virtual teams, a fine-grained assessment of the various dispersion attributes by which they are characterized is necessary.

More research is also needed to understand how virtual team members interact with existing entities, norms, and processes of their respective organizations. As we now start to gain understanding of the internal dynamics of virtual teams, there is a growing need for a better understanding of the role of their different contextual factors. Examples of issues that could be studied are the choice, acquisition and implementation of communication technologies for virtual teamwork, the integration of these new technologies with the existing technological infrastructure, members' selection and training, issues related to security and access to information, control mechanisms, and adjustments in reward policies. The sharing of "local" resources by virtual team members is a key factor that might influence the team's performance. Members rarely devote 100% of their work to the virtual team and are most likely to be involved in other projects, teams, or work assignments at their respective locations (Majchrzack et al., 2000; Maznevski & Chudoba, 2000; Sole & Edmonson, 2002). Hence, members of virtual teams are likely to engage in frequent contact with site specific resources, either human or physical, which are inaccessible to their remote partners. This can enhance the overall knowledge stock available to a local team by increasing the probability of accessing sources of unique information (Stasser & Titus, 1985). However, the interplay between local and virtual environments may pose additional coordination difficulties and hamper mutual understanding within the team. Considering these challenges, future research should address how members of virtual teams can take advantage of their respective connections with site specific resources without jeopardizing communication and coordination efficiency within the team.

Fourth, the effect of media combination on virtual team processes and performance needs further study. The empirical evidence indicates that media combination improves group processes and outcomes. Knowledge on the effects of specific combinations and how different combination affects group processes needs to be sought. This is particularly important because as virtual teams will become more widespread, it is likely that a wider range of technologies will be offered by vendors of collaborative technologies. The specific choice of technologies will become more complex. Thus, a broader understanding of the complementarities among communication media is likely to be useful for managers who must decide, under the constraint of limited budget and training resources, which technologies should be used to support virtual collaboration.

Conclusion

This chapter contributes to both research and practice by helping to articulate what we know and what we do not know about virtual teams. For practice, our review sheds light on some important challenges facing virtual team members and managers and identifies some of the mechanisms that can be deployed to deal with them. For research, the present study offers a detailed portrait of the effects of the virtual context on group processes and outcomes, complements past literature on electronic communication in distributed groups, and suggests some research avenues for future work on virtual teams. Our review raises as many questions as it provides answers and we hope that it will stimulate research on virtual teams.

References

Crampton, C. D. (2001). The mutual knowledge problem and its consequences for dispersed collaboration. *Organization Science, 12*(3), 346-371.

Griffith, T. L., Sawyer, J. E., & Neale, M. A. (2003). Virtualness and knowledge in teams: Managing the love triangle of organizations, individuals, and information technology. *MIS Quarterly, 27*(2), 265-287.

Guzzo, R. A., & Shea, G. P. (1992). Group performance and intergroup relations in organizations, In M. D. Dunette & L. M., Hough (Eds., *Handbook of industrial and organizational psychology* (2nd ed.) (pp. 263-269). Palo Alto, CA: Consulting Psychologists Press.

Hinds, P. J., & Bailey., D. E. (2003). Out of sight, out of sync: Understanding conflict in distributed teams. *Organization Science, 14*(6), 615-632.

Hollingshead, A. B., McGrath, J. E., & O'Connor, K. M. (1993). Group task performance and communication technology: A longitudinal study of computer-mediated versus face-to-face work groups. *Small Group Research, 24*(3), 307-333.

Jarvenpaa, S. L., Knoll, K., & Leidner, D. E. (1998). Is anybody out there? Antecedents of trust in global virtual teams. *Journal of Management Information Systems, 14*(4), 29-75.

Jarvenpaa, S. L., & Leidner, D. E. (1999). Communication and trust in global virtual teams. *Organization Science, 10*(6), 791-815.

Littlepage, G. E., Schmidt, G. W., Whisler, E. W., & Frost, A. G. (1995). An input-process-output analysis of influence and performance in problem-solving groups. *Journal of Personality and Social Psychology, 69*(5), 877-889.

Lurey, J. S., & Raisinghani, M. S. (2001). An empirical study of best practices in virtual teams. *Information and Management, 38*, 523-544.

Majchrzak, A., Rice, E.R., Malhotra, A., & King, N. (2000). Technology adaptation: The case of a computer-supported inter-organizational virtual teams. *MIS Quarterly, 2*(4), 569-599.

Malhotra, A., Majchrzak, A., Carman, R., & Lott, V. (2001). Radical innovation without collocation: A case study at Boeing-Rocketdyne. *MIS Quarterly, 25*(2), 229-249.

Massey, A. P., Montoya-Weiss, M. M., & Hung, Y-T. (2003). Because time matters: Temporal coordination in global virtual teams. *Journal of MIS, 19*(4), 129-155.

Maznevski, M. L., & Chudoba, K. M. (2000). Bridging space over time: Global virtual team dynamics and effectiveness. *Organization Science, 11*(5), 473-492

McGrath, J. (1991). Time, interaction, and performance (TIP): A theory of groups. *Small Group Research, 22*, 147-174.

Montoya-Weiss, M. M., Massey, A., & Song, M. (2001). Getting it together: Temporal coordination and conflict management in global virtual teams. *Academy of Management Journal, 44*(6), 1251-1262.

Mortensen, M., & Hinds, P. J. (2001). Conflict and shared identity in geographically distributed teams. *Journal of Conflict Management, 12*(3), 212-238.

O'Leary, M. B., & Cummings, J. N. (2002). *The spatial, temporal, and configurational characteristics of geographic dispersion in work teams*. MIT Press.

Piccoli, G., & Ives, B. (2003). Trust and the unintended effects of behavioral control in virtual teams. *MIS Quarterly, 27*(3), 365-395.

Pinsonneault, A., & Kreamer, K. L. (1990). The effects of electronic meetings on group processes and outcomes: An assessment of the empirical research. European. *Journal of Operational Research, 46*, 143-161.

Powell, A., Piccoli, G., & Ives, B. (2004). Virtual teams: A review of current literature and directions for future research. *DATA BASE for Advances in Information Systems, 35*(1), 6-36.

Sole, D., & Edmonson, A. (2002). Situated knowledge and learning in dispersed teams. *British Journal of Management, 13*, 17-34.

Stasser, G., & Titus, W. (1985). Pooling of unshared information in group decision-making: Biased information sampling during discussion. *Journal of Personality and Social Psychology, 48*, 1467-1478.

Townsend, A. M., deMarie, S. M., & Hendrickson, A. R. (1998). Virtual teams and the workplace of the future. *Academy of Management Executive, 12*(3), 17-29.

Warkentin, M. E., Sayeed, L., & Hightower, R. (1997). Virtual teams versus face-to-face teams: An exploratory study of a web-based conference system. *Decision Sciences, 28*(4), 975-996.

Webster, J., & Watson, R. T. (2002). Analyzing the past to prepare for the future: Writing a literature review. *MIS Quarterly, 26*(2).

Zack, M. H., & McKenney, J. L. (1995). Social context and interaction in ongoing computer-supported management groups. *Organization Science, 6*(4), 394-422.

Zolin, R., Hinds, P. J., Fruchter, R., & Levitt, R. E. (2004). Interpersonal trust in cross-functional, geographically distributed work: A longitudinal study. *Information and Organization, 14*, 1-26.

Endnotes

1 This approach is similar to the one adopted by Pinsonneault and Kraemer (1990) in their review of the effects of GDSS and GCSS on group process and outcomes.

2 Because of space limitation, the tables are not included in this paper.

Appendix I: List of Empirical Studies

Author(s)	Year	Academic journal
Sharda et al.	1988	Management Science
Smith and Vanacek	1990	Journal of MIS
Gallupe and McKeen	1990	Information and Management
Cass et al.	1992	Information and Management
Walther and Burgoon	1992	Human Communication Research
Turoff et al.	1993	MIS Quarterly
Chidambaram and Jones	1993	MIS Quarterly
Zack	1993	Information Systems Research
Hollingshead et al.	1993	Small Group Research
O'Connor et al.	1993	Small Group Research
Orlikowski and Yates	1994	Administrative Science Quarterly
Walther et al.	1994	Communication Research
Straus and McGrath	1994	Journal of Applied Psychology
Galegher and Kraut	1994	Information Systems Research
Walther	1995	Organization Science
Zack and McKenney	1995	Organization Science
Weisband et al.	1995	Academy of Management Journal
Ocker et al.	1995-96	Journal of MIS
Chidambaram	1996	MIS Quarterly
Hightower and Sayeed	1996	Information Systems Research
Walther	1997	Human Communication Research
Aiken and Vanjani	1997	Information and Management
Warkentin et al.	1997	Decision Sciences
Ocker et al.	1998	Journal of MIS
Jarvenpaa et al.	1998	Journal of MIS
Dennis and Kinney	1998	Information Systems Research
Burke and Aytes	1998	HICCS
Jarvenpaa and Leidner	1999	Organization Science
Burke and Chidambaram	1999	MIS Quarterly
Warkentin and Beranek	1999	Information Systems Journal
Weisband and Atwater	1999	Journal of Applied Psychology
Wiesenfeld et al.	1999	Organization Science
Sarker and Sahay	2003	Journal of the Association for Information Systems
Tan et al.	2000	IEEE Transaction on Professional Communication
Majchzrack et al.	2000	Information Resources Management Journal

Appendix I. Continued

Majchzrack et al.	2000	MIS Quartlerly
Maznevski and Chudoba	2000	Organization Science
Robey et al.	2000	IEEE Transaction on Professional Communication
McDonough III et al.	2001	The Journal of Product Innovation Management
Kayworth and Leidner	2000	European Management Journal
Mortensen and Hinds	2001	International Journal of Conflict Management
Lurey et al.	2001	Information and Management
Crampton	2001	Organization Science
Yoo and Kanawattanachai	2001	International Journal of Organizational Analysis
Schmidt et al.	2001	Decision Sciences
Montoya-Weiss et al.	2001	Academy of Management Journal
Kayworth and Leidner	2001-02	Journal of MIS
Baker	2002	Information Resources Management Journal
Andres	2002	Team Performance Management
Morris et al.	2002	Information Resources Management Journal
Thompson and Coovert	2002	Group Dynamics: Theory, Research, and Practice
Sole and Edmonson	2002	British Journal of Management
Huang et al.	2003	Decision Support Systems
Thompson and Coovert	2003	Group Dynamics: Theory, Research, and Practice
Massey et al.	2003	Journal of MIS
Piccoli and Ives	2003	MIS Quarterly
Ahuja et al.	2003	Management Science
Ahuja and Galvin	2003	Journal of Management
Zolin et al.	2004	Information and Organization
Panteli	2004	Information and Organization
Balthazard et al.	2004	DATA BASE for Advances in Information Systems
Yoo and Alavi	2004	Information and Organization

The chapter was previously published in the International Journal of e-Collaboration, 1(3), 1-16, July-September 2005.

Chapter XV

Deceptive Communication in E-Collaboration

Joey F. George, Florida State University, USA
Kent Marett, Washington State University, USA

Abstract

Much research within the field of MIS has been devoted to the use of collaborative technology by decision makers and the impact computer-mediated communication (CMC) has on collaborative work. Yet, there may be some unintended consequences for users of CMC, if someone involved in the joint effort decides to take the opportunity to deceive the others involved. In this chapter, we posit that CMC offers would-be deceivers advantages that otherwise do not exist with more traditional, richer media, using past research and established theories to help explain why. We review some of the findings from our ongoing research effort in this area and explain how difficult it is for computer users to detect deception, when it occurs. Finally, we discuss how the art of deception in computer-mediated collaboration potentially can affect both the current effort and future efforts of those involved, and we offer our thoughts on some of the factors CMC practitioners should consider when trying to combat computer-mediated deception.

Introduction

Work related to collaboration and computing takes many forms, from computer-supported collaborative work, to groupware, to group support systems. Yet common to all of these research streams is the idea of enabling individuals to work together as a group on some typically intellectual effort with the aid and support of information systems. Computer-mediated communication (CMC) tools are at the heart of any group effort that depends on the use of computing for collaboration. Even though many of the early efforts dealing with collaboration through computing involved small groups of individuals working face-to-face (Stefik et al., 1987; Nunamaker et al., 1991), these individuals used computing for communication and task support. As is so well known, CMC enables collaboration across space and time, and hence the name "e-collaboration" is a good fit for the type of CMC-enabled group work we take for granted today. Working and communicating through CMC has its advantages, above and beyond the ability of groups to meet across time and space mentioned above. Among these advantages are improved task performance (McGrath & Hollingshead, 1994), better access to information (Siegel et al., 1986), and flexibility in synchronicity and proximity that traditionally groups have not had.

Yet we sometimes forget that CMC still fosters human communication, and human communication, and the group work it supports, is not always a positive and enlightened activity. As Rob Kling wrote, "Many CSCW (computer-supported cooperative work) articles impede our understanding of the likely use and impact of CSCW since they rely on concepts with strong positive connotations such as 'cooperation,' 'collaboration,' and images of convivial possibilities to characterize workplace relationships, while understating the levels of conflict, control, and coercion--also common in professional workplaces....*In practice, many working relationships can be multivalent with and mix elements of cooperation, conflict, conviviality, competition, collaboration, commitment, caution, control, coercion, coordination and combat (the 'c-words')*" (Kling, 1991, original emphasis, pp. 84-85). Though Kling was speaking specifically about CSCW, he could just as easily have been writing about other type of CMC-supported collaborative effort. Computer-supported collaboration, or e-collaboration, can often be positive, just as collaboration itself can be positive, but typically, collaboration also involves aspects of working together that are less than positive, involving some of Kling's alternate c-words, like combat and coercion and caution.

One particular aspect of human communication that is often seen as less than positive, which can have an impact on e-collaboration, is deception. Although an important part of every day communication (DePaulo & Kashy, 1998), deception is often viewed negatively, as it can undermine trust (Aune, Metts, & Ebesu Hubbard, 1998) and other key elements of successful collaboration. We have been studying deception for the past 10 years, the last three of which have been spent in a concerted research effort into deception over CMC and its successful detection.

Simply put, deception can undermine collaborative efforts in any context, and it can potentially taint the final outcome if it goes undetected. However, detecting deception is not cost free. The first costs incurred follow from publicly acknowledging that one or more of the people involved in the communication event are not being honest with the others. This simple recognition may alter how people communicate and work with each other, limiting what can be accomplished through limiting trust among communication partners. A second set of costs are incurred when individuals, now suspicious about the veracity of their colleagues, add deception detection to their regular communication and work activities. The time spent detecting lies is time that cannot be spent on more productive activities. A third set of costs come from verifying the falseness of statements that have been labeled as untrue. As we will discuss later, we have found that improved detection is often accompanied by an increase in false alarms, i.e., true statements labeled as false. The more false alarms, the more suspicious statements that have to be checked out, many of which were true all along. At some point, individuals, group members, and managers have to ask whether taking the time and effort to detect deception is worth it. At the same time, communicators have to ask whether the costs of ignoring the potential for deception are even higher than the costs of trying to detect it.

Our research effort is the basis for this chapter. In the next section, we review the literature on CMC and groups, and on CMC and deception. This is followed by some of our key findings about CMC and deception that apply to e-collaboration. We end with a discussion of the implications of our findings for e-collaboration.

Literature Review

For over three decades now, researchers have devoted significant attention to the impact that computer-based media has on group work. The commonly-proclaimed advantages resulting from groups using CMC include improved task performance, the ability to overcome the time and space constraints between group members, and increased range and access to information needed for group collaboration (McGrath & Hollingshead, 1994). Likewise, practitioners and managers in business organizations tout CMC for its lower costs, better access to information, and the added flexibility of physically dispersed individuals participating in group discussions (Siegel et al., 1986). Studies in this area typically have focused on group decision-making effectiveness, which is typically measured by the quality of decisions, satisfaction of group members, length of time to reaching decisions, the number of potential solutions generated, and the amount of interaction and influence between the group members. These studies have found that CMC-supported groups are not significantly different in performance from groups without computer-support communication, nor different in the time needed for decisions or in decision satisfaction (Baltes et al., 2002). Overall, the results for group effectiveness are mixed, but CMC does offer flexibility in synchronicity and proximity that traditionally groups have not had.

Yet, for all the potential benefits CMC can provide groups, it also has the potential to be abused by groups as well. Early findings uncovered some undesired by-products of CMC, such as the lack of control over discussion and information overload (Hiltz & Turoff, 1978). For these reasons and others, technologies such as group support systems (GSS) were conceived and developed (DeSanctis & Gallupe, 1987; Nunamaker et al., 1991). Despite findings that show groups using GSS appropriately typically generate more ideas, take less time to reach a decision, and feature more satisfied members than groups that do not use GSS in the same situations (Dennis, Wixom, & Vandenberg, 2001; Fjermestad & Hiltz, 2001), the technology does not completely solve the potential for abuse; in fact, CMC may help facilitate it. While all group work has a certain amount of cooperation, it would be short-sighted to claim that all group members are similarly motivated and are all working toward the same goal. And in situations where people have different motivations and are working covertly toward fulfilling alternate goals, a commonly chosen tactic is deception (Grover, 1993).

The Motivation for Deception in Group Discussions

The group setting might seem, at first glance, to be an unlikely arena for a motivated individual to lie, since the accumulated body of knowledge within the group is larger by virtue of the group having multiple members, the differing rates of participation might allow certain group members to be more discerning than normal, and the interaction a suspicious group member has with others might be enough to expose deception to the entire group (Marett & George, 2004). But there is also the opportunity for a deceiver to take advantage of unwitting participants (O'Hair & Cody, 1994) and pre-existing factions within the group that are not available in dyadic situations. Putnam and Stohl (1990) suggest that individuals often have multiple group memberships and responsibilities, belonging to bona fide groups instead of fixed, individual groups, and these separate memberships can compete for personal attention and resources within a given group. The bona fide perspective views a work group being made up informal subgroups whose members share external commitments. Individuals often resort to deception when these different group memberships come into conflict and there is a need to resolve the issue without losing face with either one. The decision to lie to one subgroup over another is commonly made based on the membership role with which the deceiver feels a stronger alignment (Grover, 1993) or is challenged by the demands of the competing stakeholders (Takala & Urpilainen, 1999). Of course, the decision to lie to one subgroup over another occurs before choosing the communication medium for deception and before the socially-disapproved behavior frequently found in CMC-aided group work manifests itself.

The deceiver must not only believe that the end result of lying to others is sufficiently worthy to rationalize such a decision, but also must believe that their chances for success are at least reasonable. This can be difficult if the deceiver holds a minority opinion, as the views held by the majority are more often judged to be credible than that of the holdout (Maass, West, & Cialdini, 1987). However, if a deceiver anticipates conflicting opinions and facts, they will likely prepare themselves for it beforehand (Gordijn, De Vries, & Postmes, 2001), rehearsing and reviewing their arguments, fallacious and otherwise. The rehearsability and reprocessibility provided by CMC can provide the tools a deceiver believes will succeed against group stakeholders with competing demands.

Detecting Deception in CMC

The nature of computer-based media is such that a deceiver can shield more of his or her behavior from others through using CMC. Of course, the medium does not matter if discrepancies crop up in a deceiver's account, but that is not the only way a liar can give his or her true intentions away. According to deceptive communication research, upending a deceiver by detecting lies is also dependent on uncovering verbal and nonverbal behavioral indicators that accompany those lies. The Interpersonal Deception Theory developed by Buller and Burgoon (1996) relates the importance of these indicators for deception detection. Lying is described as an ongoing process of communication, with the liar's behavior changing dynamically based on strategy, and lie detection is more likely if the changing behavioral indicators are noticed by the receiver of the lie. The theory also points out that evaluating behavioral indicators is just as important for the deceiver, as the receiver's behavior can hint toward gullibility or suspicion (Buller, Strzyzewski, & Comstock, 1991). These social indicators are transmitted along with the message content over the medium being used by the conversational participants.

Meta-analyses by Zuckerman and Driver (1985) and DePaulo et al. (2003) have shown that some indicators are more reliable for deception detection than others. Verbally and linguistically, the most reliable indicators include deceivers having a higher voice pitch, providing fewer details and more irrelevant information, and using more than normal negative affect. Nonverbal indicators pointing to deception include signs of nervousness, pupil dilation, increased blinking, and others. These indicators are believed to "leak out" during discussion when the deceiver has diverted attention to composing a story and away from maintaining a credible presentation, especially when highly motivated to succeed (DePaulo & Kirkendol,

1989; Ekman, 1992). However, much of the nonverbal leakage is effectively filtered by the medium being used by the group.

Barriers to Detecting Deception

Two well-known CMC theories, media richness theory and social presence theory, posit that more social cues and indicators are available to communicators using traditional face-to-face communication as opposed to CMC (Short, Williams, & Christie, 1976; Daft & Lengel, 1986). In fact, a categorization of deceptive indicators by Rao and Lim (2000) shows that a large number of cues associated with deception are unavailable to CMC users. Paralinguistic cues should be available in computer-based media that have audio channels, but some paralinguistic cues, such as response length and speech errors, may sometimes be available in media that have text channels only. Verbal indicators and discrepancies should be available in all communication modes. Richer and more socially present media, then, should transmit more indicators of deception than leaner and less socially present media. CMC can potentially contain many reliable indicators of deception, but a crafty deceiver can take advantage of the media limitations. Intuitively, group members have revealed they are aware of these media filters, as past research shows they believe they can better detect deception with rich media than with CMC, if deception exists (Cooper & Kahai, 2003).

Yet, unless a receiver has specific reasons to be suspicious of the group member who is behaving deceitfully, he or she may be looking the other way if these indicators leak out. There are at least two reasons why this may be the case in group collaboration. First, naturally occurring human biases may prevent the receiver from becoming suspicious. The chief bias that works to reduce suspicion is the truth bias, a naturally occurring predisposition to believe that communication is truthful, until given reason to believe otherwise (McCornack & Parks, 1986). This bias has been found to exist both between perfect strangers and between intimate couples and is a major hindrance to lie detection for the average person. Yet some research has shown that this bias can be overcome. (Stiff, Kim, & Ramesh, 1992) found that the bias' effects can be reduced if detectors were warned about the presence of lies. If there is one receiver advantage for lie detection when using CMC, it is that group members using CMC are typically less trusting than face-to-face communicators, especially if they have little experience with their partners (Alge, Wiethoff, & Klein, 2003). In those situations, the effect of truth bias might be somewhat mitigated for computer-supported groups.

Another preventative factor could be the amount of activity in the group itself. This rationale follows what Maier and Thurber (1968) originally coined "the distraction hypothesis," which suggested that an overabundance of social cues in a communicative environment can distract a potential lie detector from the reliable indicators pointing to deception. Given the number of people participating in a group discussion and all the content and behavior to be monitored, it seems likely that less obvious indicators that leak from a deceiver may remain unobserved. In a group discussion utilizing CMC, the overall number of social cues are reduced by virtue of the medium's properties, but the amount of content submitted in an electronic environment is often increased and more evenly distributed among the group members (Connolly, Jessup, & Valacich, 1990; McGrath & Hollingshead, 1994). The combination of a less rich environment and more voluminous amount of submitted information (both deceptive and otherwise) can easily drown out a lone deceiver. Unless a group member fortuitously notices a suspicious indicator or discrepancy during the conversation or has a pre-existing suspicion about one of the other members, a deceiver with a convincing story can thrive within a computer-supported group.

Findings on Collaboration and Deception from Our Work

Given that deceptive communication is common, but that it could also be an issue for successful collaboration, CMC-supported or otherwise, we have recently been working on detecting deception in collaborative contexts. As part of our work focuses on deception and CMC, and another part focuses on deception in groups, many of our findings directly speak to the issue of deception in e-collaboration. Here we report on six relevant findings based on our recent work:

1. Overall human detection rates for deception are lousy. Even though the received wisdom is that people are as good as chance at detecting deception (i.e., success rates of 50%) (Miller & Stiff, 1993), we have continually found much lower rates of successful detection. Much of the deception detection literature from the communication discipline has involved receivers watching individuals on videotape and being asked either to identify untruthful statements or to provide a holistic judgment of whether the person is lying (Ekman & Friesen, 1974; Miller & Stiff, 1993). Our work has involved having dyads or groups involved in conversations where one person lies, and where the person lied to is asked at the end of the conversation to write down anything from that communication episode that was deceptive. In these studies, where a person involved in a conversation is asked to recall deception from that conversation, the rates of successful detection are far below 50%. We have reported detection success rates of 20% and 11% (George & Marett, 2004), 33% (Biros, George,

& Zmud, 2002), and 8% (both George, Marett, & Tilley (2004) and Marett & George (2005)).

2. Suspicion improves detection rates but not by much. Given that successful human deception detection is less than desirable, communication researchers have investigated how detection might be improved through content analysis and interrogator training (Landry & Brigham, 1992; Burgoon et al., 1994; Vrij et al., 2000). Another potential way to improve detection is to try to overcome the truth bias by inducing suspicion in receivers. The thinking is that receivers will be more likely to find deception if they are looking for it, which they would be if they were suspicious about what people might communicate to them. We manipulated suspicion in some of our experiments through simple warnings before the experimental session that someone in the group could be lying to advance their own causes. The good news is that we found that suspicion does improve detection. In our study of resume enhancement, where an individual who lied on his resume is interviewed over CMC about the false resume, receivers who had been warned about lying on resumes had successful detection rates of 14%, compared to only 2% successful detection for receivers who were not warned (George et al., 2004). The bad news is that even warned receivers don't seem to do all that well in detection. The worse news is that in both experiments where we studied deception and its detection in groups (George & Marett, 2004; Marett & George, 2005), suspicious receivers were no better at detecting lies than were naïve receivers. However, there is evidence that a suspicious receiver is a more inquisitive receiver (Hancock et al., 2005), which can make deception more difficult, so perhaps this area of research will bear fruit in the future.

3. Successful detection seems to be associated with false alarms. It turns out that successful deception detection comes with a price: Successfully finding deception is accompanied by labeling honesty as dishonesty. We found that suspicious interviewers had significantly more "false alarms," or false accusations about legitimate resume items, than naïve interviewers (George et al., 2004). These findings mirror those of Biros and colleagues (2002), where employees, trained to find bad data and also warned about the possible presence of bad data, found more erroneous data than their peers who had not been warned or trained, but they also had a higher incidence of false alarms.

4. Media doesn't seem to make much difference in detection. In our resume study (George et al., 2004), deceivers and interviewers were located in separate rooms and communicated through one of four possible media: e-mail, chat, chat with audio, or voice-over-IP (VoIP). In two of our group studies, groups communicated either verbally without computer support or through a GSS, all while meeting face-to-face (George & Marett, 2004). In another group study, groups met either face-to-face or were dispersed and communicated

either verbally or through a GSS (Marett & George, 2005). Across all of these studies, we found that media used for communication made no difference in detection success rate. In other words, it was no easier or harder to detect deception using one media for detection over another. In our resume study, we did determine that interviewers using VoIP were more aware of deception during the interview, as measured by the resume items they asked about during the interview, compared to interviewers using e-mail. However, by the time the interviewers were asked, at the end of the interview, to record the untruthful resume items they had encountered, there were no differences between VoIP and e-mail interviewers in terms of the numbers of deceptive items they recalled. Our conjecture is that deceivers using VoIP were better able to persuade the interviewers of the ultimate veracity of the things they questioned than were e-mail deceivers. E-mail interviewers asked about suspicious items and later recorded these as untruthful. VoIP interviewers asked about suspicious items and did not list them as untruthful once the interview was over.

5. Deceivers in groups tell more lies when using GSS than when not using GSS. In two experiments featuring three-person groups, we found that deceivers were significantly apt to tell more lies when using a GSS than when not using a GSS (Marett & George, 2005). In the latter study, when comparing deceivers who used a group support system to deceive their fellow group partners with those who communicated via face-to-face or over headphones with their partners, deceivers submitted an average of 2.20 deceptive statements to the group discussion using the GSS as opposed to the average of 1.43 deceptive statements told in the non-GSS groups. Seemingly, the deceivers felt the computer support gave them a more favorable environment to get away with lying, perhaps due to the reduced social presence with an electronic medium.

6. Deceivers seem to lie more when there are more suspicious people in the group than when there are no suspicious people in the group. We also found in our second group study (Marett & George, 2005) that, no matter what medium was used, deceivers told more lies to groups in which both of the other members were warned about the possibility of deception beforehand, unbeknownst to the deceiver. As reported above, this differs from the findings from the résumé study that showed that warned receivers were more likely to detect lies than otherwise naïve receivers. Transcripts of the group discussions showed evidence that the warned receivers were less accepting of others' submitted information, and this obstinacy may have been motivation for the deceiver to restate or rephrase their false statements. Again, catching lies was a problem for the receivers, as only eight percent of the lies told in the study were detected.

Implications for E-Collaboration

Lying to one person or to a group seems to be a protected activity, in that individuals and groups are not likely to discover lies, even when they have been warned that someone might be lying. The fact is that most people are highly trusting by nature, which is not necessarily a bad thing, but as a result, it seems that people are much more likely to get away with deception than get caught. The effects of this for dyadic and group e-collaboration would have to be judged on a case-by-case basis, but it seems that in a computer-mediated environment, the element of trust is extremely important. People need to be able to believe that their fellow collaborators will follow through on what they promise to do, that the information they are providing them is legitimate, and that their self-discipline will override the desire to stray from the agreed-upon objective. It would be an obvious betrayal of that trust to attempt to deceive in those circumstances, but there is no reason to believe it would happen any less frequently than it would in face-to-face meetings. Beyond the contamination of the current collaborative effort, lying could poison the group efforts in the future for those who had felt betrayed.

When detection is successful, it seems to be accompanied by false alarms, i.e., warned individuals find lies but also find lies where they do not exist. The practicality of using warnings may not be advisable in many situations. Organizations strive to produce a spirit of camaraderie among their employees, and managers must decide whether to disrupt the culture they have helped nurture with talk of possible deceptive behavior from within. Certainly, there are situations in which the possibility of deception should not only be made public to decision makers, but where the almost certainty of deception should be explicitly stated. An example of this would be to make human resource professionals aware of the prevalence of deception during the job interview process, a type of deception that is common and which has been widely publicized already (McShulkis, 1997). Aside from the cultural impact warnings might have, there is also a cost associated with false alarms. Managers need to decide what an acceptable rate of error would be with regard to false alarms. If false alarms are not acceptable, additional time must be taken to ensure the review process is accurate, not to mention the monetary costs that would result from background checks and research. Finally, the incidence of false alarms seems to correlate with faulty decision making (Biros et al., 2002), which is what deception detection seeks to avoid in the first place.

Finally, deceivers seem to be able to thrive in any type of communicative setting. Our GSS and group work indicates that deceivers can adjust to the medium in order to successfully lie when needed. None of our subjects claimed to have used a group support system prior to our studies, so the increase in lying may be a first time adjustment to a new media in order to accomplish the goal of lying successfully. This may be the same reason deceivers lied more to forewarned group members than to those who were naïve, in that subjects were confronted by initially suspicious partners for the first time in their group participation experiences. Although people have their own individual approaches to finding deception, for most people, these approaches have been developed primarily through personal experiences with lying in a verbal, dyadic context. As we have seen, our own systems for detecting deception in verbal, dyadic conversations do not work very well, so how much of these marginally effective systems for detecting deception can be adapted to newer media like chat and e-mail and instant messaging is an open question. Maybe the best way to tackle this problem is to not even try to adapt personal techniques for detecting deception in traditional dyadic communication to newer media. Maybe we need to devise totally different techniques for detecting deception in CMC-based e-collaborative communication, based on research such as ours and on new experiences. The first step, however, is to admit that deception is a part of collaboration, e- or otherwise, and to determine what the costs are for detecting this deception and what the costs are for ignoring it.

Conclusion

Just as information technology facilitates e-collaboration, making collaboration faster and better and more immediate, IT also facilitates negatively perceived aspects of human communication. The negative aspect of communication, and hence of e-collaboration, that we have focused on in this paper is deception. Deception is a common part of everyday human communication, and it is typically harmless, but deception can be devastating to group work. Lying can undermine collaboration through undermining the trust it is based on. Our recent research has investigated deception and its detection across various media and within groups. Some of our findings are promising: People can become better attuned to finding deception through simple warnings about its potential presence. Other of our findings are more worrisome: Finding deception seems to come with an increase in false alarms; even with warnings, people are still not very good at finding deception; and liars in groups seem to lie more when communicating over group support systems than when communicating without them. Clearly, additional research is called for to help us understand the role of deception in e-collaboration.

We need at all times to remember that deception is part of communication, whether computer-mediated or not. The potential for deception in e-collaboration should be recognized. Recognition is only the first step. The next step is deciding what costs to incur to deal with deception in e-collaboration. There are certainly times when we simply do not want to know we are being lied to, even though we know there is a cost for our blissful ignorance. But there are also times when the costs of not knowing about deception are too high, whether the costs are personal or work-related. Managers and individuals have to decide what costs they are willing to tolerate. Perhaps the most important thing to remember is that deception is reality, and that the costs associated with confronting it or ignoring it are not zero.

References

Alge, B., Wiethoff, C., & Klein, H. (2003). When does the medium matter? Knowledge-building experiences and opportunities in decision-making teams. *Organizational Behavior and Human Decision Processes, 91*(1), 26-37.

Aune, R. K., Metts, S., & Ebesu Hubbard, A. (1998). Managing the outcomes of discovered deception. *Journal of Social Psychology, 138*(6), 677-689.

Baltes, B., Dickson, M., Sherman, M., Bauer, C., & LaGanke, J. (2002). Computer-mediated communication and group decision making: A meta-analysis. *Organizational Behavior and Human Decision Processes, 87*(1), 156-179.

Biros, D., George, J., & Zmud, R. (2002). Inducing sensitivity to deception in order to improve decision making performance: A field study. *MIS Quarterly, 26*(2), 119-144.

Buller, D., & Burgoon, J. (1996). Interpersonal deception theory. *Communication Theory, 6*, 203-242.

Buller, D., Strzyzewski, K., & Comstock, J. (1991). Interpersonal deception: I. Deceivers' reactions to receivers' suspicions and probing. *Communication Monographs, 58*, 1-24.

Burgoon, J., Buller, D., Ebesu, A., & Rockwell, P. (1994). Interpersonal deception: V. Accuracy in deception detection. *Communication Monographs, 61*, 303-325.

Connolly, T., Jessup, L., & Valacich, J. (1990). Effects of anonymity and evaluative tone on idea generation in computer-mediated groups. *Management Science, 36*(6), 689-703.

Cooper, R., & Kahai, S. (2003). Exploring the core concepts of media richness theory: The impact of cue multiplicity and feedback immediacy on decision quality. *Journal of Management Information Systems, 20*, 263-299.

Daft, R., & Lengel, R. (1986). Organizational information requirements, media richness, and structural design. *Management Science, 32*(5), 554-570.

Dennis, A., Wixom, B., & Vandenberg, R. (2001). Understanding fit and appropriation effects in group support systems via meta-analysis. *MIS Quarterly, 25*(2), 167-193.

DePaulo, B., & Kashy, D. (1998). Everyday lies in close and casual relationships. *Journal of Personality & Social Psychology, 74*(1), 63-79.

DePaulo, B., & Kirkendol, S. (1989). The motivation impairment effect in the communication of deception. In J. Yuille (Ed.), *Credibility assessment* (pp. 51-70). Duerne, Belgium: Klewer.

DePaulo, B., Lindsay, J., Malone, B., Muhlenbruck, L., Charlton, K., & Cooper, H. (2003). Cues to deception. *Psychological Bulletin, 129*(1), 74-118.

DeSanctis, G., & Gallupe, R. (1987). A foundation for the study of group decision support systems. *Management Science, 33*(5), 589-609.

Ekman, P. (1992). *Telling lies: Clues to deceit in the marketplace, politics, and marriage* (Vol. 2). New York: WW Norton and Company.

Ekman, P., & Friesen, W. (1974). Detecting deception from the body or face. *Journal of Personality & Social Psychology, 20*, 288-298.

Fjermestad, J., & Hiltz, S. R. (2001). Group support systems: A descriptive evaluation of case and field studies. *Journal of Management Information Systems, 17*(3), 115-159.

George, J., & Marett, K. (2004). Inhibiting deception and its detection. *Paper presented at the 37th Hawaii International Conference on System Sciences.*

George, J., Marett, K., & Tilley, P. (2004). *Deception detection in résumés in computer-mediated interviews.* Unpublished manuscript, Florida State University.

Gordijn, E., De Vries, N., & Postmes, T. (2001). *Self-persuasion: An alternative paradigm for investigating majority and minority influence.* In C. D. Dreu & N. D. Vries (Eds.), Group consensus and minority influence (pp. 144-159). Malden MA: Blackwell Publishers.

Grover, S. (1993). Why professionals lie: The impact of professional role conflict on reporting accuracy. *Organizational Behavior and Human Decision Processes, 55*, 251-272.

Hancock, J., Curry, L., Goorha, S., & Woodworth, M. (2005). Automated linguistic analysis of deceptive and truthful synchronous computer-mediated communication. *Paper presented at the 38th Hawaii International Conference on System Sciences*, Big Island.

Hiltz, S. R., & Turoff, M. (1978). *The network nation: Human communication via computer.* Reading, MA: Addison-Wesley.

Kling, R. (1991). Cooperation, coordination, and control in computer-supported work. *Communications of the ACM, 34*(12), 83-88.

Landry, K., & Brigham, J. (1992). The effect of training in criteria-based content analysis on the ability to detect deception in adults. *Law and Human Behavior, 16*(6), 663-676.

Maass, A., West, S., & Cialdini, R. (1987). *Minority influence and conversion.* In C. Hendrick (Ed.), Review of personality and social psychology (Vol. 8, pp. 55-79). Newbury Park, CA: Sage.

Maier, N., & Thurber, J. (1968). Accuracy of judgments of deception when an interview is watched, heard, and read. *Personnel Psychology, 21*, 23-30.

Marett, K., & George, J. (2004). Deception in the case of one sender and multiple receivers. *Group Decision & Negotiation, 13*, 29-44.

Marett, K., & George, J. (2005). Group deception in computer-supported environments. *Paper presented at the 38th Hawaii International Conference on System Sciences.*

McCornack, S., & Parks, M. (1986). Deception detection and relationship development: The other side of trust. In McLaughlin (Ed.), *Communications Yearbook 9*. Beverly Hills, CA: Sage Publications.

McGrath, J., & Hollingshead, A. (1994). *Groups interacting with technology*. Thousand Oaks, CA: Sage Publications.

McShulkis, E. (1997). Job hunters resorting to questionable ethics. *HRMagazine, 42*, 27.

Miller, G., & Stiff, J. (1993). *Deceptive communication.* Newbury Park, CA: Sage Publications, Inc.

Nunamaker, J., Dennis, A., Valacich, J., Vogel, D., & George, J. (1991). Electronic meeting systems to support group work. *Communications of the ACM, 34*(7), 40-61.

O'Hair, D., & Cody, M. (1994). Deception. In W. R. Cupach & B. H. Spitzberg (Eds.), *The dark side of interpersonal communication* (pp. 181-213). Hillsdale, NJ: Lawrence Erlbaum Associates.

Putnam, L., & Stohl, C. (1990). Bona fide groups: A reconceptualiztion of groups in context. *Communication Studies, 41*, 248-265.

Rao, S., & Lim, J. (2000). *The impact of involuntary cues on media effects.* Paper presented at the 33rd Hawaii International Conference on System Sciences.

Short, J., Williams, E., & Christie, B. (1976). *The social psychology of telecommunications*. NY: John Wiley.

Siegel, J., Dubrovsky, V., Kiesler, S., & McGuire, T. (1986). Group processes in computer-mediated communication. *Organizational Behavior and Human Decision Processes, 37*, 157-187.

Stefik, M., Foster, G., Bobrow, D., Kahn, K., Lanning, S., & Suchman, L. (1987). Beyond the chalkboard: Computer support for collaboration and problem solving in meetings. *Communications of the ACM, 30*(1), 32-47.

Stiff, J., Kim, H., & Ramesh, C. (1992). Truth biases and aroused suspicion in relational deception. *Communication Research, 19*(3), 326-345.

Takala, T., & Urpilainen, J. (1999). Managerial work and lying: A conceptual framework and an explorative case study. *Journal of Business Ethics, 20*(3), 181-195.

Vrij, A., Edward, K., Roberts, K., & Bull, R. (2000). Detecting deceit via analysis of verbal and nonverbal behavior. *Journal of Nonverbal Behavior, 24*(4), 239-263.

Zuckerman, M., & Driver, R. (1985). Telling lies: Verbal and nonverbal correlates of deception. In A. W. Siegman & S. Feldstein (Eds.), *Nonverbal communication: An integrated perspective* (pp. 129-147). Hillsdale, NJ: Erlbaum.

About the Authors

Ned Kock is an associate professor and chair of the Department of MIS and Decision Science at Texas A&M International University (USA). He holds degrees in electronics engineering (BEE), computer science (MS), and MIS (PhD). Kock has authored several books, and published in a number of journals including *Communications of the ACM, Decision Support Systems, European Journal of Information Systems, IEEE Transactions, Information & Management, Information Systems Journal, Information Technology & People, Journal of Organizational Computing and Electronic Commerce, MIS Quarterly,* and *Organization Science.* He is the editor-in-chief of the *International Journal of e-Collaboration*, associate editor of the *Journal of Systems and Information Technology*, and associate editor for *Information Systems of the journal IEEE Transactions on Professional Communication*. His research interests include action research, ethical and legal issues in technology research and management, e-collaboration, and business process improvement.

* * *

Jorge Audy is a professor in the Computer Science Department and director of TECNOPUC (Technological and Scientific Park) at the Pontifica Universidade Catolica at Porto Alegre, Brazil. He holds a Doctorate in Information Systems (information systems planning). He is currently involved in several projects related to the global software development and project management, with work done with companies like DELL (USA), Hewlett-Packard, SONAE (Portugal), DB Server (Brazil) and research projects with researchers at universities like HEC (Montreal, Canada), University of Kentucky and University of Illinois, Chicago (USA). He has published in outlets such as *Engineering Management Journal, Software Process Improvement and Practice Journal* and *International Journal of E-Collaboration.* He has also published in conference proceedings such as HICSS, AMCIS, CAiSE, WER, RE, ICEIS, etc.

Henri Barki is Canada research chair in IT implementation and management and a professor of IT at HEC Montréal, Canada. His main research interests focus on the development, introduction and use of information technologies in organizations. A member of the Royal Society of Canada since 2003, his research has been published in *Annals of Cases on Information Technology Applications and Management in Organizations, Canadian Journal of Administrative Sciences, IEEE Transactions on Professional Communication, Information Systems Research, Information & Management, INFOR, Journal of Management Information Systems, Management Science, MIS Quarterly*, and *Small Group Research.*

François Bellavance is an associate professor at HEC Montréal and the director of the Research Laboratory on Transportation Safety of the Center for Research on Transportation at the Université de Montréal. He obtained a PhD in statistics in 1994 from the Université de Montréal. From 1990 to 1993, he directed the activities of the Statistical Consulting Service in the Department of Mathematics and Statistics at Simon Fraser University.

Anita D. Bhappu is an assistant professor of management and organizations in the Cox School of Business at Southern Methodist University, USA. She received a PhD in management from the University of Arizona. She studies conflict and decision-making in diverse work teams, as well as service design and delivery. Her research is published in the *Academy of Management Review, Journal of Applied Psychology, and Organizational Behavior* and *Human Decision Processes*, among others. Prior to her academic career, Dr. Bhappu worked as a chemical engineer for the Procter & Gamble Company.

Pamela E. Carter is an assistant professor of MIS in the College of Business at Florida State University, USA. Her research interests include the diffusion of complex technologies, meanings and interpretations of/within information systems, project management, and IS infrastructure management. Her work is forthcoming in *MIS Quarterly* and has been presented at numerous national and international conferences. She received a PhD from Florida State University and an MBA from the University of Maryland.

Olivier Caya is a PhD student in information systems at McGill University. His research interests include the impacts of information technologies on groups, virtual teams, distributed knowledge and expertise, electronic communication, and user adaptation.

Alan R. Dennis is a professor of information systems and holds the John T. Chambers chair of Internet systems in the Kelley School of Business at Indiana University, USA. Dr. Dennis received a PhD in MIS from the University of Arizona, an MBA from Queen's University in Ontario, and his Bachelor of Computer Science from Acadia University in Nova Scotia. His research focuses on team collaboration, knowledge management, and the Internet. He has written four books and more than 100 journal articles and conference papers. He is the publisher of *MIS Quarterly Executive* and serves on the editorial boards of *Journal of Management Information Systems, Journal of the Association for Information Systems, Journal of Computer Mediated Communication* and *International Journal of e-Collaboration.*

Roberto Evaristo is an assistant professor in the Information and Decision Sciences Department at the University of Illinois, Chicago. He is currently involved in several projects related to the management of distributed projects, with work done in Japan, USA and Europe. He has published in outlets such as *Communications of the ACM, International Journal of Project Management, Database, Journal of Engineering and Technology Management, International Journal of Emergency Management, Business Horizons, European Management Journal, Human Systems Management, Journal of Organizational Computing and Electronic Commerce*, and elsewhere. He is an associate editor for the *International Journal of e-Collaboration* and also serves on the editorial board of *Information Technology and People, Journal of Global Information Management* and *the Journal of Global Information Technology Management.*

Jerry Fjermestad is an associate professor in the School of Management at NJIT. He received a BA in chemistry from Pacific Lutheran University, an MS in operations research from Polytechnic University, an MBA in operations management from Iona College and an MBA and PhD from Rutgers University in management information systems. Fjermestad has taught courses on MIS, decision support systems, systems analysis and design, e-commerce, data warehousing, and graduate seminars in information systems. His current research interests are in collaborative technology, decision support systems, data warehousing, electronic commerce, global information systems, customer relationship management, and enterprise information systems. Fjermestad has published in *the Journal of Management Information Systems, Group Decision and Negotiation, the Journal of Organizational Computing and Electronic Commerce, Information and Management, Decision Support Systems, Logistics Information Management, International Journal of Electronic Commerce*, and several other journals and conference proceedings.

Brent Gallupe is a professor of information systems, director of the Queen's Executive Decision Center, and associate dean for the Faculty at the School of Business, Queen's University at Kingston, Canada. He also holds an on-going visiting professor appointment at the University of Auckland, New Zealand. His current research interests are in computer support for groups and teams, the management of international information systems, and knowledge management systems. His work has been published in such journals as *Management Science, MIS Quarterly, Information Systems Research, Academy of Management Journal, Sloan Management Review*, and *Journal of Applied Psychology*.

Joey F. George (PhD, University of California at Irvine, 1986; AB, Stanford University, 1979) is a professor of MIS and the Thomas L. Williams Jr. eminent scholar in MIS at Florida State University, USA. He has published in such journals as *Information Systems Research, Communications of the ACM, MIS Quarterly, Journal of MIS*, and *Communication Research*. His research interests include deception detection in computer-mediated communication, computer-based monitoring, and group support systems. He has served as associate and senior editor for *MISQ* and *ISR* and is currently editor-in-chief for *Communications of AIS*. He was conference co-chair for ICIS 2001 and doctoral consortium co-chair for ICIS 2003.

Donald Hantula is an associate professor of psychology at Temple University and executive editor of the *Journal of Social Psychology*. He holds a PhD in psychology from the University of Notre Dame, where he began working at the intersection of psychology and technology. His articles have appeared in many edited volumes and leading journals, including *Human Resource Management Journal, Journal of the American Medical Association, Journal of Applied Psychology, Journal of Organizational Behavior Management*, and *Organizational Behavior & Human Decision Processes*. His current research synthesizes behavioral economics, evolutionary theory, and technology in multilevel analyses of decision making and performance.

Stephen C. Hayne is the First National Bank research fellow and professor (CIS) at Colorado State University, USA. He received a PhD from the University of Arizona (1990); his current research involves exploring collaboration, especially when under time pressure. He has received more than $1.9 million from the National Science Foundation and the Office of Naval Research. He has published in numerous journals, e.g., *Journal of Management Information Systems, Database, Information and Management, IBM Systems Journal*, and *International Journal of Human Computer Studies*. He is co-chair of America's Conference on Information Systems (2007). He has been a IEEE member for over 15 years.

Kelly McNamara Hilmer is an associate professor at the University of Tampa in the Information and Technology Management Department. Hilmer received a PhD in MIS and a Masters of Applied Mathematical Sciences from University of Georgia, along with a BA in math/physics from SUNY, Plattsburgh. Hilmer's research interests include information exchange and decision making using collaborative technology. Her research has appeared in various journals and she has presented at numerous national and international information systems conferences.

Mark W. Huber is a lecturer in the MIS Department, University of Georgia (UGA), and is the director of the UGA Terry College of Business' Institute for Leadership Advancement's Undergraduate Certificate in Personal and Organizational Leadership Program. He has won numerous teaching awards, including most recently an Outstanding Professor Award from UGA's Student Government Association. He is also the editor of the *ISWORLD Introduction to Information Systems Course Page*. His current research interests include IS education, leadership, and group support systems. He has published papers in *Communications of the AIS* and *the Journal of Marital and Family Therapy* and is a co-author of an introduction to IS textbook (John Wiley & Sons).

Kent Marett is an assistant professor of MIS at Washington State University, USA. He holds a PhD in MIS from Florida State University, as well as an MSBA in MIS and a BS in secondary education from Mississippi State University, where he also served as an adjunct instructor. His primary research interests include deceptive communication in computer-based media and the role of technology in group decision making.

Shaila M. Miranda is associate professor of MIS at the Price College of Business, the University of Oklahoma. She obtained her doctorate in MIS from the University of Georgia in 1991. She also has an MA in sociology from Columbia University, and a Master of Management Studies and a BA in psychology from the University of Bombay. Her current research interests in information systems include electronic collaboration, outsourcing, and alternate work arrangements. She also has a strong interest in sociological theory. She has published in journals such as the *Information Systems Research, Journal of Management Information Systems, Small Group Research, Information and Management*, and *Database*.

Bjørn Erik Munkvold is a professor of information systems in the Department of Information Systems, Agder University College, Norway. His main research interests are e-collaboration, organizational implementation of information technology, and qualitative research methods. He has published articles in such journals as *Communications of the AIS, Database for Advances in Information Systems, European Journal of Information Systems, Information Systems Management, International Journal of Cooperative Information Systems*, and *Journal of Organizational Computing and Electronic Commerce*. He has authored a book titled *Implementing Collaboration Technologies in Industry: Case Examples and Lessons Learned.*

M. Lynne Markus is the John W. Poduska senior chair in information management at the McCallum Graduate School of Business, Bentley College. She is the author of three books and numerous articles in journals such as *MIS Quarterly, Information Systems Research, Organization Science, Communications of the ACM, Sloan Management Review* and *Management Science*. She was named a Fellow of the Association for Information Systems in 2004. Professor Markus holds a BS in industrial engineering from the University of Pittsburgh and a PhD in organizational behavior from Case Western Reserve University.

John T. Nosek is a professor of computer & information sciences at Temple University. He has published widely on a broad range of information technology topics. For over a decade, his main interest has been in augmenting group sensemaking. The overarching goal of this work is to develop theory based technology that will dramatically improve anytime, anyplace collaborative work by better managing the social, cognitive, and procedural complexities inherent in joint effort. Dr. Nosek's work has been funded by the National Science Foundation, several private companies and foundations, including the Lattanze Foundation, the U.S. Navy, and the U.S. Air Force. He has also worked with a number of small and large companies, including Lockheed Martin, where he helped them initiate a program to institutionalize innovation by building an innovation culture. Dr. Nosek, a retired U.S. Navy Captain, holds degrees from The United States Naval Academy, Villanova University, and Temple University.

Alain Pinsonneault is a James McGill professor and the Imasco chair of information systems in the Faculty of Management at McGill University. His current research interests include the organizational and individual impacts of information technology, user adaptation, ERP implementation, e-health, e-integration, group support systems, strategic alignment of IT, and the business value of IT. He has published papers in *Management Science, MIS Quarterly, Information Systems Research, the Journal of MIS, Small Group Research, Decision Support Systems, Organization Science, the European Journal of Operational Research*, and *the International Journal of Electronic Collaboration.*

C.A.P. Smith holds an engineering degree from MIT and a PhD in information systems from the University of Arizona. He is currently an assistant professor of information systems at Colorado State University. Prior to working for CSU, he was a senior scientist at the U.S. Navy's Space and Naval Warfare Systems Center in San Diego, also know as SPAWAR. While at SPAWAR he conducted a program of research into decision-making and managed multi-million dollar software development efforts for state-of-the-art decision support systems. He has published a number of scholarly articles in journals such as *Human Factors, Group Decision and Negotiation*, and *International Journal of Human-Computer Interaction.*

Ulrike Schultze is an associate professor in IT and operations management at Southern Methodist University. Her research focuses on the impact of information technology on work practices and she is particularly interested in knowledge work. Dr. Schultze has written on hard and soft information genres, information overload, and knowledge management. Her more recent research projects are in the area of Internet-based technologies and their implications for customer co-production. Dr. Schultze frequently relies on multi-method research designs, which include ethnographic observations, interviews and surveys. Her research has been published in, among others, *ISR, MIS Quarterly, Information & Organizations.*

Mary Beth Watson-Manheim is an assistant professor of information systems at the Liautaud Graduate School of Business, University of Illinois at Chicago. Her current research interests include impact of information and communication technologies on work; managerial, social, and technological implications of virtual work environments; and IT-enabled organizational change. She holds a doctorate in IT management from Georgia Tech. Dr. Watson-Manheim's research has been published in *Journal of Management Information Systems, IEEE Journal of*

Systems, Man and Cybernetics, MIS Quarterly Executive, Information Resources Management Journal, Information Technology and People, and *Group Decision and Negotiation*, among others. She has consulted and researched for several national and multinational corporations. Prior to joining academe, Dr. Watson-Manheim was employed in the telecommunications industry.

Michael L. Williams is an assistant professor of information systems in the Graziadio School of Business at Pepperdine University in Malibu, CA. His research focuses on the influence of information technology on decision-making, and the strategic selection, implementation, and use of information systems to gain competitive advantage. He received a Bachelor of Arts (1990) from Oklahoma Christian University, a Master of Arts (1994), and Master of Divinity (1994) from Abilene Christian University, and Master of Business (2002) and a PhD (2004) in MIS at the Kelley School of Business at Indiana University.

Ilze Zigurs is a professor and the Mutual of Omaha distinguished chair of information science and technology, in the College of Information Science and Technology at the University of Nebraska at Omaha, USA. Her research examines design, implementation, and use of collaboration technologies, particularly in virtual teams and projects. She has published in such journals as *MIS Quarterly, Journal of Management Information Systems, Journal of Organizational Computing and Electronic Commerce*, and *Group Decision and Negotiation*, among others. She has recently co-authored a book published by the Project Management Institute, *Patterns of Effective Management of Virtual Projects*. She serves as editor-in-chief of *e-Service Journal*.

Index

M

N

O

P

Q

R

S

T